Edge of Midnight:

The Life of John Schlesinger

WILLIAM J. MANN

Edge of Midnight:

The Life of John Schlesinger

HUTCHINSON
LONDON

Published by Hutchinson in 2004

1 3 5 7 9 10 8 6 4 2

Copyright © William J. Mann 2004

William J. Mann has asserted his right under the Copyright, Designs and Patents Act, 1988 to be identified as the author of this work

First published in the United Kingdom by Hutchinson

Hutchinson
The Random House Group Limited
20 Vauxhall Bridge Road, London SW1V 2SA

Random House Australia (Pty) Limited
20 Alfred Street, Milsons Point, Sydney
New South Wales 2061, Australia

Random House New Zealand Limited
18 Poland Road, Glenfield
Auckland 10, New Zealand

Random House (Pty) Limited
Endulini, 5a Jubilee Road
Parktown 2193, South Africa

The Random House Group Limited Reg. No. 954009

www.randomhouse.co.uk

A CIP catalogue record for this book is available
from the British Library

Papers used by Random House are natural, recyclable products made from wood grown in sustainable forests. The manufacturing processes conform to the environmental regulations of the country of origin

ISBN 0-09-179489-7

Typeset by SX Composing DTP, Rayleigh, Essex
Printed and bound in Great Britain by
Mackays of Chatham plc, Chatham, Kent

Contents

Acknowledgements

First and foremost my gratitude goes to John Schlesinger himself, who, despite ever-increasing physical limitations, managed to share with me the love he felt not only for his work but also for life in general. When we first began working on this biography, several months after his first stroke, he was still choosing to speak. In a whisper, he would answer my questions and offer insights into his life and career. As time went on, John stopped using his voice except on the rarest of occasions, but he continued to communicate with me through his eyes, or with a gesture of his hand or a turn of his head. When in those occasional moments he would grant me a smile, I considered myself the recipient of an exceptional gift. I am left inspired not only by his artistry but also by his generosity and compassion, and his extraordinary interest in humanity. Getting to know John

Schlesinger has been one of the great honors of my life.

I am also deeply indebted to Michael Childers, John's partner for 36 years. Michael's hospitality in allowing me to spend long stretches of time with him and John at their lovely home in Palm Springs allowed me to get to know them both, and to develop the necessary trust a project like this requires. Not once did John or Michael ever attempt to censor this work; they knew from the start that, although this might be an "authorised" biography, it would tell the full story – the low points as well as the highs – of their extraordinary lives. I am grateful for all the doors Michael opened for me in the course of this project, and for his candor, his wit, and his friendship.

John's family proved equally as forthcoming and co-operative, particularly his brother Roger Schlesinger, a kind, thoughtful man who, as I would sit with him at his home in London, gave me an idea of what John must have been like when he was well and hardy, so much did they resemble each other. Roger and his wife Sue – who left no cabinet unopened in her search for John's files and tape-recorded diaries – were incredibly generous with their time and ideas, always ready to respond to a barrage of last-minute questions emailed across the Atlantic.

Likewise, John's sister Hilary, his cousin Andrew Raeburn, and his nephew Ian Buruma (who shared his penetrating research into the family and the Jewish experience in England) were all invaluable in helping me understand and appreciate John's life.

I must thank a few others as well: John's faithful nurse, Maureen Danson, for keeping me posted, sometimes daily, on John's condition, as well as sharing the little anecdotes that offered telling insights into his final months; Gavin Lambert, for first suggesting this project and for providing an overview of John Schlesinger's place in film history; Gene Phillips, whose writings about John in the 1970s are vital for any understanding of his career and who generously shared with me his notes and correspondence; Erin O'Neill at the BBC Written Archives in Reading, who uncovered all sorts of fascinating, obscure references to John in her files, thus finally allowing the complete story of his early television career to be told; Kathleen Dickson at the British Film Institute who, when she realized my deadline, made haste to get John's early BBC films transferred onto videotape so I might view them; Sean Delaney and Olwen Terris, also of the BFI; Barbara Hall of the Margaret Herrick Library of the Academy of Motion Picture Arts and Sciences in Beverly Hills; Sue Whyte of the Royal Opera House, Covent Garden; Gisela Prossnitz of the Salzburg Festival Archive; and the staffs of the New York Public Library for the Performing Arts at Lincoln Center; the American Film Institute; the British Academy of Film and Television Arts; the Royal Shakespeare Company Archive; and the National Theatre Archive.

I also thank all of John's actors, producers, crew members, friends, and colleagues who shared with me their thoughts and memories: Luciana Arrighi, William Atherton, Eileen Atkins, Kaye Ballard, the late Sir Alan Bates, Geoffrey Bayldon, William Becker, Alan Bennett, Patricia Birch, Hart Bochner, Beau Bridges, Humphrey Burton, Julie Christie, Jim Clark, Laurence Clark, Sir Tom Courtenay, Pat Crowley, Michael Cunningham, Roland Curram, the late Noel Davis, Placido Domingo, Lisa Eichhorn, Robert Evans, Kafe Fassett, Eleanor Fazan, Scott Fichter, Sally Field, Stewart Grimshaw, Clay Griffith, Melanie Griffith, the late Conrad Hall, Sir Peter Hall, Willis Hall, Ed Harris, Jerome Hellman, Dustin Hoffman,

Peter Honess, Glenda Jackson, Anne James, Nicholas Janni, Dr David Kaminsky, Michael Keaton, Marthe Keller, Howard Koch, Jr., Larry Kramer, Andrew Kuehn, Gavin Lambert, Sonia Lawson, Twiggy Lawson, Julien Lemaitre, Joanna Lumley, Shirley MacLaine, Richard Marden, Marysa Maslansky, Ali McGraw, Sir Ian McKellen, Mike Medavoy, Sylvia Miles, Ruth Myers, Wallis Nicita, Ilo Orleans, Sean Penn, David Picker, Ana Maria Quintana, Lynn Redgrave, Vanessa Redgrave, Nicolas Roeg, Isabella Rossellini, Ann Roth, Jennifer Salt, Prunella Scales, Roy Scheider, Geoffrey Sharp, Gary Shaw, Martin Sheen, Sir Antony Sher, Ann Skinner, Jimmy Smits, John Steiner, Kiefer Sutherland, Dame Kiri Te Kanawa, Lily Tomlin, Brenda Vaccaro, Bruce Vilanch, Jon Voight, Robert Wagner, Billy Williams, Michael York, Steven Zaillian, Franco Zeffirelli, Jeremy Zimmermann.

Finally, my assistant, Matthew Capaldo, who proved enormously resourceful in every task he undertook, from researching to interviewing to transcribing; my agents on both sides of the ocean, Malaga Baldi in New York and Arabella Stein in London, who were, as always, diligent and enterprising; my editor, Paul Sidey, who remained throughout this process supremely encouraging and supportive, helping to shape the structure of this book and indulging my requests for extensions; and my partner, Dr Tim Huber, who was, as ever, my oracle of support, wisdom, and common sense.

Prologue

7 April 1970

"These are truly very exciting times"

I t was the penultimate night of Old Hollywood meeting the New. John Wayne, nominated less for *True Grit* than for a career of upholding the social law and order, sat a few seats away from Jon Voight, nominated for getting a blow job in a theater in Times Square. Up on stage, a suave Frank Sinatra was handing out a Lifetime Achievement Award to Cary Grant, while a few moments later both Ali McGraw and Candice Bergen trembled visibly as they read their respective lists of nominees. "We were all scared shitless," Voight remembered. "All of us younger stars. We had been warned to say nothing controversial, not to make any false moves. They – Old Hollywood – were watching us."

Organizers of the Oscar ceremony had reason to be anxious. The country was in turmoil. Anti-war protests were turning violent. The killing of four student protesters at Ohio's Kent

State was less than a month away. And a spate of Hollywood films had emerged in the past year that made it clear that the sympathies of Hollywood's younger generation were definitely not with the old guard.

John Schlesinger, director of the year's most controversial film, *Midnight Cowboy*, was across the Atlantic that night, awaiting the results in London. In the midst of shooting his new picture, *Sunday, Bloody Sunday*, he was nonetheless quite conscious of the drama unfolding in Los Angeles at the Dorothy Chandler Pavilion. He was keenly aware of the culture clash he'd helped bring about between the forces of rebellion and the forces of reaction. *Midnight Cowboy* might be a commercial smash, raking it in at the box office, and it might even have managed to turn the staid world of film criticism on its head as reviewers searched for fresh constructs to describe the film. But it was also an X-rated picture, the tale of two losers who turned tricks, stole money, smoked pot, and were probably fags to boot. Not exactly the kind of movie that industry stalwarts like Wayne and Sinatra and Bob Hope liked to hype.

Yet, astoundingly, the Academy had nominated *Cowboy* for Best Picture, and Schlesinger for Best Director. Old Hollywood rationalized away these nominations as simply bones thrown to the counter-culture. Indeed, as usual, the lion's share of nominations went to safe, "respectable" fare, like *Hello, Dolly!* and *Anne of the Thousand Days*, both of which could've been made in 1935. Aging Academy voters had been won over, yet again, by studio campaigns that included sumptuously catered buffets. It was enough to prompt some of the hipper critics to gnash their teeth. Grumbled Aljean Harmetz in the *New York Times*, "The fact that *Anne of the Thousand Days* received ten nominations and *Hello Dolly!* tied *Midnight*

Cowboy [at seven] had more to do with beef stroganoff, imported champagne, and three-inch prime ribs than with any quality in the films."

If New Hollywood had any chance to beat back *Dolly* and *Anne*, the bets were on George Roy Hill's *Butch Cassidy and the Sundance Kid*. No one thought Schlesinger's film was a contender, not even the director himself. "I didn't think we stood a chance of winning," he said. "Not a picture about a couple of filthy losers, no way."

But *Cowboy* producer Jerome Hellman went to the ceremony anyway, reluctantly getting his hair cut and donning the Establishment monkey suit. "I ran into George Roy Hill on the way in," Hellman remembered. "He said, 'Jerry, I just want you to know that *Midnight Cowboy* is a wonderful picture, *too*.' He was convinced that he was going to win, that we could never pull it off."

While Hellman sat uncomfortably in his tuxedo between Fred Astaire and Martha Raye, Schlesinger was thousands of miles away, having set his alarm for 3 a.m. to await word on the award with his new lover, Michael Childers, a handsome young photographer just out of UCLA. Childers had the confidence John lacked: "You're going to win," he kept saying. "I know you're going to win."

Regular telephone updates came from Schlesinger's secretary, planted backstage. "Waldo Salt won!" she exclaimed, her voice crackling across the Atlantic as the name of *Cowboy*'s screenwriter was called. That clinched it, Childers said: it was now inevitable that John, too, would take home the prize.

But Schlesinger laughed him off. Memories were still very fresh of the struggle they had spent trying to get a studio – any studio – to finance a film of James Leo Herlihy's novel about the seamy underbelly of New York. The hostility they'd faced from the old guard might have been assuaged somewhat by the picture's ultimate success, but Schlesinger knew Academy voters weren't about to reward his dirty little picture any further. After all, hadn't they given the previous year's Oscar to Carol Reed and *Oliver!* over Paul Newman's *Rachel, Rachel* and Zeffirelli's *Romeo and Juliet?*

Schlesinger's pessimism seemed justified when Wayne was announced the winner as Best Actor. Hellman clapped dutifully, hearing audible sighs of relief from those around him who were glad it was the Duke sauntering up to the stage, and not Voight or Dustin Hoffman, who'd both been so degenerate in *Cowboy*.

But then Myrna Loy took the podium to read the nominees for Best Director. In addition to Schlesinger, they were Arthur Penn for *Alice's Restaurant*, George Roy Hill for *Butch Cassidy*, Sydney Pollack for *They Shoot Horses, Don't They?* and Costa-Gavras for *Z*. Tearing open the envelope, she announced into the microphone, "And the winner is . . . John Schlesinger."

A millisecond of stunned silence followed before the audience erupted into applause for how courageous their industry seemed suddenly to have become. Voight, a loser a moment before, now strode victoriously up to the podium to accept on Schlesinger's behalf. He was gracious and brief, still apparently remembering the admonitions to behave, but nothing really needed to be said. It was clear which way the Academy voters were leaning, especially after Elizabeth Taylor announced the next award. Despite *Butch Cassidy* producer John Foreman starting out of his seat in anticipation, *Midnight Cowboy* was declared the Best Picture of 1969. Hellman, in shock, stumbled up to the stage.

"I hadn't prepared a speech," he remembered. "I think I said about six words and then acknowledged [United Artists studio head] David Picker, without whose enormous contribution the picture would never have been made. Then I walked off and called John."

In London, Childers burst into hoots, throwing his arms around Schlesinger and proclaiming that the world was theirs. Schlesinger was as stunned as Hellman. "The world did rather seem to be our oyster at that moment," he said. "Rather as if we were young turks changing the world." The sun would soon be up in London, and they decided to stay up all night. An impromptu party welcomed the sunrise: Julie Christie, Alan Bates, Tom Courtenay, Maggie Smith. The champagne flowed freely. When, a few hours later, John staggered over to the location for *Sunday, Bloody Sunday*, he'd find himself a bit wobbly on the scaffolding.

"Of course I was astonished by the Oscar," Schlesinger remembered. "In many minds, I should not have won. I had not made a picture that was approved by the old guard. We had to fight to get *Cowboy* made. Nobody wanted to make it. Then they gave us an X rating, but even that didn't stop us. We didn't cut a thing, and we said, 'This is it. This is the picture.' And then they nominated us, and then we won."

Back at the Oscars telecast, the old guard was attempting nonetheless to have the last word. Bob Hope faced the camera and intoned, "At a time when our moral values need to be restated and reaffirmed, I personally would like to see this industry lead the American people back to their true heritage of freedom — but freedom with honor and decency and a real respect for law and order and for the things that made this country great."

No amount of huffing and puffing from Old Hollywood, however, could stop the sudden momentum of *Midnight Cowboy*. The Oscar ensured that even more people would see the film and its "dazzling display of decadence and perversion," as one critic said. And Schlesinger, an Englishman, was feted as the man who had brought American cinema – finally – in tune with the times. For the moment, the last word belonged to him.

"I am very encouraged," he said, "that the climate in America, and indeed the world, seems to be set upon embracing more honesty, more truth. That can only be a good thing. These are truly very exciting times."

"I suppose I was fortunate," Schlesinger would say, years later, "to have begun making films when I did, in the 1960s and 1970s, when things were opening up, when for a brief, brilliant period films actually took chances, asked questions, probed under the surface of things, dared to have unhappy endings."

Peter Biskind, in his study of the period, has called it "the last time it was really exciting to make movies in Hollywood, the last time people could be consistently proud of the pictures they made, the last time the community as a whole encouraged good work, the last time there was an audience that could sustain it."

Indeed, Schlesinger strode like a colossus over *two* remarkable eras: the flowering of the British "New Wave" in the 1960s and the "Director's Cinema" in 1970s America. Both periods represent breaks with the past. The moribund British film industry, churning out such fare as *Sink the Bismarck!* and *Expresso Bongo* starring Cliff Richard, was startled awake by the "kitchen sink" social-realist films of a quartet of Oxford-educated filmmakers: Tony Richardson, Karel Reisz, Lindsay Anderson, and Schlesinger, who was by far the most successful of the four. His *A Kind of Loving, Billy Liar, Darling, Far from the Madding Crowd* and *Sunday, Bloody Sunday* came to symbolize a reinvigorated British cinema that offered insights into what he called "human difficulties and the illusions of love," rather than the spectacle and farce that had become so commonplace. And if, in hindsight, some critics now rank him farther down on the list of "greats" than Reisz, Anderson or Richardson, it's telling that, when the British Film Institute named the top 100 favorite British films in their 1999 poll, Schlesinger had more films on that list than any other New Wave director.

While John always insisted he was not truly a part of the "Free Cinema" movement – he retained a lifelong antipathy toward the intellectuals who were at its heart – he acknowledged that the challenge it offered to commercial cinema through its belief in "the significance of the everyday" certainly widened the possibilities of what might be explored on film. It was an exciting time for filmmaking in Britain. For a brief and shining moment, London became the hub of movie production for the Western world – it was the era of Richardson's *Tom Jones,* the Beatles films, and Roman Polanski's *Repulsion.* And no director so defined British cinema as Schlesinger.

"There was a great deal of envy toward John from the other filmmakers," said Gavin Lambert, who served as editor of the influential film journal *Sight and Sound.* "Critics, too, tended to be a bit snooty about him. Because you see, what separated John from the Free Cinema, was that he had considerably more box-office success."

Schlesinger parlayed that success across the Atlantic, arriving in Hollywood at precisely the right moment, when a similar cinematic revolution was taking place in the United States. *Midnight Cowboy*, in fact, was released two months before the film that is usually cited as kicking off the new American era, Dennis Hopper's *Easy Rider*. Critic and historian Paul Buhle has said Hollywood's "artistic reopening" of the 1970s can be traced to a single film: *Midnight Cowboy*. "Who could imagine," he asked, "that Hollywood might create an art house cinema that could also pack 'em in on a Saturday night?"

Although Schlesinger was English and would return to London to make his next picture, he was easily in sync with the new breed of American filmmakers, brash young turks like himself, who were overthrowing the studio system and wresting creative control out of the hands of the moneymen. American films of the 1970s were risky and innovative, character-driven, and defiant of traditional narrative rules. There were no gimmicks or "special effects": they were studies of the human condition, "treatises on life," Schlesinger said, "where no one can be expected to have all the answers, just some of the questions."

"We tackled subjects which were untenable before," he went on. "Subject matter exploded. I don't think we felt that we were great crusaders at the time. We just got opportunities to do things and took them."

Old Hollywood didn't give up without a fight. Despite *Midnight Cowboy*'s win — or perhaps because of it — in the next couple of years Academy voters rallied behind such standard fare as *Fiddler on the Roof*, *Airport* and *Nicholas and Alexandra*, making sure these were the pictures given record numbers of nominations. Vincent Canby of *The New York Times* cried foul, calling the Academy to task, which in turn provoked a sarcastic response from Leonard Spigelgass, one of the writers for the annual Oscar telecast.

"Let Vincent Canby and Penelope Gilliatt and Pauline Kael and Judith Crist, et. al., debate the merits of *A Clockwork Orange* and *Carnal Knowledge*," Spigelgass snarled in an opinion piece, "and we will simply accept their judgment. What a relief! We dum-dums vote for the *Airports* and the *Fiddlers* and the *Nicholases* because we just hate modern, relevant, avant-garde, impressionistic, soul-searching, violent, explicit films about rape, homosexuality, heroin, sadism, urinalysis, prostitution, and masturbation. And the reason we ignore these views of our society is that we are geriatric and conservative. We are Spiro Agnew; you are the free, untrammeled future."

His sarcasm backfired: Spigelgass and his cohorts were, in fact, not all that different from Agnew and his anti-intellectual brigade. This, despite the fact that Spigelgass, like Schlesinger, was a homosexual, but one from the old Hollywood studio school; you don't make noise about it, and you certainly don't make movies about it. Schlesinger's *Sunday, Bloody Sunday* (scripted, not coincidentally, by Penelope Gilliatt, one of the critics Spigelgass so despised) scandalized Old Hollywood in a way far greater than even *Midnight Cowboy* had. Not only did Schlesinger include – for the first time in screen history – a homosexual lead character (Peter Finch) on an equal moral plane with the heterosexual lead (Glenda Jackson), he also made sure the audience's sympathy was shared equally between the two.

Even more, unlike *Cowboy* – and *Easy Rider* and *A Clockwork Orange* and *Medium Cool* and so many of the gritty, ultra-realistic films of the period – *Sunday* was exquisitely literate, more like a novel than a film, and thus much more difficult to dismiss. No one, not even Spigelgass, could deny the quality of the picture, which endures as Schlesinger's masterpiece. In 1971, the picture received directing and acting nominations from the Academy, though not one for Best Picture.

By 1972, the war between Old and New Hollywood seemed essentially over, with the victor clear. Money talks, and the new box-office champs were pictures like *The Godfather*, *The French Connection*, *The Last Picture Show*, *McCabe and Mrs. Miller* and *Mean Streets*. While there would be no shortage of Towering Infernos and Poseidon Adventures, the 1970s marked a revolution not only in filmmaking, but in film*going*. As Susan Sontag has written, "It was at this specific moment in the one-hundred-year history of cinema that going to movies, thinking about movies, talking about movies became a passion among university students and other young people. You fell in love not just with actors but with cinema itself."

Like the work of Hopper, Coppola, Scorsese, Bogdanovich, Friedkin, Altman and others, Schlesinger's films of the period were about more than just their literal narratives, more than the action and the people on the screen. Schlesinger films, even thrillers like the blockbuster *Marathon Man*, lacked easily identifiable heroes. Their messages were ambiguous. Their endings didn't tie everything up neatly. Moviegoers were forced to ponder what they'd just seen. At the end of *The Day of the Locust*, for example, what's happened to Todd, the character played by William Atherton? Is he dead? Has he escaped? What's the little Mona Lisa smile that steals across Karen Black's face?

Or, in the famous closing shot of *Sunday, Bloody Sunday*, when Peter Finch turns to look us straight in the eye, how are we supposed to feel? "But something," Finch says. "We were something." What does he mean?

"I expect," Schlesinger once said, "that my audience is willing to work a little, not just sit there."

In 1969, in winning the Oscars for Best Director and Best Picture, Schlesinger personified New Hollywood. How quickly times would change. Before the new decade was out, the ground was already shifting under his feet, indeed, under the feet of all the young turks who had transformed the screen and the industry. The revolution was over almost as soon as it had begun, and it became clear that New Hollywood hadn't won after all. The styles and values of Old Hollywood came roaring back, and the directors of New Hollywood found themselves regarded as relics, in much the same way as the men they had replaced.

Was it *Jaws?* or perhaps *Star Wars?* What transformed the American cinema from a director's medium to a producer's corporate contrivance? When *Honky Tonk Freeway* in 1981 proved to be Schlesinger's *Heaven's Gate*, Hollywood turned on him so savagely that even today those who witnessed it still shudder. "It was as if John had done something obscene, when all he did was make a comedy they didn't think was very funny," said Schlesinger's longtime editor, Jim Clark. Worse: they didn't think it would make money, which it didn't, especially after Universal refused to distribute it, so "offended" were they by Schlesinger's blatant disregard for profits.

"They accused me of not caring whether I made a picture that would make money, that all I cared about was making a film that interested me," he said. "I stand guilty as charged."

The New Hollywood upstart of 1969 had, in little more than a decade, come to represent an increasingly antiquated system. He was a director who expected the unreasonable: namely, a producer who would fight for his creative vision, the way Hellman and Joseph Janni, his British producer, had done. And, more than that, he expected a focus on the *craft*, on the characters and the story at hand – not on how many dollars needed to be spent for television advertising or how best to make back all the money in the first weekend.

There was nowhere to turn. The British cinema, drained of its talents by the Hollywood studios, was once again stagnant, with no financing to be had. In America, asking an audience to "work" had become anathema. "There were people who wanted to believe that the shark in *Jaws* stood for something else, like man's inhumanity to man or corporate greed," Schlesinger observed. "I said it stood for a shark. That's all." And that shark made a lot of money for its studio, so more sharks were put on order.

Schlesinger's *The Falcon and the Snowman* partially redeemed him in the eyes of Hollywood. The film at least made back its cost, as well as showcasing, for the first time, the fact that Sean Penn could do a heck of a lot more than *Fast Times at Ridgemont High*. But it was a film with traitors cast as heroes in Reagan-era America, a film without razzle-dazzle, a film without romance, and (worst of all) a film without any merchandising tie-ins. Schlesinger's last work in Hollywood would be as a gun for hire, with substandard scripts and a committee of distant, uninterested producers.

"He wanted to continue to work, like all artists," said producer Wallis Nicita, a friend. "You've got to keep scratching that itch. I think he took his best shot [on these later films] but it was like putting Van Gogh around a cartoon and saying, 'Okay, make something out of it.' There was just no way."

"I think of what we have to fight for now," Schlesinger said in 1985, "the arguments about actors – not who's right for the part, but who's going to help the opening weekend, and that's it. That's all they care to talk about."

As difficult as it had been getting *Midnight Cowboy* made in 1969, it would have been absolutely impossible in a Hollywood increasingly obsessed with the bottom line. "The studios have *always* been concerned with the bottom line," said producer Andrew Kuehn, another Schlesinger friend, "but there's a difference between caring about the bottom line and not caring about anything *but*." Railing in interviews against "filmmaking by committee" did no good. What was a growing concern in the 1980s became an efficient, streamlined reality in the 1990s. Filmmaking ceased to resemble anything it had ever been before.

That's not to say Schlesinger shared no blame for the decline of his career. The heady success of *Midnight Cowboy* forever fueled a desire to achieve another blockbuster hit, a goal realized only once more, with *Marathon Man*. As Hollywood filmmaking changed, so did Schlesinger try (sometimes with a perceived sense of desperation) to change along with it, taking on projects that would have been better left to younger, more commercially savvy directors, or not made at all. He would express more than once his weariness in trying "to keep up with mediocrity," yet still he persevered, each time hoping this one might be *it*, the picture to restore him to the glory he had known in 1969. How else to explain his decision to make a movie with Madonna, the aptly titled *The Next Best Thing*?

Yet to his credit, he threw his entire self into every project he accepted, and found that in the smaller, more intimate world of television – and not, incidentally, in his native England, far away from the connivances of Hollywood – he might still craft a trio of small masterpieces: *An Englishman Abroad*, *A Question of Attribution*, and the delightful *Cold Comfort Farm*, which he paid out of his own pocket to have blown up to 35mm and distributed as a feature, earning him his last box office success and critical acclaim in 1996.

The undeniable diminution of his career has left many unsure of where to place Schlesinger in the hierarchy of filmmakers. Was he a "great director"? *The Times* of London in its final assessment, seemed to think not: "However well-crafted, his work perhaps lacked the personal stamp that marks the true cinema artist." Others from the age of great directors – Scorsese, Altman, Kubrick, Ken Russell – stamped a far more recognizable imprimatur on their films. Yet note *The Times*'s use of the word "perhaps." While John Schlesinger was certainly no Woody Allen – making the same film over and over again, varying themes and character but holding fast to the same vision, motifs, and sense of place – it can be argued that Schlesinger *did* leave a singular imprint. His description of "people pushed to an edge" can be applied to all of his work, and even in his lackluster films, what interested him was the exploration of how such people managed to live – actually, how to *survive* – in their marginalized worlds.

It's true that Schlesinger could be an obvious filmmaker, lacking the finesse of a Peter Bogdanovich or the poetry of Lindsay Anderson. Even in a film as monumentally beautiful as

Sunday, Bloody Sunday, he could still wield a clumsy hammer at times: panning down from a poster advocating the war on poverty to a refrigerator overloaded with food, for example. It was an urge toward the conspicuous instilled during his television documentary days, and as a technique it worked on the small screen in ten-minute segments. Blown up to giant size and set within the framework of a story, however, it could seem merely a glaring display of craft, the "tick, scratch, tick" that Pauline Kael would claim she was always able to discern in John Schlesinger's films.

He could also be indulgent. From that same experience in television, Schlesinger came away always craving length and time – a desire that often kept him from parting with footage, even when it might have made good films like *The Day of the Locust* or *Yanks* even better, trimmed of their fat. In later years, too, without the creative collaboration of writers such as Waldo Salt and Frederic Raphael or cameramen of the class of Conrad Hall and Nicolas Roeg, Schlesinger all too often resorted to stock reaction shots, cheap laughs, clichés instead of original twists. Few directors have known such startling inconsistency in their work, from truly transcendent, superbly realized films like *Sunday, Bloody Sunday* to muddled, incoherent wrecks like *The Innocent*.

Perhaps this unevenness prevents his elevation to the pantheon of greats. Yet Schlesinger himself was wary of such designation. Chided for accepting projects considered beneath his station, he would defend his decision: "It's very difficult to say, 'Well, I'll only do personal films, and I won't touch anything else.' There are people who have done that, and perhaps they are the top filmmakers in the world, but I don't consider myself part of that group." If being a "great" director meant that he couldn't make a film "for the fun of it" or take on a project "simply because it seemed to offer a little escapism from the world," then great director he would not be. "I was never interested in being arty," he said. "I wanted to give my audience an experience that moved them, made them think, made them cry or laugh or scream out loud. I was always most interested in telling a good story."

From the beginning, from the first little amateur films he turned out with his 9.5 mm camera, John Schlesinger wanted to be a storyteller. Though his methods would veer from the profound to the prosaic, his impulse was consistent: to use the medium of the cinema as might a bard or a minstrel, regaling his audiences like the magicians he had so admired in his youth. Kael would call his filmmaking style "mechanical," but in Schlesinger's best films there is a stunning precision to his mechanics: here is a master craftsman at work. Surely there is room in the pantheon for storytellers, for great fablers. And during the latter half of the twentieth century, John Schlesinger gave us some of our most memorable cinematic tales.

He was also, significantly, a man of his times. His films reflect who we were, where we have been, and what we have dreamed. He lived through challenging periods, years of revolution and change. His own story provides a unique mirror on the cinema of the past forty years, from both a British and an American perspective, and not just during his heyday of the 1960s and 70s. Schlesinger's early career offers a reflection of postwar Britain during an exciting period of growth and artistic expression at the BBC. His later career, marked by his struggle to stay relevant, gives insight into the realities of an increasingly cut-throat, corporate business, whose heads of movie studios hold MBAs instead of film degrees and few even bother to attend premieres anymore. ("They don't like movies," said Andy Kuehn. "They really don't. They'd rather watch a baseball game or go golfing.")

But Schlesinger's story is also the singular journey of one man who found himself at the center of his times. He presided over a glittery universe of the fabulous and fashionable in creative circles, inheriting George Cukor's crown as King of the Hollywood Salon. At the homes he shared with Childers, both in London and Los Angeles, he would mix the worlds of movies, art, music, opera and theater: Laurence Olivier, Tennessee Williams, Natalie Wood, David Hockney, Christopher Isherwood, Peggy Ashcroft, Bette Midler, Coral Browne, Alan Bennett, Michael York, Shirley MacLaine, Placido Domingo, Paul and Linda McCartney.

Undisguised about his homosexuality long before there was such a notion as "openly gay," Schlesinger lived long enough to see the very structure of one's public identity undergo a radical shift. At the time of *Sunday, Bloody Sunday*, the closest the press came to speaking the truth was to refer to Schlesinger as "a gifted director who's in touch with gay sensibilities." As he got older, and his gayness began to inform an ever-larger part of his identity, Schlesinger took the issue into his own hands. When, in 1991, Ian McKellen was criticized for accepting a knighthood from the Conservative government of John Major, Schlesinger gave his name to a letter of support published in the *Guardian* newspaper from a group of other "openly gay artists." Cheered by gay activists for his courage in "coming out," Schlesinger was also denounced by many of the same for turning around a few months later and making a political film for Major and the Conservative party.

His inconsistencies defined his life. "I feel as if I live at the edge of midnight," he recorded in his diary, an allusion to the constant pressure to prove himself, to repeat his success, to stay relevant. "I'm always on the edge of a precipice, ready for the deep end." But living on that "edge" was in truth his choice, his preferred way of life, induced by the urgency within himself to live a life both authentic and challenging. "It is in one's choices," he said, "and indeed, in one's contradictions, where definition is found."

The life he led and the choices he made offer many of the same ambiguities found in his films. Neither a hero nor a villain, neither a crusader for change nor indifferent to the world around him, John Schlesinger was a man of ideas, a lover of magic, a storyteller. Today, many film directors envy the career he had: stretching over decades, choosing material for personal rather than box-office reasons, being allowed to flourish in many different genres and styles. When Schlesinger died in July 2003, after two years of quiet contemplation following a massive stroke, his obituaries called him "one of a kind, irreplaceable." Certainly, there will be few careers like his again. In that brief, golden time when filmmakers thought they had a shot at changing the world, John Schlesinger stood shoulder-to-shoulder with the best of them. "I like to think that someday," he said, "someone will look back at my work and say, 'Here was a director who cared about movies, who did things his way, who asked some important questions, who had some ideas and vision, who left behind something that will endure."

One

"Find the Story"

Was it a comedy or a tragedy? That was the fundamental dilemma John Schlesinger was trying to
resolve, the truth that would allow him to make
sense of everything else.

"So did you ever come to any conclusion?" I asked him,
sitting on the terrace of his Palm Springs home on a warm, dry,
beautiful afternoon.

He was staring off at the mountains. "Do you mean about
life," he whispered, "or the movie?"

He was being wry. I'd been told of his humor, but flashes of
it were rare.

"Well, both, I should think," I offered.

We had been talking about *The Next Best Thing*, his last
film, starring Madonna and Rupert Everett. Universally blud-
geoned by the critics, the picture's main flaw isn't Madonna's

performance but the schizophrenic script, which never decides whether it's supposed to be essentially funny or essentially serious, a comedy or a tragedy. I knew John had struggled with that question all through the shoot, but if he wanted to get more profound with me and talk about life, so much the better.

Yet he said nothing else. He just kept his eyes on the mountains, so grand, so enveloping. Stringing more than a few words together, let alone composing an entire sentence, had become increasingly difficult since his stroke, which had left him wheelchair-bound and nearly silent. A stroke that had come not long after he collapsed during post-production of that ill-fated, contentious last film.

Looking into his room from the terrace, I could see his Oscar for *Midnight Cowboy* standing on his shelf. Beside it were pictures of people from his life: his parents; his partner, Michael Childers, still at his side after more than thirty years; actress and friend Coral Browne; and a young, handsome filmmaker John fancied, who had obligingly posed in the pool without his swimsuit.

There was also a photograph of Schlesinger himself, the way the world remembered him. It looked to be from the set of *Eye for an Eye* in 1996, but it might have come from *Madame Sousatzka* (1988), or even possibly *Yanks* (1979). Before his stroke, John Schlesinger's physical appearance hardly changed over the years. Rotund and genial, he had sparkling blue eyes, and a white beard neatly clipped to outline the lower half of his round, cherubic face. By contrast, the man in the wheelchair was thin and slumped, his cheeks sunken, one hand forever making circles against his waxy forehead.

"When John was well and hardy," one of his friends would

tell me, his voice dropping and his eyes glancing around as if he didn't want to be overheard telling the story, "he had this running gag where he would pretend to be a stroke victim. He'd slur his words, contort his face. It was really quite funny. Everyone would laugh, John most of all."

John Schlesinger sat in his wheelchair, staring at the mountains with unblinking eyes.

A comedy, or a tragedy?

"Can't it be *both?*" he once asked testily into his tape-recorded diary, fretting about some project or another. Or maybe his agitation was really about life itself, as he suggested to me that day as we sat on the terrace. "I like to think it's always about both," he recorded. "It's just in finding the right balance."

Yet balance was in short supply on the set of *The Next Best Thing*. It was the 3rd of May 1999. Schlesinger had just taken Madonna aside to tell her to lighten up, that the scene she was doing required no such heavy melodramatics. It was a comedy, he told her. A *comedy*. At least he thought so that day.

She recoiled visibly from his touch. "You're just so terribly old-fashioned," she snapped, in the pseudo British accent she'd adopted since filming began. "You don't know what you're talking about!" In front of the entire crew, she turned on her heel and walked away from him.

In the old days, of course, had Julie Christie or Glenda Jackson pulled such a stunt, the roar from Schlesinger would have shorted out the amps. Witty, cultured, polite – oh, yes, all of that – but he was also legendarily possessed of a fierce, raging temper. "He could be like Zeus, flinging down the lightning bolts," said a former crew member who'd worked with him for years.

But Schlesinger, 73 years old, his diabetes out of control, was in a funk. His back was hurting him, and there was that little problem with his breathing: he seemed increasingly unable to do it on his own. So he simply let out a sigh and retreated to his director's chair, where he sat gazing at the monitor. He would blow up later, but not then. "My dear," he would tell an assistant, "I just couldn't be bothered."

He was exhausted. That the picture had gotten this far was in itself rather miraculous. A year earlier, Schlesinger had assumed his film career was over. "So I'll rest on my laurels," he said. "There are worse things than that." Most assuredly: he knew, no matter what else he might do, his obituaries would herald him as "the man who made *Midnight Cowboy*." And maybe, if he was lucky, they'd add *Sunday, Bloody Sunday*. And perhaps *Darling, Marathon Man, A Kind of Loving*. A few cineastes would surely mention *The Day of the Locust*. All in all, a good run. Certainly laurels worth resting on.

So he and Michael sold their famous house on Rising Glen in the Hollywood Hills and bought a place in Palm Springs. "But John still wanted one more great movie," Childers said. "What director doesn't?"

It was, therefore, with considerable excitement that he listened to Rupert Everett, who'd rung out of the blue one morning with the idea for *The Next Best Thing*. Just off his starmaking turn with Julia Roberts in *My Best Friend's Wedding*, Everett was certain he could replicate its success and become, in the process, Hollywood's first openly gay leading man. The story for the new film concerned a woman and her gay male best friend (an obvious riff on the Everett-Roberts pairing) who raise a child together, an arrangement that becomes threatened when the woman falls in love with another man. Everett wanted – indeed *needed*, he said – John Schlesinger at the helm.

Giddy conversation followed over dinner, with John, Michael, Rupert and Madonna all tossing out ideas for what was certain to be a hugely successful film. "I know you can help me," Madonna said when they met, reaching across the table for the director's hand. Critics had not always been kind about her acting. John promised her that he would do his best. To the press, Madonna said "part of the attraction" of working with Schlesinger was remembering how he had guided Christie to stardom – and an Oscar. "I worship Julie Christie," she told a reporter, "and *Darling* is one of my favorite movies of all time."

Planning for the film revived Schlesinger's sagging spirits, still badly bruised from the critical drubbing he'd received over his last picture, *Eye for an Eye*. Work always invigorated him. "I'm like a bear with a sore head when I haven't got a project," he said during the shoot of *Eye for an Eye*. "I would love to know, for instance, that I'll be working, let's say, next May. The unknown can be so daunting. I'd like to keep working because it keeps one on one's toes. I'll be 70 next year and I've only got 10 more years – if I'm very lucky."

He wasn't. Since *Eye for an Eye*, there had been only one project, a production of *The Tale of Sweeney Todd* for Showtime that the critics had largely ignored. His health, too, had declined; by the time *The Next Best Thing* was rolling, John was being treated for congestive heart failure, vascular disease, high cholesterol, hypertension and an enlarged prostate – not to mention his needing regular insulin injections for his diabetes, since his blood sugar levels were in constant flux.

Principal photography began in mid April. The first day on the set, Schlesinger was amused when producer Tom Rosenberg, observing him at work, commented to the crew, "Well, he sure knows where to put the camera."

"I ought to," John replied dryly. "I've been putting it there for fifty years."

He agreed with Everett that the script, by Thomas Ropelewski, needed some adjustments, but working with writers was something Schlesinger was skilled at doing. Surely they could smooth things out. But Everett wanted to overturn one of the most basic elements of the story: instead of the two leads deciding consciously to have a child together, he suggested a drunken, unplanned sexual encounter instead. "Lots more potential there," he argued to John. "Comedy, drama, all of it."

Schlesinger knew that few people, especially not gay men, would buy that premise. He argued that the original idea of the two friends making a deliberate choice to raise a child was more interesting *and* more believable. Then they could either attempt awkwardly to have sex (as pulled off hilariously on the television programme *Will and Grace* a few years later) or resort to the old turkey baster, as many mixed gay-straight parents have done.

Everett, however, was adamant. The film's original producer, Leslie Dixon, would later assert that the version of the script John signed on to direct was not what made it to the screen. In a letter to the *Los Angeles Times*, she would call Everett an "egocentric actor" who rewrote the screenplay (Ropelewski was her husband) with the blessing of Tom

Rosenberg. Yet John, too, had given his approval even though he remained fundamentally uncomfortable with the idea of the drunken lovemaking. "This script is going to need major work," he told Childers. "We are going to have to completely reshape it."

In the past, John Schlesinger had loved that process, the "what if" phase of moviemaking: hammering out the story, imagining the look and the feel of the film with the writers. And he'd worked with some of the very best: Waldo Salt, Alan Bennett, Frederic Raphael, William Goldman, Penelope Gilliatt, Willis Hall, Keith Waterhouse. He had always been known for his eye for a story. "I can't actually sit down and write good dialogue," he said, "but I always know when it's not right, or when a 'beat' is missing. So much of human relationships deals with what isn't said, with the subtext, that you've got to make sure that it's there."

But Everett dismissed any input from a man whose opinion had been gospel to the likes of Salt and Bennett and Raphael. At another emergency script discussion over dinner at Café Les Deux, the mood was still cordial, but Childers said he could smell panic in the air. Everett suggested they all walk off the picture together: "It's going to be a disaster," he kept repeating. Madonna, however, wasn't so ready to throw in the towel. She looked to John for salvation: she still had hopes he could work his magic on her. The director concluded they should carry on, rewriting as they went along.

"John was very aware what the problem was," said Scott Fichter, his assistant on the film. "The script jumped from comic to serious without much reason or balance."

Comedy or tragedy? Schlesinger's skill was for the latter, though he'd given comedy his best shot a couple of times, succeeding once (*Cold Comfort Farm*) but also very famously falling on his face (*Honky Tonk Freeway*.) He originally saw this new picture as drama, but had allowed himself to be swayed over to the comedy side by Everett, who wanted to keep his *My Best Friend's Wedding* fans happy by giving them some slapstick. Yet the story's essentially tragic nature was inescapable: the alternative family, no matter how touted by the film's marketing campaign, comes undone. No one winds up happy in the end.

Which, of course, was practically Schlesinger's stock-in-trade. Billy Liar deliberately misses the train to London; Ratso Rizzo dies before stepping foot in Miami; both Alex and Daniel (*Sunday, Bloody Sunday*) end up alone. "I don't know if I'd call my endings unhappy," John observed. "They're ambiguous, and I like ambiguity. I've almost always had ambiguous endings. I let the audience figure it out for themselves."

But this was 1999, and Hollywood didn't do ambiguity anymore. "Everybody's so busy now trying to explain things," John said, "making sure that the audience doesn't have to ask 'how did that happen?' They're putting captions on the most obvious things."

In Schlesinger's opinion, the script for *The Next Best Thing* had become terribly obvious and increasingly melodramatic: Robert's the father; then he isn't the father; then the real father comes back; then he's gone; and so on and so on. At rehearsals, John would read Everett's green and pink revised pages with growing exasperation, but he also had a few ideas of his own. If his star was going to be intractable on the drunken lovemaking scene, then why not make Abby into more of a seductress? John argued that even though she knows Robert's gay, Abby could still, deep down, have a hankering for him, the only man in her life who's ever been good to her; honest and constant. One night she gets him a little drunk. They wrestle. She goes down on him. The camera moves over to Robert's face. Eyes closed, head back, he would have resembled Joe Buck in *Midnight Cowboy*, thinking about Crazy Annie while the college kid played by Bob Balaban busied himself in his lap. In this way, John argued, taking the sex act to the next step might at least be seen as *somewhat* more possible.

"Absolutely not!" Madonna insisted, allegedly horrified at the idea despite having performed fellatio on a bottle in her backstage documentary *Truth or Dare*. Some who were involved in the talks thought her opposition was due less to any aversion to the act than to her strongly held belief that any man, gay or straight would ultimately find Abby irresistible. Everett backed her up, sharing none of John's concerns about the unlikelihood of the drunken moment of passion. To a *New York Times* reporter visiting the set, he said he viewed Robert as having had a physical attraction to Abby years ago, as he said he himself had once had for Madonna. "Their loneliness reignites that spark," he explained, "and they have sex, which I think is a genius event."

Maybe to Everett such sexual flexibility seemed genius (indeed, he scripted a scene in which Robert tells his gay pals that he's had sex with Abby, and instead of any "ick factor," they respond with "Cool!" and "Was it hot?") but to gay audiences the entire basis of the film was undercut by that premise. In a drawn-out, hokey dance of seduction, Madonna emerges from a closet wearing a slinky 1930s ballgown; before long she's being mounted by a randy, if intoxicated, Everett. "Yeah, right," said John's assistant Gary Shaw, "like that gown was supposed to do the trick to get a gay man turned on enough to fuck her."

When the film was finally released in March 2000, the forthright Michael Musto of the *Village Voice* stated the obvious: "Every single queen I know has been getting drunk, sleeping with their female best friend, and then fighting to get custody of the resulting baby. Oh wait a minute – that's not real life, that's the plot of the new Madonna movie." Without the expected core audience of gay men to build the picture up by word of mouth, *The Next Best Thing* never stood a chance.

There was a time, of course, when John Schlesinger was listened to, when his instincts were trusted and his ideas put into practice. "I wish Jo Janni were still alive," Childers told me, shutting the door to Schlesinger's room so he could rest. Our little talk on the terrace, even though he'd uttered not more than half a dozen sentences, had tired him out. His younger partner – the 22-year-old golden boy was now an indefatigable 57 – ushered me into the living room to fill in the blank spots. "Oh, yeah, Jo Janni, the stories he would've been able to tell. Like how John had to fight to get that scene in *Sunday, Bloody Sunday*. Penelope Gilliatt didn't want that kiss included. It's not in the original script. She tried later to claim credit for it, when everybody called it groundbreaking. But it was John's idea. All John's."

I'd known from the start that Childers would be the guardian of the flame, the sentinel keeping watch over Schlesinger's legacy, and that I would need to take that into account. It was Childers, after all, who had summoned me here, albeit at John's request, to write the story of the director's life that he'd always planned to pen himself, but because of his stroke would now never be able to do. Almost from the moment we'd first shaken hands, Childers had been making grand claims about John and his films, admitting later, with a mischievous glint in his eye, that when he couldn't remember things exactly, he'd "exaggerate and make them even better."

Yet, in the story of the famous close-up of a male-to-male kiss in *Sunday, Bloody Sunday*, Childers was one hundred percent accurate. In London, I would go through John's files, meticulously kept and labeled, each revision of every script preserved for posterity. And there, in Gilliatt's first draft submitted to Schlesinger and Janni, Daniel (Peter Finch) and Bob (Murray Head) *do* kiss – but in long shot and in silhouette. "That kiss was going to be in close-up or not at all," Schlesinger said. "I wanted it as big and as natural as any kiss that's been on the screen."

Long discussions ensued between director and screenwriter at John's home on Victoria Road in Kensington. Schlesinger felt as proprietary over the script as Gilliatt did; it was, after all, his story. For several years in the mid-1960s, Schlesinger had been the Peter Finch character, desperately in love with a young man who remained frustratingly footloose, dividing his time between John's flat and that of a woman. The object of Schlesinger's *amour* would never choose between the two of them and, like Finch, John never asked him to. The relationship ended when the boy went to Italy (not America, as in the film) but the story had haunted John ever since.

"Penelope Gilliatt was rather against the fact that this doctor and his lover were going to actually greet each other with an extremely fond kiss," Schlesinger said. "'Can't we do it in long shot, in silhouette?' [she asked]. And I said, 'No, it's got to be done absolutely as if it's an everyday occurrence with everything totally natural and normal about it.' If we had done it any other way, it wouldn't have worked."

There was nothing particularly political in Schlesinger's insistence on the scene: though Gay Lib had been making headlines, especially after the Stonewall riots in New York in June 1969, the director wasn't attempting to blaze a trail for homo sex on the silver screen. It was simply about finding and serving the story, which *demanded* that the kiss be seen in close-up, no matter the objections of Gilliatt. Daniel, a physician, has just come home from seeing a patient. His lover, Bob, is waiting for him; they hug as Daniel rattles on about his day at the clinic. That hug is the first provocation, the first signal to audiences that something lives between these two men. Moviegoers sat up and took notice; some grew uneasy, though they weren't entirely sure why. Schlesinger then upped the ante by having Bob rub Daniel's neck as they continue the small talk. In this easy, natural build-up to the kiss, audiences could both sense something coming as well as deny its inevitability: "No," some told themselves, "he can't possibly be going *there* . . ."

But, of course, he was. In 1971, few could imagine such a payoff. Schlesinger gave it to them anyway, in a large, full-mouth, ardent kiss, Finch's strong hands gripping both of Murray Head's cheeks. "That's the way John said it had to be done, so it was," said the film's editor, Richard Marden. "No questions asked, and Jo Janni backed him up."

No grumbling, either, from Finch or Head, though Schlesinger recalled hearing a sound of horror at the moment of contact from one of the camera operators, traditionally one of the few domains of macho heterosexuality on a movie set. "Yes, one or two of the crew members had a problem with [that scene]," said cinematographer Billy Williams. "You have to remember this was something new. No one had seen something like it before."

Gilliatt, for her part, stayed away from the set that day. In her revised script, she had eliminated the directions for the silhouette but had stopped short of calling for a close-up. All it reads in her second version is "They kiss," leaving it up to John to determine how, in fact, they go about doing it.

Thirty years ago, a romantic, close-up kiss between two men was far more provocative, far more risky, far more pushing to the edge than any implied fellatio between a man and a woman would be in 2000. "But, you see," Marden said, "John took chances, and they paid off. He insisted on that kiss because he wanted to make a film about the people. Otherwise the thing wouldn't have been valid at all. He was not trying to be sensational. It was a look at the way things are, and Jo Janni saw that and trusted him and that's why, in the end, it's as good a picture as it is."

A different set of producers – *The Next Best Thing*'s Tom Rosenberg, Gary Lucchesi, and Richard Wright (who John took to calling "Richard Wrong") – never trusted Schlesinger. Or maybe they did, in the beginning at least, trust his reputation as an actor's director, a writer's director. But thirty years after the creative sparks of the one-on-one, director-producer relationships that Schlesinger had so cherished with Janni and Jerry Hellman, the dynamic had become obsolete. Jo Janni, and Jo Janni alone, had produced *Sunday, Bloody Sunday*. Jerry Hellman said he couldn't ever imagine sharing ultimate producing responsibility on a film. By contrast, *The Next Best Thing* was produced not only by Rosenberg, Lucchesi, and Wright, but also by Ted Tannebaum, Lewis Manilow, Linne Radmin, Marcus Viscidi, Meredith Zamsky, and, nominally,

Leslie Dixon – producers, executive producers, co-producers, associate producers. This was John's much-despised "film-making by committee," and he never would learn how to negotiate his way through.

"Perhaps we should have known from the start it was a bad match," said Ruth Myers, brought in by John as costume designer, "between those of us who were used to doing things one way and those who expected something else."

On her first day on the set, Myers – a two-time Academy Award nominee whose credits stretched back to 1967 and included such films as *Isadora*, *The Addams Family*, *Emma*, *L.A. Confidential* and *Iris* – brought her sketches to present to Madonna. "She looked at me in amazement," Myers said, "because what she was used to was rails and rails of clothing coming in for her to choose from. At the time, however, I couldn't understand what she was talking about. I'm not a fashionista, and here she was expecting [racks of] Stella McCartneys and Donatella Versaces. In her defense, that's the way modern films go, and I think what happened in a small way for me happened with the whole film for John. There was just no comprehension about how things had changed."

Sitting with him in Palm Springs some two years later, I asked Schlesinger, "Do you think maybe it was hopeless from the start, just the collision of two different worlds?"

His response was surprisingly swift. "But why ask *me* then?"

That one's not hard to answer, and I told him so. John Schlesinger stood for something; something many in the *new* "New Hollywood" seemed to be forever chasing after: prestige, certainly, but also challenge, innovation, fearlessness, intelligence. They wanted him because John Schlesinger understood story and character, even if what he'd end up telling them was not what they wanted to hear.

"John wasn't a writer but he thought like a writer," said producer Wallis Nicita. "He could draw out every single possibility in his head and then write out to the end of the line the possibility of everything. He was brilliant like that."

In the myriad scripts of *Sunday, Bloody Sunday* there are scrawlings in the margins in John's handwriting, whole passages circled with arrows pointing to the next page: "Isn't this what we're after?" or "What's her motivation here?" He employed his own idiosyncratic story-boarding before each film: "Funny little hieroglyphics which only I can probably read."

In his head, he carried an entire movie. "This goes here," he'd say, finding the perfect place for a vignette he'd observed in Piccadilly Circus or Times Square – like the crazy street lady singing at the end of *Darling* or the toy mouse in the automat in *Midnight Cowboy*. He loved "laminating" such small moments behind the main action. In *Cowboy*, Joe and Ratso are talking about the afterlife, having just visited Ratso's father's grave. They're ruminating over reincarnation when, behind them, a woman bursts in, blathering in a loud "Noo Yawk" accent: "I don't know, my husband parked the car, they've moved us on and I got in a lot of trouble, and I mean, what is this place coming to?" Absolute absurdity, yet the stuff of daily life.

"So you laminate the two," Schlesinger said. "There's this serious conversation, there's this woman complaining, and then in come two weird-looking people who take a photograph of it all. They're all wonderful, totally disparate things happening, and it's constantly interesting."

He never claimed auteurship, however. He found the whole

notion silly and pretentious. He respected the writer far too much to ever claim authorship of a film. "The process of working with a writer is so extraordinarily complex," Schlesinger said. "A writer may very often think of a totally visual idea which kicks off an entire way of shooting a scene, or a director may think of the content, saying we need a scene in which such-and-such happens. I've many times improvised a scene with a writer, but I would never claim that I am the sole auteur of a film. Absolutely not."

A good director, he said, "in some way pursues his own personal vision, and makes whatever sacrifice necessary to do it. And the great enemy of demographics – and the great friend to those of us who are trying to make something special or perhaps something different from the mainstream – is the reality that every now and again what everyone thought was going to work *doesn't*, and something out of left field suddenly *does*."

John Schlesinger both loved and hated what he did. Shooting a film was nearly always difficult and unpleasant. In some ways *The Next Best Thing* was a walk in the park compared to making *The Falcon and the Snowman*, shot on location under a brutally hot Mexican sun with a belligerent, uncooperative Sean Penn (ironically, about a year before Penn would marry Madonna).

"I was not happy, to put it mildly, during the making of that picture," Penn admitted to me. "John and I saw the character and the script very differently. But I'll tell you this much. At least he had a vision. Maybe it wasn't mine, but today most directors haven't given any thought to having a vision. If I were making a picture today with John Schlesinger, even if it meant fighting like hell again, I'd get down on my knees in gratitude."

Fight like hell? Schlesinger *itched* for a good fight if it meant he might get what he wanted. A film was his baby, he'd often say, and he was its father. If *he* wasn't going to fight for it, who would?

"I think part of the problem on that last film was that John had no one to battle," said Ruth Myers. Her husband had been the legendary production designer Richard MacDonald, collaborator with Schlesinger on *Far from the Madding Crowd*, *The Day of the Locust* and *Marathon Man*. "I remember Richard telling me that all through *Locust* he could hear John and [cinematographer] Conrad Hall going at it tooth and nail. John's m.o. was to battle his way through, but he had no peers here, no one who really understood him well enough for him to fight with."

Not that he didn't rant and rave on the *Next Best Thing* set, often to anyone who happened to be passing by. "It becomes irritating when you've got three producers with earphones looking at your every move on the set," he told a reporter. He was infuriated when Everett began incorporating changes to the script without running them by him first, especially after he'd spent the previous night drawing out his "funny little hieroglyphics" for the next day's work. He'd be handed the revised pages at the same time as the prop people and lighting technicians. "I'm the director here!" John would bellow, but he found that complaining to the film's gaggle of producers did little good. They had given Rupert their permission, completely maneuvering John out of creative control.

"It's sickening to watch how producers and other execs kiss-ass the talent," said Scott Fichter – talent, defined here, being movie stars, not a veteran director of bygone classics. "All it really took was someone to take issue with something [in the script] and then of course the producers were thinking, 'This is going to halt the schedule,' so they were put into a corner and manipulated in that regard [to go along with Everett's changes.]"

Everett had a lot riding on the film. This was his big chance, possibly his *only* chance, to prove himself a major box-office star. As filming went on, with scenes so painfully falling flat, he seemed to panic. He threw things. He shouted and cursed. Once, complaining that John wanted him to shake his butt too much, Everett stormed off the set, yelling back over his shoulder: "I'm not Julie Christie in *Darling*!"

And afterward, he stewed about it. "He'd walk around with such a face on, that mouth coming down," said Gary Shaw, another assistant. Pretty soon wags on the set dubbed him "The Incredible Sulk."

While relations soured fairly quickly with Everett and the producers, a certain equanimity lasted longer with Madonna. Schlesinger felt she was a "scared little child"; her acting, he told Childers, was "adequate," and in some places even quite good. Which she is: of all her starring pictures, *The Next Best Thing* shows her to her best advantage, and that has to be credited to Schlesinger. Although many of her scenes still fall horribly flat, in some – particularly those where her character is angry or indignant – she comes alive.

For the most part, she respected John's views on the character. "Madonna saw him as a sort of mentor," said Fichter. The director adored the star's two-year-old daughter, Lourdes, and early in the shoot Madonna presented him with a gift she rarely gave anyone: a framed photograph of the girl to keep on his desk.

But increasingly the star turned cold and distant; by June, when they were shooting the New Year's Eve party scene in Silverlake, a *New York Times* reporter described a very chilly set indeed, with both Everett and Madonna hustling off immediately after their scenes were completed and John walking around grumbling that no one was "focused." The article quoted Madonna as saying about John, "He has high expectations. He's very to the point. I would say that sometimes he verges on being insensitive, but I suppose that's his style."

Toward the end of the shoot, she seemed to detach from the entire project, suddenly fixated on landing a new role: that of Sayuri in the planned Stephen Spielberg adaptation of Arthur Golden's novel *Memoirs of a Geisha*. Completely subsuming herself into the part, she gave herself a Japanese name and liked to be addressed in that way. Reportedly, the call sheet would report that "Katsu" or "Sayuri" and not "Madonna" would be needed for that day.

"Of course it became the biggest joke in the world," Gary Shaw said. "John absolutely refused to address her as [a Japanese name]. He thought she was mad."

The absurdities only mounted. Late one evening, Schlesinger hitched a ride home with one of the screenwriters Everett had brought in. But the gate in front of his rented house was stuck, and he couldn't get inside. The screenwriter suggested John climb over. "That's exactly what she said to him, *climb over*," said Gary Shaw. "And John – the dignity and pride that he had, his age and body type – still he climbed up over that gate and, of course, he fell and broke his ankle."

For the rest of filming, he'd hobble his way through: a fitting image for his last, compromised work for the screen.

Broken ankles or stars throwing tantrums, it was always something. The actual shooting of a picture had always been Schlesinger's least favorite part of the job. "I get my knickers into a terrible twist during it," he said. "I need a lot of bolstering up, and I lose courage and confidence many times during the process of making something; panicked and nervous."

Every one of his friends and coworkers would have some version of this story: Schlesinger, consumed with doubt, insisting that what they were doing was "a pile of shit." He said it on his first dramatic film, *A Kind of Loving*, in 1962. He said it on *Cold Comfort Farm*, his last success. He said it even on *Midnight Cowboy*, at the height of his powers. That insecurity, I would learn, was an essential part of Schlesinger's nature. In those moments, he was once more the son who was never as good at games as his father wished him to be; the student who never really excelled at anything particular in school; the aspiring filmmaker who could never compete with the intellectual sparring of colleagues like Lindsay Anderson or Karel Reisz.

But when it was just him and the writer and maybe a few other trusted collaborators — when he allowed himself to dream, to imagine, to ask himself "What if?" — *then* there was confidence. Supreme, total faith in himself and his vision.

"I love the moment when you're dreaming up a project," he'd say, "when you're working with a writer and saying, 'Supposing we set this in the Paris Opera' — I mean, *whatever*. All is a wonderful fantasy. Then comes the agony of actually having to set it up, and wait for the money, which starts being depressive, and the fight begins. And the actual shoot, which is very often tense because of the pressures that the director's under, is really my least favorite part. I mean it's exciting, but also there is the feeling of, 'God, will I ever be able to triumph over the odds?' So it's a sort of personal agony."

Schlesinger once said the three most expensive words in the movie business were: "Let's try this", but that he'd never stop using them. After the blockbuster commercial success of *Midnight Cowboy*, he could have made any picture he wanted. He chose *Sunday, Bloody Sunday*. "I knew from the start that it was really a piece of chamber music, that not everyone would appreciate it," he said. "But it was a film I believed I had to do. Not *wanted* to. *Had* to do."

At that first dinner with his stars of *The Next Best Thing*, when hopes were still so high and the future looked bright for all of them, Everett had said the reason they needed John – not wanted, *needed* – was because he knew how to make movies. "He said John had *passion*," Childers remembered. "That John took risks, and that nobody took risks anymore."

Certainly, his body of work is evidence of that. "I like to make films about people pushed onto an edge," Schlesinger mused. "People pushed into decisions." It was why he was drawn to make a film of Thomas Hardy's *Far from the Madding Crowd*. "I believe in Hardy's vision, that man is a little creature constantly struck down by all sorts of things of his own making, or of natural disasters or whatever. Life consists of picking yourself up and trying to go forward. I believe that's a privilege." Survival, he said, was sometimes life's only reward.

I'm reminded of that thought as his devoted nurse Maureen Danson, so slight herself, lifted his frail body from his wheelchair and eased him into bed.

"In several of my films," he once said, "I've dealt with this idea of the 'if only,' of somebody wanting to be other than they are. You know, if he weren't a cripple, what would he do? If he were attractive, what would happen? The idea that if he were an operator, a really smart operator, he would do something else. It's the Miami fantasy in *Midnight Cowboy* or the dwarf in *The Day of the Locust* – 'I want to be a big man!' Hence the cockfight. It's about that little man wanting to be treated as a normal-sized human being. That was the underlying theme of that scene to me. Subtext is something which not only interests me but which I think is essential to all drama."

Was that why the producers of *The Next Best Thing* had wanted him? Subtext?

"If they'd wanted a trendy little modern picture, as they seemed to be going for, without all the nuances that John brings to a film, why did they use him?" asked Ruth Myers. "Why employ someone of the legendary status of John Schlesinger and then not use what he has to offer?"

Neither Rosenberg nor Lucchesi nor Wright agreed to requests to be interviewed for this book. Rupert Everett sent an official decline through his manager. Madonna never responded at all.

The final indignity for Schlesinger was the ending of the film. Robert has lost his son and his friendship with Abby. Horrible words have passed between them. Yet, in the final few frames of the picture, Abby stops the car and allows the boy to run across the street to his father. A couple of badly written postscript titles inform us that, despite all the lies, deceits and betrayals, everybody found a way to live happily ever after, with the child loving all of the members of his "alternative family" equally.

Schlesinger's friends and associates were appalled. "How could you have allowed them to force you into this *Brady Bunch* kind of ending?" Gary Shaw asked him. John was too exhausted to answer.

Imagine, for a moment, the effect of a similar title after Peter Finch's last fade-out in *Sunday, Bloody Sunday:* "Bob came back to England and spent lots of time with both Daniel and Alex and everybody loved each other very much and lived happily ever after." In other words, all the angst and heartache of the film had meant nothing.

"Endings are absolutely the most important thing," Schlesinger said. "And mine are about people having to make compromises in their life." Question marks, he insisted, were much more interesting than full stops. "And isn't that true of life, really? I don't think we all join hands and walk into the sunset. I know that Hollywood would like that, but that's not my view of the world. I think that although I regard myself as a reasonably happy person, our lives are very often a compromise. Relationships are difficult, not ideal, and have to be worked at . . . And that's what I want to make films about. I want to make films about *life*."

Schlesinger was fond of often pointing out that movies would be around for a lot longer than their makers, and those that would stand the test of time wouldn't be those that bore the heading, "This Film Was Brought in Under Budget and Under Schedule." No, he said, the films that would last would be the ones that took chances, that broke the mold, that did things "the director's way."

Michael Childers and I were looking down at him from opposite sides of his bed, where John was drifting in and out of sleep.

"He helped change all the rules thirty years ago," Childers said, "but then the rules got changed again." He moved toward the door. "You've got your work cut out for you. I only wish he were able to talk more and tell you everything you need to know."

Then he left us alone.

On 22 November 1999, while post-production on *The Next Best Thing* was taking place in Los Angeles, Schlesinger collapsed outside his flat on Gloucester Road in London. He was taken by ambulance to Chelsea and Westminster Hospital, where he was admitted with heart palpitations and pneumonia. As he would write later in his diary, from that moment on, he was "completely out of" the film. On 6 December, while still in hospital, an angiogram was carried out, and doctors became alarmed over the blockage of several arteries to his heart. Three days later a triple bypass was performed.

Several friends recalled visiting John in hospital and his gesturing to the wall of flowers, saying, "But nothing from *her*," meaning Madonna. No card, no word, no further communication between them. From various sources John had heard that she was already badmouthing the picture, even before its release, saying it had become "too gay."

Everett, for his part, sent flowers, and a note wishing John a full recovery and expressing his hope that the difficulties on the set hadn't led to his collapse. In a cheery reply dictated to his secretary, John assured Everett that "despite everything, I feel good about the movie and your part in it. It's a beautiful performance and one that I can't help thinking should do you a great deal of good, the range is so extraordinary."

A number of John's friends felt he was being overly gracious to a man who they thought had treated him very poorly, and the same number of them wasted no time in pointing the finger at the stars and producers of *The Next Best Thing* as the cause of John's collapse and, eventually, some thirteen months later, his stroke. That's probably unfair, and certainly John did his best not to carry a grudge in those first weeks of 2000. He saw a rough-cut of the film soon after returning to Los Angeles at the end of January, and thought it wasn't so bad; indeed, there were things he really liked about the film, such as the moment when the boy wonders what the word "faggot" means and is told by a friend that it's a person who cuts his father off in traffic, and he was encouraged by enthusiastic previews.

He wasn't aware that, even then, Everett (with the permission of the producers) was still rearranging and taking things out. When he learned of it, John immediately rang Richard Wright. The last involvement he had with *The Next Best Thing* (until it came time to promote it, which he reluctantly agreed to do) was that telephone conversation, which ended abruptly when he screamed "You amateurs!" and slammed down the receiver.

Why had they hired him?

"I think that a good director wants to give the audience a special experience," he once said. "You want to affect them in some way, whether to alarm them, or make them think about something. That's what I hope films are doing."

He did have a passion for movies. The story goes that when *Far from the Madding Crowd* was playing to uninterested American audiences, John followed it around, trying to drum up support for the picture. He insisted it was true that he once actually *vacuumed* a movie screen so that the film would look better to the audience. "It was a small theater in New York," he said. "It had a really filthy screen, and nobody had bothered to clean it. So I said, 'If you won't clean it, I'll get a ladder and a bucket of water and do it myself.' I think most directors would have done the same."

No, not most directors.

His eyes were open.

"John?" I asked.

He was attempting to speak. I leaned down closer.

"Find the story," he whispered.

"What did you say, John?"

But that was it. One time only. He wasn't a man who liked to repeat himself, even when he was well.

Find the story. Had he been dreaming, imagining he was back on the set with Waldo Salt or Frederic Raphael or even Penelope Gilliatt? Or was he really talking to me, offering me my own "Rosebud"? Not so much a command but rather a *clue* to understanding the story of his life.

Find the story. The way *he* had, so many times, on so many films. Films that would survive him. Films that would last. Films whose stories still matter – and whose budgets and schedules are the last things any of us will remember.

Two

1926–1946

"Good at practically nothing"

"We never played, you understand," Hilary Schlesinger told me, referring to her brother John's relationship with his younger siblings while they were growing up in Hampstead, in north London. "We were always *directed* by John right from the moment we could walk."

When last I saw him, John was very much anticipating a trip to London, his homecoming. Nearly two years now he'd been away. But at the last moment his doctors had advised against the plan: he was too fragile to travel, they said. When Michael broke the news to him, John fell into a depression; Maureen later told me she felt this disappointment contributed to his second, milder stroke, occurring not more than a week later. How much John had wanted to return to England. This was where he hoped to be when he died.

So I went on my own, on a mission to track down his past, and found, as ever, past serving merely as prologue.

"Oh, he would have us all out in the barn doing numbers from the latest revue from London," Hilary said. "Songs and things which were far beyond any of us. But we would do them anyway, and John would invite the local people and get everyone involved."

From the time he was a very small boy, John Schlesinger was staging productions at the family's Hampstead home. Gathering his sisters, his brother, his cousins, his friends – sometimes even his grandmother – John would build shows around them: little plays, song-and-dance revues or the occasional melodrama, complete with a velvet curtain hung across the entrance to the drawing room. As a teenager, he'd also direct shows at Mount Pleasant, the family's small Queen Anne country house in the village of Kintbury in west Berkshire. These more elaborate shows were staged in the Mount Pleasant barn, where – like Mickey Rooney and Judy Garland in films he never saw – he'd stage the "Kintbury Follies," himself at the piano, signaling backstage for Hilary or Roger or Wendy or Susan to come in and do their bit.

"One of my earliest memories of John," said his brother Roger, "was being four years old and having to light some magnesium ribbon to produce a flash so he could come on stage. It was his version of *Macbeth*, and he played all three witches."

"Sometimes Roger or I would have ideas, and we'd suggest them to John," Hilary said. "Cold water was always poured on them. John was the director. Nobody else."

When he was in his early teens, he'd get his hands on a 9.5 mm home-movie camera. The little playlets became films, two or three or five minutes long. While their celluloid has long since crumbled into nitrate, Hilary Schlesinger discovered a series of letters that document her brother's first adventures in motion pictures.

"I hope sincerely we can arrange some sort of show for next holiday," John wrote to her, while both were away at school, detailing a script for a film called *Three Generations*. Another time, in planning for a "full-length play" he called *Doctor's Orders*, John laid down the law about the necessity of his siblings' cooperation. "One thing must be settled at the start," he wrote, "and that is that everyone must be cooperative and keen about it, otherwise it will be well nigh impossible to do. You will all have parts to learn — some of them quite long — in your spare minutes at school, and there will be lots of rehearsals. So I want you all to pledge to help as much as you can, [and] cooperate with me in every way."

John Schlesinger was fifteen years old.

He had, as he would describe it, a "perfectly normal middle-class English childhood." His father was a pediatrician, his mother an accomplished violinist. There were five children in all, John the eldest, and a staff of servants usually more numerous than the family. The children grew up in a separate wing of the house, sometimes seeing their parents for only a few minutes a day. Meals were taken separately; chores and discipline were handed out by the servants.

"When one looks back at that time before the war," said Roger Schlesinger, "it was a very different type of life. All professional families had staff. We had a cook and an undercook, a parlor maid, a nursery maid, a chauffeur, and a governess. Our parents had their lives, we had ours. That was just the way it was."

His own children, in and out of the room a half dozen times to check about dinner, movie plans, and using the family car, grew up much closer to their parents, Roger believed. "But you know," he said, reflecting on his own childhood, "in some ways it made it much more exciting going on family holidays to have that special time with the parents." Holidays, to Italy, Yugoslavia, and the annual summer trip to Switzerland, were taken together as a family until 1956, when John was 30.

In all of the profiles of John Schlesinger, in all of the interviews he gave about his family and early years, there is a determined insistence on how special his parents were, how supportive, cultured and admirable. "I was terribly fortunate with parents," he said often. "They were tolerant and enormously encouraging." His childhood, he declared, was "very privileged and very happy."

No doubt all of that is true. Dr. Bernard and Winifred Regensburg Schlesinger gave their children a sense of the possibilities of life: that there was an enormous world out there beyond Hampstead and they were entitled to it. It was an assumption that was integral to the experience of their class, a belief that their children needed only to declare their particular talents and the world would make a place for them. And, to their credit, an awareness of their privilege *was* conveyed to their children: certainly John would make his mark with films about people who, through the accident of birth, grew up with few of the assumptions he did, and none of the expectations.

From the time they were very young, the Schlesinger children were imbued with an appreciation of the arts: music, literature, the theater. There were discussions of books and plays, Shakespeare and Wagner, Chaucer and Brahms. John's mother long nurtured a dream of conjuring family chamber music, with John on piano or oboe, Wendy on cello, Roger on French horn, Hilary on violin, Susan on clarinet. Though the result rarely materialized as harmoniously as she might have hoped, the beauty was in the effort.

Yet exacting parents, for all their best intentions, for all the tremendous gifts they give their children, can sometimes leave inadvertently painful marks. Once, as Wendy played cello in her primary school orchestra, the praise of the other parents left her mother decidedly uncomfortable. Winifred insisted, in full earshot of everyone present, that there was still something wrong with the cadenza. The message was plain. Too much praise wasn't good. Recognition, John would remember all his life, should be kept to a minimum. "Parental pride?" he'd ask. "We could never be sure."

Behind the encouragement, behind the cultured foundation and the conferring of life's possibilities, there was something withholding, even a little cold, about John Schlesinger's childhood. "Rise above it," his father would insist when John, almost in tears, would complain about being bullied at school. "You've got to endure." After all, that's how he, Bernard, had gotten by, how he had made his way. "Never take no for an answer" was Bernard's lifelong motto, a creed John would adopt and one that would prove both a blessing and a curse. As a film director legendary for his refusal to take no for an answer, he got an awful lot done — his budgets raised and his contracts signed — but, like his father, there would be little time or patience for simply appreciating his accomplishments, for feeling satisfaction or contentment.

Dr. Bernard Edward Schlesinger cast an enormously long

shadow over his son's life. A pediatrician at Great Ormond Street and, later, at University College Hospital, Bernard specialized in childhood rheumatic disorders, and his views on the subject were highly respected. He published frequently and lectured at gatherings of the British Medical Association; in 1959, he was flown to Malta to investigate and treat illnesses found among the children of British servicemen stationed there. Labelled as being "ahead of his time," Dr. Schlesinger opened the first hospital unit in London for the care of premature infants and was among the first physicians to arrange for mothers to stay with their ailing children at a London teaching hospital.

He was also a classic example of a pre-war English gentleman, an archetype that is rapidly disappearing even from memory. On Saturdays he always wore a tie; before the war, he and his wife always dressed for dinner even when simply dining on their own – Bernard in black tie and dinner jacket, Winifred in full-length evening dress. Nicknamed "Jumbo," Bernard was warm and gregarious, hale and hearty, his "only concession to winter," *The Times* would report, "a small scarf around his neck." His grandson, the writer Ian Buruma, wrote of him: "I would watch him as a child, as he worked in his Berkshire garden, picking vegetables or pruning the fruit trees, dressed in corduroys and tweeds. He seemed to belong to the landscape."

The son of a Jewish immigrant from Germany, Bernard was nevertheless more English than many an Anglo-Saxon. He had served in the British army during both world wars, in the trenches in France for the first one, later marching through Palestine with General Allenby. That he was of age for both wars – a private in World War I and a Brigadier in World War II – was hugely significant in Bernard's life. "I think it gave him a certain obstinacy," said Roger, "but it also made him a great egalitarian."

Bernard's father, Richard Schlesinger, had come to England from Frankfurt in the 1880s. He was a stockbroker who spent several years building up his own personal wealth before marrying Estella Ellinger, born in Manchester, the daughter of a German-Jewish father and a Dutch-Jewish mother. Estella would be the grandparent who doted on the children most, who got down on the floor to play with them, who became for John an extraordinary influence. He would tell one interviewer that Estella was one of the "most indomitable women" he ever knew. Indeed, she was the grandmother who, legend has it, bought him that first 9.5mm camera, but John would say it could just as well have been a gift from his parents. His grandmother would, however, prove a benefactor in other ways. It would be she who financed his first amateur features, *Black Legend* and *The Starfish*.

By the time her grandchildren were old enough to visit, Estella lived on Fitzjohns Avenue, a then largely Jewish enclave in North London that the Schlesinger children dubbed "Fitzjews" Avenue. Her home was only a few blocks from John's first school, The Hall, which he attended as a day-boy. A stop at Grandma's on the way home became a habit. Richard Schlesinger was by then in the last stages of Parkinson's disease (John remembered only a dribbling, incoherent, frightening man), but his wife was a bundle of energy and high spirits. Tiny, nicknamed Dolly, she was prone to malapropisms: "maternity plays" instead of "nativity plays." Her grandchildren adored fooling with her. "She used to get tired of us slamming doors umpteen times," Roger Schlesinger said, "so she'd say, 'I'll give you a penny every time you close the door quietly.' So we'd stand by the door, opening and closing it quietly, and collect our pennies."

Estella raised her son Bernard much as he would raise his own children a generation later, in a house in Hampstead surrounded by servants (the 1901 census showed the family of three had four: parlor maid, housemaid, nurse and cook). They remained very connected to their Judaism, keeping all the Jewish holidays; Estella in fact helped found one of the first liberal synagogues in England. Yet, as Buruma wrote, they "lived in that peculiar North London world of German émigrés who spoke English to one another, ate roast beef on Sundays, sent their sons to public schools, and listened to Beethoven and Wagner."

Bernard would grow up with none of his parents' religious convictions. Attending a traditional English prep school, he went on to Uppingham in Rutland, which, then as now, prided itself as classically English, "in the heart of England." Bernard would, in fact, point out to friends that his mother was, after all, "English," having never known any other country.

It was not really a repudiation of his Jewishness; it was, rather, an embrace of his Englishness. "To my grandfather," Buruma wrote, "England was not only the country he was born and raised in; after Hitler, it was, in his mind, the country that had saved him, and his family, from almost certain death."

To his children, Bernard taught that all religions were equal. During school holidays, he would take them to synagogue in St. John's Wood, less out of any adherence to Judaism than based on the idea that some faith, some tradition, was better than none. "And if we grew up to choose another religion, that would be fine, too," Roger Schlesinger said.

Indeed, neither he nor John were ever bar mitzvahed. The

family never kept kosher, and the children loved to tease their grandmother with strips of bacon at the breakfast table. They were brought up as thoroughly English, with their bacon and roast beef and Christmas plays. In their smart coats and hats, Wendy and Hilary looked almost identical to photographs of the King's daughters: "Here come the little princesses," the neighbors would chortle as the little girls approached. And John's attendance at St. Edmund's prep school left him more religiously familiar with the language of Thomas Cranmer than of Maimonides or Joseph Karo. He would sing in chapel the great old Christian hymns like "He Who Would Valiant Be" without any sense of detachment or obvious irony.

Ian Buruma considered that Bernard and his family dealt with their Judaism, as many others of their era and class did, "as something that was inevitably there but should not be made too much of." Especially not by the 1930s, when there was a new wave of Jewish immigrants streaming into London, this time from Russia and Poland, who were regarded as less educated and "cultured" than their predecessors from Germany. Buruma remembered his great-grandmother declaring these new immigrants were the type "who gave Jews a bad name."

Yet as English as they had become, the Schlesingers remained aware that their status could not be taken for granted. Family tradition had passed down the story of Richard Schlesinger being denied a commission in the German army because he was a Jew. In 1938, refused a position at a prominent hospital, Bernard, too, blamed "the old, old story," by which he meant anti-Semitism. Still, he was "too proud, too patriotic," his grandson Buruma said, ever to complain about prejudice: "It would not have fitted his ideal of England."

John Schlesinger's Jewishness, no matter how tangential his

relationship to it, nonetheless fundamentally imprinted his life in ways both large and small. He would, on the one hand, long for a greater cultural adherence to his heritage, and on the other, rue his very name for setting him apart, for making him feel outside – "other" – as a boy.

The history of his family had prepared the way for that. The music that served as the soundtrack for his childhood was largely German. His father, a great Wagnerian, and his mother, with an education in music, owned an enormous collection of gramophone records dating back decades. Music, in the Germany from which Richard Schlesinger had come, had been seen for generations by Jews as an emblem of education and status. "To be educated," wrote Buruma, "to know your German classics, to be musical, was the secular route to assimilation." Richard Schlesinger, denied his commission in the German army, would nonetheless pass on to his children his love of Wagner, a composer who had believed the only hope for Jews was in the "annihilation" of their heritage.

If anything, music was even more important in the family of John's mother, Winifred Henrietta Regensburg. The daughter of Hermann Regensburg, like Richard Schlesinger, a stock-broker from Frankfurt and his wife Anna Alsberg, Win's life paralleled that of her future husband in many ways: a Hampstead childhood, four servants, an early education in the arts and music. She left school at fourteen to study full-time at Trinity College of Music; after World War I, she spent three years studying languages at Oxford. Marriage and family would be put ahead of a professional musical career, but Winifred did play with the Newbury Symphony Orchestra in Berkshire and, during World War II, with Gerald Finzi's acclaimed string orchestra.

Her passion ensured that the house was always filled with music. Among John's earliest memories was standing on the veranda outside the drawing room of their house in Hampstead, his little hands gripping the window sill, watching his mother's string quartet inside and hearing the music lilting out into the garden.

It had been, appropriately enough, through music that Winifred met Bernard. Playing the violin at a wedding anniversary party, she noticed a young man with a cello across the room, a nephew of the honoree, smiling at her. Win's parents insisted, however, that at seventeen she was too young to think about love. Flash forward a year: war had broken out, and Winifred, like so many young women of her age and class, was part of the Voluntary Aid Detachment. Working at a military hospital in Brondesbury, she looked up one day to see Bernard, there with a nasty case of boils. Having volunteered for the army straight out of school, Bernard now found himself under Win's tender care, and a romance bloomed. A photo of Winifred still treasured by the family is dated 1915 and inscribed to Bernard: "To remind you of the only thing the war has brought us – our friendship."

They wed in 1925, after a nine-year engagement dictated by the war and the fact that interns were not allowed to be married. Theirs would be a great and enduring love affair that lasted nearly 60 years.

"Their love for each other was a model that was very hard to live up to," said Ian Buruma. Indeed, meeting the bar set by Win and Bernard on what a successful relationship should look like would prove daunting for all of the Schlesinger offspring. By seeming to fulfill each other so completely, by appearing so thoroughly to meet each other's needs and expectations, Win and Bernard set a standard for perfection that often seemed unattainable – and success in personal relationships was only one small part of that. In every aspect of his life, John Schlesinger would grow up trying to please his parents as much as they pleased each other. "I think, without meaning to, they raised the stakes very high for their children," Buruma said.

Yet they were tolerant of failure, not opposed to change, and incredibly resilient in the face of adversity. What mattered to them was the endurance of the family unit their marriage had created. "They bounced back many times from setbacks," Roger said. "I'm sure it must've been a shock to them when they found out John was gay, but ultimately they were fine. My older sister, Wendy, died of cancer when she was 43. They bounced back. My sister Susan committed suicide. They bounced back. My sister Hilary converted to Catholicism but my father learned to joke about that. I think what shocked my parents the most, more than anything, was my divorce from my first wife. Because they were so conscious of family and I was breaking up my family. Family was the most important thing."

Standing in front of the house at 15 Templewood Avenue in Hampstead, I could picture them, John and Roger and Hilary and Wendy and Susan, playing in the garden. I could imagine – almost hear – Win in the drawing room with her string quartet. I could visualize the servants, calling the children in for tea. I could see Bernard, arriving home from his practice, tired and bleary-eyed, but nonetheless preparing to spend the evening going over lesson plans for the courses he taught.

"That was John's and my room, there," Roger Schlesinger said, pointing to an upper window in the red brick house, two ornately carved chimneys rising from its four-sided roof. Around the side of the house, the basement opened onto a sunken garden that had changed little in the passing decades: hedgerows and stonework, rosebushes and heather. The lowest windows in the house, Roger told me, looked into the schoolroom where their governess taught them to read, write, and do simple sums.

"There was also an alcove with a little stage," Roger said, as we tried to peer into the windows from the road, "where John, when he was quite small, put on his very first shows."

He wasn't born here; John Richard Schlesinger first saw the light of day on 16 February, 1926, at 53 Hollycroft Avenue. But Templewood Avenue would be where he grew up, learning his sums, putting on his little plays, and cowering under his sheets in fear of moths.

"Yes, moths," Roger recalled. "John had a great fear of them. We shared a room, and if they got in he would start crying. I would have to get out of bed and kill the moths."

When the lights went out, the authoritarian director of the Kintbury Follies wasn't so self-assured. And it wasn't just moths that terrified him. Loud noises could send him into a panic. He couldn't abide fireworks. He didn't learn to ride a bicycle until he was eleven, and horses made him terribly anxious. Whenever the children's riding instructor would attempt to lure John over, the boy, no more than five, would simply shake his head and say, "No time to trot, no time to trot." And if some of the neighborhood boys were ever to suggest a friendly game of football, well, little John Schlesinger would run as fast as he could in the opposite direction. "I never felt part of the herd when I was young," said John. "I was always an outsider."

His son's timidity was enough to try Bernard's patience. He

never openly berated John for his fears but the boy felt his displeasure nonetheless. "I could never quite live up to his extraordinary example," John said. "He was good at all the things I wasn't good at. I wasn't gregarious with people. And I certainly wasn't good at games."

John's schoolmates taunted him for his ineptness and lack of interest in things that boys were supposed to be good at: running, jumping, kicking a ball. He was miserable being sent away to school: first, from the age of nine, St. Edmund's, a high-church prep school at Hindhead, Surrey, in the former country house of George Bernard Shaw; then, at age thirteen, Uppingham, following in his father's footsteps. At Uppingham, John said, he was "good at practically nothing."

Uppingham had played a long and well-established part in British life. Founded in 1584, the school could boast an impressive list of alumni: James Elroy Flecker, poet and playwright; E.J. Moeran, composer; Lt. General Sir Brian Horrocks, Commander of the 13th Corps under Montgomery; A.P.F. Chapman, captain of the England cricket team 1926-1930; Sir Neville Faulks, High Court judge; John Aldridge, Royal Academician; the film actor Boris Karloff; and Sir Patrick Renison, Governor of Kenya. That's not to mention Dr. Bernard Edward Schlesinger.

Down the corridors of Uppingham John would walk, passing photographs of previous rugby teams, his father "leading the pack." It was a constant reminder that Bernard was "terrific at all those heroic kinds of things" that his son could never manage. "It seemed to me that I couldn't get away from being reminded of him . . . I couldn't live up to what his reputation had been."

John's lack of athletic prowess, especially when his younger brother turned out to be every bit as much the sportsman as his father, permeated his perception of himself. "It was a feeling that I would never amount to much because at school – in games, in sports – I was always seen as less than a success."

Of course, had John Schlesinger been a star athlete, had he been his father's son in every way, we would never have had his films. There would be no Vic Brown, no Billy Liar, no Joe Buck or Ratso Rizzo. "I suppose," he acknowledged, "had things been different, I wouldn't have concentrated so much on life's losers and failures." Another time he observed, "The bleaker part of me, the pessimistic side of my films, probably comes from this source. During childhood, I was a failure at a great number of things."

That observation offers a key insight: despite the great fun of the Kintbury Follies, despite the increasingly detailed little 9.5 mm films, despite the magic act that delighted everyone, despite accomplishments in music and art, John Schlesinger viewed himself a failure. Part of that, friends and family insist, was simply his personality, and may have been congenital. "There's something in our family called the 'Curse of the Regensburgs,'" Roger told me with some amusement, "because on my mother's side of the family everyone is terribly pessimistic." Throughout his life, John would consider the glass half empty, his family shaking their heads and muttering about the family curse. Jo Janni loved to tell the story of John at the Berlin Film Festival. Waiting as the jury viewed *A Kind of Loving* downstairs, John paced anxiously, finally exploding into a fit of despair: "Why did we ever bring this film here? It will never win! Everyone will hate it! You stupid Italian cunt, what were you *thinking*?" Meanwhile, downstairs, the film was winning the Golden Bear.

Yet any inherent tendency towards pessimism was only exacerbated by a family dynamic that taught that too much praise was worse than none at all. Even the wisdom imparted by his beloved grandmother carried a fatalistic ring: that one must simply do one's best in life in order to "get through," which, in the end, is all you can really hope for. "Take half a loaf if you can get it," John said, "because you might not get any bread at all."

It's an odd attitude for a child of privilege, yet John spent his youth feeling shamed for the things he couldn't do and unappreciated for the things he *could*. In an environment where praise was rationed, heroes on the football team at least had cheering fans. "Games were the most important thing, above everything else," John said. "If you were a boy and you weren't good at games, you simply weren't good." Moreover, measuring success by how much he could emulate his self-sufficient, heroic father proved hopeless. "I just never felt he was ever proud of me," John admitted in a number of interviews.

John's family would insist that *of course* Bernard was proud of John, that he was absolutely thrilled and delighted by his son's success in the cinema. "I know John worried about it," said Michael Childers, "but I would tell him, 'Of *course*, your father is proud. How could he *not* be?'"

Later, John would muse that he thought his father eventually became "really quite pleased with the way things were going – at least I hope he was." In 1980, when John was profiled on television for *This is Your Life*, Schlesinger's parents were part of the programme. Their pride in their son is quite apparent on the telecast. John wrote to a friend: "It was so wonderful that both my parents were able to be part of it, and I know how much it meant to them. They have now become celebrities themselves and fan mail reaches my father from ex-patients from long ago, and my mother seems to be recognized whenever she goes shopping in London or Newbury, so I think that must give them some extra pleasure."

Yet the doubts lingered. After we'd completed our interview about John's 1993 film *The Innocent*, the actor Hart Bochner rang me to say he'd thought of something else. "I'm not sure this is of interest," he said, "but I remembered a conversation John and I had. We'd been talking about my father when John brought up his own. He told me that he never felt he had his father's approval, that he had never known if his father was ever really proud of him. It was quite extraordinary, his opening up like that. I remember he was quite serious, quite sad about it, and I sensed it was something very deep inside him. That it was something he had carried around with him for a very long time."

There's a scene in *Yanks* that tears one's heart. A little boy, away at school, hounded by ruffians, writes plaintively to his mother: "Please let me come home. I hate it here. They bully me because they say I don't try hard enough at games. But I do my best. I don't want to let you and Daddy down but I want to come home so much. I don't fit in here. You must understand. Please."

The boy's mother, played by Vanessa Redgrave, is conflicted. She clearly feels for her son, but her husband, away at war, would never approve of his running away from a challenge. Her friends counsel her, "Don't give in to him." Meanwhile, shots of the boy being swung by his arms and legs by bullies are intercut into the scene.

The mother's lover, played by William Devane, takes the opposite approach. He tells her he doesn't think a child should stay somewhere he's miserable, that tradition doesn't mean much if there are no feelings behind it. In a bit of wish-fulfillment, of rewriting history and mending his past, Schlesinger the director gave his celluloid alter ego an outcome he certainly wished for but never enjoyed. The boy in the film runs away from his school, and his mother, moved by her lover's compassion, allows him to remain home with her.

"Before we began shooting," Vanessa Redgrave told me, "John took me aside and said, 'I want you to know you will be playing my mother in this film.'" Certainly Winifred Schlesinger never had a wartime affair with an American officer, but still she informs Redgrave's character of Helen in every scene of the movie. Helen is how John saw his mother: beautiful, poised, noble. Helen might be the lady of a great house, but she treats her working-class staff as equals. In wartime she becomes a Mrs. Miniver figure, working the land and volunteering for the Red Cross. She might have yearnings of her own but ultimately she sacrifices them for the good of her family. In his most obvious tribute to his mother, John made Helen a musician, part of a regional orchestra, a cellist to Winifred's violinist.

Yet Helen is also highly sexual, and without any apparent shame of it. John even gave Redgrave a nude scene to play, which they both felt was integral to understanding the character as a fully-fleshed woman, not just as a mother and wife. It suggests that John was able to view his parents as individuals, with their own needs and desires, virtues and flaws. It is significant that Helen, no matter how moved she might be by her son's letter, does not bring him home. The boy must save himself. She allows him to stay with her when he runs away, but she does not take action on her own.

"John hated school, was bored by it," said his sister Hilary. From Uppingham he wrote her: "Life is as boring and lonely here as ever and I'm really rather fed up." He had been hoping to start work on some sculpture and oil-painting but the house captain had him painting puppet heads instead. So he would wander off on his own, away from the other boys, dreaming up scenarios for the plays and films he'd make during school holidays.

For many gay men, it is a familiar tale: the dreamer, the child apart, the "different" boy. No matter what era, no matter where in the world, it is the same: different children are singled out, and that's especially true for boys who don't "act like" boys. But John Schlesinger wasn't only a poofter: he was also a Jew. At Uppingham, John remembered feeling his Jewishness "very keenly" when the papers filled with accounts of pogroms in Germany. The taunt of "Let's chase Schlesinger" became a rallying cry of his schoolmates. Sometimes he eluded them, scurrying up a tree or hiding in his room. Other times they caught him, though his tales of being "beaten fiercely" may have been exaggerations; his family and longtime friends remembered nothing quite so traumatic.

Yet, clearly, he felt persecuted for being different. Children respond to such feelings in many different ways. Some attempt to conform. Some withdraw into a world of fantasy and make-believe. Others act out, become violent. Still others channel the experience into art, somehow maintaining a sense of their own self-worth, placing themselves into the role of "observer" or "commentator." John Schlesinger fell into this last category. Despite feeling a failure, despite growing up without any conviction of his father's pride in him, he never resorted to self-loathing nor apologized for who and what he was.

A story he would tell of his first sexual experience is illustrative. He was about ten or eleven, at St. Edmund's. He and another boy were in the changing room, getting into their games clothes. They "fiddled" with each other – touching each other's penises – before hurrying outside. Later, playing the organ in the school's chapel, John was horrified by a discordant sound he couldn't identify. He was suddenly certain it was a sign from God, punishing him for doing something bad. But when he discovered that the kneeler had simply gotten caught on the pedals, all fear evaporated, and he never felt any guilt about his sexuality again.

History is filled with stories of gay men who did not manage such easy acceptance of themselves, especially in the 1930s, a time of often savagely enforced conformity in response to the perceived excesses of the previous decade. While it's unlikely that, at such a young age, John actually thought of himself as homosexual – adopting such an identity for oneself, even nowadays, usually comes much later – his awareness of his difference had always been very strong. It wasn't just that he was bad at games and that he recoiled from the idea of physical violence. From an early age, he recalled, he also "fell in love with boys." He would tell his nephew Ian Buruma that it was, ironically, the only thing that made him feel that he "fit in" at school. Deep, passionate friendships were tolerated in English public schools; the headmasters surely knew how often these friendships led to sexual experimentation, but they looked away, an unspoken acceptance of a bit of buggery in one's youth.

"At school, everyone did it," said Geoffrey Sharp, who lived in John's house at Uppingham, "so it didn't mean as much."

Sharp would remain a lifelong friend. Yet while both would turn out to be homosexual, a specific consciousness of that part of themselves was not what bonded them as youngsters. It was a more generalized sense of being different, a connection forged by sensibility and shared interests. "We were both musical," Sharp said. "I remember walking back together to our house from the music school, holding hands and singing a bit of 'Madame Butterfly' together."

Together John and Geoffrey would skip out on games, play their records until the needles wore down, and exchange details of their latest "crush." No good at sports, John Schlesinger was, however, *very* good at male bonding, and his devotion to his mates was actually applauded by his teachers. "That was the one thing at school," said Buruma, "that he could *more* than share with the other boys."

Of course, it was fully expected that such nonsense would ultimately be abandoned; when, in E.M. Forster's novel *Maurice*, the character of Maurice Hall wants to continue a homosexual relationship into adulthood, his former school lover, now married, is aghast. Like Maurice, John Schlesinger would never repudiate that part of himself, and would eventually find a fulfilling relationship with another man.

The foundation for that sense of self was laid by his parents. Despite their initial discomfort with the idea of homosexuality, it is to Bernard and Winifred that credit must be given for bestowing upon John his genuine, fundamental sense of self-worth. Though Bernard may have withheld, by his very nature, a show of his pride in his son, he and his wife nonetheless gave all of their children perhaps the greatest gift any parent can give a child: a sense that they are inherently *good*.

If that seems at first glance to be a contradiction – that, consciously or not, Bernard and Winifred may also have made their children feel never quite good *enough* – consider what else the Schlesinger children received from their parents: a belief in their place in the world. John grew up with a profound sense of entitlement. It was not presumptuous, never overbearing or arrogant. It was simply that his parents taught him that, no matter who or what he was – Jewish, the grandson of immigrants, homosexual – he deserved to succeed. He was worthy.

The sharp smell of briny water hit me even before I saw the sea. Gulls called from overhead, making arcs in the overcast sky. It was here at Brighton that John made one of his first little 9.5 mm pictures, a day in the life of St. Edmund's school. It began with the gates of St. Edmund's opening as if by magic (John had rigged the gate with ropes and instructed fellow students to pull them open when he gave the command) and went on to follow the school on an outing to the seashore. He caught one shot quite unexpectedly: the headmaster changing into his swimming costume under a towel. Later, after screening the picture for him, John remembered the headmaster failed to see the humour: "He thought it was *lése majesté*," he said. The offending scene was ordered trimmed before permission was given to show the film to the school.

It was John Schlesinger's first brush with censorship. In admonishing John, the headmaster said the young director seemed to be poking fun at discipline – an accusation which John, of course, denied. When, of course, he *was*.

That little subversive tweak would crop up in nearly all of his films. It can also be spotted in the second film he made out at Brighton, a little piece for the BBC's *Monitor* series called "On the Pier." It was supposed to record simply a lighthearted day at the beach, but John was far more fascinated with the peepshow than with the families romping in the surf. "What's this, an octopus?" the narrator asks, as John himself is seen peering into a viewer. No, not an octopus: it is a girl removing her stockings.

Here, in the sand, on the promenade, is where John stood, a young boy, an iconoclastic documentarian. Finding his story meant following the steps he took as a filmmaker; steps stretching from Hampstead to Kintbury to Hindhead to Brighton, then on to the north country, London, Dorset, Wiltshire, New York, Los Angeles – all around the world. To find John Schlesinger's story, I still had a long way to go.

"I had a Box Brownie camera when I was nine years old," he said, remembering the beginnings. "And my father, who was a great encourager of all of us children, said you mustn't only take photographs, you've got to learn to develop and print them. So I did that for a time, until I had my first movie camera, when I was about eleven."

He began experimenting. "My head was filled with the possibility of what one could do with film," he said. There were some rudimentary stop-motion effects: Grandma appearing as if from nowhere, the family cook, Laura Ford, seeming to disappear and then rematerializing across the room. "Childish things, really," he'd say with a laugh, "but nevertheless the fantasies were there."

Projecting those first little films for a captive audience of family and servants, John sometimes aimed colored lights at the screen to enhance the pictures. The seaside was infused with a soft blue tint, holiday scenes would glow with red and gold. He was forever playing with lighting, filming in shadows or flooding a scene with bright light. Curious, really, that he should be so inventive, given that he'd hardly seen any real movies at all.

Trips to the cinema were rare for the Schlesinger children. Indeed, even the theater was only an occasional treat, not more than once a year usually. Appropriately enough, John's first theatrical memory — and an experience that would make a lasting impact — was a performance by the magicians John Nevil Maskelyne and David Devant, conjurers famed for their "honest" illusions, with none of the quasi-religious, "spiritualist" trickery so common at the time. In the world of Maskeyne and Devant, as well as in the *oeuvre* of John Schlesinger, magic needed no rationale other than entertainment, plain and simple. Soon, John was perfecting his own magic routine in front of his bedroom mirror. Rabbits being pulled out of hats became a staple of the Kintbury Follies. Later, he'd credit this early interest as "the first glimmering" of wanting to create "illusions of life" in the way he would eventually manage on the screen.

From the very beginning, what always piqued John's imagination was the inexplicable, the mysterious, the eerie, the weird. "I've never been able to understand my attraction to the macabre," he'd admit, a fascination that stretched back at least to Maskelyne and Devant and probably earlier: to *Struwwelpeter* — the often cruel German fairy tales, in which thumbless children abounded and little girls set themselves on fire, and which John and his grandmother both loved. Indeed, the theater outings that would remain the most vivid in his mind were those with some scary, dark element: Charles Laughton as a foppish, menacing Captain Hook in *Peter Pan*; Anton Dolin as the mysterious, cloaked figure of St. George in *Where the*

Rainbow Ends; Engelbert Humperdinck's opera *Hansel and Gretel*, wherein the Witch captures the children and then ends up in the oven herself.

Visits to the movies, usually the Tatler cinema on Tottenham Court Road, were less frequent than to the theater. Few cinematic memories, outside of Mickey Mouse cartoons, would remain from this early period. What Schlesinger found more intriguing than anything he saw up on the screen was the organist, bathed in pink and green light as he waved to the audience and descended down below the stage.

For all his eventual success in cinema, for all his love for the art of filmmaking, John Schlesinger was never really a movie buff. "I do love movies, though I don't slavishly go to them," he'd admit. "I'm not very good on the history of movies. There are many famous classics that I've never seen, because there have been other things in life that have interested me." He wasn't like his friend Martin Scorsese, who, John said, "devoted his life to seeing every film imaginable." John would remember a call from Scorsese, who was all excited about having just seen a restored film by the silent film director Rex Ingram. "I could never be like that," John said. "There are other things I enjoy far too much, like opera, like ballet, like music. I want different experiences because they all inform each other."

Certainly that attitude had its roots in his childhood, when filmgoing was rare, when his family held a decidedly high-minded approach to culture. His mother, with her classical background, would sometimes despair of her son's habit of listening to popular music radio programmes. Even more adamant in this regard was his uncle, Walter Raeburn, "for whom anything later than Mozart was looked down upon," John said.

Uncle Walter would have considerable influence on his nephew. A circuit judge, Raeburn wrote plays for the children, who included seven of his own. "I think had it been more fashionable to go into theater during those days, Walter would have," Roger Schlesinger remembered. Terribly eccentric, Raeburn left behind at his death a box filled with little wrapped packets: every blade he had ever shaved with, together with a description of what sort of shave it had been.

John enjoyed this eccentric uncle, who, to his nephew's great satisfaction, preferred children of a more musical or artistic bent than those with a proclivity for games. An actor in student productions at Oxford, Uncle Walter displayed an enthusiasm for the theater that would nudge John toward his own interest in acting. He wouldn't articulate that goal to his parents for several years, but by the age of 10 John had already decided that his life's ambition was to work in the theater.

He found further inspiration from a teacher at Uppingham known as "Cud" Wright – "a rather eccentric schoolmaster," John remembered, "who I will always be grateful to. He believed Shakespeare should not be read sitting at our desks, but rather acted. So consequently we were always on our feet with the text, acting the plays as we were examining them."

It was through this same teacher that an interest in film was, at last, cultivated. Wright brought in films, usually German, often silent, the first of which, Robert Wiene's *The Cabinet of Dr. Caligari* (1919), would leave a major imprint on John Schlesinger's mind and talent. *Caligari* appealed to John's love of the macabre (with its gruesome themes of mind-control, insanity, kidnap and murder, *Caligari* still sends chills today) as well as his fascination for the possibilities of cinema. The influence of the film's expressionist sets, framing narrative, and kinetic camerawork can be seen in *The Day of the Locust*, particularly in its surreal ending.

During this time, John also saw G. W. Pabst's *Kamerad-schaft* (1931), the story of a mine disaster on the French-German border. He would later recall the pioneering use of sound in this early talkie: the tapping of the miners as they try desperately to signal their rescuers, the use of voices in the distance. It taught him a great deal about the subtle power sound could achieve on film.

Wright also brought in F. W. Murnau's *Der letzte Mann/The Last Laugh* (1924). At the time, John failed to appreciate the film; he recalled that he and his classmates practically laughed it off the screen. Without dialogue or even any intertitles, the film seemed one giant, unruly pantomime, especially with the enormously fluid camerawork of Karl Freund. But *The Last Laugh* would persist in John's memory. Several years later he saw it again, and came away feeling Emil Jannings exemplified what "great acting could do in the cinema." Further, Murnau's pioneering use of *mise-en-scène* would become a roadmap for many filmmakers who followed, Schlesinger included.

He brought this newfound appreciation of cinema back home during holidays, taking far greater care with his 9.5 mm. He no longer simply demanded obedience to his direction; now his siblings had to be *artists* as well, actors serious about their craft. At Mount Pleasant, he turned a pigsty at the bottom of the garden into an office, where he planned not only his own productions but a new tradition for the family: regular film screenings. A penny a week was collected from everyone so he could rent the films, and he'd hound those who failed to contribute – fretting over movie budgets even at this early age.

Family film schedules consisted mostly of Mickey Mouse

cartoons or Charlie Chaplin shorts, but there were some dramatic classics as well: Fritz Lang's two-part *Die Nibelungen* (1924) was a favorite, particularly the first installment, *Siegfried*. With its homage to Nietzsche's idea of the superman and a pageantry that was eerily similar to the Nazi rallies going on in Germany at the time, Lang's film seems an odd choice for a Jewish home. But not really, given that the Siegfried legend also inspired Wagner's opera cycle *Der Ring des Nibelungen*, and the Schlesingers, great Wagnerians, had already mastered the knack of separating their Jewishness from their Englishness – even from their German-ness. Indeed, John would accompany the silent films with his parents' 78 r.p.m. recordings of Wagner's opera.

But it was the artistic triumph of Lang's film and not any perceived inherent fascism that left the mark. Schlesinger cited *Siegfried*'s extraordinary photography, with the "wonderful effects of light coming through the trees," as one of the greatest influences on his filmmaking. This attention to visual detail can be seen in every one of his films; John's relationship with his cameraman would be second only to his partnership with the writer. Just a few frames of *Far from the Madding Crowd* are evidence enough to show how he used photography to visually impact his narrative. In fact, there are moments in the film where the "light coming through the trees" is almost a direct replay of *Siegfried*, some 40 years earlier. "One is a great borrower working in films," John said. "You cannot help it."

Yet in those last years leading up to the war, no one, except perhaps himself, could have foreseen such a future. John Schlesinger was a moviemaker, yes, of increasingly detailed little narratives with an ever-expanding repertoire of camera tricks. But as pressure mounted to decide on a career path, he declared suddenly for architecture. How serious he ever was about this is debatable, but it was a career choice that pleased his father. Architectural schools were investigated, and the idea of "John as architect" would persist for many years.

"Find the story," John had instructed me, and it's small moments like these wherein lie discoveries. I don't believe John Schlesinger ever truly wanted to be an architect. Even as his father was pursuing schools for him, even as John himself made a great noise of interest, he was already calculating how a study of architecture might enable a career as a movie set designer. By his own admission, his reading material at the time was more likely to include Edward Carrick's books on film design than anything on modern city planning. John had no intention of ever becoming a draughtsman at some stuffy London architectural firm. He simply saw no other respectable, middle-class route into the theater or cinema, even if the way would inevitably be roundabout.

Of course, the war put everyone's plans on hold; in 1939 no one could say with any confidence what lay ahead. In that year Bernard Schlesinger, well into his 40s, volunteered to don his army uniform once again, this time as a medical officer. After taking part in the disastrous Norwegian campaign at Narvik, he was posted to India.

World War II "changed everything" for the Schlesinger children, Roger remembered. Gone were most of the servants. Food was rationed. Bernard's orderly discipline was replaced by Winifred's less rigid authority. "My father came back to a strangely changed and ribald, noisy family," John said, "which slightly shocked him, I think."

The great national common effort of the British people during the war years uprooted an ancient class system determined by background and deference. Servants, social standing, customs, tradition – all were thrown into the air to land where they may. The nation was suddenly filled with immigrants, usually with brown skin, hailing from one of those faraway Commonwealth countries. Conservatives would lament this change, loudly nostalgic for the old order that Peter Hitchens has called a shared culture of "beliefs, attitudes, prejudices, loyalties and dislikes. Yet John Schlesinger was an example of one who, though born into the privileged class, would have found it impossible to thrive under the old ways. For him, change was good: he would always love England and English manners, but he would find a greater sense of self in the American wilderness of individual determination and achievement. The proscribed pre-war English way of life would never have offered as much opportunity for him to come into his own.

It was during this period that John developed a particularly strong bond with Winifred. She had come to see her eldest son as artistically gifted with talents that needed to be encouraged, and she indulged him in his interests. With great affection, John would recall how his mother gave him Stella Gibbons' novel *Cold Comfort Farm*, which he loved for its satire and the "extreme eccentricity" of its characters. They discussed the novel at length, enjoying their shared appreciation. Half a century later *Cold Comfort Farm* would prove to be John Schlesinger's last cinematic success.

During Bernard's absence, Winifred used their shared love of music as a way to connect the children with their father. She made recordings of their music lessons to send to her husband so he could hear how they were progressing. "Often we would add a personal message to him," John said, "just to let him know he was in our thoughts."

Listening a world away to his children's scratchy, sometimes discordant but always heartfelt musical attempts must have been bittersweet for Bernard. His children may have worried for his safety, but he was also concerned about theirs. Frightened by Nazi advances across Europe and reports of Jews being interned and sent to camps, Bernard wired his wife with the suggestion they consider the heretofore unthinkable: that they break up their family and send the children to America.

Winifred received the idea with horror. It wasn't that a German occupation of England was unimaginable; what was far more difficult to envision was being separated from her children. The pain of that kind of break had already been seared into her mind, for in 1939, soon after the war began, she and Bernard had been instrumental in bringing twelve Jewish children from Germany to England. Although emigration into Britain was tightly controlled, the horrors of Kristallnacht had led to a governmental exception: ten thousand Jewish children could enter the country, providing they came without their parents. The Schlesingers arranged to take twelve: six boys and six girls between the ages of nine and twelve. Meeting them at Victoria Station, Winifred saw up-close the look of stunned fear that remained stamped on their faces. Taken hastily from their parents in Germany, sometimes without any preparation or explanation, the children had been put on trains, then boats, then trains again, carrying them to a foreign land. With despair, Winifred read the letters from the children's mothers, grateful beyond words for her help yet nonetheless devastated by the dawning reality that they would never see their sons or daughters again.

But the children lived. Winifred and Bernard Schlesinger had saved twelve young lives from certain murder. Extraordinary people in extraordinary times, and their young wards would remain forever indebted. Winifred's daily visits to the house that she and Bernard had purchased for them in Highgate were eagerly anticipated by the children. A trained staff was present at all times to care for them, and a rabbi visited to tend to them spiritually. All but one of the children would remain in close contact with the Schlesingers for the rest of their lives; reunions have been held every ten years.

Then came the Blitz. In September 1940, when German bombers began raining 57 nights of terror over London, Winifred packed up the house and moved her children out to Mount Pleasant. The twelve German children were also moved further away, separated and placed with various families – another traumatic experience for them, and precisely what Winifred feared for her own children if she sent them out of the country. Accordingly, she resisted her husband's entreaties for the duration of the war.

"My mother believed that had we been sent to America or Canada," John said, "we would never have gotten together as a family of our own again. She finally decided she'd rather stay here and take the risk."

It was a risk that ultimately paid off, but in 1940 no one had any guarantee of how the war would end. "It was a terribly, terribly frightening time," John said. For a sensitive boy, afraid of moths and fireworks, the idea of bombs falling from the sky was traumatizing. He was just fourteen at the time of the Blitz; he would lie awake at night, staring at the ceiling, listening for sounds, dreading adulthood – when he, too, would have to march off, like his father, into a war he didn't understand. "I used to think about my father out there," he said, "the possibility he might be killed. It was terrible to imagine him never coming home."

Yet of course Bernard *did* come home, once again the hero. And, in a gesture that underscores the extraordinary character of both him and his wife, that Christmas they invited two German prisoners of war to share dinner with them at Mount Pleasant. Six years of death and revulsion, with full knowledge of the atrocities the Germans had inflicted upon the Jews, and still Bernard and Win made this remarkable overture of kindness and civility.

"John would tell me such extraordinary stories about his family," said the writer Alan Bennett. It was soon after their enormously successful collaboration on *An Englishman Abroad* in 1983, and John proposed a film based on the lives of Bernard and Win. "It would have been a fictionalized memoir of how the family came through the war," Bennett said, "of bringing the children over from Germany, and it would have included a son coming out as gay. It would've been a good thing to have done, an intimate, wholly English film."

Bennett made a few notes and John was tremendously excited but, in the end, nothing ever came of the project. Instead, in one of those maddening choices that came to characterize John Schlesinger's later career, he chose to go with the supernatural thriller *The Believers*, one of the worst films he ever committed to celluloid.

In truth, as good as he was at directing those small, intimate, "wholly English" films, John Schlesinger always had a hankering for his dark, macabre thrillers. It's significant that,

just at the moment when he had nominally become an adult —
having left Uppingham and been conscripted into the army — he
made a ten-minute film (with a new, upgraded 16 mm camera)
called *Horror*. Officially, the plan was still to become an
architect; he had, in fact, signed up with the Royal Engineers
with this purpose in mind. But during basic training in
Clitheroe, while cleaning latrines, he had met John Marples,
who shared his interest in mystery and the supernatural.
Together, they revived John's boyhood magic act and secured
a gig at the local Methodist church hall, where they knew they
could at least count on a free supper.

A screening of Jean Renoir's *The Southerner* at one of the
local theaters inspired the two young men to try making a film
together. At first glance, it's difficult to see how *The Southerner*,
the best of Renoir's American films, might have led to *Horror*.
The story concerns a poor southern farmer's struggle to raise
his crops and support his family. That's really all there is to the
film: the farmer perseveres despite all sorts of disasters and
obstacles. Its theme is survival, certainly a dominant motif in
both John's life and his films. He would clearly have been
impressed by Lucien Andriot's fluid, often panoramic
photography, not to mention the lighting of the film, with its
deep shadows and bright cotton fields. But it was likely the
more gruesome, violent scenes that inflamed John's imagination: a jealous farmer wrestles the hero (Zachary Scott) to the
ground and stabs him in the chest with a knife; in another scene,
a crooked bartender emerges from the shadows holding a gun.

These are the scenes which apparently inspired *Horror*,
made shortly after Schlesinger and Marples had finished basic
training and begun their studies at the School of Military
Engineers at Chatham. Once again, John corralled his brother

Roger and trusty family cook Laura Ford, along with a friend, Paul Vaughan, to fill the roles in the film. Sadly, *Horror* no longer exists, but all who saw it recall fondly John's opening shot of two hands reaching out from the darkness toward the audience. The story, such as it was, concerned two escaped convicts, played by John and Roger, who witness the stabbing to death of Ford by Vaughan. That was about it: an exercise in Grand Guignol.

Ultimately, the Royal Engineers aside, John set his sights on becoming a filmmaker. *Horror* was a kind of calling card for him; he would take it along with him, as well as his camera, when he shipped out to Singapore.

He detested the army. By the time he arrived in Singapore, the Japanese had already surrendered, making any actual combat unlikely. Still, John abhorred the regimentation of military life. Basic training had been particularly loathsome: "I was frightened to death of obstacle courses," he said. He broke his ankle attempting one stunt but his sergeant insisted he carry on. John swore at him, finding all of this military discipline absurd. From that day on, he resolved "to rebel against any kind of organized group."

Indeed, later, when he was up against the board for officer selection, John would, quite unsolicited, volunteer the information that he was a Jew and "proud of it." It was less an insurgence of cultural pride than his own defiance of authority. Bernard took his son's comment in stride, assuming it to be the reason that John never received a commission, much as it had been for his father. Meanwhile, John Marples *did* become an officer, and was sent to Ceylon, while John Schlesinger was posted to Singapore as a private.

Sailing in convoy through the Mediterranean, John had no

clue where he was being sent. When khaki drill-clothing was issued he assumed it would be the desert, but when the ship continued through the Suez Canal, and suddenly the khakis were replaced with green fatigues, all bets were off. Arriving in Singapore, the troops were housed on the racecourse until suitable billets were found. John watched in fascination as hundreds of stoic, dispirited Japanese soldiers were marched through the town by just a few British guards.

Without much else to do, his skills as a draughtsman were put to use designing loos. Writing back home, John suggested perhaps architecture wasn't his future after all. With his parents' blessing, he managed a transfer from the Royal Engineers to the Combined Services Entertainment Unit. Enter Kenneth Williams, later the outrageous comedian of the *Carry On* films. In his diary, Williams would record his first meeting with John on 30 April 1947, calling him a "charming fellow." Together they were part of the campy entertainment staged for their fellow troops at Singapore's Victoria Theatre. John regaled audiences with his magic act, and occasionally joined Williams in drag for farcical plays.

"That's where John really came out, where he blossomed," said Michael Childers. "You couldn't get much gayer than [the CSE]."

In his memoir, Williams would remember the men of the CSE having "little or no regard for military discipline or protocol," which was a great relief to John. "Our interests and activities were totally alien to regimental procedure, [arousing] the antagonism which invariably exists between the conventional and the eccentric," Williams wrote. The garrison theater was dubbed "The Gaiety," and "dark mutterings about the arty-crafty CSE fairies" were heard: "Long-haired flamboyancy contrasted strangely with martial stiffness."

If conscription had offered the unexpected advantage of escaping from architectural school, it also gave John something else: his first real exposure to a community of homosexual men. In the CSE, John encountered gay men who were not only comfortable with their sexuality but often rather boastful about it. John was especially delighted by Barri Chatt, who came from London as part of a civilian show and performed in a number of revues for the CSE. Kenneth Williams remembered the day Chatt arrived in Singapore, jumping out of a Jeep and pirouetting before a brigadier. "Tell your mother we're here, dear," Chatt announced, as he disappeared into the barracks in a cloud of perfume. Chatt would eventually be given honorary officer status; when soldiers would heckle his act, John remembered, Chatt would retort: "Don't bite your tongue, dear, you'll get blood poisoning."

Among the other soldiers John befriended in the unit were the comedian Stanley Baxter – who'd go on to become the first person to do a drag imitation of the Queen on British television – and the dramatist Peter Nichols, who'd remember John's "semi-civilian life in the equatorial city, passing his time till his number came up." John even managed to slip away to do some radio drama for Radio Malaya.

It is to Nichols' brilliant satirical farce *Privates on Parade* that we look for our best glimpse into John's army experience, and certainly for insight into the shaping of his gay identity. Nichols gives us such characters as Acting Captain Terri Dennis, who rechristens his men with girl's names (even Jesus is referred to as "Jessica Christ") and Corporal Len Bonny, undisguised and unapologetic in his relationship with another man. As Nichols makes plain, homosexuality was an integrated, condoned, even celebrated part of the fabric of life in the CSE.

That perspective would make a lasting impact. John Schlesinger had found, in the unlikeliest of places, a community of other "different" men, a place where so many of the old mysteries suddenly made sense, where the loneliness and isolation that had haunted him since childhood was finally dissipated. "I knew at that point that I had found my way at last," he remembered. Halfway around the world he had gone, finally to find his way home.

Three

"Never anything else"

Every Easter weekend, Palm Springs is the setting for the White Party, a gathering of several thousand gay men, a bacchanalia of sex, drugs and high-energy dance music. On Sunday night John and I, along with his nurse Maureen, had just finished supper at a restaurant near the park where the closing party was being held. As we were wheeling John outside, fireworks began exploding in the night sky, a pandemonium of color and sound.

I remembered his boyhood fear. "Are the fireworks bothering you?" I asked John. "Is the noise too much?"

He shook his head "no." All through dinner he hadn't spoken a word, yet he'd remained very involved with the proceedings, eager to look out the window each time I signaled that another attractive, shirtless man was passing by.

"Do you want to head over and see the party?" I asked.

His whisper was in the affirmative. Men rushed past us toward the throbbing music, clueless about the identity of the old man in the wheelchair. Surely some of them had seen *Midnight Cowboy* or *Sunday, Bloody Sunday* – or *The Next Best Thing?* I didn't tell John that the electronic vocals getting stronger as we approached the park belonged to Madonna. If he recognized her voice, he gave no clue. He was too interested in watching the men – watching *life*, really, quite literally rushing past him.

Fireworks no longer frightened him, that much was obvious. When we stopped at the corner, I watched as he lifted his eyes to the sky, following the trail of the latest burst of gunpowder, red and gold reflecting on his face. Not much scared John Schlesinger anymore. Not here, not among these men. "John likes being around other gay men," Maureen said. "It makes him feel he's still a part of things."

I looked down at him. John was smiling, his eyes moving back and forth slowly, between the fireworks and the crowd of men.

"What set John apart from so many of his contemporaries was that he was really quite comfortable with the gay part of himself very early on," said his cousin, Andrew Raeburn, the son of John's eccentric uncle Walter. Andrew would later share a house with John on Peel Street in London. In those days, he said, one didn't formally "come out" as such: the obvious would simply and eventually make itself known. "I remember when I moved in, John asked me if I would worry if there was occasionally a stranger at the breakfast table. That made it perfectly clear to me that John was gay."

Andrew, gay himself, cited John as influential in his own journey to self-acceptance. "I owe him a tremendous amount of gratitude. I was so terribly shy about it all, and I remember when I was going to Amsterdam once he said to me, 'If you come back and you haven't gone to the Turkish baths, I am going to kick you out.' He showed me that you can't go through life not doing anything about it."

In the 1940s and 1950s, however, many men (and women) did just that, denying their basic sexual orientation, sometimes even to themselves, marrying, having children, leading furtive double lives. "That would have been completely unacceptable to John," Andrew Raeburn said. "It would never have even crossed his mind to follow that route."

In 1947, after demobilization from the army and with architectural school no longer an inevitability, John chose to read English at Balliol College, Oxford. If his parents harbored hopes that he might still find his way to a draughtsman's respectable future, they made no such entreaties. At the age of 22, John seemed free to chart his own course, and at Oxford he threw his energies into theater, joining the highly regarded, long-established Oxford University Dramatic Society (OUDS) as well as the newer, edgier Experimental Theatre Club, of which he would serve as president.

"I remember him as extremely energetic," said William Becker, a chum of John's from Oxford. "Very funny but very serious too, very *into* things."

Postwar Oxford was an incredible cauldron of roiling talent and ambition, "fast, piratical and quite clever" in the words of Kenneth Tynan, who was there. Tynan, along with Lindsay Anderson, was a few years older than John, but their presence at the university would not have gone unnoticed, Tynan especially, with his ever-present Mickey Mouse watch and the foppish Anthony Blanche outfits he always wore. Although in different colleges, they were all part of the world of OUDS, where even if one were straight, homosexual sensibilities and mannerisms were often adopted as a shorthand for chic.

In fact, even more than in the CSE, there was an obvious, flamboyant gay presence at Oxford; when John was there, friends remember, the leader of the pack was Edward Montagu, later Lord Montagu of Beaulieu. Although John was not a part of Montagu's more extravagant circle, he was nonetheless quite open about his own sexuality, which was not the case for certain others. Soon after arriving at university, John met a tall, willowy young man from Yorkshire with a love of theater and an energy that rivaled his own: Tony Richardson. That the two never became friends might strike an outside observer as curious, but to those who knew them, there were never two people more different. "Everyone knew John was gay," said William Becker, "while no one was ever sure just what Tony Richardson's story was."

Richardson would live much of his life in a state of ruse. "He placed his female lovers center stage and relegated his male lovers to the wings," Gavin Lambert observed. Richardson would justify such an arrangement when he told Lambert, "The price of repression is extremely high."

Yet, at Oxford, the repression of homosexuals that was building in postwar Britain would have felt very far away indeed. Those who moved in the world of OUDS and the Experimental Theatre Club prided themselves on sophistication and tolerance. Among John's other fellow undergraduates were his cousin, Christopher Raeburn, a veteran of the Kintbury Follies; Michael Codron, later the famed theatrical producer; future actor Nigel Davenport; Peter Parker, the future chairman of British Rail; and Shirley Catlin, who played Cordelia to Parker's King Lear and would later become Labour MP Shirley Williams, then a co-founder of the Social Democratic Party and, still later, leader of the Liberal Democrats in the House of Lords.

"For the first time, I was very happy with my life," John said. At Oxford, he found a community of like-minded peers, and finally indulged his dream of working in the theater. He would win a student directorial competition (besting, among others, Tony Richardson) with his adaptation of Thornton Wilder's *The Happy Journey to Trenton and Camden*, an experimental forerunner of Wilder's *Our Town*. Staged without scenery and with a minimum of props, *The Happy Journey* proved an effective laboratory piece for John, using as it did an apparently pleasant road trip to explore the underpinnings of emotion and conflict in an American middle-class family. "I was able for the first time to really look at how acting might get to the heart of the human condition," he said.

Most of his time at Oxford, however, was spent as an actor. Several Sandy Wilson revues, some with Kenneth Tynan; the Troll King in *Peer Gynt*, directed by Tony Richardson; Dame Nuisance in the Christmas 1949 pantomime, *Babes in the Wood*; and Merlin in a 1950 Experimental Theatre adaptation of Henry Fielding's *Tom Thumb the Great*. With Michael Codron (who wrote and directed *Babes in the Wood* and produced *Tom Thumb the Great*) John played in a farcical number called *The Kosher Kids*.

John's most noted student performance came in 1949, as Trinculo in Nevill Coghill's production of *The Tempest*. Coghill, a distinguished English don, had been an influential tutor of W.H. Auden and, with C.S. Lewis, J.R.R. Tolkein, Owen Barfield and Charles Williams, he'd comprised the informal "Inklings" literary group. Idolized by Oxford students, who were thrilled when he would agree to direct one of their plays or operas, Coghill had considerable, if indirect, influence on the development of British theater and film: dozens of important artists would train under him, John Schlesinger and Richard Burton being but two.

For *The Tempest*, Coghill pulled out all the stops. "It was truly spectacular, unforgettable," said William Becker, who played Caliban. "All the theatrical journals of the day had photos of it." Staged on the lawns of Worcester College, the play offered the spectacle of Caliban making his dramatic entrance right out of the lake. Trees walking as men transformed themselves into whips; a lighted galleon emerged from behind the bushes, startling the audience. Ariel ran fleetingly across the surface of the lake by means of a wooden bridge rigged up just underwater, and vanished into a dazzling shower of sparks.

That kind of spectacular illusion would remain a fascination for Schlesinger, the boy who'd first been mesmerized by Maskelyne and Devant. If he'd had his way, more of his films would have been magical, illusory spectacle. He claimed not to enjoy films with a preponderance of "special effects," but his comments always seemed somewhat disingenuous, as if that's what he thought a "serious director" was supposed to say about a cinema that had been overtaken by Spielberg and *Star Wars* and *Titanic*. Certainly, he was always interested in making movies that explored character and the relationships between people, but if he could pull off some wonderful illusion as part of that — as he managed to do in *Billy Liar* and *The Day of the*

Locust, and even in the dream-fantasy sequences of *Midnight Cowboy* – he was always very pleased.

All one needs to do is look at the amateur films he made on his own to see where he positioned himself as a filmmaker. *Horror*, then *Black Legend* and *The Starfish*: John Schlesinger saw himself right from the start as a director of thrillers, with magic and illusion and the macabre defining his art. At Oxford, he made films about ghosts and witches, while Lindsay Anderson's first amateur work, *Meet the Pioneers*, was a bleak documentary about coal miners in Yorkshire.

Yet there is another key difference between the two: the same year as *Black Legend* and *Meet the Pioneers*, Anderson was writing in his diary about his torment over his sexuality, trying to choose between a life of celibacy or a life of anonymous lavatory encounters. He could apparently see no third way. Meanwhile, John Schlesinger was falling madly, obviously, publicly, in love. And while not a perfect relationship by any means, John was at least able to entertain visions of forming a lifelong, fulfilling partnership with another man, something Anderson at that point simply could not bring himself to consider.

"There's a handsome one, John," Maureen said, as the last of the fireworks illuminated a stocky man standing not far away from us, his hairy, muscular arms crossed over his chest.

"No," I said, leaning down to John. "That's not your type, is it?"

He shook his head. "Too big," he whispered, his first words all evening.

John had always preferred his men slender, smooth and smart. All of the great loves of his life had fit this description, including Michael.

"John never had any trouble getting men," said Richard Marden, who had known Schlesinger since his Oxford days and edited a couple of his best pictures, *Sunday, Bloody Sunday* and *The Falcon and the Snowman*. "John was John. He was an entertainer, and so if he was attracted to somebody, it's more than likely that he would make them attracted to him."

This despite a supposed handicap that has sent many another man into self-imposed exile. Soon after entering Oxford, at the age of 22, John, to his horror, lost most of his hair.

"I felt terribly self-conscious about it," he said, refuting Marden's perception of confidence. His twenties would be spent, he insisted, feeling shy and awkward, never knowing what it was like to look like a young man. "Everyone thought I was older than I was. It wasn't until I got to be 30, never having known what it was like to look younger, that I started to come into my own. I was always a late starter at everything."

That's a bit of an exaggeration, for as Marden and many other friends point out, there were plenty of amorous adventures before John hit his third decade. "John was always incredibly handsome," said Michael Childers. "Such beautiful eyes. But I think what made him most attractive was his sense of humor. The way he could tease you, make fun of anything. It was captivating."

Indeed, his humor – his wit, his mischief, his sense of play-fulness – was the very first thing that every single interviewee cited as what they loved and remembered most about John. "There was a way he had of being able to make all of us laugh, anyone, on a movie set, at his home," said Alan Bates. "It was the gift of laughter, and he gave it to everyone."

"What I remember most is how provocative he could be," said Julie Christie. "He was a mischievous character who delighted in taking the piss out of everything and anyone. He had an amazingly rude vocabulary, which he took great pleasure in using in a very loud voice in public spaces, despite having inherited the most exquisite manners from his family."

The classic example is the stunt John pulled on her during the filming of *Far from the Madding Crowd*. "I had one scene," Christie remembered, "where I had to open the coffin of the dead mistress of my husband. I knew the coffin contained a terrible secret about my husband and I had to prise it open dramatically to discover it. I went into one of those actorly things: I needed to be very intense and serious and be on my own to get into the mood. I was getting very ratty with everyone who made a noise on the set. We eventually got around to shooting it after I had been indulged with 'time' to build up to it. I slowly prised the lid off the coffin. Inside, instead of a dead mistress and baby as there should have been, there was a small, smirking props man holding a huge dildo."

That kind of irreverence was cultivated early. Stories of practical jokes on his brothers and sisters are numerous. There were hilarious imitations of Noël Coward and Peggy Ashcroft, and, yes, that ironic running gag of pretending to have had a stroke. "He had a vulgar, wicked sense of humor, and he took glee in making jokes he knew would embarrass people," said Ann Skinner, his longtime continuity assistant. "But he could usually use enough warmth that he didn't offend anyone."

"He could be so naughty," agreed his friend Stewart Grimshaw. "I remember when he was living in Peel Street, across the way lived this gay couple, very distinguished actors, Gary Bond and Jeremy Brett, who was of course married to Anna Massey. And John would be spying out the window at them and then come running up the stairs shouting, 'They're doing it, they're doing it!' A dirty joke was always funnier to him than a non-dirty joke."

Kenneth Williams found one of John's jokes so hilarious he recorded it in his diary for posterity: A girl asks the designation of the uniformed fellow with whom she's dancing. "I'm a Gurkha officer," he tells her. "I thought they were black," she says. "No, only our privates are black," he replies. To which the girl smiles and says, "My dear, how *fantastic*."

"John loved to laugh and even more, he loved to make others laugh," said Roland Curram, a friend since the early 1950s. "It was an earthy humor, very ribald, very red-blooded. Quite decadent. The one thing I hope that you gather from all of this is John's enormous humanity, and his attempt to make the world appreciate life, and he did that mostly through laughter."

Curious that a man so highly regarded for his ability to make people laugh would prove such a tragedian as a director, with most of his ventures into comedy falling flat. "It wasn't a humor that translated well," said Jim Clark, his most frequent film editor, who cited *Honky Tonk Freeway*, John's reviled farce of 1981, as a prime example. John's humor – often quite black, always very English, and with a healthy dose of camp – had a hard time, Clark said, "playing to mass audiences."

Yet his charisma was nonetheless very apparent in person. Even as a young man, before he had become famous and "someone to know," men and women alike would gravitate to him at parties, charmed by his wit. "He drew people to him," said Roland Curram. "He was incredibly magnetic."

"John sitting in a restaurant was very compelling," said Stewart Grimshaw. "People who didn't know him would always say, 'Who is that?' He was a very powerful presence in a room or party. He was the one people listened to."

Still, he remained always a bit ill at ease, never quite sure of his own attractiveness. Part of the reason, as he suggested, may have been his baldness, but most of the nagging self-doubt stemmed back to his earliest days when he felt inadequate at games and so unlike his gregarious father in social conversation. Those old boyhood feelings, so powerful, never really went away, and it would be humor he'd use to deflect this sense of inferiority. For all his apparent ease in making friends, John Schlesinger was never one hundred percent certain of the impression he made on people. He would remember being invited to a "rather smart dinner party" in Belgravia around this time, walking "round and round" the house trying to summon the nerve to go in. "Oh, God," he kept saying to himself before steeling himself to ring the bell, "I don't want to go in there."

This essential conflict between self-confidence and self-doubt would show up in all areas of his life, including his film work, so perhaps he should be taken at his word that he spent his twenties feeling somewhat adrift and it wasn't until he hit 30 that he felt he'd "come into his own." Certainly, when we consider the relationships he pursued during this time, we're left with what modern psychology might label "self-defeating" behavior: fancying men who would remain always out of reach, never fully available to him. Sex was one thing; affairs of the heart quite another. And John Schlesinger would not have the success in the latter that he enjoyed in the former until almost two decades later. "I think," he said, "I was afraid to love."

At Uppingham, he had developed crushes on several of his schoolmates; later there would be a brief, unrequited longing for the staunchly heterosexual John Marples. But it was during his first year at Oxford, directly after his experience in the CES where he had seen first-hand the possibility of forming an undisguised relationship with another man, that John really fell in love for the first time.

His name was Alan Cooke, and he was handsome, cultured, witty, and interested in all the same things as John: theater, film, music. Born in London and educated at St. Paul's School, Alan read English at Merton College; by 1949 he was president of OUDS, while John was president of the Experimental Theatre Club. They complemented each other perfectly, John felt, two sides of the same coin, the yin and yang of Oxford student dramatics.

"John was completely mad about Alan," said his friend Geoffrey Sharp. "But I don't think it was ever entirely reciprocated from Alan's end."

For John, Cooke would remain frustratingly noncommittal, unwilling to avow homosexuality in the way he himself had done. "Alan had some sense he might be bisexual," said Gavin Lambert. "He was certainly not 'out' in the way John was."

For weeks at a time, John and Alan would be inseparable, talking film and theater, dreaming of the future. Then, abruptly, Alan would move off, back to his own room, wracked with guilt for having had gay sex. He would refuse to see John or have anything to do with him, insisting he had "gone straight" and was now dating a woman. John would simply have to accept that fact, he said, and move on. Yet before long, Alan would be back in John's house – and in his bed. John took him back every time, without question.

Their frequent separations were agonizing. Dragging Geoffrey Sharp along, John would walk past Alan's window to see if the lights were on. "He wanted to know if Alan was home, and who was with him," Sharp said. For his entire three years at Oxford, John would be absolutely besotted with Alan Cooke.

In the summer of 1948, however, he latched onto the perfect arrangement, one that would not only keep Alan in his life — indeed, bind them together — but also further his own ambitions for a filmmaking career. While spending the school holiday at Mount Pleasant, Alan listened to John's enthusiastic proposal that they make a film together. They could blaze a trail for independent feature filmmaking in Britain, John argued, revolutionizing the staid British film industry. Alan was intrigued and agreed to give it a try.

Taking their cue from Edward Dmytryk, the American director who'd recently criticized the "closed entrée" that he'd observed in the British film industry, Schlesinger and Cooke vowed to break down the walls. They issued statements to the press announcing that their new venture would prove "a worthwhile film can be made on a natural location with only a very small capital." They hoped to engineer a foothold in the business by convincing a producer to invest a few thousand pounds in their enterprise. "Every young director or camera-man realizes that enthusiasm is not enough," Cooke told the film journal *Sight and Sound*. "But we want to be given the chance to learn, not to be thrust into the cutting-room for too long."

Such ambition, they hoped, would be rewarded, but first they needed a product — and, of course, it would be something macabre. One of the earliest tales to inflame John's young imagination had been the legend of Coombe Gibbet. Near the village of Kintbury stood a stark pole on the top of a hill where, as John was told by the villagers, the lovers George Broomham and Dorothy Newman had been hanged in 1676. Their crime had been the brutal murder of Broomham's wife and son. As a boy, John would wander through the chalk downs imagining the grisly tale, visualizing the dead, broken bodies of Broomham and Newman dangling from the gibbet. Now, with Alan, he combed through the spidery handwriting of the Western Circuit Gaol Book to uncover the details of the story.

The picture would be called *Black Legend*. John rounded up his usual cast of actors: his brother and sisters, cousins, the family cook Laura Ford and her boyfriend Bill May, and even John Marples, who played Broomham. He also scored a bit of a coup: for the role of Broomham's wife he secured Ena Morgan, a family friend who, as Ena Evans, had had a brief career in the silent cinema, playing in such Stoll Picture Productions as *Fighting Snub Reilly* (1924) and *A Daughter of Love* (1925). John lured her back before the camera; since they couldn't afford a soundtrack, Ena felt right at home.

Still, it was important to Schlesinger and Cooke that, though their film was silent, they did not resort to silent-film techniques. "If we reverted to the ham acting of *The Great Train Robbery*," Cooke said, "the effect would be hilarious but unconvincing. On the other hand, the subtlety of expression in close-ups might be meaningless without dialogue." He and John argued over how best to work around this problem: they decided to use modern camerawork and aim for comedy as well as thrills, since people would probably laugh anyway at a bunch of amateurs emoting without dialogue. A musical accompaniment (since lost) was also recorded on discs.

"We started from scratch," Cooke told *Sight and Sound*.

"There was not a technician amongst us, nor at that time had any of us had more than a fleeting glimpse of a film studio. What we knew we had learned from our stalls in cinema after cinema."

The cost of the film, which came in at just under 250 pounds, was financed by Grandma Schlesinger. Costumes had to be made and sets built. Fortunately, a local mill donated all the wood, and the various friends who came up from Oxford were willing to sleep in tents in the Schlesingers' back garden. Alan acted as producer, coordinating call sheets and property lists, while John was in charge artistically as the director. As would ever be the case, he found the planning stages – those nights sitting up late with Alan, imagining what they could do – far preferable to the actual shoot, which proved quite arduous. Again foreshadowing future movie sets, John was stricken by "the Curse of the Regensburgs"; his daily pessimistic laments finally unnerved Alan to the point where he blew up in rage. "The strain upon everybody's patience is fearful to recall," Cooke would remember. Particularly trying was the experience of watching the climactic hanging scene go awry, bringing down the gibbet and wrecking the camera. They lost precious days having to take it up to London for repair.

The result of their endeavors is an entertaining little film, ambitious yet fully conscious of its own limitations. For all the talk of repudiating silent-film techniques, however, there are a number of iris shots and old-fashioned fades to black, making *Black Legend* feel more like 1918 than 1948. The performances are, as the filmmakers expected, quite overblown and clumsy, with the actors occasionally looking self-consciously into the camera. There are long stretches of inaction and shots held too long, although the English countryside is lovingly captured, anticipating the bucolic scenery of *Far from the Madding Crowd*.

John's technically accomplished camerawork is the film's best feature. Having already been peering through his lens for at least a decade, he had completely mastered the craft of matching his shots and framing his subjects creatively. He also displayed a sure hand at editing; sitting at the dining room table of Mount Pleasant, he spliced disparate shots together to create some very effective scenes, notably the sequence of a carriage careening out of control. By intercutting close-ups of the wheels spinning and a woman falling, he conveyed the impression of the carriage overturning without actually having to overturn it. In another scene, he depicts a rainstorm by showing the surface of a pond, with one, two, three, and then dozens of drops.

The narrative of the film is framed by a modern prologue and epilogue: a group of cyclists come upon the gibbet and meet a cloaked stranger, who relates the legend for them. Throughout, there are some nice cinematic touches. As Broomham's wife waits for his return, the candle burns down, with the lighting changing accordingly. The spread of gossip through the village is handled in a rapid, amusing montage. The actors, despite their clumsiness, were obviously instructed carefully and personally, as everyone, foreground and background, has something to do. And the final mob scene is well managed, prefiguring even in its crude interpretation the riot in *The Day of the Locust*.

John clearly reveled in the gruesome flourishes he was able to give the film: the young boy's death scene, with his hands in the air, going limp as he dies; the bloody gibbet discovered by the village idiot, Mad Thomas; the final hanging of the murderers, filmed with very expressionistic, *Caligari*-esque shadows. The final revelation of the cloaked storyteller turning out to be the ghost of George Broomham, complete with his stop-motion disappearance, is a bit corny, but it surely produced the intended reaction, a little thrill and some laughter.

Indeed, when the finished picture was shown that autumn at the cinema in nearby Newbury, the locals were bowled over by what the young filmmakers had accomplished. In February they showed it at Oxford, in an exhibition hosted by the Experimental Theatre Club and held in the lecture theater of the Geography School. A correspondent from *The Times* was in the audience and gave *Black Legend* a generous review, saying the film showed "promise." With its top-of-the-page placement, the review was extraordinary exposure for the first-time student filmmakers. A screening was then arranged in London at the House of Lords, through a friend of Bernard's who was a peer. In the audience this time was the esteemed film critic Dilys Powell, who hailed the film in her *Sunday Times* column as being made with "brains, not money."

This was heady encouragement for the novice movie-makers. Powell was one of the *grande dames* of film criticism, having written about movies for decades. John was thrilled to receive her blessing – "the only rave I've ever had from her in my life," he'd say wryly, looking back – but at the time a good word from Powell was enough to convince him that success was assured. All of the youthful chutzpah in planning to bypass apprenticeships in the cutting room and go straight to the director's table seemed to be paying off.

Indeed, Dilys Powell's enthusiasm persuaded a publicity man from Ealing Studios, then the most prominent British production company, to set up a screening for his boss, Sir Michael Balcon. With great anticipation, John and Alan trekked out to suburban west London with their film and their twin turntables. Balcon, encouraged by the advance reviews, arranged for all of his studio department heads to attend the screening. Enthusiastic introductions were made all around, and then they settled down, the lights were shut off, and the projector began to hum.

When the phonograph records failed to play, however, Balcon suggested they just watch it silent – "a terrible blow," John would remember, "because it didn't work. We live in the age of sound films." Still, he expected *some* reaction from the assembled movie people. But nothing. No gasps of the kind that had been uttered by the local people of Newbury when poor little Robert Broomham was killed. No expressions of awe in response to all the hard work they'd done to stage the hanging. Nary a ripple when the cloaked figure at the end disappeared in a camera effect as old as Georges Méliès.

When the lights went up, the audience walked out in silence. John hurried up to Balcon, who turned to him and said, "Thank you for showing us your amateur film."

Of course that's what it *was*, an amateur film by a couple of university students. But Balcon's expectations had clearly been raised too high by the effusive praise of Powell and his own publicity people. All that was left for John and Alan to do was to pack up their film and their records and return dejectedly to Oxford.

"It's just as well to know that success doesn't mean a thing in terms of what you really want to make," John would say, years later. "I learned early on the frustration of not getting what I wanted off the ground."

In a career that would be, as he quipped, constantly "up and down like a whore's drawers," John Schlesinger had to inure himself early against his critics. That's a daunting challenge for someone predisposed to seeing the glass as always half empty. "There were many times, and it still happens," he said, toward the end of his career, "when I suffer from a sense of frustration at being made to feel inadequate or unequal to the job. Therefore, when success comes it's all the more enjoyable. It also means that I'm not very good at dealing with failure."

How much accuracy there is in the story of John's rejection by the great Sir Michael Balcon is debatable. It makes for a colorful legend – youthful hubris humbled, returning to Oxford with his tail between his legs – but it seems a bit fanciful, at least in the abrupt rudeness shown toward the young filmmakers. The tale neglects to factor in the overall slump facing British film studios at the time. To have secured a position at Ealing, John would have had to have made a film so dazzling that Balcon would have, in the midst of an economic downturn, created a job for him at the studio.

Had *Black Legend* been that sort of film, so impressing Balcon that he *had* found John a job as an assistant, we might have seen a career very different from the one that emerged: a studio-molded John Schlesinger, a director of thrillers and mysteries. Just because they would have been products of a studio doesn't mean they wouldn't have been good; John's skill would surely have prevailed, and he might well have given a boost to the ailing British cinema, anticipating the Hammer horrors of a decade later. Schlesinger's eventual emergence into the ranks of "kitchen-sink" realist filmmakers was not an inevitability in 1948. Had Balcon signed him up, John might have been quite happy as a steadily employed director of popular thrillers.

At some point, however, he would inevitably have itched to do something more, to inject a bit of the human condition into his ghost stories and mysteries. Even in *Black Legend* there is the pathos of the father witnessing his son's death at the hand of his mistress. "I don't want to preach," John once said, "but still, if one goes through all the agony of making a film, you do want it to say something in the end."

What set Schlesinger apart from some of his peers was that his initial urge was always toward the visceral experience rather than the cerebral. Yes, he wanted his audiences to *think*, but more importantly, he wanted them to *feel*, be it terror or revulsion or compassion or pity. It is why, of the Oxford quartet who came to define British cinema in the 1960s – Schlesinger, Anderson, Richardson and Reisz – John would be the most prolific and the most commercially successful.

Yet not the most acclaimed. Of the four, he was the least intellectual, usually considered by critics as less of an *artist* than the others. Indeed, much of the critical elite would attempt to dismiss him in the course of a career that spanned half a century. Even Dilys Powell, after her initial support, never again found much good to say about John Schlesinger, even as she boosted Lindsay Anderson and Tony Richardson to the forefront of British cinema. David Thomson always famously disliked Schlesinger, largely on the basis that John preferred "story" above all, and that he tended to use anecdotes Thomson found "shy of thematic coherence"; in other words, he could see no larger "meaning" to John Schlesinger's pictures beyond the stories of his characters.

In much of the negative criticism leveled at Schlesinger over the years, there was an undeniable hint of intellectual snobbery. John himself always felt that Anderson and Richardson looked down their noses at him, all the more envious of his commercial success because, to their minds, he didn't deserve it: he didn't participate in the discourse on film, never pontificated about auteurism or cinema semiology. At Oxford, while John was off hanging dummies on gibbets, Anderson and Reisz were founding the film theory magazine, *Sequence*, to which Richardson was a frequent contributor. Endless hours were spent writing about and debating the role and nature of cinema, while John, for his part, was utterly bored by such dry, brainy discussions. "You only really learn by doing," he said. "I'm not really a great theorist. I haven't a lot of theory. The practical experience is the most important thing."

Later, he'd criticize the others, especially Anderson, for being idle, for not putting all those grand ideas into more frequent practice. Instead of theorizing, John would spend the 1950s acting or, when he wasn't on stage, *observing*. "People ask me sometimes, 'What do you do when you are not making a film?'" John told an audience in 1981. "I think I am always doing what a lot of film directors do, or should do, which is to observe. We live off life. I love watching people. It's like sitting with a sketchbook. You store away incidents in your mind, never quite knowing when you're going to use them."

Simply *living life* was John Schlesinger's best training for making films. Intellectual theorizing was, to him, a waste of precious time; time that could be spent traveling, or attending the opera, or laughing with friends, or making love. Or, as he would demonstrate in his long career, making *movies*.

"I do love to work," he said. "I'm not really happy unless I've got a project on the go, and am thinking about the creation of something . . . I don't want to make 'important' films all the time. I like to do different things . . . a small picture here, a big picture there."

He would be criticized for making his thrillers, as if the director of *Sunday, Bloody Sunday* was too good for them, too literate; as if a literate man shouldn't enjoy a good roller-coaster ride as much as anyone else. "[The critics] always wanted me to be doing something more high-minded," he said. "I think sometimes I was too busy living life to ever be a great artist."

Indeed, there is a school of thought that suggests that unless one is suffering for one's art, one is not truly an artist at all. It is true that many of the great artists of all disciplines – theater, painting, music, literature, cinema – have been beset by personal demons, tormented souls whose art became their cries for humanity. Many of these figures were also gripped by an all-consuming narcissism, making them desperate for the love of an audience to fill the deep and abiding emptiness in their lives.

John Schlesinger had no such cravings of the ego. Yes, he desired success; he was ambitious; he wanted to make lots of money, especially as he got older. But he was not a tormented man. His quirky pessimism notwithstanding, he lived a life relatively free of personal demons. He did not abuse drugs or alcohol. He did not come from a dysfunctional family nor find himself trapped in long-term destructive relationships. There was no internal struggle over his homosexuality, as there was for Anderson and Richardson and so many others. His art came, not from discontentment with life but, rather, from a love of it.

Perhaps that partly explains the prejudice that sometimes existed against him. What drove John to filmmaking was the desire to tell stories of the human condition, not a need to exorcize his inner devils or send bold political messages about society. "I'm with Goldwyn on that," he said. "If you want to send a message, use Western Union." Though his desire for popular success would lead him occasionally into some rather unwise career decisions, his making of commercial films was not in any way a repudiation of his art. "I want to have some fun out of making films," he said. "It's a great source of pleasure to me. And therefore I don't think one's got to get too arty-farty about it."

He would learn, despite his kneejerk pessimism, to distance himself from criticism and rejection, for they would become the ever-present background chorus to his career. "I've often been dismissed," he told his diary. "I think some critics are uncomfortable with me because they have never been able to put me into a nice little slot. They haven't been able to place me. But I've long since ceased to lose sleep over that. They've got their jobs to do, and I've got mine.

"I don't rush out [to get the reviews] anymore," he said another time. "I think it's very sad that David Lean actually admitted that the New York Critics' Circle rendered him impotent for fourteen years. You shouldn't let them know it *ever*. Even if you think it, don't ever let them know that they have any power at all."

Such equanimity, however, was not yet developed by 1948. Balcon's rejection was devastating to John. The fact that Mount Pleasant Productions didn't crumble in its aftermath must likely be credited to Alan Cooke rather than to John, who was convinced that all his self-doubts had simply been proven correct: their film was terrible. Alan, on the other hand, wanted to give their venture another try.

Cooke would remain defensive about their first film.

Writing in *Sight and Sound*, he offered a response to the naysayers at Ealing Studios, acknowledging *Black Legend*'s "ineptitudes" but also pointing out that they had proven "a valuable point for amateur film groups: that a film can be made in a fortnight on a budget of £250 or less." He was eager to commence a new film, and during Easter break in 1949, on holiday together in Cornwall, he and John came up with the idea. All they knew was that they wanted a witch in it, they wanted to use Nigel Finzi, the boy who had played George Broomham's son in *Black Legend*, and they wanted it set in the present "if only to remove the endless complications of trying to avoid telegraph wires and metalled roads in our camera angles."

Charmed by the rocky coast and crusty fisherfolk of the village of Cadgwith, John concocted a fable of a sea witch who, caught in the net of a fisherman, secures her freedom by granting a wish: all of his catches from now on will be prodigious. To make sure she keeps her end of the bargain, the fisherman takes from her a magic charm: a glass starfish.

John's spirits revived quickly once he had a new project at hand. He once again called on his family and friends to serve as actors and crew. His aunt, Margaret Webber, would play "Witch Meg"; his sister Susan took the substantial part of Wendy, the little girl who arrives in the village with her parents only to uncover the secret of the sea-witch. To play Wendy's brother Tim, they brought back Nigel Finzi (who was, incidentally, the son of Gerald Finzi). Geoffrey Sharp and John Marples arrived to oversee the production, and Richard Marden, who would later cut *Sunday, Bloody Sunday*, served as editor.

The Starfish, which began shooting in August of 1949, is a far better film than *Black Legend*. John would never think so; he would say he made two films while at Oxford, the first "good" and the second "terrible." Yet *The Starfish* benefits from acting that is far superior to the first film. In the role of Jack Trevenick, the fisherman who catches the sea-witch and must ultimately rescue young Tim from her clutches, John and Alan cast a professional actor of some reputation, Kenneth Griffith. At the time of *The Starfish*, the Welsh-born Griffith had just come from playing the villain in the film *Bond Street*; he was recognizable enough, he remembered, that people would often refuse to sit in railway compartments with him. Griffith had also received considerable notice as the conniving blackmailer in the BBC production of Edward Percy's *The Shop at Sly Corner*; he would later make controversial documentary films criticizing British involvement in Ireland.

Although Griffith didn't mention *The Starfish* in his auto-biography, he recalled it was a period when he was "reverting to the gypsy thing, playing any part to make a living." With the help of Grandma Schlesinger, John and Alan managed to pay Griffith a wage comparable to touring companies, and their investment paid off. As the moody Trevenick, Griffith was good, first eliciting fear and distrust then, finally, admiration. Nigel Finzi also justified the filmmakers' faith in him, turning in a believable, competent performance. The most pleasant surprise, however, was John's sister Susan; her acting was very naturalistic, and she had a very engaging screen presence. Largely based on her experience with *The Starfish*, Susan Schlesinger announced to the family that she, too, wanted to pursue a career in acting and the theater.

The film also had the obvious advantage of sound. Convinced that part of *Black Legend*'s problem lay in its silence,

John pleaded with his grandmother once again to come up with financial backing. This time she gave him enough to secure a soundtrack that would include several snatches of dialogue and a specially composed score by his friend Roy Jesson, who later became a professional musician. In his first use of sound on film, John demonstrated a sharp ear: footsteps approaching, the crash of the surf, voices echoing in the cove are all very effective.

There are also some very nice, closely observed scenes that have a distinct documentary feel: the fishermen awakening early in the morning, drinking coffee and smoking cigarettes; young Tim heading out on a lobster boat and being teased with one of the creature's claws. Yet again, however, there are long stretches of near inaction that do nothing to advance the story, as if John couldn't decide whether he was making a fairy tale or a fishing documentary. The first glimpse of the witch doesn't come until nearly halfway into the film, but when it does, it's striking: caught in the net, she's hideous looking, and it's a tribute to John's love of the macabre that the scene remains as creepy as he intended.

Seen later, in full daylight, however, Witch Meg looks far less frightening, coming across pretty much as what she was: John's aunt in a bad mask. After its atmospheric buildup, the film rushes toward its conclusion, revealing more and more of its amateur construction in the process: clumsy acting by the locals, awkward jump-cuts, and a resolution that seems none too clear. Still, there's no discounting *The Starfish*'s sense of story, or its visceral thrill.

For the film's release, Alan Cooke struck a deal with a Manchester-based producer-distributor outfit called Butcher's Film Service ("Rather aptly named, I'd say," John would remark, years later.) Butcher had made its mark mostly with *Old*

Mother Riley cheapies and now spent much of its time providing independent films to the provinces. Blown up to 35 mm, *The Starfish* was sent out to a number of regional cinemas in early 1950, and was heralded with a two-page feature in *Sight and Sound* that positioned Cooke and Schlesinger as bright young hopes for the British cinema. "Mount Pleasant Productions have convinced many of us that with very little encouragement a worthwhile experiment could become a reality," the piece said.

But suddenly it was all over. John would remember attending a screening of *The Starfish* at the Odeon, Staines, cringing as the audience hooted at the film. When it was over, he heard someone remark, "Well, somebody must have had fun making *that*." He convinced himself it was a terrible film – and so that was that, he said, explaining why he disbanded Mount Pleasant Productions. *The Starfish* was a "terrible" film, he said, over and over again, and so he abandoned his dream of making movies and decided instead to concentrate on his "second string" – acting.

That explanation simply doesn't ring true. After all the hopes and dreams of Mount Pleasant Productions, after the hype in *Sight and Sound*, after the encouragement from Dilys Powell, it seems unfathomable that John would simply give it all up so quickly and switch to acting. It's true that *The Starfish* wasn't exactly setting the provinces on fire; there was no follow-up review from Powell; Michael Balcon didn't come around begging John's forgiveness and asking for another chance. But neither was the film a disaster: *The Starfish* was what it was, a short, independent, film making the rounds of regional cinemas, with a recognizable star to boot. Mount Pleasant Productions certainly could have made further pictures for Butcher Films to distribute.

But it didn't. It was over. John would finally offer a more believable reason for the six-year sidetrack he took away from moviemaking. "A tortured relationship" had so depressed him, he said, that upon graduation from Oxford he joined a theater repertory company "to get out of England." What had happened was, in the summer of 1950, soon after *The Starfish* had gone into distribution, John and Alan had traveled to the United States as part of a student production tour of American universities. They were housed separately, and by the time the trip was over, so was their relationship. Alan had decided finally that he was not homosexual after all; there could be no more dallying with John, or any man. Utterly devastated, John didn't have the heart to carry on making movies alone.

In *Midnight Cowboy*, Joe Buck's portable radio becomes almost a character of its own. When he is forced to pawn it, we actually feel sad, the way we might if watching a little boy surrender his beloved teddy bear. The radio has been Joe's companion, his friend, his oracle.

When John Schlesinger went to America in 1950, he took with him a portable radio much like Joe Buck's. "Listening to that radio, I learned about American culture, really for the first time," he said. It was one thing to watch American movies like *The Southerner* which, after all, had been made by a Frenchman. It was quite another to listen to call-in shows, with beauty tips and health advice being doled out to American housewives. Farm reports crackled into his ear as his tour bus rattled across the long flat Midwest highways. A cacophony of rock-and-roll, rhythm-and-blues, and country-western blared out from nearly every station — and *hundreds* of them, not just the handful he might listen to in England. Yet he could find precious few that played the classical music or opera he so loved.

As guests of the American National Theater Association, the Oxford students performed *King Lear* and *The Alchemist* at various Midwestern universities. Their trip began and ended in New York, where they were housed individually by different sponsors. John's first glimpse of America was a rundown basement flat in Chinatown. "I remember rats crawling outside, and the awareness of considerable violence going on, strange screams in the night," he said. The future director of *Midnight Cowboy* – perhaps the best film ever made about New York's street life – was too terrified to leave his flat and venture outside.

After the tour was finished, the students returned to New York. This time John was lodged in a nicer apartment whose owner was away. To his delight, he found little messages left all around the flat: "Englishmen welcome," one read. Another said, "Tea here" and another "Shower here," with an arrow pointing to a rubber contraption that was rigged up to allow a shower in the bathtub. More pleasant this stay might have been, but the city remained blisteringly hot. John lay awake at night, sweating into his sheets, listening to the sirens and more strange screams in the night. As he was on a charter flight back to London, he had to wait day by day, hourly in fact, for news of when the plane would be able to take him home. He paced the flat anxiously, depressed over the separation from Alan, feeling very much a stranger in a strange land. At this point, he was not fascinated enough by American culture to want to explore it. "New York for me at the time," he remembered with considerable dread, "was not a place to be holed up."

Back home, he found some work as a radio actor at the BBC,

but he remained heartbroken over the loss of Alan Cooke. Before the year was out, he was planning to ship out with the British Commonwealth Theatre Company, founded in 1949 by New Zealand crime novelist and producer Ngaio Marsh as a "synthesis of Commonwealth talent." John's parents were once again outwardly supportive of his decision, even after they were told the company would soon be spending six months or more in Australia and New Zealand. "Privately, they were very worried about John, whether his going into acting was a good idea," Roger Schlesinger said. "But we never knew they felt that way until John was successful and they admitted they'd had some doubts."

The tour lasted until the end of October, about nine months, enough time for much of John's heartache to heal. It was "hard work, often frustrating, but valuable and interesting," he said, and he'd had fun playing Feste in *Twelfth Night*. When not on the stage or on the radio with the New Zealand Broadcasting Service, John would busy himself shooting home movies on visits to several South Pacific islands: geysers shooting in a mountain gorge, steam rising off water, volcanic rock, molten lava. Watching these snippets, it's easy to see Schlesinger's fascination with capturing moving images on film. He wanted to see how they would appear, what kind of effect they might have on the screen.

In another scene from these home movies, John focuses on a young man walking along a riverbank into the fog. He turns to the camera with a knowing look on his face. In the next frame, we suddenly catch a glimpse of John himself, laughing and clowning around. The identity of the young man with him is not known, nor is the reason for John's levity. But the images offer further proof that the trip to the South Pacific had done exactly what John had intended it to do: it got him over Alan Cooke.

He returned to England in November 1951, sorry to see the repertory company disbanding, "for it was a splendid idea, if badly mismanaged." He once again performed in some radio plays for the BBC, but radio work couldn't be counted on for a living. Accordingly, he signed with the Wilson Barrett Company, a Scottish troupe that took him on the road for six months, culminating at the Edinburgh Festival in August. It was a good run, but once again he returned to London, in the fall of 1952, without any promise of a job.

"Might you ever have done anything else?" I asked him, as Maureen helped him settle into his wheelchair, his eyes particularly open and alert this day. "Gone back to architecture? Maybe become a musician?"

It was taking him longer and longer to answer questions. Minutes passed. Maureen left the room to get his lunch. I'd just about concluded he wasn't listening, wasn't present, when finally he answered, simply and obviously:

"There never was anything else."

Four

1952–1958

"Don't you think it would be better if . . . ?"

The Written Archives of the BBC are stored in a small country house on a residential lane in Reading, surrounded by flowering bushes and clover fields. Not what I expected at all: I imagined the world's largest broadcaster would keep its records in a modern building with elevators and air conditioning and bright fluorescent lights. Instead, it was in a shaft of sunshine that I read the letters of a young and eager John Schlesinger, while outside the window a songbird chattered noisily.

"I have just completed a tour of Australia and New Zealand," John wrote, "and I would appreciate it if you would bear me in mind when you are casting . . ."

"I wonder if you remember meeting me at a showing of my film *Black Legend*. I am most anxious to have the chance of doing some TV work . . ."

"I have recently returned from six months in Scotland and was hoping you might have some work for me . . ."

"Things are rather quiet at the moment. Can you find anything for me . . . ?"

"Please remember me when you are in need . . ."

"I stand ready at all times . . ."

Some of the letters were handwritten. I examined his penmanship: youthful and precise, so unlike the scrawl I'd come to recognize from reading his adult diaries. The headings at the top of the stationery gave witness to the movements of these years: Kintbury, Berks; Balliol College; the British Commonwealth Theatre Company; Inver Court; Cornwall Gardens.

And filed neatly behind John's letters (the BBC kept everything) were the flimsy, smudgy, carbon replies: "I am afraid there is nothing I can offer you at the moment . . ." "We will keep you in mind . . ." "Things have gotten very competitive here . . ." "Thank you for writing, but I have nothing at hand . . ."

Undaunted, John kept writing – to A.E. Harding, to Reggie Smith, to Caryl Doncaster, to Val Gielgud – to any producer with whom he might have had contact. In the course of just two months in 1952, he sent fourteen letters to the BBC, looking for work. He was always unfailingly polite, articulate and gracious, but such attributes couldn't hide mounting desperation as months, then years, went by. Writing to Douglas Cleverdon of the BBC Features Department, John recounted how he'd performed in Michael Flanders' revue in Cheyne Walk more than a year previously, and he'd heard Cleverdon had seen the show. "I realize that this is rather a belated opportunity to remind you of this," John wrote, "but I should greatly appreciate it if you could spare the time to see me." For once, there was no reply attached.

His persistence did occasionally pay off, however, first with radio work, then with television assignments. In 1953 his parts ranged from singing on the children's programme *The Rose and the Ring* (for which he was paid £12) to *Will Shakespeare* (for which he was paid a whopping £40 for two performances).

"So, John," I said, fanning out in front of him copies of his youthful letters of appeal, "didn't you ever feel like giving up?"

He stared off at the mountains. Finally he whispered, in an echo of his father, half a century earlier, "Never take no for an answer".

It was during his tour of Scotland in 1952, John recalled, that Bernard, after a long day in the hospital, took the night train up to Glasgow in order to have dinner with his son and see him perform the following night. No matter any private doubts, his father "made a great effort to encourage, even if I was in some terrible thing." Encouragement wasn't necessarily approval, of course, but John was grateful for his father's gesture nonetheless. "When I was depressed, which I often was, he'd say, 'You've just got to put your head down and keep pushing.'"

John admitted later, however, "there are moments when one gets tired of pushing."

Certainly he was tired of the grind he found himself in by the mid-1950s. A British actor's choices were severely limited in those years. Repertory and radio work could offer only so much and, by 1950, the British film industry had nearly sputtered out, despite a newly launched government tax on movie tickets to create a fund to subsidize production. The problem was that British cinema attendance was beginning its sharp decline in reaction to the introduction of television. With the coronation of Elizabeth II in June 1953, television became a permanent fixture in the lives and homes of most people. The increase in television licenses (343,000 to 10 million) would directly correspond with the decrease in movie audiences (1,396 million to 515 million) between the years 1950 and 1960.

An actor's hopes, then, rested with the burgeoning television industry, which at that time was still in the exclusive grip of the BBC. When John first started making the rounds, the head of television drama was Michael Barry, who presided over a wide variety of quality television productions in the early 1950s, some of which (*Will Shakespeare*, for one) featured bits by a young John Schlesinger. Out to Shepherd's Bush John would trek, to the BBC's production studios at Lime Grove, "a rabbit warren of studios and offices connected by tortuous corridors and filthy fire escapes." Additional early television work included playing Amiens in *As You Like It* and a "one-man band" on the programme *Your Own Time*, for which John received a note thanking him for his "lovely" performance: "Everyone here admired it very much." He'd also make appearances on the popular TV series *The Grove Family* and *The Peter Brough Show*. But there was never any guarantee of work: despite playing in various BBC productions over a period of three years, John could still get a letter in March 1955 telling him there were already "too many actors on our books," and there was nothing for him.

Another option was to take radio work in the provinces through the West and Midland Home Services; the BBC paid for lodging and food if John was willing to make the journey to Plymouth or Birmingham. There was also occasional stage work to be had. In June 1953, as part of the coronation festivities, John performed at Westminster Abbey in

Christopher Hassall's *Out of the Whirlwind*; in March 1954, he was playing Isaac Mendoza in *The Duenna* in Scarborough.

But film remained the holy grail. John took heart from a recent spurt of filmmaking activity at British studios by American producers, their eyes on favorable tax breaks. These Anglo-American productions offered British actors a chance for employment as well as possible studio contracts. In January 1952, Twentieth Century Fox secured the cooperation of the British Navy in filming C.S. Forester's novel *Single-Handed*, the story of a heroic British sailor in World War II. For the first time since the war, Wembley Studios in London would be used for feature production. The producer of *Single-Handed* was Frank McCarthy, a retired U.S. Army colonel (later named Brigadier-General) and a deeply circumspect homosexual whom John would later come to know (and disdain) in Hollywood.

At the time, of course, McCarthy would hardly have noticed John among the many British actors lining up at Wembley Studios hoping for a job. John would be one of only a handful of actors chosen to play sailors; the rest were actual men of the British Mediterranean fleet. In a little twist of irony that John found amusing, he was cast as a German sailor because of his last name; he actually has one line of dialogue, spoken in German. He would ring his grandmother during rehearsals to practice saying the line with an authentic-sounding German accent.

In September, the cast and crew shipped off to the Mediterranean, John on the cruiser HMS *Manxman* (rigged up as a Nazi raider), for six weeks of shooting. He confided to the director, Roy Boulting, that he'd like to direct films someday himself; Boulting told him to stick around, even when he wasn't in a scene, to pick up some tips. That gave John ample opportunity to moon over the star of the film, Jeffrey Hunter, who had the kind of masculine, dreamy, matinee-idol looks John would always be soft for. As ever, John had brought along his movie camera, and recorded (with color film) lots of shirtless sailors lounging about, a homoerotic tableau right out of a Paul Cadmus sketchbook. He even managed to get Hunter to pose for him against the striking backdrop of a blue Mediterranean sky.

He also had his still camera with him. Having enjoyed still photography nearly as much as motion photography since childhood, John was forever taking pictures, and he spent his downtime during the shoot capturing his shipmates in all sorts of dramatic "artistic" poses. Director Boulting took a look at the resulting photos and pronounced John a "frustrated filmmaker."

Single-Handed (retitled *Sailor of the King* in the United States) was released in the summer of 1953. The experience galvanized John's desire to work in motion pictures. He quickly scrambled for additional parts: a ticket-taker in Ealing Studios' *The Divided Heart* (1954); a gentleman in *Oh . . . Rosalinda!!* (1955), an adaptation of the Strauss operetta *Die Fledermaus*, directed by Michael Powell; and, once again, a German officer in Powell's war epic, *The Battle of the River Plate* (1956), which had blockbuster worldwide success as *The Pursuit of the Graf Spee*. This last film introduced him to Peter Finch who would, of course, make a significant return appearance in John Schlesinger's life.

If there was irony in his frequent essaying of German parts, John was also playing considerably older than his age, supporting his contention that he didn't "come into his own" until his thirties. "As an actor, John had a kind of middle-aged quality, even as a young man," said Peter Hall, who directed him onstage in *Mourning Becomes Electra* in 1955. "He was cherubic, but still he seemed much older than his years."

John might have made a career as a character player in movies, but as heady and exciting as he found acting in films, he was barely earning enough money to last a few months at a time. He eked out his living with television, radio and stage work, but these were lean years; if not for the generosity of his parents, he would most likely have had to give up acting altogether. Deciding once to throw a party and invite several well-placed theater acquaintances, John and his flatmate, another struggling actor, named Noel Davis, rented some expensive furniture and a few pieces of art to hang on the walls in an attempt to give the impression they were doing well. But most people saw through their little ruse.

"My early life on my own was a difficult period," John said. "Making a living, getting by, getting work. And one had to be very careful. It was after all, the Fifties."

When the decade began, John was living with his family at their flat in Inver Court. In those days, London was a gray city, gray and brown, not yet the center of swinging rebellion it would become just a little more than a decade later. Not much of a nightlife existed outside of well-known cafes and restaurants; gay nightlife, what little there was, was distinctly underground and hidden. Engaging in homosexual acts was still a crime in Britain; no establishment would openly identify with queers.

During the war, it had been different, with less rigid

enforcements on behavior. "I remember London then being the gayest place on earth," said Geoffrey Sharp, "in telephone boxes and lavatories, just wild." The bar at the Ritz Hotel had been an "upper market" gay hangout; Leicester Square and Piccadilly Circus offered dozens, if not hundreds, of cruising soldiers and sailors. It was part of the "wartime morality" the Archbishop of Canterbury would rail against by war's end, exhorting the nation to return to decent Christian standards.

By and large, the nation did, but the gay subculture survived, only now in extremely circumspect conditions. Sharp recalled a few pubs where it was understood one could meet other homosexuals; occasionally he and John would venture out to one of these, though John was pretty shy about approaching anyone. "He was great at sending someone else out [to strike up conversation]," said Sharp, "but not so courageous about it himself."

His caution was understandable. By the early 1950s, Britain was in the midst of what Sheridan Morley has called "one of its periodic fits of hypocrisy." Anti-gay repression had become a national sport. In the summer of 1953, John's old Oxford classmate, Edward Montagu, along with film director Kenneth Hume (he'd made *Hot Ice* with Michael Balfour in 1952), were accused of sexual assault by two teenage Boy Scouts. When the case against them seemed ready to crumble over the Scouts' conflicting testimony, a whole new charge was introduced, that of "indecent assault" on two airmen. This time the net had also snared the *Daily Mail*'s diplomatic correspondent Peter Wildeblood (an ironic name, given that he was definitely of Wilde's blood), as well as Montagu's cousin, Major Michael Pitt-Rivers. On through the winter the headlines raged, culminating with Montagu being sent to prison for a year. It was all completely outrageous; no one had expected the peer to pay more than a fine. He had the support of many in the theater community; Kenneth Tynan had posted bail. But postwar Britain had been seized with an anti-homosexual paranoia; judges were out to make lessons of sodomites who had, until now, escaped much public scrutiny.

It is vital to understand the context of the period in which John Schlesinger came into his own, a time of intense oppression. It's been observed by several historians that the forces which led to the crackdown on homosexuals could be linked to reactions to the national postwar decline and loss of Empire. The popular press, in fact, conflated homosexuality with treason, especially after Guy Burgess and Donald Maclean, British spies who defected to Moscow, were revealed to be homosexual. "Buggery" was therefore a cancer that needed to be rooted out of British society, and examples were found in all walks of life: Alan Turing, the brilliant mathematician who'd cracked the Enigma codes during the war, was sentenced to hormone therapy for his "homosexual offenses." William Field, a member of Parliament, was arrested for soliciting sex from men in Piccadilly Circus. The number of "indecency between males" offenses recorded by the police in 1952 was 1,686; for comparison, consider the five-year period of 1935-1939, when that figure had been just 299.

The facts make John Schlesinger's attitude all the more remarkable. There was never any pretense at marriage or even dating. Roger Schlesinger remembered John escorting the actress Janet Suzman a few times, even calling her a "woman he could have considered marrying." But this was years later, and "could have considered" is far removed from actually saying "I do," which many other gay men uttered willingly in an attempt to conform.

Traces of the secure, grounded, homosexual sensibility that John nurtured in life show up in nearly all of his films, even his earliest: sly little winks to the subculture. In *Sunday in the Park* (1956) he included a scene of a muscle man flexing his biceps and then, quite astonishingly, there's a shot of two men admiring him, eating (of all things) bananas! In his first feature, *A Kind of Loving* (1962), there is a glimpse of a theater marquee heralding Dirk Bogarde in *Victim*, the sensational, controversial film by Basil Dearden that, for the first time in cinema, treated homosexuals sympathetically. As John's career progressed, these subtle little nods grew even more obvious. Not only would he take on major gay themes in *Midnight Cowboy* and *Sunday, Bloody Sunday*, but he would insert minor gay characters into films in which their sexuality had no relevance to the plot: the photographer in *Darling*, the neighbors in *Madame Sousatzka* and *Pacific Heights*, the undercover detective in *Eye for an Eye*. In *Honky Tonk Freeway*, he gave us a Jeep filled with hunky gay men. "John thought if gay characters weren't going to be seen in other people's films, he'd put them in his," Childers said. "It was kind of a signature of his."

A signature of connection to a community for which he had long felt an affinity. While he had never identified with the more flamboyantly gay Oxford crowd, John was always nonetheless aware that, to the public at large, his own "perversion" could be easily associated with more overt, less discriminating homosexuals. It was a dynamic not unlike that between his parents and the louder, more obvious, Eastern European Jews of Whitechapel. It didn't matter that Bernard Schlesinger wore a tie on Saturdays and ate roast beef and lived in Hampstead; he might still be denied a placement at a prominent hospital, one more telling of the "old, old story."

"I remember when the whole Montagu affair was going on," William Becker said. "John was quite sympathetic, refusing to pass judgment. He said he saw it as a persecution."

Yet Schlesinger was never any kind of activist. When Wildeblood was released from prison a few years later and published a book about his experience, calling for "homosexual rights" and publicly naming himself as one, John felt it all a bit melodramatic. Still, there was resonance in Wildeblood's description of being spat upon by a woman who, in his words, "did not look eccentric or evil; in fact she looked very much like the country gentlewomen with whom my mother used to take coffee on Saturday mornings. She looked thoroughly ordinary to me. But what did I look like to her? Evidently, I was a monster."

Had he been less discreet in his life, it is not inconceivable that John might have found himself in Peter Wildeblood's position; their ages, their education, their backgrounds were not so different. And surely John knew that was the case, understanding the commonality between himself and those hauled before magistrates, a connection far greater than that between his parents and the Jews of Whitechapel. When Lord Montagu, a peer, could be so humiliated, when so esteemed an actor as John Gielgud, arrested in a public lavatory in 1953, could be made into an example, no one was safe.

Accordingly, for all his acceptance of self and rejection of the closet, John remained very careful in public. "I was going around saying 'darling this' and 'darling that,'" recalled Geoffrey Sharp. "John would shush me and say, 'Don't call me *darling.*'" Nearly twenty years later, of course, that particular gay affectation would prove to be his ticket to fame.

John was more successful at meeting people in less obvious circumstances. On 6 February 1952, while on a tour of *Twelfth Night*, he met Noel Davis, a young actor with whom he established an immediate and lasting bond. "I will always remember it, because it was the day the King died," Davis said. "We just took to each other, just like that. It was a connection that was obvious to both of us, and it would last a lifetime."

John had just turned 26; Noel was about to turn 25. They were never lovers, yet Noel Davis would become John Schlesinger's intimate companion, his life partner – in many ways his spouse, save for the fact they would never have sex. This forming of family is part of the unique beauty of the gay experience, of being in a relationship to someone where definitions are rewritten and established models become irrelevant. "We were one hundred percent devoted to each other," Davis said. "I knew what he thought. He could finish my sentences."

Noel Davis was born Edgar Davis in Liverpool, the son of a piano salesman. After service in the merchant navy, he moved to London and changed his name in honor of Noël Coward. Every bit as determined as John to make a career for himself in the theater, Noel Davis was bright, outrageous, and very, very funny.

"He made John laugh, that's why John loved him so," said their mutual friend, Eileen Atkins. Noel's humor could be terribly cutting – never toward John, of course, who was like a god, but to almost anyone else. His sarcasm, delivered with the most precise timing, appealed to John's ribald sense of humor. At parties, if someone arrived in some outrageous, pretentious outfit, Noel would nudge John with an elbow and the comment,

"What kind of statement is *that* supposed to be making?" The Schlesingers took the impecunious Noel in to live with them in Inver Court; later he and John would move into their own flat at 52 Cornwall Gardens.

Not everyone liked Noel. He could be insulting, particularly toward women. He resented John's boyfriends, especially the ones that lasted, like Childers. He demanded a good deal from John, especially after John became famous — and John always delivered. When character parts on stage and television started drying up for Noel in the 1970s, John helped launch his friend on a new career as a casting director, beginning with his own *Yanks* in 1979.

Through it all, however, theirs was a very successful home life, with Noel playing host to John's colleagues and actors, arranging dinners and parties and generally keeping everyone entertained. "He was like John's wife in many ways," said one friend. Another colleague from John's BBC days always assumed that John and Noel had been lovers, and was surprised to learn they weren't.

So why *weren't* they? Even as I raised the idea, I already knew the response. "Not John's type," I was told. Noel was too flamboyant, too effeminate. John, on the other hand, may have been *exactly* Noel's cup of tea: bright, ambitious, with a background far more cultivated than anything a piano salesman's son from Liverpool might have otherwise known. For Noel, the relationship with John was paramount: he would make a point of celebrating their anniversaries, and reminding John when the date had slipped past him. In 1982, he cabled John in Johannesburg to wish him a happy thirtieth; John, traveling with Michael Childers, received the news warmly. "I can't resist telephoning [Noel] to see how he is and to give him all my love," he said into his tape-recorded diary. "It's so wonderful to look back on relationships that have lasted so happily for so long. It suddenly gets me back to my roots which I don't think about while I'm away, but miss when suddenly they're brought to mind."

While John may not have remembered their anniversary, he was certainly, as ever, on Noel's mind. Had John been so inclined, some friends felt, Noel would have been right there, ready and eager to be his spouse in more than name only. "Noel loved John more than anyone in the world," one friend said. "John always came first."

Like so many caught up in a professed search for love, John Schlesinger could not, at that point, return it fully when offered it straight on. He could not see past the image of his "perfect man" that he cherished in his mind, still personified by the handsome, masculine, bisexual Alan Cooke. Like many who are "afraid to love," John would find appeal in those who were unavailable; those who stood at hand were often left unconsidered. His relationship with Noel Davis would endure, wonderful and solid just as it was — and yet, might it have been more had John been so willing?

By 1955, tired and often broke, Schlesinger had lost his zeal for acting. "I was limited to what I could play by size, shape, voice," he said. Looking back, he doubted he was very good anyway: "I wouldn't have cast myself for most of the roles I played had I come up before myself as an actor. I enjoyed the experience, but I knew I was not going to make Ralph Richardson abandon the stage."

Yet his experience on the other side of the camera offered

him invaluable insight into the actor's craft. "I think what my film acting experience did," he said, "was to make me sympathetic to the problems of having to get out there and do something in front of that nasty bit of glass – the camera lens – and having to play a high emotional scene at 8:30 in the morning. I understood the problems of being shoved into the middle of something without having been able to work up to it because we were shooting the end of the story first. I suppose I have a natural sympathy for actors, though they can madden me often. They can behave like spoilt brats, but by and large I would never take the attitude that a lot of directors more famous than I have taken, that they are puppets or cattle."

If acting wasn't meant to be, then what else? Surely it was too late now for architectural school. John was nearing the end of his twenties; fellow Oxford classmates had already begun making names for themselves in their various professions. Lindsay Anderson had, in fact, just won an Oscar for his short film, *Thursday's Children,* while Tony Richardson had been accepted into a filmmaking training program at the BBC. John was encouraged by friends like Noel Davis and Geoffrey Sharp to return to independent filmmaking: "Go back to doing what you really want to do," they said.

A few months before, he had signed with an agent, Basil Appleby, a former actor with producing aspirations, who agreed that John should return to filmmaking. Instead of another thriller, Appleby insisted, what John needed was a documentary, the kind that was proving so popular with the features department at the BBC. And if not with the "Beeb," there would soon be another option: on 22 September 1955, the BBC's monopoly was broken with the launch of ITV – Independent Television.

It was early summer 1955, and John, stretched out on a Sunday morning in Hyde Park, seized upon an idea: he'd make a film about the park, about the crisscross of humanity he saw there, the dozens of little stories going on all around him. The resulting film, running just fifteen minutes, is a delightful kaleidoscope of human vignettes. His eye for detail, so confident in all of his films, is readily apparent here: a small child tottering into the park is immediately followed by a woman in a wheelchair; a shot of a man showering is juxtaposed with a shot of a swan grooming itself. As ever, there's a defiance of convention, his usual tweak of propriety: he singles out from the crowd black and Muslim faces, a definite departure for 1955. And those shots of the muscle man being watched by the banana eaters were quickly followed by another little nod to the gay subculture: a fat older man cruises a younger man, who smiles back at him. If John's goal was to capture a cross-section of what went on in the park, he certainly wasn't going to exclude one of its most common activities.

Even more enjoyable about the film are the humorous narratives he incorporates. A man posing his girlfriend for a photograph, elaborately arranged, is at the last moment thwarted by the sudden intrusion of another couple walking right in front of his lens. An old woman is horrified by what she thinks is a man urinating against a tree. When the man suddenly moves away, the camera reveals he's been shielding a child, who's actually the one relieving himself. John cuts back to the woman, who's bemused now rather than outraged.

Of course, capturing such specific moments unplanned was unlikely, so John trooped his stock company into the park for a few set-ups. His brother Roger and cousin Barbara Webber played the couple with the camera; his nephew Ian Buruma was one of the little boys. He also needed a man with a bowler hat – how could one make a film about a London park without a man in a bowler hat? – so he persuaded Roger's friend Robert Stinson to drop by, as Stinson was the only person he knew who actually *had* a bowler.

It was at this same time that John won a small part ("a spit and a cough") as one of the townspeople in Peter Hall's production of Eugene O'Neill's *Mourning Becomes Electra* at the Arts Theatre. Onstage at 9 p.m., he was back off at five past, leaving plenty of time before the curtain call to edit the film on his portable movieola. Peter Hall remembered seeing John backstage, hunched over, consumed by his work.

The play closed after a short run, and John was again out of work. He couldn't afford to finish his film, which he was now calling *Sunday in the Park*. "I had a tape recorder with a rough sync mark with a little bit of Sellotape on it," he remembered, "and I would give performances for anybody who cared to look at it." Appleby finally convinced a BBC representative to take a peek; though impressed, he said it needed a score. John persuaded them to commission his friend Serge Lancen to write one, and the result was the perfect match to his images. Marching music keeps time with the people entering the park; an African-inflected beat accompanies a shot of a black man preaching at Speakers' Corner. John managed to insert some sound effects as well: birds chirping, water splashing, cars honking, dogs barking. It is the sound that really ties the short film together.

It was with considerable jubilation that he gathered the family around the telly at 3:00 p.m. on Sunday, 5 August 1956, to watch its transmission. Shown with a concert by the Band of the Scots Guards in Kensington Gardens, *Sunday in the Park* proved a diverting little program for the BBC. Certainly the exposure helped guarantee the film's placement at the Edinburgh Festival a few weeks later, where it was grouped with work of new, up-and-coming directors. *The Times* singled out *Sunday in the Park*, along with Lionel Rogosin's *On the Bowery* and Denis Sanders' *A Time Out of War*, saying that although the filmmakers' ideas were still unorganized, "their influence may be as strong on the cinema of the 1950s and 1960s as was the influence of the group who brought realism to filmmaking in the 1930s." More prophetically, the newspaper linked John's film with, among others, Lindsay Anderson's *Thursday's Children*, saying the filmmakers shared "a similarity of ideas."

Such praise might not have equaled Anderson's Academy Award, but John enjoyed a rare stretch of optimism that summer of 1956. The relative success of *Sunday in the Park* convinced him that, freshly 30, he just may have finally come into his own.

"I'm glad I didn't have a quick success in my life," John would say, smack in the middle of his greatest period, between *Midnight Cowboy* and *Sunday, Bloody Sunday*. "I think for a long time I felt a failure, but I don't know that I really was. I don't think that I've become ruthless, though I'm absolutely ruthless in fighting for what I believe is right within my own work. I'll fight to the teeth for that. I just hope I continue to have that energy for some years to come."

The close observation of life so charmingly captured in *Sunday in the Park* was paralleled by an equally close involvement in all aspects of his filmmaking. Schlesinger's collaboration with Serge Lancen over the score of the film predicted a career of working closely with his composers. Because he knew a thing or two about music – he was, after all, Winifred's son – he would prove to be either "a bane or a help" to those scoring his films: "I can tell them immediately what I do not like or what I think works. Many directors are very wishy-washy at this stage, but it is one of the parts of filmmaking I find the most exciting. To me the score must add another color to the film. The music should not be adding pink to crimson but rather something that elevates a scene or sequence to the right dramatic temperature."

Never would Schlesinger be the type of director to turn a score over blindly to his musicians. Neither would he allow a cameraman to set up angles entirely on his own, or permit a production designer to shape the picture's look without any input from him: he had been photographing and designing his own little productions far too long for that. As late as 1990, Clay Griffith, set decorator on *Pacific Heights*, recalled John's "fastidiousness" about everything in the picture: "I met with him about all the characters – what kinds of things they'd have, where they would live. It was great to have that kind of interest from him. A lot of directors don't have responses to pieces of furniture."

John had responses for everything in his films. He could visualize their mechanics even before they were made. Peter Honess, his editor on several films, once visited John on an elaborate outdoor location shoot in New York City for his 1987 picture *The Believers*. "All sorts of cameras, streets cordoned off, all these extras," Honess said. "I thought it was quite impressive. John said, quite casually, 'Yes, I suppose it is.' Then he paused. 'Won't be in the movie, though.' He could already see that. But it was too late to call everything off!"

With such an instinctive eye, John should have been a natural for the BBC filmmaker's training program, the same one that had taken Richardson a season before. In June 1956, a couple of months before *Sunday in the Park* was broadcast, John had interviewed with producer Ian Atkins, who recommended him in an internal memo: "Although not wishing to spend his life producing drawing-room comedy, he is keen to learn the technique of live television production as well as the making of films for television. I think he has something to offer to the Television Service and that the wider the insight into its workings we give him, the more he will give us."

However, a subsequent meeting with producer Royston Morley did not go nearly as well; Morley told colleagues he was "not so impressed" with Schlesinger. By this time *Sunday in the Park* had been shown, and was being hailed in Edinburgh, but still John was not selected for the September training program. He was also passed over for the January session. Writing to explain their decision, Michael Barry said that "vacancies are few and far between, and there is considerable competition." He held out the possibility, however, that Schlesinger could still be called in for yet another interview for a future program.

Why was John turned down? He would remember a curious question that kept arising in the course of the interviews: "What sport do you play?" That season the BBC had a particular interest in more athletic programming, wanting to find someone with an inclination for games. The ghosts of his childhood had made a reappearance. Thirty years later, John had the perfect comeback for such a question: "When I feel like exercise, I lie down till the feeling's worn off." But at the time he merely launched into an impassioned argument that there were plenty of other interesting film subjects beyond football and cricket. It was an argument no one was listening to.

Undeterred, he made the rounds with *Sunday in the Park* under his arm, but his burst of optimism was quickly dissipating and he was soon once more crying woe. In rapid succession, he was turned down by Edgar Anstey at British Transport Films and by Barbara Hammond at the BBC. Letters in his files revealed he was willing to do anything for a job. To Hammond, he had pitched an idea for a game show called *Alibi*. The studio would have been laid out as a courtroom, with the quiz master dressed as a judge. Celebrity guest stars would be accused of some "crime", e.g. the "abduction of the receptionist at Lime Grove", and then given five minutes to come up with an alibi. The jury would be made up of six members of the public, whose job it would be to reach a verdict after the "defendants" were questioned. Fifty years later, in the era of reality television, it might have sold but, at the time, Hammond wrote that she was unable to convince anyone at the BBC to give it a shot.

John was finally hired by James Carr of Worldwide Pictures, known for its documentary short subjects; its recent release, *Foothold on Antarctica*, had scored both British and American Academy Award nominations. Yet John's initial assignment for them was inauspicious enough: a film about cheese commissioned by the Milk Marketing Board. The job was (perhaps thankfully) brief. "They didn't seem to have more for me," John recalled. "I suspect because they felt I had ideas above my station. Somebody obviously had overheard me saying, 'Don't you think it would be better if . . .' at the movieola, and the door was very rapidly closed." From his short tenure at Worldwide Pictures he did get one thing: union membership.

To keep a few pounds in his pocket, he took some acting work at ITV. In December 1956 he had a bit on *The Adventures of Robin Hood*, directed by none other than Lindsay Anderson. The following February, he played "a most unpleasant little Frenchman" in *The Magpies*. A small part in the BBC's *A Woman of Property* followed, for which he was paid the princely sum of 46 pounds. Bits in several films kept him busy through the middle half of 1957: *The Last Man to Hang*, *The Brothers-in-Law* (starring Richard Attenborough), *Stormy Crossing* (in which John played a garage mechanic) and *Seven Thunders*, one more war picture for Herr Schlesinger to employ his German accent in.

Perhaps in some expiation for the way they had kept John dangling about the training program, the BBC hired him in early April 1957 to film a few segments for the new topical programme *Tonight*. Premiered on 18 February at 6.05 p.m., *Tonight* ran for 40 minutes and was presented by the engaging Cliff Michelmore. Historian Asa Briggs opined that the programme "deliberately blurred traditional distinctions between entertainment, information, and even education; while through its informal styles of presentation, it broke sharply with old BBC traditions of 'correctness' and 'dignity.'" The perfect vehicle, it would seem, for a man like John Schlesinger.

At the time of his hire, *Tonight* was still finding its feet, struggling to disprove a *Daily Telegraph* quip that it was "reminiscent of those interminable repetitious morning programmes in America designed to catch successive waves of the breakfast audience." A *Tribune* review on 18 March called on the producers to add more variety and humor. Accordingly, the BBC's Deputy Director, Cecil McGivern, who had met with John about the training program, suggested to *Tonight* producer Donald Baverstock that he give Schlesinger a try.

It was an exciting period. New technology had increased the opportunities available to television filmmakers; cameras had been freed from their fixed bases and entanglement of cords, with portable lamps making lighting of subjects easier than ever. By late 1956, outside broadcasting – the filming of real events – had become a TV buzzword. The new capabilities dovetailed with the expansion of the BBC Television Service by fifteen hours a week, thereby creating a need for new, original programming. Old American films, mostly westerns, had been filling the void, but such programmes as *Panorama* quickly proved the popularity of topical magazine series. By March 1957, too, there had been a tremendous spike in the audience: the British "television public" was now nearly 19.5 million, excluding children, with viewers spending at least 40 percent of their evening watching telly.

John's first assignment for *Tonight* was to capture some images of London's famous Petticoat Lane. He did as he was told, traipsing off with veteran BBC cameraman A.A. "Tubby" Englander to find interesting faces in the crowd and little bits of business between customers and merchants. It was silent, shot in no particular order, and after John gave the footage over to Baverstock, he never saw it again. "It was like working for a newspaper," Schlesinger recounted. "You just made something and turned it in, and they did what they wanted with it." The film was cut down by editor Jack Gold to 431 feet, or about six minutes. A spoken commentary was placed on top of it without any input from John, and the piece was transmitted as part of the programme on 23 April.

The experience left John unsettled. "I resolved never to let that happen again," he said. He would remember making "about a dozen" films over the next eight months for use on *Tonight*; BBC records can confirm only nine. Despite the regular paychecks – he would make between £8 and £12 per film – it was not a pleasant period. John clashed repeatedly with Baverstock and his assistant producer Alisdair Milne over creative control of his work. Infuriatingly, they would address him as "boy" – as in, "Doesn't work, boy."

Still, he turned in some interesting material. He caught some witty scenes of rush hour, shot with the foreknowledge that they would be used to illustrate the narration of "The Charge of the Light Brigade." A day's jaunt to Uppingham resulted in scenes of the school breaking up for the holidays. For a film on Wakes Week, the annual holiday in the Lancashire cotton towns, John captured a lovely slice of life in the town of Blackburn: a montage of closed shops, children running out of school, holidaymakers filing onto trains, a solitary watchman walking down an empty street.

And despite his memory to the contrary, he was able to manage some creative authority as the months went on. Several of the films credit Schlesinger himself as dubbing, and some-times writing, the commentary; for a piece on an unnamed holiday resort in bad weather, he brought in Noel Davis to narrate. By November he was making two short films that bear the unmistakable John Schlesinger imprimatur. One was "Armistice Day," which contained a new twist on a very old theme: instead of the "hackneyed" (his word) approach to most war tribute films, John shot scenes of the Imperial War Museum as seen through the eyes of a little boy, for whom, he said, "war was just a series of exciting models." This is contrasted with the reality: an old man, walking with a stick and carrying a wreath to the war memorial, his bare-headed shadow falling across the names of the dead.

Schlesinger's most ambitious film for *Tonight*, however, was "Song of the Valley," a little dramatic narrative based on a popular song by Dorothy Squires. Running just about four minutes, the film illustrated Squires' lyrics about a recently released prisoner returning to his mining valley home. Halifax in Yorkshire served as the setting, a north-country glimpse that anticipates *A Kind of Loving* and *Billy Liar*. "Song of the Valley" contains little more than a montage of power-station chimneys, scrap heaps, and terraced houses intercut with shots of an actor portraying the ex-con as he returns to the arms of his family. Yet the film was effective enough for the BBC to rerun it fairly often, as late as 1960 and perhaps beyond. It was the first time John had directed actors in a fiction film since *The Starfish*, and he thoroughly enjoyed the experience.

There was now, however, a final falling out with Baverstock, who said to John, "You're worth it when it works and not worth it when it doesn't." His insistence on mixing his own films was slowing down production, Baverstock argued, yet it's fair to say that John's work had been one of the factors that had boosted *Tonight*'s standing. Asa Briggs felt that *Tonight*, in its first year, had shown the public "that the BBC could be just as sprightly and irreverent as ITV." It would continue to be so, but without John Schlesinger.

"I hate television," he would say more than 30 years later. "I think it's one of the worst things that's happened to civilization because it's been misused. I'm a television addict when it comes to documentaries or music or things on The

Discovery Channel. I hate films on television, though. There's no comparison between the way you view a film in a cinema and on television. It's rather like reading a book — you can put it down if the phone rings."

Working small always frustrated John Schlesinger. Even then, doing his little bits for *Tonight*, he had his eye on bigger things. He had watched with some envy as, under the banner "Free Cinema," the short documentary films of Tony Richardson, Karel Reisz and Lindsay Anderson had been shown at the National Film Theatre in various programmes starting in February 1956. The films were publicized with a manifesto that read, in part: "No film can be too personal . . . Perfection is not an aim. An attitude means a style. A style means an attitude."

Free Cinema would become the name not just of an exhibition but of a movement — espousing the ideas advanced by Anderson and Reisz in their magazine *Sequence*. Free Cinema challenged commercial moviemaking to embrace "the importance of people and the significance of the everyday." Although the terms are often used interchangeably, it's important to keep in mind that Free Cinema is not synonymous with the British New Wave. Free Cinema was a specific documentary movement that advanced the realist views proposed by John Grierson some 30 years earlier. It would, however, engender many of the ideas and visions that helped inaugurate the New Wave; indeed, Free Cinema blazed a path that enabled its founders — as well as others, like Schlesinger — to *become* the New Wave when they entered the world of dramatic feature filmmaking.

In fact, as pointed out by Gavin Lambert, co-editor with Anderson of *Sequence* and the longtime editor of *Sight and*

Sound, "Free Cinema was never a genuine movement, just an effective publicity move invented by Lindsay to distinguish the group from the older, 'establishment' directors – Asquith, etc. – and to exploit the value of a label."

Accordingly, as part of its mission to confront the stagnant British film industry, Free Cinema took every chance it could find to hype its ideas. In January 1958, *The Times* published a long letter from Anderson in which he wrote passionately about the urgency facing the national cinema: "When we talk of 'art,' [people] think immediately that we are proposing a diet of thin, grey, neo-realist gruel, or of stale, dressed-up literary classics. Of course these are not what we need or want. If young audiences are to be brought into the cinemas, we will have to learn to make films which are relevant to them . . . And this can only be done by accepting the world in which we live, instead of running away from it."

Such polemics made the Oxford triumvirate of Anderson, Reisz and Richardson the "new hopes" for British cinema. Richardson's direction of John Osborne's *Look Back in Anger* at the Royal Court Theatre, and his subsequent forming of Woodfall Films, came to define "the atmosphere and subject matter" for cinema, John would remember: defiant, realistic, and yes, *angry* drama was the order of the day. It was a worldview shared to a large degree by Schlesinger; certainly he was in complete accord with Anderson's sentiments as published in *The Times*. Films needed to be relevant, he believed; they needed to reflect the changing society. In many ways, John would have fit in well with the Free Cinema people, if only they hadn't been so *serious* about it.

It was never in John's nature to discourse on the meaning of "art." Intellectuals and their arguments always made him distinctly uneasy, even those with whom he'd work successfully later on, like Frederic Raphael and Alan Bennett. "I don't know what they're talking about," he'd complain to friends.

"John wasn't really all that well-read," said Stewart Grimshaw, who shared a flat with him for a few years and remained a lifelong chum. "He got his knowledge vicariously through his friends. I think he arrived intuitively at things, emotionally."

In the cinematic debate that raged in the 1950s, John Schlesinger sent no tracts to *The Times*; his voice was not heard in the din raised by the Free Cinema clique. "I was considered an outsider by that group," he said, "even though I'd been at Oxford with several of them . . . I was making films, too, but I didn't go in for all that intellectual argument about attitude and style."

"I think that because John never joined the movement," observed Gavin Lambert, "they brushed him aside as an artist. There was a very militant feeling in the case of Tony and Lindsay – not Karel – that 'if you're not with us, you're against us.' I never heard Lindsay attack John's work directly. Like Tony, he just shrugged off any mention of his name. This was naturally very irritating to John."

Indeed, John felt their disdain: running into Anderson around this time, he was told condescendingly by his colleague, "Really, Schlesinger, you've got to set your sights higher than television."

Anderson's belief that films ought to be personal was a point on which John would agree, but might a film in fact be *too* personal, thus refuting the Free Cinema position? John thought so: "I believe that one must make films for more than just oneself. One has to tell a story that reaches people, that has some universal resonance, not just resonance for a select few. I don't mean to suggest in any way playing to the lowest common denominator, but there is definitely a place for a film that reaches as wide an audience as possible."

Still, the buzz surrounding Free Cinema – which, informally, also included cinematographer Jack Clayton, whose upcoming directing debut, *Room at the Top*, was already being chattered about in film circles – was enough to prompt Schlesinger into action. His sights were indeed set higher than television. "My eye was always fixed on the big screen," he said. "I saw what others were doing, and I wanted a chance at it myself." He asked for permission to show his *Tonight* work to feature film producers, only to be refused. "Why should we cut our nose to spite our face, boy?"

"So I used to steal them," John said. A good thing, too, because with a few of his early films, only he owned a surviving print some 40 years later. He'd sneak off with his films under cover of night and give showings to his *Single-Handed* director, Roy Boulting, over at British Lion Films, or to Edgar Anstey at British Transport, all in the hope of getting the kind of break Clayton and Richardson had managed.

But there would be no screenings at the National Film Theatre for Schlesinger – not for another twenty years anyway, when a retrospective would be held of those very films he was then churning out for the BBC. Yet neither would there be any grandstanding or theorizing; he would just keep plugging along, learning by doing. Television, John admitted, taught him a basic film grammar "like being in weekly rep does for an actor." He learned how to trust his instincts: "There was no time for second thoughts. First thoughts were the only ones you could do."

His apprenticeship paid off. The little films he made for *Tonight* turned out to be solid pieces of work, and they hadn't gone unnoticed at the BBC. At the time of John's final blow-up with Baverstock, another producer, Huw Wheldon, was already considering him for a new project in development, a series devoted to the arts, called *Monitor*.

Producer Humphrey Burton, already on board, said Wheldon "poached" Schlesinger from *Tonight* to work on *Monitor*, but John's own recollections on the subject always included a very definite break with the first programme before starting on the second. He would admit, however, that Wheldon was "waiting in the wings" with an offer he found very appealing. Fortuitous, for Schlesinger had been forced back to acting (an episode of *Ivanhoe*) in an effort to keep the money coming in. *Monitor*, however, would offer him a chance to keep making films – and longer ones, too, with greater creative authority. "I was extraordinarily excited by what Wheldon was offering," John remembered. "It was everything I had been looking for."

Described in internal planning memos as a "highly sophisticated type of magazine without necessarily appealing only to Third Programme types," *Monitor* was planned from the start to reach the widest possible demographic. The brain-child of producer Kenneth Adam and the BBC's formidable Assistant Head of Television Talks, Grace Wyndham Goldie, *Monitor* used language far more colloquial than other BBC serious arts programmes and paced itself in a lively, informal manner. One early critic described the series as "more Network Three than Third Programme", yet the subject matter of *Monitor* was likely to include profiles of composers, poets, operas, and artists, definite Third Programme territory. This very marriage of style and substance was what made *Monitor* so successful – indeed, what turned it into the legend it has since become.

In January 1958, John was signed to a six-month contract at £40 per week. Wheldon served not only as producer but also as presenter. For the first show, John suggested going backstage at promoter Tom Arnold's annual circus at Haringey Arena; it was the first time the Russians were taking part and interest was high. Wheldon liked the idea, so John hustled up to Haringey with a small crew, capturing some intriguing scenes: the clowns putting on (and then taking off) their makeup, trapeze artists swinging, ballerinas preening. Impressive camera angles were maneuvered by shooting from the rafters, looking down.

Even more than his stint on *Tonight*, John's time at *Monitor* proved an invaluable training ground. "He learned a great deal about montage," Humphrey Burton said. "He loved editing, and was very involved in that process. He was very involved in all aspects of production, for which he was thrilled."

Huw Wheldon was as generous as Donald Baverstock had been possessive. "Huw was my first producer in the best sense of that word," John would say, linking Wheldon to the tradition of happy collaboration he would enjoy with Jo Janni and Jerry Hellman. "He would scribble notes on the back of a used envelope during the screening of a rough-cut and invariably they made good sense at moments of panic and chaos as transmission loomed."

Wheldon (later controller and then managing director of BBC television) was indeed a thoughtful, intelligent man who recognized that *Monitor*'s strength lay in the diverse talents of those he assembled; he himself needed to be the strong and supportive "cement [that holds] the thing together." A high-spirited Welshman, Wheldon would be remembered for shouting, "Warm! Warm! Warm!" behind the cameras when interviewers came across as too staid or reserved. His own warmth was legendary, with a laugh so loud and boisterous that one friend said it was "famous from one end of Britain to the other." Wheldon's optimism would often prove a happy foil to Schlesinger's bouts of doom and gloom.

"John and Huw sparked off each other very well," said Humphrey Burton. "It was a very productive relationship, and interesting, too, because of their reverse backgrounds." While John had gone to Oxford, Huw's higher education had been at the London School of Economics. Huw was also "very straight," Burton said, while "John was gay, and quite open about it." But their mutual interests drew them together. "Huw loved the theater, and he loved what John could bring to *Monitor*."

It was Wheldon who gave John what he'd been looking for, "the freedom to fail." Over the course of the next six months, John made eight more films, ranging in length from twelve to twenty minutes. He looked back at this period as the happiest and most carefree of his professional life. "There was no one looking over your shoulder to see if you were going to come up with a hit or a miss," he said, "because the next one could always be better."

"The Circus" kicked off the very first episode of *Monitor* on 2 February, 1958, along with such other offerings as "Sam Wanamaker at Liverpool" and "New York Reactions to John Osborne's *The Entertainer*." Broadcast fortnightly on Sunday evenings, usually from 10:15 to 11:00 p.m., *Monitor* quickly grew into a tremendous audience favorite. John had a ball. He got to travel: Paris, Brussels, Cannes. He got to cover things of interest to him, like opera and classical music. In March, "a wonderful Italian scratch company" was performing an opera at the Theatre Royal, Drury Lane, and Wheldon agreed to John's request to cover it. As John remembered it, the theater's policy refused to allow cameras backstage, and BBC higher-ups called on Wheldon to cancel the assignment. "It was my first brush with the front office," Schlesinger recounted, "but Huw, who was nothing if not as determined as I was to break the rules, supported me." They found a "renegade" cameraman, Charles de Jaeger, who was willing to sneak with him behind the curtain and capture some images. "The Italian Opera" was broadcast on 30 March.

John was soon off on a tour of the continent with writer Robert Robinson, with whom he'd been at Oxford. They sent back several items including a satirical look at the Cannes Film Festival. Robinson, with his sardonic humor, became one of John's favorite collaborators at the BBC. "We were at Cannes for several days, feeling just about as jaundiced then as we do now about it," John remembered. They caught Jayne Mansfield arriving, Anthony "Puffin" Asquith holding forth at a cocktail party, and desperate actors doing anything to be noticed, like model-singer Rosalie Ashley "posing like mad" (Robinson's notes) in a ring of photographers.

Perhaps the best of John's early *Monitor* work, however, is a piece on Benjamin Britten, taken as the composer prepared for the annual Aldeburgh Festival. The sense of place is strong and immediate: the seaside, the fishermen, the sea shanties on the soundtrack. Place would always be an important element of John Schlesinger's films, whether it be Lancashire in *A Kind of Loving*, Dorset in *Far from the Madding Crowd*, New York in *Midnight Cowboy*, or Hollywood in *The Day of the Locust*. In fact, for a profile, the film spends precious little time on its subject; Britten appears onscreen infrequently. Rather, we get a sense of the man and his art through his work: long close-ups of the children singing in a rehearsal for *Noye's Fludde* (Noah's Flood) – among them, and perhaps glimpsed by John's camera, the sixteen-year-old Michael Crawford. When Britten *is* onscreen, he is usually watching and listening to the children, an expression of wonder and joy on his face.

Grace Wyndham Goldie was never a supporter – John recalled having "permanent rows" about various films with her – and, indeed, she criticized this film as too "self-indulgent." But for the rest of the BBC brass, "Benjamin Britten at Aldeburgh" was a small masterpiece. "It's a very telling film with great emotional power," Burton said, pointing out that the lyrical ending, with Britten walking along the beach with his dog, has been pinched by many a documentarian since. For John, it was a meeting with a man he greatly admired, and the mention of Britten's *Peter Grimes* was prophetic: Schlesinger's production of that opera would be his last work before his stroke.

Yet John's favorite *Monitor* film, I suspect, was not "Benjamin Britten," as good as it was. Far more self-indulgent, at least from the filmmaker's point of view, was "On the Pier," shot in July in Brighton. With its quirky little twist on the traditional day at the beach, taking us not along the sand but into the dark confines of the arcade, the film has the mocking humor John so prized, his trademark subversive wink at convention. It bears some resemblance to *Sunday in the Park,* opening with people arriving at the pier, focusing on the grotesques and slightly tacky among them. A woman in ear-rings stuffs her face with pastry; girls pose in revealing bathing suits; an old salt sleeps under a newspaper. There's the requisite hunky shirtless man, but the world of sunshine doesn't hold John's interest long. Under the pier, "down below the madding crowd," as he puts it, he shows us the rusting, rotting posts and piles. And with his love of the macabre, he couldn't resist a sideshow called "Hades." Commentator Robert Robinson intones, "The very gates of hell, greeted by an Anglo-Saxon equanimity."

John clearly wrote this one. Inside the arcade, he forces us to see the hideousness behind the humor: "those dead little teeth" in the smile of a cracked porcelain doll; "the horribly dead life of dummies," who move "like sleep walkers, blind or terribly crippled, jerking their artificial limbs." Not surprisingly, he focuses in on a strange hermaphrodite doll that has a female face but wears male clothing – dreaming, John tells us, "all the terror of painted toys."

"I enjoyed myself," he would remember of his *Monitor* years. "There's no doubt about that. But still I knew there was more for me to do. As much fun as this was – more fun, in fact, than I'd ever had professionally or would ever have again – I knew making these little films was only what it was: a moment in time."

Five

1958–1961

"So intent upon getting the effect"

J
ohn was in the midst of a walk from his wheelchair to the arms of his physical therapist when I came through the door. Maureen cheered when he made it. I did, too.

Safely back in his chair, John was beaming, obviously thrilled that I had witnessed him take those few small steps.

"That was excellent, John," I said, stooping down beside him. Across the room, Michael was crowing that John just kept amazing them all, defying his doctors' predictions. John's grin seemed permanently fixed on his face.

"You'll show them, John," Michael called. "You always showed them."

Later, alone on the terrace, I asked John if he was trying so hard to walk again because he wanted to go back to work.

"Yes," he answered strongly.

It was hard to imagine it, though by then I had learned

enough about John Schlesinger not to put anything past him.

"What is it you still want to do?" I asked him.

"*Hadrian*," he said.

Ah, yes. *Hadrian VII*, John's white whale. A film he chased for many years, almost snaring it more than once. Baron Corvo's novel told the story of a man who, confined to his room, imagines himself the Pope, and lives in a fantasy existence free of the boundaries and obstacles imposed on him in real life. First Dustin Hoffman, then Daniel Day-Lewis, then Geoffrey Rush: each came close to playing the would-be Pope. Hoffman's attempt at the part was immortalized in a photograph taken by Michael that hung on John's wall, the actor dressed in clerical robes with a miter on his head and a crazy smirk on his face.

In 1987 John had been asked by a reporter what film he wanted to be making in the year 2001. He named *Hadrian*. "We would follow him out from his real-life spartan room to an imaginary land where he is Hadrian VII," John enthused, "surrounded by members of the Sacred College and cardinals in full purple."

His days now so silent, yet his eyes still so wide, so seeing. What did he think about as he sat there? Where did he go? Was he really plotting his next film, as he seemed to want us to think? Was he really trying to get back to work? Or was he just living his own fantasy, playing his own Hadrian?

"I don't think he ever forgave me for not doing the part," Dustin Hoffman told me. "We screen-tested and I was mistaken not to do it. I was just afraid, I guess. I felt a profound sense of doubt that I could pull it off. Could I believe myself as the Pope? I remember John being so extraordinarily passionate about it and I just wasn't. I didn't get it. It seemed like a very

English sensibility. I should've done it simply because John's an artist."

"There are two kinds of directors," said Gavin Lambert, "those who create the same world with variations in it and those, like John, who create a different world with each film yet show the same person behind the different worlds. But at some point in John's career the struggle to make what he wanted became so difficult and, because he didn't want to give up working, he ended up making films he didn't want to make. That was very difficult for him. Times changed, and it wasn't a question of directors like John not being able to keep up with the times. The times couldn't keep up with them."

He wanted one last great film. Even a good film. Something, *anything*, to wipe away the stain of *The Next Best Thing*. In those early, carefree days at the BBC, it hadn't mattered so much: if one film flopped, the next one could always be better. "Now you're only as good as your last film," John said, not long before his stroke, "no matter how many other brilliant things you've done." Asked by a reporter in 1995 if it bothered him that so many younger film executives weren't aware of who he was, he paused for a moment, then said, "Well, yes, of course it does. But I'm too old a hand to lose any sleep over it. Do they realize I made over twenty films? I don't really care that much. Well, I do, but I don't. You know what I mean? It upsets me, but I say, so what else is new?"

In the summer of 1958, far from being forgotten, John Schlesinger's value was just beginning to be recognized.

His six-month contract was up, and John was playing hardball. *Harper's Bazaar* magazine, impressed with what they'd seen on *Monitor,* had approached him to direct a fashion film. They would need his services for eight to twelve weeks in the autumn. Accordingly, John laid down the law to A.G. Finch in the contracts department: if *Monitor* wanted to keep him, they would have to make it worth his while. He demanded £50 a week and a flexible enough schedule that would allow him to work in other markets.

"He has a pretty shrewd idea of his value to us," Finch wrote in a memo to his colleagues, including Huw Wheldon. "At the same time he has a reasonable regard for realities, and appreciates that the type of films he has been recently making for us, while of near-unique quality, can probably attract only one market for some time to come."

In the end, John accepted a compromise: £45 a week for eighteen weeks. But in truth he got most everything he wanted, not least of which was an affirmation of his worth to the BBC. He was no longer just a freelance filmmaker; he was an artist under contract, and as such, would be entrusted with bigger, more ambitious projects. In addition, since they recognized that artists periodically needed to spread their wings, he would be allowed some freedom: "He emphasized that to maintain his usefulness to us he would have to go off for a couple of months and do something different as a refresher," Finch wrote. "It would be as much in our interests as his to accept this situation." The only restriction imposed by the BBC was to forbid any outside work for the competition, ITV.

Finch added, however, that they "could not again tolerate being forced to make decisions like these at a few days' notice under circumstances that could be interpreted as pistol brandishing." Yet the fact remained that the pistol had been brandished and they had ducked, giving John what he wanted.

At age 32, John Schlesinger had finally claimed his own artistic and professional power.

The Corporation's faith in him was justified by his first film under his new contract, "The Innocent Eye." A look at the art of a child, it was filmed at a secondary modern school in Brixton, and is really Schlesinger's wistful memories of his own childhood. His camera focuses on a timid little boy who has painted a colorful and fanciful mural. "It was a shape and a song and a poem that a little boy of five was thinking about when he painted the creation of the world," commentator Michell Raper says on the soundtrack. The five-year-old delights in his art, but the older students are frustrated in their attempts. "At fourteen, the world is suddenly difficult," Raper says, as John inserts a shot of a fight in the schoolyard. Inside, a teenager is crumpling up his effort: "You see too clearly – not only the world but the inability to express it." The film ends with a sense of yearning for the innocent eye lost.

"Extraordinary success," Wheldon wrote in a memo to John, a sentiment echoed by everyone, including Goldie. "This is the kind of direction we are very pleased to have," she wrote. The film would go on to win a Diploma of Merit at the Edinburgh Festival.

John was certainly gratified by the response, but later, not unlike the fourteen-year-old who crumpled his drawing, unable to discern any wonder left within, he'd distance himself from the piece. "I suspect it's dated frightfully," he said, twenty years on. "Probably very sentimental by today's standards. I would probably do it all quite differently now." And most likely make a film not nearly as good.

He would always eschew sentiment, preferring the less vulnerable expressions of parody and irony, which is surely why he remained more fond of a later *Monitor* film, "Hi-Fi Fo Fum." Transmitted in April 1959, it was made at the height of the stereophonic phonograph, or "hi-fi," craze. Teaming up again with his favorite BBC writer, Robert Robinson, John mocked the growing consumer demand for everything in high-fidelity, but the humor of the satirical re-enactments is nearly lost today. Satirizing a fad dates far more quickly than honest sentiment. The most interesting bit in the film is the glimpse John offered into the highly intricate technicalities of recording for hi-fi: using his cousin Andrew Raeburn's membership in Philomusica of London, John showed the elaborate set-up needed to record a quintet of classical musicians.

Pistol brandishing wasn't needed at the conclusion of his second contract with the BBC. By the spring of 1959, it was clear that John Schlesinger was a star filmmaker, and the producers would now have to take what they could get. That meant one 45-minute film a year, to which the entire pro-gramme would be devoted. John was in demand by other producers now, including the competition; they couldn't keep him off ITV forever. Wheldon offered to put him on a full-time salary but, with outside offers piling up in his mail, John refused. "I never would have been a good corporation man at the Beeb," John said, looking back. "Never would have been able to adapt to that corporate attitude."

He recalled a contretemps with Grace Wyndham Goldie that summed up his feelings. "I felt I was making *films* at the BBC. They were shot on 35 mm, cut the normal way, dubbed the normal way, and still she would say, 'You're making tele-vision.' And I would say, 'No, I'm making a film for television.' But she insisted, 'No, you're making television.' I never have been able to understand the difference."

His former agent, Basil Appleby, now working for Sapphire Films (producers of the ITV series *Four Just Men)*, hired John as second-unit director under Basil Dearden. It was a fortuitous encounter, as Dearden was also a film director of some note, then working on his groundbreaking film about race relations, *Sapphire*. Dearden would also, of course, direct *Victim*, a film which greatly inspired John. Working with Dearden proved similarly inspirational: "He taught me a great deal," John recalled, especially grateful for the insight Dearden provided about the relationship between a director and his actors, and the subtlety necessary for film acting.

Four Just Men was, however, a trifle for both of them. The weekly dramatic series featured four revolving stars: Dan Dailey, Jack Hawkins, Richard Conte, and the legendary Italian director, Vittorio De Sica. Dearden sent John to Rome to shoot exteriors for De Sica's episodes.

"I was terrified about directing De Sica," John said. "He was one of my gods." The relationship was uneasy at first: De Sica was suspicious of this young substitute for Dearden, figuring him a lowly assistant good only for filming a few car chases. But the Italian master was soon impressed with John's eye for small moments and background. It was, in fact, the first time John was being paid to work in a non-documentary setting with actors and a script, and De Sica appreciated the sharp observational skill he brought to the task. When John was injured in a minor auto accident and spent a few days in a Roman hospital, it was De Sica who, alone among the crew, came to see him. They remained friends. In 1971, De Sica would be one of the greatest champions of *Sunday, Bloody Sunday* at the Venice Film Festival.

In many ways, De Sica's career resembles Schlesinger's. He

began as an actor and directed a body of films that isn't easily defined except by its variety. There were influential neorealist pictures (*Shoeshine*, *The Bicycle Thief*), satirical fantasies (*Miracle in Milan*), light popular fare (*Marriage Italian Style*), brilliant character studies (*Two Women*), and the elegiac tragedy *The Garden of the Finzi-Continis*. De Sica's demand for excellence was often frustrated by his parallel quest for commercial success, a battle which also came to shape John's career.

Freelancing kept him busy during 1959–1960. Another second-unit assignment for Sapphire Films came his way, this time for *Danger Man*, the series starring Patrick McGoohan. Following this, producer Patrick Macnee snared John for a couple of episodes of *The Valiant Years*, the documentary series on the early life of Winston Churchill produced by the American television network ABC. Among those who trooped before John's camera were Lord Mountbatten and Field Marshal Bernard Montgomery; John then edited the footage and spliced in newsreel clips to form two entries for the 26-episode series.

It was back at the BBC's Lime Grove studios, however, that he once again flexed his creative muscles. For his first annual *Monitor* offering, John chose to follow four painters on their artistic journeys, an idea first proposed by Michell Raper, who'd written "The Innocent Eye" and who would take on scriptwriting duties again this time. According to John's notes, the film was structured around the question, "What does it mean to be a young man or young woman who wants to break into the art world, to live by painting?"

They would call it "Private View," and it would be Schlesinger's first long professional film, running just over 40 minutes. The artists he profiled were a diverse lot: Anthony Whishaw, who painted old people, dancers, and bullfights; James Howie, who painted his native Scottish landscapes; Sonia Lawson, an abstract artist from Yorkshire; and Allan Rawlinson, a metal sculptor, who lived in a Northolt housing estate. "They are all trying to break through," John wrote in a letter to Huw Wheldon. "It is a personal, private intrusion into their world."

"Private View" is a satisfying film, quiet and intense like its subjects. John lets the art speak for itself, the contrasts in the artists' techniques and styles are striking, yet the film is held together by their commonality of purpose. They are ambitious without being grasping, innocent without being naïve, committed to their art without pretension.

John's "enthusiasm was catching," remembered Sonia Lawson. "So on camera, off the cuff, I spoke fast and keenly about my work and ideas. The following week, John returned, saying what I'd said was just what he wanted but could I repeat it all again more slowly? Of course I couldn't remember in depth what I'd said, so rather ponderously I talked of what I believed I'd touched upon previously. A few years later, I was miffed to hear Patrick Moore speaking at a vast speed of knots on BBC TV's *Sky at Night*. How quickly things change and often for the better."

John suggested he could help Lawson get into films if she was interested: "At that time I did not know he was gay," Lawson said with amusement, "so the vision of the casting couch spelled too much hassle, so I turned down the proposal!"

"None of them suffer dramatically or with any tinge of self-pity," John observed of the artists, a characteristic he admired.

Indeed, John Schlesinger would never have much patience for the myth of the artist suffering for his or her art.

The film was transmitted on 8 May, 1960. Higher-ups at the BBC were once again thrilled by Schlesinger's latest offering, including Goldie, who Wheldon reported was "delighted with it." John certainly proved prescient in his selection of artists: Whishaw went on to win several prizes and awards during a prolific career and become a member of the Royal Academy; Lawson likewise won several awards, and had a painting commissioned by the Archbishop of Canterbury to give to the Pope in celebration of their ecumenical accord in 1989.

Soon after filming was complete on "Private View," John accepted an offer from Carl Foreman, the blacklisted American screenwriter-turned-producer who had set up a company, Open Road Films, in London. Foreman wanted Schlesinger to make a promotional film about his upcoming war drama, *The Guns of Navarone*, then starting principal photography in Greece. John accepted, hopeful this might prove an entrée into feature filmmaking, and set off for Athens in February 1960. He immediately ran into conflict with the film's director, Alexander Mackendrick, who resented a second crew following him around – in effect, filming him filming. "Sandy M. isn't exactly overjoyed with our presence," John wrote to Huw Wheldon. "Thank God for the zoom lens, which Carl very sensibly let me persuade him to get."

Foreman had tentatively agreed that John could fashion some of the footage into a piece for *Monitor*. "I think almost certainly there will be something for the BBC out of all this," John reported, "though how long, and what shape, it's difficult to yet know." He spent his first week in Greece covering the various units struggling to get their equipment up into the mountains. "Carl is a glutton for having anything and every-thing covered," John said, particularly the arrival of the film's stars, Gregory Peck, Anthony Quinn, and the voluptuous Gia Scala "showing her measurements."

Navarone turned out to be a most unpleasant experience: "The frustrations are endless," John wrote Wheldon. "By nature the position of an 'observing camera unit' with a full-feature one is invidious to say the least, and we have very much been treated like the poor relation." He wasn't happy with the crew he'd gotten either ("I really boobed when I picked these two") and he longed for the BBC's Ken Higgins or Charles de Jaeger.

Though MacKendrick was soon replaced by J. Lee Thompson, John would still write to Wheldon of increasing tension and chaos: "Frankly, I don't think Carl will ever be happy until he's directing it all himself." In March he sailed from Athens to Rhodes, where he shot considerable footage on the C.G.S. *Courier*, and filmed some promotional scenes of Gregory Peck with his wife, Veronique. But John was becoming increasingly disillusioned with the whole project. By April, still holed up at the Miramare Hotel on Rhodes, he couldn't see how the past three months had in any way helped his ambitions. A month later he was still trying to assemble his copious quantity of celluloid ("bits of rubbish") into some kind of finished whole.

In the end, various short films would be assembled from John's footage to promote *The Guns of Navarone* in cinemas and on television; in October 1961, the U.S. Coast Guard, in a bid to sell itself as much as the film, distributed a twelve-minute short to American TV stations of Mr. and Mrs. Gregory Peck touring one of their ships.

So it was that, when John finally returned to Lime Grove, he had the distinct sense of coming home. Despite his long time away, relations with Wheldon were still warm; the producer looked on Schlesinger almost paternally, addressing him in letters as "my dear old bronzed top hat" after John had burned his scalp in the hot Greek sun. No hard feelings were harbored over the fact that John never managed to get a *Navarone* feature for *Monitor*. John immediately began casting about for ideas for a new film.

Given that "Private View" had successfully profiled young, up-and-coming painters, John decided to take a similar approach with a subject closer to his heart: actors. "I wanted to do a film about drama students at Central School, Swiss Cottage," he said. "About their lives, about the pleasure and the freedom and the apparent security of college life, particularly with a difficult profession [ahead of them]." His ten-year-old memories of life at Oxford had faded into a kind of nostalgic reverie about simpler days, days of hope and dreams. "I thought young actors would have interesting stories to tell. Actors are fascinating creatures, living so many different lives in their careers, needing to be ready at all times to embrace something brand-new."

So he took a notebook and a cameraman and headed over to the school on Eton Avenue to look around, not realizing he himself was about to embrace a whole new direction in his own career.

Several shorthand descriptions would be used for John Schlesinger over the years: "keen observer of the inter-personal drama"; "master of atmosphere and detail"; "portrait artist of the human condition." But the simplest, and most common, was this: "actor's director." John loved working with actors, and they with him:

"He had a genuine respect for people's abilities," Glenda Jackson said. "He never would pretend that he knew more than his actors. One of the things I found most endearing about him was his willingness to listen to other ideas."

"He was always more the collaborator than the dictator," Alan Bates agreed. "But he was still quite the searching director. John loved that process with actors, trying to get to every corner of it."

"He was interested like a scientist," said Joanna Lumley. "And I don't mean that clinically because he was not clinical. It's the oldest adage, rather, which is, truth is beauty and beauty truth. John looked for the truth in a performance and was not afraid of what form it turned out to be. He was an artist, a great portrait painter."

"John gave his actors a lot of freedom to find the character and find the moment," said Martin Sheen. "He's not close-minded. He has an image of what he wants but he's not married to it. He always invited us to go with our instincts."

"He was so generous to his actors," said Isabella Rossellini. She remembered that during the filming of *The Innocent* (1993), she felt distant from her costar Anthony Hopkins. "So John came up with an idea. He gave Tony and I an hour to improvise a scene not in the script. It was just to build connection. No other director I know would give his actors that much room to analyze and explore."

"John always encouraged a lot of improvisation," Sally Field concurred. "He would just let you go, but he'd be sitting right there watching you intensely. I never felt I was out there alone. We developed a shorthand, where I'd look over at him and know from his expression if I'd gotten it right. I can still hear him, 'Too much, my dear. Too much.'"

"For a young actor, he was very inspirational," said Jimmy Smits, an unknown when John cast him in a pivotal part in *The Believers* (1987). "It was scary stuff that I was putting myself through, but it was all a lesson. I kept looking to John for permission to do it, and he was always right there saying, 'Just fly, just jump off the branch and go for it.'"

"He knew what he wanted from his actors, and you knew he was going to keep working until he got it," Jon Voight remembered. "That was the deal with John. That's what we counted on. He would talk to us in our own language."

He could also be imperious. Editor Jim Clark recalled many times when John, fed up with one of his actors, would simply say, "Oh, go ahead and do it your way, my dear, but don't forget we have the scissors."

Still, he'd admit if he was wrong, said Brenda Vaccaro. "He wasn't wrong often, and he'd throw a fit about it, but he'd finally admit it."

She remembered a scene in *Midnight Cowboy* where her character, Shirley, reaches into her purse to pay Joe Buck for his services. "I was supposed to say, 'How much is it? Twenty? Oh, yeah, right,' and then I was supposed to hand him the money. Well, John was all impatient and he took my hand and shook it and said, 'Oh, *please*, let's just get on with it. Give him the money and then he leaves.'

"John thought that was that," Vaccaro said. Instead, the young whippersnapper stopped the set cold when she said, "Excuse me, but I think you should try shooting it *both* ways." By this time, John had directed four feature films and led Julie

Christie to an Academy Award, and here was Vaccaro, in just her second picture, challenging his direction. "Yes," she said courageously, anticipating his wrath, "there's a moment here for Shirley and we ought to see it."

More than thirty years later, Vaccaro still remembered the look John gave her, and she shivered. "He is *such* an Aquarian. He can just completely turn on you. That look – oh, I wanted to run! But even though he blew up, he shot the scene both ways. He did it for me. And then, when I was leaving the rushes, he stopped me as I walked up the aisle, and he said, very kindly, 'Brenda, you were quite right. We should do it your way.'"

It's true that John's own early acting experiences helped shape his relationship with his actors, enabling him to better appreciate their craft and the work they needed to do for him. But watching John's second long *Monitor* film, a picture that would be called "The Class," I found yet another piece of his story: this was the guiding principle, the formative encounter that, perhaps more than anything else, turned John Schlesinger into "an actor's director."

"Here," says the acting teacher, handing his student a crumpled newspaper and instructing her to pass it along to her classmates. "I want you to handle this as if it were a wounded bird you cared about."

The teacher watches as the students carefully pass along the precious bundle of crinkled paper. "I don't want to see a lot of emotion and tenderness," he warns. "I don't want you to express your feeling at all. I want all that to go into your contact with the bird. You've got to keep it outside there. Anything of you which is left over to express your feelings with is *ham* – precisely that bit which is not engaged in solving the problem. The only way you can dramatize, or see what's going on inside somebody, is by seeing how they deal with something *outside*."

In John Schlesinger's best films, this is precisely how he instructs his actors: we do not see great theatrics of emotion. Rather, the dreams and fears and regrets and hopes of his characters are conveyed to us through what they do, how they simply *are:* Tom Courtenay getting off the train to buy milk and making no attempt to get back on; Peter Finch playing "Cosi Fan Tutte" in *Sunday, Bloody Sunday*; Shirley MacLaine listening to her pupil play the piano in *Madame Sousatzka*; Coral Browne watching Alan Bates walk off alone at the end of *An Englishman Abroad*.

What had begun as an idea to profile acting students became instead a primer from an acting *teacher*, and in many ways John was a pupil. Sitting in on a class taught by Harold Lang, whom he'd met while both were actors at ITV, John was struck by how riveted the students were by their teacher's style and presence. He arranged for Huw Wheldon to return with him, and they watched Lang's near-hypnotic effect. "I decided this was my film," John said. "Harold Lang and this particular class."

At first, Lang, a rather arch, imperious man, thought he was mad. "You're with *Monitor*, are you?" he sniffed. "I can't think why you want to sit in. I would never want to be a part of this."

He came around, however, when it became clear that John was making him the star of the film. "Harold was an extraordinary man, extraordinary personality," John said, and it comes through in "The Class": telling one student she is actually a child murderess, he is almost a Svengali. It is a wonderfully quirky little film: not quite a documentary, for Lang and the students were re-enacting a class for John, stopping action when he called cut and positioning themselves for the best camera angles; but it is not a fiction film either, for these were the lessons Lang would have used anyway, and the students had no idea ahead of time what he was going to ask of them. Moreover, for all their cooperation with the camera, they were already good enough actors to seem completely unaware of it.

At one point, Lang pairs different students to perform the scene between Shylock and Portia from *The Merchant of Venice*, but using their *own* words, not Shakespeare's. His motive is to get at the truth of the scene without reliance on the script; without that understanding, he instructs, even Shakespeare's words aren't sufficient. "As wonderful as they are," Lang said, uttering a credo that would echo throughout the making of Schlesinger's films, "words by themselves are never enough. We must know what they are intended to do, to whom, against what resistance. The words aren't great drama just because they tell us eternal truths about justice or mercy, or because they tell us about Portia's character, but because *they pass between people* in a particular dramatic situation. That's what makes them live."

If John took any lesson from Lang to heart it is this: his best films would resonate with the power of human relationships. There is no greater exploration he could make as a filmmaker: the drama that *passes between people*. Vic and Ingrid. Joe and Ratso. The triangulated lovers of *Sunday, Bloody Sunday*. Faye and Homer. Christopher Boyce and Daulton Lee. Coral Browne and Guy Burgess.

What makes "The Class" a brilliant film is not, however, its thesis. Proving Lang's point, John did not simply rely on words for the film's success. Though it distinctly lacks a musical score and the camera remains largely still, it is nonetheless filmic in its approach, from the starmaking turn by Lang, who keeps viewers as enraptured as his class, to its little moments of verisimilitude, such as the glimpse we get of a ballet class through a glass panel in a door while "our" students take a short break in the hallway. We hear the instructor and the music, the scuff of ballet slippers. Once back in the classroom, John frames Lang beside a NO SMOKING sign for several shots. The message is clear: This man has authority. He gives commands and we obey.

"It is the best film I made for *Monitor*," John said. "One of the best I've *ever* made, in fact." He would close it with a flair fitting his sensibilities and which would have its own resonance throughout his career: Peggy Ashcroft, who had attended the Central School from 1924 to 1926, is heard reciting Portia's speech as the credits roll. In her voice we can hear all of the lessons Lang was endeavoring to teach. Ashcroft would herself go on to be directed by John Schlesinger, not once but three times.

John had no idea at the time that this would be the end of his tenure with *Monitor*. Controller of Programmes Kenneth Adam described "The Class" as "splendid," even inquiring if they could get Lang to collaborate with Schlesinger on other projects. But destiny was already conspiring to move John's career in a new direction; he would soon be working on a project for British Transport Films which would lead directly to his fateful meeting with Joseph Janni. Although he would discuss a few ideas with Wheldon over the course of the next few months, John never did get back to the BBC – at least not for another twenty years.

He retained a lasting affection for his time there. The BBC was his film education, after all, his graduate study: Ken Russell would call *Monitor* "the only British experimental film school." Russell followed in Schlesinger's footsteps, arriving at Lime Grove in early 1959. By that time, John was already a star at the BBC; when he graduated to making just the one long film per year, Russell took up the slack, churning out films that were every bit as inventive as Schlesinger's had been. John would, in fact, unofficially anoint Russell his successor, pronouncing "A House in Bayswater" – the story of a demolished Edwardian mansion broadcast in December 1960 – "a modern master-piece." With John's departure, Russell went on to become *Monitor*'s new major star.

As much as he had enjoyed his *Monitor* years, John was eager to break into feature film production. He was elated to receive a call from Edgar Anstey at British Transport Films asking for a meeting. More than once John had gone to Anstey in search of work; now, impressed by what he'd been seeing on television, Anstey summoned him, adding, "Bring something to show." This time there was no need to steal footage: John lugged several of his *Monitor* films over to Anstey's office, including a rough cut of "The Class," which had not yet been broadcast.

If he experienced any flashbacks to that day, nearly twelve years earlier, when he'd threaded another film (*Black Legend*) into a projector to show another producer (Michael Balcon), they were quickly dissipated by Anstey's obvious approval. "I think," he said, turning around to John as the lights came on, "you should come and make a film for me."

British Transport Films was a film production outfit formed in May 1949 by the newly nationalized rail industry to promote rail travel. Edgar Anstey, a protégé of the pioneering documentary filmmaker John Grierson, was BTF's first Producer-in-Charge. Though essentially producing propaganda, Anstey attempted to bring an artistic sensibility to his pictures, conscious of his place within the British cinema. Indeed, these were some of the most-seen British-produced pictures in the country; Anstey wouldn't settle for simple, overstated travelogues.

John's first idea was to do a piece on Brighton; he was still intrigued by the stark contrasts of the place. A treatment was prepared but Anstey ultimately nixed the idea; it was more about the *place*, he said, than it was about *getting there*. Over lunch, they bantered other ideas back and forth. On the spot, John suddenly had the idea for a day in the life of a railroad station. "It's a microcosm of what's going on in a city," he told Anstey, who was thrilled by the idea and told him to run with it.

John chose Waterloo Station. For several weeks he hung around, doing what he said a director needs to know how to do: *observing*. "Under one roof," he said, "we found all the misery, happiness, loneliness, bewilderment and loss to be found anywhere in the world." During his weeks of observation at the station, John witnessed several moments that he knew absolutely had to be in the film: an old woman demanding why a certain train was not leaving at a certain time; handcuffed prisoners being led onto a train, destination Parkhurst or Dartmoor; and, in what would become the heart of the film, a child crying in the middle of the station, terrified after being separated from his mother.

It was clear he was going to need actors. In the days before portable synch cameras, he would've needed to run along with "a wild tape recorder" if he were to get all the sounds he needed to match up with the action. How much easier to just re-enact a scene with actors. In the final film, called *Terminus*, John estimated that the ratio of actual footage to re-enactments was about "50-50." It's a figure that may surprise many who remember the film fondly, because when *Terminus* was released, it was assumed everything in it was real. Part of the film's original appeal, in fact, was the apparent magic Schlesinger had worked in capturing real events and making them dramatic. In retrospect, his magic was really about filming drama and making it look real.

The shoot took just about two weeks. For the old woman he brought in the aunt of his friend Roland Curram, who said "Aunt Gertie" had a wonderful time working with John, hitting all the marks and sounding every bit as bewildered as he wanted her to sound. He also brought in actors to play the gang of prisoners and photographed them through a fence, foreshadowing their life behind bars. Then there was an actress who quite beautifully essayed the part of a young woman carrying flowers to meet an incoming train.

John had considerably more trouble, however, finding his little lost boy. He tested a few children from drama schools, but found them all so "hardboiled they couldn't care less if their mothers left them." He finally settled on his brother Roger's wife's nephew, who seemed to have the right sensitivity. Even if John needed to nudge him into some theatrical tears, he figured it was in the kid's blood: he was also the grandnephew of Peggy Ashcroft.

The scene would be shot backwards, John decided. "We had pre-lit the railway station office, where the lost child was taken to wait until his mother could be found," he recalled. "We sat him on a case. And it was then that the mother actually went away and the crying began." Cinematographer Ken Higgins, whom John had borrowed from the BBC, quickly moved in with his camera. "I suppose," John reflected later, "one is so intent upon getting the effect one wants that one ceases to be a humanist at that moment."

But more was still needed. "We needed him really bawling," John said. The boy was old enough to realize they were shooting a scene; the camera was right there, and Mummy couldn't be too far away. So he offered the boy a bite of chocolate. When the child wanted more, John withheld it: "That's when he cried best, and the camera was ready, and we got all his facial reactions, which we used." That's the shot we see at the start of the scene, the desolate little boy in the middle of the station, all alone, crying furiously. Except that his tears aren't ones of terror: they're of rage.

No matter: it works, and stunningly. *Terminus* is a near-perfect little film, the best John had done up to this point. The re-enactments are mostly all topnotch; the only drawback is some of the wooden non-actors like the station manager who calls on the telephone. Mostly, however, the film buzzes with the kind of activity one would expect from a picture that opens with the rather obvious metaphor shot of a beehive. John's sense of place is sharply maintained; except for an establishing aerial shot of London, we are never outside of the station. We glimpse nuns bustling through the crowd, a group of men laughing heartily, and, typically, a couple of handsome young sailors sharing a smoke. As he had with *Sunday in the Park*, John offers a real slice of humanity: there's a bag lady, a forlorn young woman looking for an umbrella, and a number of black faces, who usually appear to the cadences of Jamaican music on the soundtrack.

The subtle score, always attuned to the crowd scenes, was the work of Australian composer Ron Grainer. Lyrics to a couple of the songs were written by John's old pal from *Monitor*, Michell Raper. Along with cameraman Ken Higgins, it was a crew he worked well with; he had learned from his harrowing *Guns of Navarone* experience that camaraderie with his crew was vital for a successful picture.

Like his tenure at *Monitor*, John's brief experience with British Transport Films was also a happy one. "Edgar was a very good producer for me," John reflected, looking back a decade later. "He said what was necessary to say in an objective way, but identified himself with the project, which in my opinion is the best possible way of producing films. I've been very fortunate in having good producers to work with who have been able to keep objectivity when I'm losing it." He added Anstey to a list that began with Huw Wheldon and continued with Jo Janni and "most recently, Jerry Hellman." Little did John know then, in 1971, that that list would end there.

Terminus, with its candid-camera survey of human relationships, stands as a prologue for much of John's later work. Many of the themes touched on so quickly here – the despair of lost children, the bewilderment of outsiders, the fate of misfits who find themselves at the end of the road – would be carried to fruition in his dramatic feature films. This, clearly, was a filmmaker to watch: indeed, late that summer, *Terminus* won a Golden Lion Award at the Venice Film Festival.

"To actually win an award," John said, "was quite unbelievable." He'd remember that some British critics, especially after the win in Venice, were a bit "snide" about the film, though he'd say, "That's something I've gotten used to from critics here at home." Still, the public was queuing up outside cinemas to see it. His three years of nonstop activity seemed finally to be paying off. "Suddenly I felt on the fast track," he said, "but to where, I wasn't quite sure."

His destination would come courtesy of a fast-talking, heavily accented Italian who had first contacted John a couple of years before: Joseph Janni. The producer, then with the Rank Organisation, had happened to catch John's *Monitor* piece on the Italian Opera. Calling on the director afterward, Janni complimented him for his witty yet never condescending depiction of his countrymen. "I think I should like to discover you," Janni said grandly, in his rich Milanese accent.

John laughed. "Be my guest," he replied.

It would take *Terminus*, however, to bring them back into each other's orbit. In the spring of 1961, Janni was still steamed over losing the rights to Karel Reisz's *Saturday Night and Sunday Morning*, which had become the most talked about film in Britain. But Janni was somebody else who never took no for an answer; he was never down for long. In his hands he held a couple of projects which, he hoped, would leave *Saturday Night* in the dust. *Terminus* convinced him it was time to make good on that promise of "discovery." He rang John and announced, "I want to make a film with you."

Six

1961–1962

"This is a ruse of Richardson's to get rid of me"

"I t was all such a long time ago," said Alan Bates, as he ushered me into his house in St. John's Wood. He seemed reflective, philosophical even, about the past: "John and I were both young. Everything seemed ahead of us."

Alan Bates, the fresh-faced, north country lad of *A Kind of Loving*, had just turned 69 years old. There was a stoop to his walk, and he moved with some difficulty. He hadn't been well; inquiring after John's health, he was saddened to hear that his old friend was still in the wheelchair. In a few days' time, Alan Bates would receive his knighthood from the Queen; he and Glenda Jackson, he told me, were still pushing for a knighthood for John.

"It was such a wonderful experience, such an opportunity for me, getting the chance to make *A Kind of Loving* with John." Bates smiled fondly as we sat in his small living room. "It was his first film and he got so into it, really relished it. I remember the sheer joy of it, great fun and laughter. There was such a sense of promise then, such a sense of future."

A future for all of them, John, Alan Bates, and British cinema, too, just then flowering into its new golden age. "The British producer is finding that his pictures are in greater demand than ever before," the trade publication *Box Office* noted at the time. Indeed, postwar trends were being stood on their heads: "It is the Hollywood pictures," *Box Office* reported, "which are failing to please the customers and the home-grown features which are breaking the records."

A Kind of Loving shot John to national acclaim nearly over-night. After years on the sidelines, suddenly the name Schlesinger was grouped with that of Anderson, Reisz, Richardson and Clayton and, for several critics, it was Schlesinger who came first. At a party one night, during that halcyon period when *A Kind of Loving* was showing in nearly every cinema in Britain, John walked up behind Lindsay Anderson, clapped him on his back, and said, "I guess I finally managed to think higher than television."

"Of course, John wasn't always so confident," Bates said, laughing. "Once the first few days of shooting were over, he started in with his usual, 'Oh, God, I can't do this. It's all terrible. What was I *thinking*?'" He laughed again. "But of course he *could* do it, and he did it brilliantly."

They'd make four pictures together, Schlesinger and Bates, a record for John with any one leading man. "There was a certain simpatico with Alan," John would say. "Maybe because we started out together . . . It is one of my few actor friendships that has really endured, because working with actors is rather like a shipboard romance: you are all thrown together very closely for a short time, swear undying loyalty and love, then you're jolly glad when the thing's over. But Alan and Julie Christie and a few more have become good friends . . . He is just such a good, intuitive actor. Yes, I love working with Alan."

"John's very particular as a director," Bates told me. "He'll go for quite a long time to get nuance and detail. He has a huge sympathy for the acting process. I remember another director once taking me through a huge number of takes and finally I said, 'If you're looking for something and I'm not doing it, you'll have to tell me what it is.' And he said, 'No, I'm not looking for anything, I just wanted to see if you would come up with something on your own.' I thought that was pretty unfair. John wasn't doing that. He'd search *with* you. He'd be trying to find nuance and meaning and he'd work with his actors to bring that out."

"I was so very, very fortunate," John said, "to have gotten in at a time when the British cinema was really opening up, when new things were being tried, when we could actually find financing for homegrown projects. There was such an energy, such an excitement. I never thought I'd have to go to America to make films. In the early 1960s, it truly seemed as if the British cinema would go on forever."

Joseph Janni may have wanted to make a film with John Schlesinger, but he was shrewd enough not to plunge into any partnership blind. "He had some doubts," John admitted, "over whether I could handle actors." The crude theatrics of *Black Legend* failed to reassure the producer; even the second-unit work John had done on *The Four Just Men* had been primarily exterior scenes, car chases, and establishing shots.

But Janni had a hunch about John. He had him direct some commercials – several for Polo Mints, a couple for Fray Bentos meats, a quartet for Kellogg's – and gave him a copy of Stan Barstow's novel *A Kind of Loving*. Janni owned the film rights; in fact, at that moment, playwrights Willis Hall and Keith Waterhouse, the successful co-authors of *Billy Liar*, were hard at work on an adaptation. Janni felt the subject matter – a boy from a northern industrial town gets a girl pregnant and is forced to marry her – was perfect for the sudden vogue for realistic, working-class films kicked off by Clayton's *Room at the Top* and Reisz's *Saturday Night and Sunday Morning*. John, headed to Switzerland for a skiing holiday, promised to read the book and let Janni know what he thought.

"When I read *A Kind of Loving*," John said, "I thought it a particularly human story which I could tell well. I sent a card to Jo Janni saying that I was desperate to do this. That I really felt I could."

The producer remained unsure. To prove John could handle actors, his agent, Richard Gregson, suggested that he direct one of the Edgar Wallace mysteries then being churned out at Merton Park Studios. But John refused. "I wouldn't do an Edgar Wallace thriller," he said, "because I knew that I couldn't possibly do it any better than anybody else at that time."

Fair enough, but might there have been another reason for his opposition? For among those "anybody elses" then making Edgar Wallace thrillers was one Alan Cooke; at that very moment, John's ex-lover was shooting a potboiler called *Flat Two*. A few years earlier, Alan's career had seemed to be outpacing John's. He'd gone to New York to helm live TV dramas, including "Robert Montgomery Presents" and "Studio One," while John toiled away in obscurity in London. In 1956

Cooke had taken the plunge and moved to Hollywood, directing several episodes of NBC's "Matinee Theatre." He also married and had a son. By the late Fifties, however, Alan was back in Britain, churning out pedestrian fare for ITV while John had begun his classy documentaries for the BBC. *Flat Two* was Cooke's stab at breaking into features; John refused to go that same route.

So Janni hatched another idea. He also held the rights to *Billy Liar*, which was then enjoying a successful run at the Cambridge Theatre. Would John be willing, Janni asked, to do a screen test with Tom Courtenay, who was slated to play Billy on film? Courtenay was preparing to take over the part from Albert Finney on the stage, but hadn't yet done so; Janni wanted to see what Courtenay might do with the role. John was savvy enough to understand that the test would be as much for him as it was for Courtenay. If he acquitted himself well, he would not only get *A Kind of Loving*, but also, quite possibly, the eventual assignment to direct the *Billy Liar* film – a job presumed to be in the pocket of Lindsay Anderson, since he was directing the stage version.

Janni wasn't happy with the test John turned in. "To tell the truth," he said, "I hated it." But he "shut his eyes" and signed both Schlesinger and Courtenay to contracts anyway.

It was, as they say, the start of a beautiful relationship. Six films together, among the best ever produced in the British cinema, with at least two becoming influential, international hits. To the end of their lives, the two men would retain enormous affection for each other: to John, Jo was "a mad Italian, a renegade"; to Jo, John was "a brilliant filmmaker and practical jokester." They made an odd pair, Schlesinger round and soft, Janni lean and angular. While the producer was sociable and gregarious, John still found it painful to make conversation with strangers. But they shared traits in common as well, among them a volatile temper: huge explosions would erupt on the sets of their films, with scripts being tossed and chairs being kicked and invectives being hurled. "You Italian cunt!" "You ridiculous faggot!" Thirty years later, John would smile, remembering the madness. "The crew would imagine we were about to come to blows," he said. "But the storm would pass as quickly as it had begun and Jo never bore a grudge for long."

"Their rows were classic," remembered editor Jim Clark. "They loved each other, worked very well together, but the screaming! The yelling! We were running [an early cut of] *Darling* and we never got much past reel two because Jo was yelling, 'Stop the projection!' He was screaming at John, 'How could Julie do that? She'd never do that!' And John got all red and started perspiring and they were both pacing around the room. Their rows would always end with Jo saying, 'What do you know about women, you're a homosexual!' To which John would reply, 'A great deal more than you, you wily Milanese philanderer!' And then they'd laugh and calm down and work it out."

Temper wasn't the only thing they shared. Both had fits of melancholy that alternated with bouts of raucous humor. "I can remember, as a boy," said Jo's son Nicholas, "watching my father and John at the Berlin Wall. They were jumping up and down all over the place, pulling faces at the guards." On the set of *A Kind of Loving*, the two would double over in laughter at private jokes. "They had names for all the girls who tried out for parts," Nicholas Janni said. "They were always egging each other on."

What bonded them was their sense of being outsiders. "My father felt very outside of English society," Nicholas said. John did, too, despite having been born in Hampstead and educated at Upminster and Oxford. He had never quite fit within the traditional English social system; it's not surprising that his patron, his creative soulmate, would turn out to be a passionate foreigner. "Both John and my father were very anti-snobbishness and all that kind of English nonsense," said Nicholas Janni. "They delighted in their rebellion."

Joseph Janni had been born in Milan in 1916. Though he started out studying engineering at Milan University, he would later attend the Centro Sperimentale in Rome, the famous film school founded by Mussolini, then in its first years. In 1939, in opposition to the Fascist regime, Janni left Italy for America, where he had arranged for a job at the Disney studios. But during a stop in Britain on his way to Hollywood, war broke out; Jo decided to stay where he was, though he'd spend part of that time in an internment camp.

Janni never felt in accord with England. Being an Italian during the war meant he was subject to mistrust and hostility. Yet he would make films that helped define British cinema and, by extension, British society. His first job was as assistant to John Sutro, who produced Michael Powell's *49th Parallel* with Leslie Howard and Laurence Olivier. Janni would later work with John Corfield, but he was itching to make his own films: he would say later that he was filled with the desire to "produce in England the sort of films that were being made in Italy" – the works of Visconti, De Sica, Rossellini. This admiration for Italian neorealism would profoundly influence Janni's artistic vision.

In 1947, he formed his own production company, Victoria

Films; he'd later chop the name down to the more mod "Vic." Yet Janni's early films do not resemble the gritty realistic dramas of the Italian masters as much as they do the patriotic, postwar British studio product. His first film was *The Glass Mountain,* an odd yet lovely hybrid of war film and musical directed by Eduardo Anton and Henry Cass, starring Michael Denison and Valentina Cortese. Set in the Dolomites, it proved popular enough to be reissued twice, in 1950 and 1953.

This initial success brought Janni into affiliation with the Rank Organisation, for which he produced a wide range of films, from *Romeo and Juliet,* directed by Renato Castellani and starring Laurence Harvey and Susan Shentall, to several lightweight comedies and actioners helmed by Jack Lee. The most successful of these was *A Town Like Alice* (1956), but Janni's ambitious Eskimo drama, *The Savage Innocents* (1960), directed by Nicholas Ray and starring Anthony Quinn, failed at the British box office. He would later say the flop was the spur that set him back on course toward producing the kind of realist, socially aware films he'd been wanting to do now for more than a decade.

In light of this, a break with Rank was inevitable. The story of his termination is pure Janni: called in for a producers' conference with his boss, John Davies, Janni was asked to remain after the meeting had concluded. "I have bad news for you, Jo," Davies told him. "We are not renewing your contract." Janni gave little reaction, simply continuing to make conversation as he walked toward the door. Finally, with his hand on the knob, he turned, and said, "Oh, and John – what was that bad news you were going to give me?"

He loved telling stories like that about himself, and others loved telling them nearly as much. One of John's favorites was

Winifred Schlesinger always had a particular soft spot for her sensitive, creative first-born son John.

Schlesinger was filming short subjects from the time he was a teenager, first with a 9.5 mm camera and later graduating to a 16 mm.

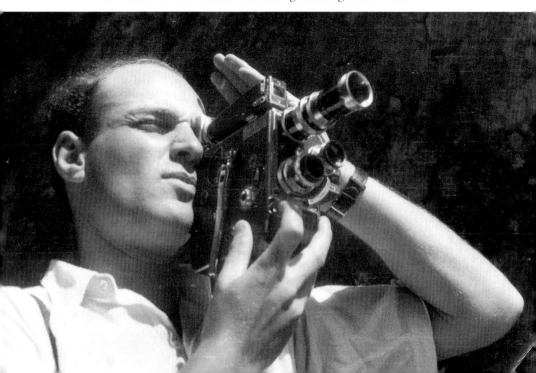

The young director (*far right*) and three members of his stock company for the Kintbury Follies: (*left to right*) his sisters Wendy and Susan and brother Roger.

John found his calling in the farces and plays put on by the Oxford University Dramatic Society and the Experimental Theatre Club.

Fascinated by magic since he was schoolboy, Schlesinger performed a magic act during his time in the Army. Magic, he said, was what inspired his desire to create illusions on the screen.

Schlesinger (*right*) with his first love, Alan Cooke, discussing a scene for their first film, *Black Legend* (1948). Their next one would be set in the present, if only to relieve them of the difficulty of avoiding power lines like the ones here.

Schlesinger became a star director for the BBC's classic programme *Monitor*. Here he is directing young players for his treatise on childhood, *The Innocent Eye*.

John's best film during his BBC years was *The Class*, featuring the dynamic acting teacher Harold Lang (*right*).

On location for *A Kind of Loving*, John developed a fancy for his leading man, Alan Bates. They would become lifelong friends.

Although *Billy Liar* failed at the box office, it launched the film career of Tom Courtenay and made Julie Christie a star.

John called Joseph Janni (*left*) 'a mad Italian,' but their tempestuous, utterly devoted partnership resulted in some of the best British films of the 1960s and 1970s.

In Capri, filming *Darling*, his first international blockbuster: Schlesinger at the camera, Julie Christie and Roland Curram at the table wearing sunglasses.

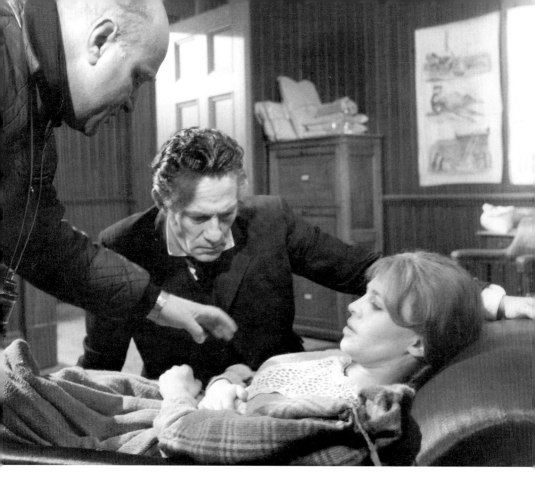

Critics scratched their heads trying to figure out why the director and star of *Darling* next chose Hardy's *Far From the Madding Crowd*. John would wonder later on himself. Of the four leads, John felt only Peter Finch (here) was on key.

Schlesinger loved goofing on the sets of his films, but soon the laughter had disappeared between the director and his star, Terrence Stamp.

the time he found himself a passenger in Janni's car as they hurried to some location or another. Impatient with the single-lane traffic, John remembered, Jo overtook them all to form a second line at the lights. With drivers shaking their fists and honking their horns, a policeman charged up to Janni's window.

"I've been watching you," the cop growled.

Janni merely lifted an eyebrow in response. "I pay you," he said, "so when you've learned to be a good policeman and keep the traffic moving, *then* you may complain about my driving."

Janni was always in a hurry, a fast, reckless driver, mostly of Jaguars. He was blunt and aggressive, a shrill hypochondriac, and exactly the right man to guide John Schlesinger to his fame. Jo, as much as John, wanted an opportunity for critical and commercial success. Forced into a routine at Rank, Janni would break out, pursuing projects he thought might fit the vogue. He wasn't simply trying to cash in on what was already being known as the British New Wave; in fact, he had been at the forefront of the trend, optioning Alan Sillitoe's novel *Saturday Night and Sunday Morning* back in 1958 for £3,000. But Rank considered its commercial prospects unlikely, and, without the necessary financing, Janni agreed to sell the rights to Woodfall Films, where Tony Richardson and Karel Reisz were anxiously waiting to get their hands on it. The film's eventual blockbuster reception merely solidified in Janni's mind that Davies' termination of his contract had, in fact, been fortuitous.

However, Janni's new backer-distributor, Anglo-Amalgamated, a small but feisty company, carried none of the prestige Rank enjoyed. Anglo's chief claim to fame was the series of lowbrow *Carry On . . .* films (*Sergeant, Teacher, Nurse*) starring John's old Army buddy, Kenneth Williams. The year before, Anglo had distributed Michael Powell's brilliant and notorious *Peeping Tom*, only to dump it after the critics of the time savaged it as pornographic.

Head honcho at Anglo was one Nat Cohen, who was eager to move out beyond the legacy of *Carry On* . . . and *Peeping Tom*. "Anglo-Amalgamated was glad to be a part of what we were doing, getting out there on the edge," John said. Indeed, the partnership would transform the company from a distributor of plebeian comedies into a major international player, perhaps the most recognizable purveyor of British film abroad. "The forces were all in alignment," John said, looking back. "All of us, Jo Janni, Nat Cohen, Alan Bates . . . we all came together in the spring of 1961 and all our lives were forever changed."

It is difficult to describe now, some 40 years later, the excitement felt in British cinema in the early 1960s. For the first time in decades, as the very social fabric of Britain was being rewoven, filmmakers discovered a motherlode of untapped potential. Suddenly available to them were subjects previously forbidden, experiences and dramas which had never been exploited. In the struggles of the working class, in their sense of claustrophobic anger, there were stories to be told, and the filmmakers of the British New Wave took full advantage. While the rest of the nation was in the midst of a rebirth, as postwar austerity was replaced by affluence and consumerism, the working classes, especially in the provinces, felt left behind. Britain's decline as a world power could serve as a metaphor for their lives: trapped within the small islands of their existence, nowhere to go, no chance to spread their wings. In this very despair, British filmmakers found their greatest hope.

If that sounds cynical, it may well be: for the New Wave, despite all its debt to the socialist, anti-consumerist principles of Free Cinema, was in truth a commercial movement. These films made money, and that's why they continued to be made: after nearly a decade of decline, people were again queuing outside the nation's cinemas. The anti-hero, or "angry young man" became, paradoxically, a heroic figure for British middle-class audiences eager to see films that dealt with adult subjects: unwanted pregnancies, divorce, racial issues, economic struggle, and homosexuality. This was what so excited the filmmakers of the New Wave, including Schlesinger: the medium of the cinema, so long a tool of spectacle or farce, could offer a compelling sense of life's immediacy.

It could also make them money. As Peter Hutchings has observed, "Realism might well in some instances involve a 'moral' commitment to serious social issues but in the 1959-1963 period it also sold films." That nearly all of the New Wave directors, Schlesinger again among them, would very quickly move on to new genres after the vogue for kitchen-sink drama was over, seems testament to the fact that their commitment was never purely about message. Indeed, John would have recoiled at the idea that he was making movies for a "cause"; he made movies because he wanted to tell good stories — and yes, he wanted them to make money.

That's not to take away from any artistic impulse: certainly Schlesinger was thrilled to be able to challenge "a nation of conformists," which was the way he saw Britain, especially British cinema. Like the other filmmakers working within the New Wave, John was inspired by the social upheavals going on all around him: class rebellion; the women's movement, new immigrants from the old Commonwealth, greater visibility of homosexuals – all of this contributed to the world view of a generation then coming into its own.

Indeed, the Macmillan years were informed by the Prime Minister's embrace of the "winds of change" – winds which would carry round the world a new sound called Merseybeat, named for the musical movement that began in Liverpool. In February 1961, about the same time John Schlesinger began negotiating with Joseph Janni, a group called The Beatles performed for the first time at Liverpool's Cavern Club. By the time *A Kind of Loving* was released a year later, other Liverpool bands such as Gerry and the Pacemakers were already hot on the heels of safe, establishment rockers like Cliff Richard and Frankie Avalon. The long-neglected working classes and provincial towns were pushing their way to the forefront of music and film and, indeed, all of popular culture; a revolution of style and attitude was underway.

It's interesting that the film most often cited as launching the British New Wave, Jack Clayton's *Room at the Top* (1959), did not come from one of the Free Cinema proponents, though, like Schlesinger, Clayton benefited from a climate of fresh ideas and a willingness to explore new ground. Over the next few years, moviegoers worldwide would be introduced to places like Manchester, Oldham, Burnley, Leeds, Lancaster and New-castle, places that had rarely, if ever, been captured on film. "Directors were certainly enchanted with the north," said Keith Waterhouse, scriptwriter for *A Kind of Loving* and *Billy Liar*. "At one time you couldn't walk around the slag heaps without tripping over a light cable." Regional accents were suddenly heard in cinemas throughout Britain, and not just for comic effect or background color. These were the voices of the new stars: Alan Bates, Albert Finney, Tom Courtenay, Rachel Roberts.

Yet the burst of cinematic interest in Britain in the early 1960s, while significant, has often been overstated: the New Wave did not, in fact, reverse the overall postwar trend of decline. The number of British-made features actually decreased from 79 to 69 from 1960 to 1965; the number of cinemas also dropped dramatically in that same period, from 3,034 to 1,971. Yet net box-office receipts remained virtually unchanged; there was, apparently, enough of an increase in the numbers of moviegoers to offset other industry trends. This small uptick was not, however, a surge of the general populace leaving their television sets and returning to the movies. Rather, this was a movement of *young* people who, like John, had come of age after the war, for whom the old traditions held little relevance, and who were looking for new ways, new ideas, new paradigms. Filmmakers like Richardson and Anderson and Schlesinger gave them what they were looking for, visions of life that were recognizable as well as probing. As the critic Samantha Lay has written, the British New Wave offered films that did not merely "reflect the surface realities of everyday life, but [also] penetrated that surface to reveal human truths."

Schlesinger was keenly aware that he had been thrust into a position of some responsibility, and he believed the new British directors held in their hands the power to embolden a traditionally timid Wardour Street. "Perhaps we may see," he said in 1962, uncharacteristically optimistic, "a fully supported national cinema emerging."

Yet there remained some daunting challenges to that dream. Britain had never had a tradition of cinematic enthusiasm of the kind found in France, for example, where the directors of the *Nouvelle Vague* enjoyed tremendous official and public support. "The heritage we have had in Britain is a patchy one," John said, reverting to his more familiar pessimism. "I don't think this country has really ever been addicted to films. We've had *periods* – periods of great documentaries, the Korda period, the Ealing period under Balcon – but I think that entrepreneurial talent is thin on the ground in this country. It's the thing we lack most. It's no use making a film unless it's going to be seen. I think Britain on the whole is rather embarrassed by the process of selling or marketing: they think it's a bit vulgar. Wardour Street has always had a tradition, it seems to me, of not being very good at selling."

In the early Sixties, however, there was considerable optimism that those traditions might be changing. By the time John inked his contract with Jo Janni to do *A Kind of Loving*, there had been five films released that could be considered New Wave, all of them successful. Three of them had been directed by Tony Richardson, the third, *A Taste of Honey*, proving one of Britain's biggest moneymakers that year. The film (the screen version of Sheila Delaney's hit play) featured a sympathetic if sad-eyed homosexual, an odd young man who "acts just like a woman" and who takes care of his teenage friend when she becomes pregnant. John, as one might expect, was impressed and inspired by Richardson's handling of the subject; he hoped to find a project that would enable him to inject "a similar sort of character" into his own work.

For all of Schlesinger's distancing from the Free Cinema adherents, it is notable how often their careers would intersect. John had acted for Lindsay Anderson at ITV; now he snatched from him the film of *Billy Liar*. In April 1962, at the same British

Film Academy ceremony where John won Best Short Film for *Terminus*, Tony Richardson took home the award for Best British Film for *A Taste of Honey*. Their careers were following each other, and their paths would cross socially as well. Taking a holiday in St. Tropez with Geoffrey Sharp around this time, John ran into Richardson. "Tony came up to John, and with that north country accent of his, told us he'd just bought a village in the hills," Sharp remembered. "John thought he said 'villa,' but Richardson said no, a '*village*.' It was a group of houses about ten miles from St. Tropez, and he was in the process of doing them up. He invited us to a party and though John was reluctant, off we went. It was very dark, no sign of anything, and we were driving through the hills lost when John turned to me and said, 'This is a ruse of Richardson's to get rid of me.'"

Richardson and Anderson would, according to friends, grow jealous of Schlesinger's commercial success; for his part, John came to envy the exalted regard in which they, and Reisz, were held by critics and historians. In his unease over Richardson's invitation, there was insecurity as much as disdain: John feared he would not be able to keep up with the intellectual sparring he assumed would go on. Friends of Richardson laughed away that perception, insisting Tony's gatherings were less geared to theoretical pursuits than raucous horseplay. In that case, John may have felt more at home than he imagined, for his idea of a holiday weekend meant lolling about in the sun, winking at boys, and taking joy in irreverence – such as the time he and Alan Bates sat in a Parisian café speaking with northern accents and convincing everyone they were Yorkshire miners.

The ambivalence Schlesinger felt toward the other New

Wave directors would be reflected in the choices he was inevitably asked to make about films he found inspirational. Never would he name a single film by Richardson or Reisz, except to say that their films had opened a door that allowed him to take on subjects that interested him. In 1963, John cited Anderson's *This Sporting Life* as exciting him "enormously," primarily because it was "the first of a new batch of films that had a marked style of its own." That the film should be a commercial success was important for everyone, John said; indeed, his own *Darling*, then in production, would take a similar shift away from social realism to psychological drama.

When asked in 1969, at the height of his career, to name his favorite directors, John made a show of protest but then gave it a shot. "First and foremost," he said, "Renoir." There was a long pause. "Kurosawa, Satyajit Ray, Fellini, Kubrick, René Clair – though not necessarily in that order." He hastened to add that it was the earlier Fellini films he liked, not the more recent: he had loathed *Juliet of the Spirits*. John was inspired by humanist directors directing very human films; thus, he discounted most of the newer French directors, who he considered "unreal and overintellectual." He made an exception of Truffaut, however, calling *Les Quatres Cents Coups* (*The Four Hundred Blows*) "the warmest film made by a recent French director." Note, however, that among the names of his favorites he included not one Briton.

Privately, he admitted that he saw himself as "part of a new trend in British cinema" and that *Saturday Night and Sunday Morning* had had "a tremendous impact" on him. "I do think this is a beginning of a new upsurge in British films," he wrote in his diary, but added, with considerable foresight, that there was a limit to social realism: "We have not yet started in any way to explore the techniques used by Antonioni, Resnais, Godard or Truffaut."

Schlesinger once shared a memorable dinner in Tokyo with Kurosawa. Actor Toshiro Mifune was present, too, and they were all talking about how to get pictures made. "Quite a lot was drunk," John said, "and Kurosawa was saying, through an interpreter, 'We have to fight. We're all in retreat. We've got to link arms and fight.'" John laughed, struck by the memory. "At the time I said twaddle. I believe it now." Indeed, almost from the moment he first called "Action!" on the set of *A Kind of Loving*, John Schlesinger would realize that to get what he wanted, he was going to have to fight.

On the first day of shooting in November 1961, John arrived by car on location in the town of Stockport. Sitting beside him was Alan Bates. Rounding the corner of the street where he would film his first scene, John gazed upon the dozens of crew members setting up their cameras and recording equipment. He suddenly felt sick to his stomach. Looking over at Bates, he said, "Let's turn the car around while we still have time and get the hell out of here."

John had come to quite fancy Alan, a tall, strapping young actor from Derbyshire. Bates had exactly the qualities John would always find irresistible in a man: classic good looks, boyish charm and a certain sexual ambiguity – not to mention the fact that he was fundamentally unavailable. Friends said that, had Alan been willing (and not then smitten with another young man), John would have jumped at the chance to have an affair with his star. Yet despite his "crush," John was able to enjoy Bates' company and the friendship would last a lifetime.

Bates brought solid "New Wave" credentials to the set of *A Kind of Loving*. His appearance in 1956 as Cliff in John Osborne's *Look Back in Anger*, directed by Tony Richardson at the Royal Court Theatre, had brought him to wide attention; Richardson would go on to cast him in *The Entertainer*, in the small role of Laurence Olivier's son.

But it would be *A Kind of Loving* that turned Alan Bates into a star. By the time the film started shooting, it was already generating a buzz: John Schlesinger, the documentarian from the BBC and director of *Terminus*, was making a fiction film, and he was raiding Richardson's Royal Court of talent. Janni had hired Miriam Brickman, formerly with the Royal Court, as casting director for the film. "They all screamed in horror when Miriam came to work with me," John remembered. Brickman brought in not only Alan Bates but also June Ritchie, a strikingly lovely young actress from Manchester, straight out of drama school. *A Kind of Loving* was Ritchie's first part in a major film.

"I remember when June Ritchie came in for a test and I turned her down," John said. "She'd been to the dentist and her face was still puffy. I thought she looked too fat." He then tested Barbara Ferris but was drawn back to Ritchie who, on second glance, was exactly the kind of peaches-and-cream English girl he wanted: beautiful but unaffected, appealing but unfamiliar. He knew the two lead roles, Vic and Ingrid, had to be filled by unknowns; audiences needed fresh faces onto whom they could project their dreams and illusions.

A Kind of Loving is the story of Vic Brown, an ordinary working-class chap making his way through life, still living at home with his parents, working as a draughtsman at a factory. It is not an unpleasant life; what sets the film apart from the rest of the New Wave is that Vic is not rebelling against anything. He is not Colin Smith in Richardson's *The Loneliness of the Long Distance Runner*, nor does he have the upwardly mobile aspirations of Joe Lampton in *Room at the Top*. There is a vague longing to move away, a sense of wonder about the possibilities of his future, but his family life is not unhappy and Vic feels no resentment about his station or his community. Indeed, Schlesinger would say he wanted to make a break from the unrelievedly drab and gritty atmosphere of other New Wave films; northern life, he insisted, was not always so uniformly dreary – an impression given by London-based filmmakers making supposedly realistic films. John, on the other hand, insisted on a clean and modern factory for Vic and Ingrid's workplace, offsetting the one in *Saturday Night and Sunday Morning*. He also gave Vic's sister Christine, a bright, modern flat, and a happy marriage.

The major anomaly of *A Kind of Loving*, however, is that its story rises not from character or setting in the way the other films had – angry young men reacting against a society that oppressed them – but rather from a *situation*. Alexander Walker described this as the film's "documentary predicament," and it was handled by Schlesinger with skills he'd acquired from "swiftly annotated news reportage." It is true that the story hinges on the consequences of Vic's desire to get Ingrid into bed – which he manages to do in a wonderfully wrought, terribly pathetic scene – only to find out, a few weeks after he's dumped her, that she is pregnant. They marry, they fight, they separate, and finally they reconcile, with the unstated understanding that they have no other choice, that "a kind of loving" might be better than none.

It was a tenet John believed himself, that survival was often the best one could achieve. *A Kind of Loving* is not a hopeful film; it is about making the best of what you've got. It is filled with brilliant little moments of heartbreaking honesty. Sitting in a café as Ingrid blathers on nonsensically, Vic looks around and sees his past, his future, and what might have been: laughing mates sharing a few pints, a silent staring older couple, and a pair of lovers, gazing into each other's eyes as they experience what Vic (and Ingrid) will never know: true love. When they marry in a drab Register Office ceremony, the lack of joy, the sense of lost opportunity, the misery of squandered futures, is unbearably palpable. Both Bates and Ritchie are astonishing; their subtle expressions and simple gestures convey all of the disappointment and regret their characters feel yet do not show. If Janni had any lingering reservations about John being able to work with actors, they disappeared after seeing the performances he pulled from his two stars.

It would become Schlesinger's particular talent, this exploration of human relationships. He was equally fascinated with the other interactions in the film as well: Vic and his parents, Vic and his sister, and, most particularly, Vic and his mother-in-law, played superbly by Thora Hird. In her cat's-eye glasses and obsessive television watching, she personifies the film's theme of faded dreams. It is clear Mrs. Rockwell once had ambitions of grandeur; failing them herself, she had hoped she might live them out through her daughter. But Vic has ruined all of that. He is an intruder in her house after he marries Ingrid and moves in. She won't even give him his own key.

In perhaps the film's most famous moment, Vic comes home drunk and is sick all over the carpet. His mother-in-law witnesses his degradation; her face, in a tightly framed close-up, reveals all of her loathing and disgust for this man who has destroyed her daughter's (and her own) life. John saw the moment as Vic's rebellion against his mother-in-law's tyranny; it can equally be seen as the moment Mrs. Rockwell is proven right in her opinion of her son-in-law.

"I remember Thora did that scene and she did it brilliantly," Alan Bates said. "But John said, 'Again,' and she was quite surprised. She said, 'One-take-Thora, that's me. I don't do more than one.' But John insisted. I think he wanted to rile her a bit."

In fact, he wanted to rile her a great deal. Alan Bennett recalled John telling him the story of that scene, how he "called for more sick – probably Crosse and Blackwell's scotch broth – and even stirred it himself." To Hird's revulsion, John had Bates get sick not once but twice, leaving her still with only one line in response: "You filthy disgusting pig." She would have to improvize, John told her, since he was intent on extending the scene.

"Now this was not a technique Thora had ever had any occasion to acquire," said Bennett, who was a friend of the actress. "Her job was to say the words, not make them up. However, she did her best. Having a text, 'You filthy disgusting pig,' she proceeded to play variations on it. 'You pig.' 'You're filthy. Disgusting.' Thora thought that would be all but John kept the cameras rolling. She said the magic phrase no less than eleven times, with all her frustration at not being able to think of anything better feeding into the anger she was supposed to feel as the character. And it's a wonderful scene."

Most critics, looking back on the film, have offered a curious appreciation for its "objectivity." Praising Schlesinger's documentary style of filmmaking, these critics have insisted that the film provides balance between the two main characters, keeping audiences from "choosing sides." I'm not sure what film they saw, for in *A Kind of Loving* it's clear right from the start whose eyes we're looking through. This is Vic's film; Waterhouse and Hall wrote their script from his perspective, and John directed it from his perspective. We are expected to feel Vic's entrapment, not Ingrid's despair. We follow Vic on the pub crawl; we don't stay home to listen to Ingrid pour out her grief to her mother. We are supposed to see Mrs. Rockwell as a meddlesome, domineering old harridan, not as a mother hen ferociously protecting her young.

Looking back on the film years later, John would comment on a changing morality that would tell Vic, "Leave her, for God's sake. Give yourself a chance." But what might that new morality say to Ingrid? *Kick the bum out?* He'd cajoled her into having sex with him, after all, then dumped her. Once they were married, he came home drunk and tried to force her into the bedroom: who should leave *whom* here? But John never got around to seeing the film from Ingrid's perspective; in fact, he was hardened against it, especially after Penelope Gilliatt wrote a scathing review of the film in the *Observer*. Schlesinger's picture might have been worthwhile, Gilliatt wrote, if it had owned up to "the misogyny that has been simmering under the surface of half the interesting plays and films in England since 1956."

Those were fighting words, and John never forgot them. He would have a long and tempestuous relationship with Gilliatt, who that year would marry one of the chief architects of New Wave misogyny, John Osborne. Yet she was correct that, in most of what had been produced so far, women were seen as obstacles to freedom, the ball-and-chain around the legs of male protagonists. Even more than that, they were, in the words of

Samantha Lay, "the social agents of consumerism" – the very devil that Free Cinema had been established to oppose.

In her review of *A Kind of Loving*, Gilliatt wasn't far off the mark in calling the female characters "monstrous"; even Ingrid, with her insipid chitchat and shopping sprees. That does not, however, negate the film's power nor its beauty. It is credit to Bates' performance, Schlesinger's direction, and the screenplay of Waterhouse and Hall that, despite Vic's loutish behaviour, we do sympathize with him. We do indeed care about him and hope he finds a degree of happiness at film's end. He is not an uncaring man, just an immature one: in the final scene with his sister, when she upbraids him for his lack of duty, we see a glimmering of the man he might become, a flickering of the soul within. It is the surest sign that we are watching a John Schlesinger film.

The other clue that it's Schlesinger we're watching is, of course, the number of hot buttons being pushed. "Is it true, John," I asked him, concerning a rumor that had held currency, "that John Trevelyan, the British censor, was a voyeur, and so you'd get him to approve certain scenes by inviting him onto the set and letting him watch you film them, up close and personal?"

The question provided an opportunity for one of his rare smiles, stretching slowly across his gaunt face, revealing his teeth.

A Kind of Loving did indeed raise some hackles for the censor. The films of the past few years had been constantly pushing the envelope, and Schlesinger's picture had gone a few steps further. "The censor asked for 30 cuts," John remembered for his diary. Considered especially objectionable was the scene where Vic goes into a chemist shop to buy condoms, which made even some of the crew anxious: "It had never been done before," John said, "never ever, and there were people on the set who said I was ruining a beautiful film by including such a filthy scene." In his diary he ranted about "the fucking idiots . . . When is the cinema going to grow up?"

Also rousing Trevelyan's concerns was a book of naked pin-ups that Vic shows first to his mates, and then to Ingrid in an attempt to get her aroused. "We argued greatly with Trevelyan that it was a question of how things were done," John said. "His argument back was that if he allowed it in the film, it would open the floodgates and allow anyone to cash in. Fortunately we won the battle. Now that all seems a dim and old-fashioned memory."

None of the cuts were made – thankfully, because the chemist-shop scene, especially, is amusing and poignant, with Vic emerging too embarrassed to have bought the condoms from the female clerk. (Of course, it was also an important plot point, in that his failure to use protection leads to Ingrid's pregnancy.) Whether they staved off the censor through John's skills of persuasion or through a shrewd invitation to Trevelyan to watch the filming of June Ritchie disrobing for the cameras, we may never fully know. Trevelyan, who presided over a period of great liberalization, reforming a system that had become, by 1960, so restrictive as to be impractical, would recall it took "courage" for his office to pass the film. Yet *A Kind of Loving*, Trevelyan said, "was undoubtedly sincere and a film which would be helpful to many young people."

Unlike many British films of the period, which were snipped, cut, or outright rejected, *A Kind of Loving* went out as made. It was only censored in Australia, which received the picture in September. "Bloody" was excised whenever it was heard; "Oh, stuff security" became simply "Oh, security"; and the shot of Vic and Ingrid in bed, asking whether it's too dangerous to have sex while she's pregnant, was eliminated.

Making his first dramatic picture had been, overall, a happy experience. John had especially enjoyed scouting out actual locations in Manchester and nearby towns, and attending a Saturday night dance at a local hall in Oldham, with the whole cast and crew, even the cameramen. Like a true "New Wave" filmmaker, Schlesinger cast local residents in small parts; something of a place was "rubbed off," he believed, on people "who belonged to the setting." The camera picks this up, notably in the wedding scene that opens the picture. John instructed his extras to say what they would have said had they been at a real wedding. Little snippets of their conversation, from the mouths of wonderfully eccentric real-life characters, are heard on the soundtrack as the titles are superimposed onto the scene, greatly assisting the authenticity Schlesinger wanted to capture.

Location work was rewarding, but John was equally at home working in a studio. Much of what he had to say about filming on location reads now as simply lip service to the New Wave credo that deemed studio work artificial and limiting. Even as early as 1963 he was taking issue with that way of thinking. "I disagree with those who say it is impossible to reproduce something realistically in a studio," he said, pointing out that a cramped suburban flat posed its own severe limitations. It was a direct rebuke to Richardson, whose antipathy to studios was widely known and whose films (at that point) had nearly all been shot on location and inside actual houses.

There were times during the filming of *A Kind of Loving* that John felt a part of a dream: this was, after all, a major motion picture, and he – the boy with the 9.5 mm camera, the director of the Kintbury Follies – was at its helm. His usual moments of despair and self-doubt cropped up from time to time, but mostly he enjoyed himself. The adage that a happy experience making a film meant disaster (and vice versa) would not become true for Schlesinger for another several years.

John enjoyed good relations with his crew, working well with cameraman Denys Coops, eliciting some excellent photography that was appropriately straightforward and conservative to match the story. He also liked the writers, Hall and Waterhouse, though, since the script had been largely prepared by the time John arrived on the scene, he did not have much input into the basic structure of the screenplay. If he had, he mused, he would have started it at an earlier point in the novel to give more history to Vic's character.

The shoot also hammered out what would become John's working relationship with Janni. As producer, Jo was never far away from the set. Ensconced one day in the sound van listening to John filming a scene between Bates and Ritchie, Janni kept poking his head out to cry, in his Italian accent, "It's a too slow! Too slow!" He had no monitor, just a hookup for sound; he could hear the dialogue but not see the action.

Finally, John had enough. "Getta your arse outta here and then maybe you'll unnerstanna the pacing!" he shouted back at him, mocking his accent. And when Janni did emerge to watch the actual shoot, he agreed John was doing it right.

Janni's habit of "advising" his director and writers – some might call it meddling – was an example to John: "Jo was absolutely insistent on long, detailed, sometimes exhausting re-examinations of the script, quite ruthless in fact. He'd be ready to cut the whole leg off when there was only something wrong with the knee." Still, John came to value this kind of collaboration: "It was clear why we all cared so much. One reason: we wanted to make a good picture."

Interference from producers would become a bane of John Schlesinger's life, but not with Jo Janni. He could meddle with the script, call out "too slow" from the sound van, question why John was shooting from a specific angle, but Schlesinger — though he'd battle with him, sometimes fiercely — tolerated his intrusion. "We were partners," John said simply. "We were making the film together."

Later, he came to realize just how special a gift Janni had given him. Jo protected him from any financial worries, kept him insulated from any concern that might distract from his making the best film he could. It was a situation John took for granted in his early career — wasn't this how all films were made? — but one which became an increasingly rare experience in his later years.

"Jo made deviousness a fine art," John said. "He managed to conceal a growing over-budget from the backers as long as possible so their complaints came too late to prevent us from completing the shoot. It was wonderful to have that sort of support."

In 1961, money was simply not an issue. "I made *A Kind of Loving* when you could be happy to be paid £4,000 to make a picture," John said years later. "And you could make it for £180,000 and still get eleven weeks to shoot it, *and* make the money back in our own country. That's how I started. The funding came from a British company, with no reliance on American money at all."

How times would change. *A Kind of Loving*, released in April 1962, made back its cost three times over; £500,000 qualified as a gigantic hit in those days. It was the sixth most popular film that year in Britain, and nearly all of its gross was British.

On its release, many of the critics took a snide approach to the film, dismissing it as a crass attempt by Anglo Amalgamated to cash in on the New Wave. Indeed, there was a developing backlash against gritty "kitchen-sink" drama. Gilliatt, quite apart from her accusation of misogyny, offered her famous quip that *A Kind of Loving* "goes out on a limb that is already creaking with other people's weight." *The Times*, meanwhile, called the film "impersonal"; Dilys Powell, memories of *Black Legend* apparently long forgotten, found it "glum and minatory."

But then the picture was discovered by writers for the magazines and film journals who, contrary to their newspaper colleagues, saw in *A Kind of Loving* something different, a little twist that set it apart from the rest. Gordon Gow called it a "remarkable film about unremarkable people"; Philip Hartung wrote that Schlesinger departed from the "angry young man school" by tempering his story with "warmth and humor."

A Kind of Loving was nominated for Best Picture by the British Film Academy; it lost to *Lawrence of Arabia*, but the nomination – a nod to the director, not the producer, as in the United States – was rewarding enough on its own. After all, it was given to John for his very first dramatic outing, an unusual recognition.

The film opened in New York on 2 October. Although it would receive only a very limited distribution in the States, John did a swing through New York to promote it. It was the first time he'd been back in America since his unhappy tour with OUDS twelve years earlier. At lunch at Sardi's with the *New York Post*'s Irene Thirer, John said he had no desire to "go Hollywood" or make "big" pictures: he was happy, he insisted, with "medium-priced" budgets and making small, intimate pictures.

Bosley Crowther of the *New York Times* lent his observation that *A Kind of Loving* was "a kind of *Saturday Night and Sunday Morning* only not so vigorous and harsh." Indeed, the film's lack of polemics is what ultimately sets it apart from other New Wave films, and why, even with its archaic sexism, it holds up better than so many other films of the period.

"Ours is a gentler film," John said. "It's about love in a general sense. It had no particular political axe to grind. I think it's a film about human difficulties and the illusions of love. It is a film about compromise, which is what many of my films are about."

"But what are the limits to compromise?" I asked him, on a good day, when the sun was shining and he'd been able (and willing) to offer a few sentences to those around him. "When does it become simply giving away too much?"

His response was swift. "That's what's interesting," he said.

Does Vic give away too much? Does Ingrid? Does Joe Buck? Daniel Hirsh? Faye Greener? Guy Burgess? Madame Sousatzka?

That's what makes John Schlesinger's films interesting.

Seven

1962–1964

"What's half a loaf?"

"**J**ulie's coming by for lunch, John," Maureen told him. Something flickered in Schlesinger's eyes, but then it was gone. The past couple of weeks hadn't been good for him. He'd been in hospital again, having aspirated while eating. The experience frightened him badly, and when he returned home he was even more silent than usual. Maureen felt he was depressed.

"The stroke affected his left side," she said. "It shouldn't affect his speech."

"So he's *choosing* not to speak then," I ventured.

"Yes." She reached over and took John's hand. "When he feels motivated enough to say something again, he will. Won't you, John?"

A visit from Julie Christie, everyone hoped, would do the trick. Julie: John's darling. Of all his actors, Julie was the one who remained most special, most precious to him. It had been months since he'd seen her last; she'd been in London but was now back in California, living in Ojai. She was making this trip into the desert specifically to see him.

We had a couple of hours before she arrived, so we popped in the DVD of *Billy Liar*. And there it was, one of the greatest and most poetic star entrances in cinema history: Julie Christie walking down a dreary provincial street, backed up by a mod, ultra-cool beat composed by Richard Rodney Bennett, swinging her purse, dodging traffic, checking out her reflection in shop windows, radiating from her every pore a sense of *joie de vivre*.

"How soft in silks our Julie goes," the *Observer* would rhapsodize, looking back on Christie's jaunt into stardom. "Methinks we hear the liquefaction of her clothes." Indeed, she didn't just walk down that street, the *Observer* said, she *floated*: "She didn't just ooze happy self-confidence, she flaunted it unselfconsciously. She was sexually free, emotionally free, carefree."

Billy Liar was a black-and-white film, but in memory that scene, at least Julie herself, is in Technicolor – the golden sun in her auburn hair, the rosiness to her cheeks, the redness of her lips – all set against the stark grays of the background. If the Sixties didn't produce transcendent movie stars in quite the numbers previous decades had done, it didn't matter: we got Julie Christie.

"It had nothing to do with acting," she would say, looking back. "There was a certain charisma between my face and the screen. You can't plan for it. It's something magic that happens with certain people who become film stars."

She arrived at John's house in a kerchief and wearing no makeup. Out on the terrace, she sat with John, chatting about the drive, about the boutiques she'd stopped at, about London, about Alan Bates and Terence Stamp. John said not a word. He didn't even lift his eyes to look at her, keeping them cast down into his lap.

I told her about John's biography.

"Well, I remember nothing," she said immediately. "You shouldn't even bother trying to interview me. I'd be of no help to you at all. Isn't that right, John? Isn't it true I have no memory?"

He began rubbing the side of his head with his hand. It was an indication he was tired, Maureen said, and she came to wheel him in for a nap.

"Goodbye, John," Julie said. "Sleep well."

When he was gone, she started to cry.

"What I remember," Julie said, looking up fiercely, "is a man of great humor. He was irreverent. He made me laugh. He loved shocking people."

And she proceeded to recall, despite her protestations, a great deal about working with John, about being part of his family for 40 years. She even perused a Schlesinger filmography, circling names of cast and crew she remembered, sharing memories of working with them.

"I just love him," she said, when it was time to leave. "Always have."

And then she was gone, walking off through the garden — deliberately now, slower, not the bouncy walk we'd seen in the film. But, as ever, transcendent.

Tom Courtenay was being bombarded by crumpled balls of paper. It was the prison scene in *Billy Liar*, where Billy imagines himself a political prisoner, typing up his manifesto, ripping page after page out of his typewriter, crumpling them up and throwing them onto the floor. "John called 'cut,'" Courtenay remembered, "and suddenly the entire crew, egged on by our esteemed director, was throwing wads of paper at me."

John was having a ball. "He was never one who said, 'You have to suffer for your art,'" Courtenay said. "He wanted to have a good time making pictures."

Another time, for the scene where Billy fantasizes a shooting spree, John arranged to have the prop man drop a dead duck down from the rafters. "He was like that," Courtenay said. "You know, there was this great contrast in John. On the one hand, he liked culture, great music, theater, opera, things that were fine – but he also liked a little vulgarity. He loved nothing better than startling the whole crew with some outrageous prank."

It was a happy period. Nat Cohen had given John and Jo Janni practically a blank check with *Billy Liar*. The profits from *A Kind of Loving* were still rolling in, and the film won the Golden Bear at the Berlin Film Festival in February. Riding high, John was enthused over his larger budget – £230,000 – which would be necessary if he was going to pull off making Billy's fantasies look real. Early on, he and Janni had decided that the film would take a different route than the play, which didn't show the fantasies but simply allowed Billy to act them out on stage. Given the nature of cinema, however, John saw the tremendous possibilities of actually bringing the imaginary kingdom of Ambrosia to life, and in CinemaScope, to boot!

It was an approach initially opposed by Courtenay, who wanted to play the role exactly as he had done it in the theater.

"But of course John saw how to do it for film," Courtenay said, "and he was exactly right."

By removing the stark, grim realism of the play, both producer and director knew they were venturing away from a successful formula, but at least they'd be embarking on a limb that, if it were to creak, would only be from their own weight. All the usual trappings of a social realist film are there: urban north atmosphere, a satire of the British working classes, and a seemingly angry young man who rebels against his situation. But Billy Fisher is a rebel only in his dreams. Like Vic Brown, Billy's rebellion is not about his social status; he is not Joe Lampton, trying to climb out of his class. Rather, Billy's struggle is more universal: it is about compromising one's ideals in exchange for security. Billy's misery is due less to his social class than to choices he himself has made: living with his parents instead of moving out on his own, leading on two girls at the same time, daydreaming and messing up on the job. In *Billy Liar*, as in all his films, Schlesinger was less interested in the social realism than in the human story found within the setting.

In this way, the film has a much greater resemblance to Keith Waterhouse's novel than to Lindsay Anderson's stage production. Comedy is much more frequent in the film than in the play, and its explicit fantasies turn *Billy Liar* into an authentically cinematic piece with little of the stagebound residuum that has marred other stage-to-film properties. Wisely, John eschewed the dissolves or other gimmicks traditionally employed to indicate the onset of a "dream sequence." Instead, the fantasy is layered straight onto the reality as Billy's flights of imaginations arise out of real situations, thus preserving a very realist look for the film. John had in fact been quite critical of the gimmickry in Richardson's

A Taste of Honey, and found Alain Resnais' *L'Année Dernière à Marienbad* boring.

Willis Hall once again worked with Keith Waterhouse in adapting the script. The action takes place in a single day. Billy Fisher, an undertaker's clerk, awakes one morning in his parents' house in a northern provincial town. He tells his parents and grandmother that he's been offered a job in London; he's received what's probably a standard form letter of encouragement from the comedian Danny Boon, to whom Billy had sent some material. His parents are skeptical and discouraging, and when Billy tries to resign his job, his boss points out that he's aware Billy had failed to post some calendars and then pocketed the money he'd been given. He's not going to be able to leave until he pays that back. At a dance that evening, the two girls Billy's been stringing along come to blows, and Billy takes off with Liz, his true love, a free-spirited girl who convinces him to escape to London with her. But then Billy's grandmother dies (John would recall in his diary that he "exorcized the experience" of watching his beloved Grandma Schlesinger die by recreating it in *Billy Liar*) which triggers a reaction of fear and guilt. Though Billy manages to get on the train with Liz, he finds an excuse to get off, and deliberately misses his chance for freedom.

Not much of a story. But what makes it fascinating are Billy's daydreams. In some ways, he has already escaped his life: he has created the imaginary world of Ambrosia, where he rules as a benevolent dictator. We see Billy marching with his army, the crowds cheering him, a beaming Liz at his side as first lady of the land. Sometimes the stimulus for the fantasy provokes less exhilarating images: the prison scene, for example, or when he imagines himself not as a leader but as an ordinary foot soldier. Billy's deliriums sometimes also turn violent, as when he guns down his family at the breakfast table after they've thrown cold water on his plans. In a brilliantly funny scene, he imagines barging into his boss's office and telling him off in grand style, only to have his boss in real time show up behind him; Billy has to cover his grandstanding with a sudden coughing fit.

John assembled a fantastic cast: Wilfred Pickles and Mona Washbourne are terrific as Billy's parents; Helen Fraser, straight off her small comic turn in *A Kind of Loving* as Ingrid's talkative friend, is letter-perfect as one of Billy's grasping girlfriends. Leonard Rossiter, then best known for the television programme *Z Cars*, was cast as funeral director Shadrack; he'd go on to several memorable comic film roles, including Kubrick's *2001* and *Barry Lyndon*. The ancient Councillor Duxbury was played by 85-year-old Finlay Currie, a veteran of more than 100 films but perhaps most famous as Magwitch in David Lean's *Great Expectations*.

For the grandmother, John had to convince Ethel Griffies, who'd originated the part on stage, to return to England from Hollywood, where she'd gone to make Hitchcock's *The Birds*. She is marvelous as the cantankerous old lady, whose death allows some real feeling to emerge from Billy but also plays a part in keeping him stuck in his life.

For Liz, John tested several girls, including one he remembered from seeing in a play at the Central School of Speech and Drama while he was there making "The Class." This was Julie Christie. John arranged a series of three screen tests for her. The tests made her seem "cold," he thought, but the real reason he decided against her, later stories to the contrary, was because he wanted Topsy Jane, who had played opposite Courtenay in *The Loneliness of the Long Distance Runner*. Both John and Janni thought a continuity between the two films would help box office. In true iconic movie fashion, however, Topsy Jane got sick after a few weeks of shooting and needed to be replaced. John was immediately on the phone to Christie.

"It was such a wonderful part," she told me. "I was thrilled to get it because I wanted so very much to be a part of that exciting period in British film." She was terribly inexperienced; her major credit at that point was as the android in the BBC science-fiction serial *A for Andromeda*. "Of course, John didn't think much of me as an actress then, and he made sure he told me so. I wasn't his first choice. I knew I had a lot to prove."

It was his way of keeping her on her toes. Schlesinger would behave similarly with many of his actors, deliberately with-holding praise so they didn't become complacent: Jon Voight, William Atherton, Lisa Eichhorn. But prove herself Christie certainly did: Liz is the soul of the film. Without her, Billy's dreams would be merely pathetic; but because she loves Billy, we do, too. The glimpse we have of Liz as the train pulls away, with Billy making a great show of pretending to catch it, is priceless: on her face we see her determination but also, significantly, her compassion. To Billy she offers one last wistful smile as she vanishes into the dark.

Liz's ambition to leave behind her roots has not turned her into an "angry young woman." Rather, she is enthused by life's possibilities. She represented a new kind of youth, rebellious still, but without the rancor that had marked characters like Joe Lampton and Jimmy Porter. Liz was a harbinger of the young people who would soon transform London from its gray Fifties façade into the heartbeat of a swinging revolution, who realized that in their own hands they held the power to change society.

Indeed, even in her small town, Liz has already broken convention: she is not a virgin, and feels no shame about the fact. The original dialogue had her telling Billy that she was not "virgo intacta," but the censor switched the line to "You know there have been others, don't you?" – the meaning still clear, and the poetry of the scene perhaps even enhanced. In claiming her sexual power, Liz goes a long way toward exonerating Schlesinger of Gilliatt's charge of misogyny. "Do you remember what you asked me to do and I said, 'Another night'?" Liz asks Billy. She smiles. "Well, it's another night." It is Liz who has the courage to defy the rules, to break out, to escape.

Unlike with *A Kind of Loving*, John was intimately involved with the script of *Billy Liar*; early drafts are filled with his handwritten notes and rewrites. As originally planned, it is Billy who cajoles Liz into going to London, not the other way around. She agrees, on one condition: "I just want a wedding ring." In the original script, that demand was intended to provide the opportunity for Billy's fear of commitment to show itself. It's implied that Billy will go on to London alone, and Liz says she'll settle for "postcards" instead of a ring.

John clearly saw the need for a rewrite. He crossed out the "wedding ring" line, recognizing this as out of character for Liz. It also placed a false dilemma onto Billy, making it seem as if the idea of marriage and commitment was what kept him from going to London when, of course, it was far more than that. It was his fear of taking *any* leap in life, any change. The ending was rewritten to make Liz the instigator for change, with a wedding ring the furthest thing from her thoughts. Billy and Liz board the train together, and then John and the writers came up with the whole elaborate ruse of Billy rushing off to buy milk. The original line had Liz saying, "It doesn't matter" when Billy asks her if she wants any; John changed it to read, "Don't really want any", a subtle change, but one that underlines her determination to stay on the train and go to London. We get a clue that she's going to be okay on her own by the enjoyment she gets from flirting with a group of traveling musicians. Billy, meanwhile, in a scene perfectly executed by Courtenay, stands at the milk machine counting in his head until he hears the train begin to chug away. That last frantic jog back onto the platform is one of the greatest exhibitions of pathos ever captured in the cinema.

Again, with *Billy Liar* John sought some distance from other New Wave films, choosing Bradford for its newly renovated city centre, a deliberate move away from the usual cobbles and mill chimneys. The opening credits establish the setting, a city being torn down and rebuilt. "There was a sense of impending change in Bradford," John said, "which was just what I wanted in the picture." The film was actually shot in several different towns: the famous introduction montage of Julie swinging down the street was compiled from various shoots in Bradford, Manchester and London, where construction along Tottenham Court Road provided a perfect backdrop.

In 1999, the British Film Institute ranked *Billy Liar* seventy-sixth in its list of the one hundred favorite British films, ahead of *Oliver!*, *A Clockwork Orange*, *In Which We Serve*, *Women in Love* and *A Hard Day's Night* – not to mention Schlesinger's own more commercially successful films, *Darling* and *Far from the Madding Crowd*. Today *Billy Liar* has become a latter-day masterpiece: Leslie Halliwell in his influential guide has called it "seminal in acting, theme, direction and permissiveness." In hindsight, *Billy Liar* has become "one of the great movies of the 1960s," according to A.O. Scott in the *New York Times* – "pure ambrosia!"

"The reviews came too late," groaned Tom Courtenay. "Thirty years too late."

Once again, John had to endure the initial sting of the notoriously grudging British newspaper critics, a withering, lifelong assault to which he'd eventually become inured. *The Times* grandly opined that Billy's fantasies were "repetitious," lacking "any real flair and gusto" – an incredulous assessment, no matter how subjectively the reviewer defined terms. Penelope Gilliatt, weighing in once again in the *Observer*, wrote that *Billy Liar* didn't so much look *down* on working class life as look *up* at it "from under a rubbish heap of working-class claptrap." Yet it wasn't working-class life that John was commenting on, but rather *any* kind of prison, working class or middle class, external or internal, that kept someone from pursuing their dreams.

As they had with the first film, magazine critics came to the rescue, but not nearly so unanimously this time. Peter Harcourt wrote that *Billy Liar* proved that the northern industrial film could reveal "the light-hearted as well as the drab," but Elaine Rothschild considered the whole thing "wretchedly" written, directed and edited. When the film opened in America in December, Andrew Sarris judged that John's direction was so wrong "that the accumulation of errors resembles a personal style." Sarris went on to rather famously doubt that fantasy could ever be transferred successfully to the screen because of the fantastic nature of the medium itself: "Fantasy piled upon fantasy," he wrote, "yields only banality."

Indeed, at the end of shooting, neither Schlesinger nor Janni felt the film had come together as well as *A Kind of Loving*. There were great doubts expressed by both of them, sending John especially into one of his familiar spirals of despair. The film's mixed reception and the resulting poor box office – Schlesinger was told by Anglo Amalgamated that the film never made back its cost – simply confirmed his doubts. Even the occasional glowing review – John Coleman in the *New Statesman* called the film magnificent, saying John was now "a creative world away from Reisz or Anderson or Richardson" – failed to lift his spirits.

Who can explain the vagaries of the box office? *Billy Liar* should have been a smash. It is a better picture than *A Kind of Loving*, more self-assured, more daring. It has dark flights of fancy that anticipate *The Day of the Locust* but also contains wonderful bits of humor – Schlesinger's best comedy, in fact, until *Cold Comfort Farm* some 30 years later. It offers a more honest and far more relevant reflection of working-class lives than most other films of the period. And though Billy fails to break free of his life, it also signals real hope: Liz gets away, after all, and even Billy, for all his failure, is not truly unhappy. There is victory on his face as he marches back home, his invisible army behind him. He has found his own way to survive.

Billy Liar was nominated as Best Picture by the British Film Academy; it lost to Tony Richardson's *Tom Jones*. Tom Courtenay and Julie Christie were also nominated.

In later years, like the rest of the world, John would learn to embrace *Billy Liar*. "The film wasn't a commercial success," he admitted, "but I don't think it is because of a 'downbeat' ending. I don't think it is a downbeat ending at all, because Billy stayed with his fantasy. He funked going to London, missed the opportunity with the girl and with life and everything else, but he still had his fantasy and he returned in triumph to his house, marching along with that invisible army. I thought that was wonderful."

What doomed *Billy Liar* at the box office was the times. "Moviegoers are getting a bit bugged by that same scummy old roofscape and the eternal kitchen sink-drome," quipped *Time* magazine after the picture's U.S. premiere. "They sometimes find it hard to believe that things are really all that bad in Merry England."

Indeed, the vogue for social realism had peaked, and although Ken Loach would pick up the torch and carry it with some success into the next decade, he marched pretty much alone. Nearly all of the New Wave directors moved on to new genres: Jack Clayton brilliantly adapted Henry James with *The Innocents*; Tony Richardson's delightful exuberance in *Tom Jones* replaced his youthful rancor; and Karel Reisz pulled out all the stops with *Morgan!* (1966) and *Isadora* (1968), becoming, in the process, "the Cecil B. DeMille of social revolution," according to the *New York Times*. Only Lindsay Anderson would stick to his "ill-tempered artistry," though his *If . . .* (1968) and *O Lucky Man!* (1973) depend far more on the surreal than the real.

Schlesinger, too, had charted new territory: *Billy Liar*, while from the school of realism, defies easy categorization. It is a film about compromise, about dreams, about failure and success. It is serious, it is funny, it is real, it is fantasy. "I'm very proud of it," John would say. "I am pleased to see that after all these years it has endured."

In the months following *Billy Liar*'s release, however, John slid into a dark depression, and the derisive reviews were the least of it. Rather, he was still reeling from a telephone call he'd received on the morning of 18 July, while the film was in final preparation. His sister Susan had been found dead in her flat on Beaufort Street in Chelsea, having taken an overdose of barbiturates the night before. When her flatmate came in to wake her, she found Susan lifeless, a suicide note beside her bed. An inquest at Hammersmith on 24 July 1963, ruled that Susan's death had been "self-administered, while her mind was temporarily disturbed." A friend testified that she knew Susan had been "grieving over the death of a friend."

That friend was the playwright John Whiting, who had died the previous month of cancer. Whiting was perhaps the most important figure in the "new British drama" of the early 1950s, a kind of forerunner in sensibility and impact to the New Wave artists in the cinema. Whiting's *Saint's Day* had been produced at the Arts Theatre and won the top prize in the Arts Council's Festival of Britain play competition; Peter Brook called it "the product of a new and extraordinary theatrical mind." Whiting's biggest success had come when he was commissioned by Peter Hall to write the first new play for the Royal Shakespeare Company, *The Devils*, based on Aldous Huxley's *The Devils of Loudun*. He was in the midst of a career renaissance when he died, working with the RSC and finishing up two screenplays. "The British theatre," wrote *The Times*, "can ill afford to lose the plays he might have written had he lived long enough to achieve his full potential stature."

Schlesinger had known that his sister was involved with Whiting; theirs was a great and passionate romance, "one for the ages," friends said. But Whiting was married, with children, and at his death Susan had been bereft, her place in Whiting's life unacknowledged in all the official grieving.

Susan's career as an actress, inspired by her brother's early experiments, had been just beginning to take shape. Determined not to ride John's coat-tails, she used the stage name Susan Maryott; just a few months before her death, she had played a lead part in the BBC drama, *The Continuity Man*, with her photo featured prominently in the magazine *Stage and Television Today*. For several years, Susan had alternated between television (*Negative Evidence* with Peter Wyngarde and the science-fiction thriller *Target Generation*) and the Royal Shakespeare Company, through which she met Whiting. Most recently she had played Luciana in *The Comedy of Errors* in September 1962.

Susan's death was devastating to the family. John was completely staggered by it; her death would remain a lingering pain for the rest of his life, a wound that never really healed. At a *Billy Liar* release party, less than a month after Susan's death, Tom Courtenay remembered being asked to sing a few songs he'd recently performed on a television programme. "One was about a girl who wasn't coming home again," Courtenay said. "I looked up and saw John had burst into tears. He had to walk out of the room."

In Susan, John saw reflected something of his own life: the heartache, the loneliness, the impossible love affair. He was now 37 years old. Despite numerous enjoyable sexual encounters and the occasional casual boyfriend, he had never known the kind of deeply felt, mutual relationship with another person that Susan had known with Whiting. He wanted it, however, and badly: one man, now in his late seventies, told me how he'd dated John a few times in the late 1950s and sensed how much John wanted a relationship. When the man, an American, left for home, he found waiting at his ship a dozen red roses from John – a romantic goodbye from a man who was craving a little more romance in his life.

By this time, John's brother Roger and sister Wendy had married and started families of their own. John was lonely; his ongoing relationship with Noel Davis, rewarding on many levels, was clearly not sufficient. His loneliness wasn't unusual, of course, for a gay man in the early 1960s; social restrictions limited not only opportunities to meet new people but also hampered efforts at integrating a new lover into one's life. It was difficult to build a relationship when it meant arriving at events in separate cars or maintaining separate homes.

Still, John had only to look around to see plenty of examples of homosexuals in the world of theater and film who had managed to find longterm companions: Binkie Beaumont and John Perry (who'd been John Gielgud's lover first), Gielgud and Paul Anstee, Christopher Isherwood and Don Bachardy, Noël Coward and Graham Payn, Somerset Maugham and Alan Searle, Gore Vidal and Howard Austen. As early as 1958, when he was filming the piece on Benjamin Britten for the BBC, John had recognized Britten's partnership with Peter Pears: "It seemed to me they had made quite the commitment to each other." Such a relationship was exactly what he wanted for himself.

His lack of personal fulfillment spilled over into a generalized ague of regret and impatience. The story of Billy Fisher came to resonate for him. Calling his protagonist both irritating and imaginative, John said: "He lacks the effort to concentrate on anything he really wants to do . . . There seems to me to be so much of all of us in this. It is for me a highly personal theme."

All those years he'd spent between graduation from Oxford and signing with Jo Janni now felt wasteful, as if he'd been simply spinning his wheels. Never mind the valuable lessons or creative license of his BBC years; never mind the laurels of *Terminus*. John saw himself as a director of scripts and actors, and as such, he had a lot of catching up to do. He considered that he was a good five to ten years behind where he *should* be in his career; had he been more focused, more determined, less sidetracked by acting – or by agonizing over Alan Cooke – he felt he would have had this kind of success a lot earlier.

It seems an unfair assessment; as usual, John was being too hard on himself. True, if he hadn't taken his detour into acting, he might have produced a *Sunday in the Park* in 1951 instead of 1956. Maybe he would have secured a job at the BBC earlier, or gotten hired by Ealing or Rank, or gone to Hollywood. Yet none of those scenarios would necessarily have resulted in the kind of success he was enjoying by the mid-Sixties, which not even the disappointing returns of *Billy Liar* could affect. The BBC didn't start making the kind of short films John specialized in until the later part of the Fifties; had he gone to Ealing or Rank, he would have been stuck making comedies or actioners at a time when the British film industry was becalmed in the doldrums; and a try at Hollywood may well have turned out not much differently than it had for Alan Cooke, who wound up being just one more cog in a highly competitive entertainment machine.

No, John Schlesinger's breakout came at the only moment it could have occurred, with all forces precisely converging: a renewed energy in the British cinema, a moviegoing public ready for new experiences and visions, a shift in the national social and political consciousness, and the heightening of his own reputation, built up through his years at the BBC. Fretting over time lost was, however, an integral part of his nature, and no doubt his own personal grief and disappointments colored much of his perspective in these years.

It was around this time that Roger Schlesinger remembered John speculating about marrying Janet Suzman, a member of the Royal Shakespeare Company. He would escort her to a number of parties; it was the expected protocol. "We all lived double lives," recalled John's friend Larry Kramer, later the playwright and AIDS activist who was then working as the London assistant to the head of production at Columbia. "I duly brought a young woman with me for Monday-night executive screenings."

With the spotlight now suddenly turned toward him, John felt obliged, for the first time in his career, to resort to such subterfuge. But the speculation about Suzman remained just that; watching as Tony Richardson married Vanessa Redgrave in 1962, John could not imagine ever taking such a step himself.

His parents had, of course, figured things out by now. He never officially made an announcement to them, or to his siblings, about being gay, Roger said: "We just came to realize it in due course."

"John never compartmentalized his life," said his friend Stewart Grimshaw, a young man from Scotland who moved in with John in Peel Street after Andrew Raeburn moved out. "At that point, Noel Davis was living in New York and John had nobody consistent in his life. I think he liked the idea of company, so I moved into the top of his house."

One night, Grimshaw recalled, John's sister-in-law ran into John and a group of his gay friends, and was somewhat put off by their irreverent behaviour. Talking with his brother later,

John refused to apologise for them. "These are my friends," he said plainly. "These are the people I live my life with."

"His friends were part of his household, part of his life," Grimshaw said. "I loved being part of a household where people came and went. It was a very open, happy household. I've never been in a house where people talked about so many things."

Eventually, many of John's gay friends became close with his family, and these relationships, especially as they deepened, helped John's parents adjust to their son's sexuality. In fact, Bernard Schlesinger had a great friend of his own, a fellow physician, who helped very much in that regard as well. This friend was also a homosexual, and early on had spotted John's special qualities. When Bernard shared his concerns about his son, his friend told him to stop worrying: someday, he promised, Bernard would be "very proud" of John. "Of course," Roger said, laughing, "we had to tell my father that this great friend of his was actually gay himself. Sometimes one just didn't see these things."

Nearing 40, John was still handsome, with a perennial, cherubic youthfulness, but his hair was nearly gone and he'd let himself get a bit chunky; interviewers routinely described him as "stocky." Still, Larry Kramer found him goodlooking enough, and they began an affair. Ten years younger than John, Kramer was handsome, witty, charismatic, and passionate about film and theater. It's not difficult to see how John may have been smitten: Larry possessed all of the attributes John found irresistible including being unavailable. Kramer's very noncommittal was, in fact, a draw for John, whether he was fully conscious of it or not. Like Alan Cooke, Kramer's unavailability fit a pattern that had come to define John's love life.

That dynamic would be repeated in his relationship with Peter Buckley, another attractive, ambitious American who Kramer described as "an early version of Michael Childers." John met Buckley soon after his affair with Kramer was over and, once again, was mesmerized by his lover, the 26-year-old editor of *Plays and Players* magazine. But this, too, would soon pass, and John, as ever, was left alone.

In September 1963, despite the middling response to *Billy Liar*, John and his stars were greeted like royalty at the Venice Film Festival. Arriving with Julie Christie and Tom Courtenay, John felt for the first time the rush of international celebrity. While Courtenay remembered the Festival being "indifferent" to the film, fans and reviewers were ecstatic at Christie's presence; she had become, quite literally, a star overnight. On the strength of that one saucy walk, David Lean decided to cast her in his epic *Doctor Zhivago*.

John's next project, for the moment, was uncertain. There was talk of him making a film in South Africa to "give colored actors a chance": his idea, tossed around with Janni, was to make "a sad but sharp comedy," featuring the confusion and hypocrisy that ensues when the South African government allows a Japanese delegation to use public transport reserved for whites only. When he was confronted with the boycott of production in South Africa then being led by playwright Arnold Wesker, John insisted it was the wrong approach: "Let's go in," he said, "and teach by example."

Nothing came of the idea, but what was clear was Schlesinger's determination to find something new to do, something challenging, something that wouldn't pigeonhole him as he feared was already starting to happen. Lindsay Anderson's *This Sporting Life,* in many ways the most unsparing of all the British social realism films, had been even less successful at the box office than *Billy Liar.* John wanted to break out of the mold of "angry young director" as quickly as possible; a suggestion to film Stan Barstow's second novel was therefore quickly brushed aside.

One of the stark differences between John and his New Wave contemporaries was that he had come from television, they from the theater. It was part of the unstated snobbery that persisted in some of the criticism of his work; to some, he was still a telly director working with a lowbrow distributor. So it was with enthusiasm, early in 1964, that John accepted an offer from Peter Hall to direct a play for the Royal Shakespeare Company. Not just any play, but an unproduced one-act script by John Whiting called *No Why.* In many ways, it was as a tribute to his sister Susan, who had been a member of the RSC, that John undertook the assignment; it would also hopefully establish him as more than just a director of social realist pictures.

He had remained friendly with Peter Hall since *Mourning Becomes Electra,* expressing an interest in working with the RSC soon after Hall took it over in 1959. The company was devoted not only to Shakespeare but also to modern drama; "only thus," Hall explained, "could we develop the kind of protean actors, alive to the issues of the day, that Shakespeare deserved and that would give his plays contemporary life." It was a radical new concept, designed to compete with the Royal Court Theatre and to counter the looming establishment of a National Theatre under Olivier; as such, the RSC, with homes in both Stratford and at the Aldwych Theatre, London, appealed greatly to John's mind and heart.

"When John started directing movies," remembered Hall, "I felt the logical thing for me to do was to try to get him to direct in the theater." That Schlesinger had no theatrical experience outside university productions caused Hall no worries: "John had a very keen intelligence and a strong visual sense. What more could I want?"

No Why was an experimental play; bringing in a director with fresh ideas seemed right. The experience was nerve-wracking for John, however, who found that directing actors for a live performance carried with it far more risks than film, and surrendering control was always a difficult task for him to manage. He steadied himself by concentrating on Whiting's play, which he admired a great deal: the story of a little boy in his pyjamas who is harangued by his parents in the attic for some unnamed offense. The parents clearly stand for society attempting to punish and control the individual; in the boy John clearly saw himself, an elfin child who didn't follow the rules or adhere to convention.

His cast was topnotch. Tony Church and June Jago as the parents were unsparingly good, and in the role of Max (a "languid mummy-fixated cousin," according to *The Times*), a young man named John Steiner proved exceptional. Tall, blonde, extraordinarily goodlooking, John Steiner captivated John Schlesinger's heart and libido; they were soon lovers.

No Why premiered on 2 July 1964, sandwiched between two other productions, Fernando Arrabal's *Picnic on the Battlefield* and Jean Tardieu's *The Keyhole*, grouped together for a program of one-acts under the collective title "Exhibitions One." In the press there was considerable hoopla about the event: as part of the RSC's policy of presenting new, experimental work, seat prices were reduced to attract younger playgoers. Debates raged about who could be more "avant garde," the RSC or the Royal Court Theatre, with John's status as a movie director attracting much of the attention. Wags asked breathlessly if Julie Christie or Alan Bates might turn up for the premiere, but John's stars let him have the spotlight to himself. And he certainly took his bows in it: *No Why* was the best reviewed of the three plays, "the most satisfactory experience of the evening," according to *The Times*.

The depression of the year before had lifted. John had given himself a major artistic challenge and risen splendidly to the occasion. Even more importantly, he was in love, and with a passion he hadn't felt since Alan Cooke.

"I had coffee yesterday with John Steiner in L.A."

John was in bed. He hadn't been getting up much the past few weeks, his days of physical therapy apparently over. Sometimes he seemed to disassociate from life around him completely, but now, with great effort, he turned his face to look at me.

"I can see why you made a movie about him," I said. "He was very charming. And still very handsome."

In many interviews given over the course of the years, John Schlesinger had said that *Sunday, Bloody Sunday* was his most personal film. In his tape-recorded diary he had insisted at one point, "It's my story, my own bloody Sunday – my affair with a young man." I asked Michael Childers if he knew who that man was. But of course he did; and not only did he know, he had his number. It really *was* as sophisticated as the movie made out.

"His name is John Steiner," Childers said, smiling. "I told

him once, 'You may have gotten the movie, but I got the real estate.'"

John Steiner laughed as he remembered that quip. "Oh, yes, Michael has said it to me several times, and each time he forgets he's said it before. Of course, it was *great* real estate. I remember going up to their house on Rising Glen for a party. David Hockney was there, and Glenda Jackson . . ."

His voice trailed off as he thought back to that night. Glenda had played with Steiner in Peter Brook's *Marat/Sade* (1966), her first starring part; she would also, of course, play the woman at the third end of the *Sunday, Bloody Sunday* triangle – in effect, she was playing John Steiner's lover.

"It must have been quite the rush to have a movie made about you," I said.

Steiner seemed uncomfortable with the observation. "The relationship was what it was," he said, choosing his words. "Whatever may have happened as a result after that, I think it was John's property. Great artists will use whatever happens in their lives with extraordinary results, and that movie was not only a great movie, it was a watershed. In fact, even though *Darling* was more successful, this was in essence John's greatest film. But I must say that I really didn't have anything to do with that at all."

I asked if John had let him know he was doing a script that, at the very least, had sprung from their time together.

"Yes, he did. I knew that the movie reflected something of me in it, but as I say, it really has nothing to do with me. It has everything to do with John's artistry."

"But you were the muse for that artistry."

He smiled. "Yes," he said softly. "I suppose I was."

For two glorious years, in the midst of John's peak in British cinema, John Steiner had been his lover. Whatever the specific differences between real life and movie script, the basic structure was the same: Steiner was involved with a woman at the same time he was involved with John; both knew about the other; and all three accepted the situation with a degree of equanimity and open-mindedness. It was a breakthrough experience for John: as much as he felt passionately about John Steiner, he felt no need to control the situation or possess him in the way he had with Alan Cooke.

Never would he describe this relationship as "tortured" the way he'd described the one with Cooke, even if Steiner ultimately remained as unavailable as any of his former lovers. The difference now was that John was fully engaged in his career; in the past he'd had no footing either personally or professionally. During his time with Steiner, John was being challenged creatively on his most exciting project yet, the original screenplay for *Darling*. So there was a place to channel his emotional energy, an outlet for his passions: he did not feel the need to direct all of it at Steiner.

It was also, significantly, the onset of the sexual revolution, the birth of Swinging London. "I think John was fascinated by that idea, that relationships could be so open," said Steiner. "That was part of the Sixties. No definitions, and I suppose at that time, that was me, too. I had no definitions, no preconceived notions."

"Steiner was quite the serious young actor," John's friend Stewart Grimshaw recalled. "The relationship was very important to John, and to Steiner, too, I suppose. *Sunday, Bloody Sunday* was really pretty faithful to what I saw in that relationship."

They moved with relative ease from flat to flat, John

occasionally taking Steiner to industry functions, showing up with him at parties, and then also understanding when he needed to go off for a night or two with his female lover. "It was terribly sophisticated," John observed for his diary. "Those were the times."

Yet underneath there was a longing for something more, reflected in the stories John's friends and family told me of how he would drive past Steiner's flat to see if his lights were on – an echo of behavior from his Oxford days, when he'd do the same thing with Alan Cooke. For John Steiner was not only who he loved, but in many ways, who he wanted to be: young, handsome, desired. Steiner, just 22 when he met John Schlesinger, was the kind of golden boy John never was, confident, clearheaded, on-track in his career. Born in Cheshire, Steiner had been educated at Gordonstoun before entering the Royal Academy of Dramatic Art. He toured India with the Bristol Old Vic company, playing Fortinbras in *Hamlet* before making his debut in 1963 with the Royal Shakespeare Company in *Edward IV*. Just before *No Why*, Steiner had proven he could handle modern roles as well, playing in David Rudkin's *Afore Night Come*, directed by Clifford Williams.

"It was a very exciting time in the theater, very creative, the best," Steiner remembered. There was the RSC and the Royal Court and the establishment of the National. New genres and formats were being experimented with; London was shedding its dour reputation and beginning to blossom once again as a theatrical hub. "Everyone was finally getting over the war, even though it had been fifteen years earlier. People were beginning to have fun again. It was really an extraordinary explosion."

During his time with Schlesinger, Steiner appeared in *Marat/Sade* on stage, perhaps the most buzzed-about theatrical production of 1964, and would later recreate his part in the film. He also appeared in Christopher Marlowe's *The Jew of Malta* before moving mostly into cinema, taking parts in Stanley Donen's *Bedazzled* and Peter Hall's *Work is a Four-Letter Word*. By this time he was spending considerable time in Rome, where he would eventually move, beginning a long-running career as a character player in Italian crime pictures and spaghetti westerns, starting with *Tepepa* (1968.)

The relationship with John dissolved gradually. In another correlation between life and film, John discovered Steiner's plans to leave London via his answering service, the same way Glenda Jackson discovers Murray Head has left for America. The experience left a tremendous impression on him. "It was a very heavy time, very intense," Stewart Grimshaw remembered. When Steiner left, John felt a void, a wistfulness — not because he ever really expected to change Steiner, to own him or find in him the kind of longtime, committed partnership he so craved, but rather because with Steiner gone, he was forced once again to confront his own loneliness. Steiner had offered a refuge, a chance to believe, if only fleetingly, that he had found some love in his life. After all, he had learned long ago to consider something better than nothing, and so it was.

"When you're at school and want to quit," Daniel says at the end of *Sunday, Bloody Sunday*, "people say you're going to hate being out in the world. Well, I didn't believe them and I was right. When I was a kid, I couldn't wait to be grown up and they said childhood was the best time of my life and it wasn't. Now I want his company and people say, what's half a loaf, you're well shot of him; and I say, I know that, I miss him, that's all. They say he'd never have made me happy and I say, I am happy, apart from missing him."

Words written by Penelope Gilliatt, but they come from John Schlesinger's heart: "All my life I've been looking for someone courageous and resourceful, not like myself, and he's not it." Pause. "But something. We were something."

Eight

1964–1965

"Plenty of room at the top"

Outside the Piccadilly tube stop, three young women in *Austin Powers*-inspired miniskirts and knee-high latex boots were tossing about lots of "groovys" and "smashings" in their speech. One of them wore a gold marijuana leaf around her neck; another had pasted decals of Mick Jagger and Madonna on her purse.

We've come so far that rebels now go *back* in time rather than forward, when the youth culture borrows relics of the past and jumbles them together into a pastiche of expression and attitude. When one of the girls asked me for a light, I couldn't resist asking back, "Have you ever seen *Darling*?"

"*Darling*?" Her eyes lit up. "With Julie Christie?" She seemed pleased at the comparison she presumed I was making. "No, luv, never seen it, but it was *smashing*, I hear. Set the whole of London swingin'."

She was right on that point. Whenever there's talk about "Swinging London," the movie that invariably comes up is John's 1965 smash, the success that took him around the world and transformed him into a director of international stature. *Darling*: "the Sixties in aspic," according to writer Jeffrey Richards, and the worldwide symbol of Swinging London, even though it was made a full two years before the city got into a serious swing.

"*Darling* was definitely an influence on the scene," Twiggy told me. She would know. In the mid-to-late 1960s, Twiggy was the personification of Swinging London, emblazoned in all her pencil-thin glory on the covers of magazines and showing up to brilliant parties in the latest tie-dyed frocks. "Julie Christie in miniskirts, everybody being so free," Twiggy said. "It was kind of revolutionary. You look back now and see what an enormous impact that film had."

In the mid-Sixties, London was transformed. Suddenly there were places to go and be seen, nightspots and galleries and discotheques where one might spot Terence Stamp, Lulu, Manfred Mann, Jean Shrimpton, Mickie Most, Vidal Sassoon, Peter Noone, Marianne Faithfull, footballer George Best, and, if you were very lucky, an odd Beatle or two. John Lennon met Yoko Ono for the first time at the Indica Gallery in Duke Street; at Bazaar in King's Road, fashion maven Mary Quant gathered together trendsetters like photographers David Bailey and designer Terence Conran. In Camden Town, Arnold Wesker opened the Roundhouse, where patrons remembered naked girls walking around as guests watched movies and got stoned on pot. "It was probably the first time in London," one man said, "when strangers broke the ice and said hello to each other."

With the money he made on *Darling*, John invested in Le Carrosse, a hip new restaurant opened by his old friend Geoffrey Sharp in Covent Garden. "We made a point of staying open late at night so that actors, or anyone else, could come in and have dinner at ten," Sharp said. Decorated by the renowned designer David Hicks, Le Carrosse was a move away from the "starchy stiff" eateries of the past – "no tie code or any of that," said Sharp. People came in wearing the trendy garb of Carnaby Street: love beads, kaftans, velvet suits and miniskirts – not unlike those *Austin Powers* girls I encountered outside the Tube station.

A new kind of glamor was found at Le Carrosse. John became a vital part of the city's pulse, with such diverse luminaries as Peter Brook or Peggy Ashcroft or Michael Caine dropping by. In the thick of the scene, too, was the Royal Shakespeare Company, with which John had continued his involvement; articles about RSC productions and their new visions for the theater turned up frequently in the pages of the city's two "avant garde" journals, *IT* and *Oz*. It was a mind-blowing new world, far removed from the grimy urban landscapes of the English north, and John was one of the first to chart it with *Darling*. By 1965, London was aglow with color, its drab browns and grays replaced with neon pink and psychedelic orange.

It was no coincidence that October 1964 marked the end of thirteen years of Tory rule. Change was happening quickly: a new culture bloomed overnight centered on youth, preoccupied with pop music, fashion and sexual freedom. The British youth explosion was always far more relaxed and easygoing than the American one: musicians, actors, models, disc jockeys, producers, and footballers were equal in this new royalty, sharing drinks on the rooftop of the Ad Lib club, posing for tabloid photographs, flashing the peace sign. Articles would appear in *IT* predicting a new economy based on rock music, drugs, and free love. The mindset of Swinging London soon made its way around the world. "For a few years," wrote the historian Shawn Levy, "the most amazing thing in the world was to be British, creative and young."

Sometimes there are accidental segues in life so poetic that they seem predestined. At the end of *Billy Liar*, Julie Christie's character is seen heading on a train south to London. Writing in the *New Yorker*, Brendan Gill offered the hope that in her next film Christie would be found in the capital city, "in a charming flat, wearing exquisite clothes and speaking sentences that parse."

John was, in fact, already well into the first drafts of a script for a film about London's jet-set when Gill wrote those words, but it wasn't by any means a foregone conclusion that Christie would be his star, despite the near-universal orgasm with which the critics had greeted her performance in *Billy Liar*. Nat Cohen made some noise over whether Julie was a big enough name to carry the picture but, in hindsight, no one else could have played Diana Scott, whose story spun John's career – and indeed all of British filmmaking – into a giddy new game, away from the sordid realism of the north and toward the glittery, sophisticated satire of London. "With Julie Christie," Alexander Walker observed, "British cinema caught the train south."

Even before *Billy Liar* was completed, John had begun work with the novelist Frederic Raphael on the story. In December

1962, he told a reporter from the *Observer* that "if we're to give a picture of Britain today, it's just as important to make realistic films about the rich as about the poor." The idea was suggested by radio journalist Godfrey Winn, who had played himself in the "Housewives Choice" opening of *Billy Liar*. Winn had recounted for John a scandal that was currently making waves in London: the mistress of a syndicate of showbiz and corporate men, kept in a swank Park Lane flat, had finally thrown herself from the balcony, tired of the sordid state of her life. John's penchant for the macabre and ghoulish was aroused. "I thought this was an interesting, nice-nasty subject," he would remember. One can almost hear him rubbing his hands together in glee.

Janni paid Winn for a ten-page synopsis, but Winn wasn't a screenwriter; they were soon knocking on Frederic Raphael's door to shape the idea into something filmable. They both knew Raphael had a reputation for prickliness – in his diary John would call him "an intellectual snob" – but they also knew he was brilliant at witty, sparkling dialogue: indeed, those very "sentences that parse."

The first thing Raphael did was completely toss out all of Winn's ideas, telling John he was "perfectly capable of writing something totally out of his imagination." John would always wish they'd kept the original story, but after the Profumo Affair reached a crisis point in June 1963, it seemed in bad taste: Secretary of State for War John Profumo had confessed to misleading the House of Commons when he denied an "improper" relationship with showgirl Christine Keeler. Keeler would also be revealed to have been carrying on with Yevgeny Ivanov, an attaché at the Soviet Embassy, and possibly others – a "syndicate" of men, some might have called it. Suddenly a script that had a Keeler-like character kill herself (not that Keeler ever did) seemed too close to home, and both John and Jo Janni told Raphael to switch gears.

Where to go next? Janni suggested they visit a woman he knew; just *how* he knew her was never made clear. It was a significant shift: in the original idea, the woman is a victim; in the new concept, based on Janni's friend (called only "Jennifer" in memos and early drafts) the woman is very much in charge of her own life. She is witty, ironic, extremely fashion conscious, and highly ambitious, with numerous lovers and gay male pals – very modern, really, very *Sex in the City*. The story moved from tragedy to ironic comedy; by early 1964, Raphael was cautioning that they ran the risk of turning the film into a "tuppenny-ha'penny dolce vita", a reference to Fellini's gigantic hit of 1960, *La Dolce Vita*, to which *Darling* would inevitably be compared.

Writing the script was "a long slow process," John wrote. It was the first time since *The Starfish* that he had been involved in creating an original screenplay. "It is difficult to start from scratch; we are so unused to doing so. It seems an automatic reflex action to start with someone else's basic story." He found himself in a peculiar situation for a British filmmaker, he said: "Practically every film that is made in Britain is a borrowed idea, based on something that has been successful in another medium. We rarely seem able to conceive an idea in cinematic terms; and this is a depressing thought."

Working with Raphael, John observed, was like a tennis match, with both of them straining to return each other's ideas successfully. Raphael did not find the process enjoyable; he'd eventually describe it to a reporter from the *Daily Mail* as "two years, five scripts, and countless bitter moments."

Originally the character, already named Diana in early drafts, was to end up with a wealthy older husband named Timothy, who was running as a Labour candidate for Parliament. Raphael's notes on the character suggest he may have been a more interesting figure than the Italian prince Diana eventually landed in the film. "Timothy is not a fool," Raphael wrote, "but he is a weak, even sentimental man; his Socialism springs from a sense of guilt . . . Though he looks ludicrous wooing Diana – most people look ludicrous wooing someone who doesn't want him – he is not a silly man. He is a man who has, through sexual passion and a kind of weakness induced by wealth, come to act in a silly way."

Raphael added that it was vital they find "an actor of real stature to convey the inner, silent scream for help which this civilized, elegant, pampered man is putting out." Early talk was focused on Maximilian Schell, but by May 1964 they had to "rethink the whole of the Timothy character," as "Jennifer," in the process of divorcing her husband, was suddenly fearful she'd told the filmmakers too much. Before they knew it, she had issued an injunction against the film. All the material they had gotten from her had to be scrapped.

It was this move that ultimately robbed the film of much of the comedy John had initially envisioned for it. A home-burgling scene, much of the bantering with her gay friends, even the satire of British politics as enabled through the character of Timothy – all of this would have given the final script a lightheartedness that *Darling*, as it was made, lacks. "It came out more bitter than we expected," John said.

He remained almost obsessively involved in revising the script all through the late part of 1963 and into the spring of 1964. His files, as I discovered them in London, were stuffed with carbons of letters sent to Raphael, with suggestions big and small. In a detailed two-pager written on 5 June 1964, he outlined twenty different changes he wanted; his tone wasn't collaborative but directive, insisting on revisions of even little moments like, "page 36, establish empty flat, otherwise who is he ringing?" He told Raphael to scratch entire scenes and come up with more motivations for characters. By the time Dirk Bogarde was cast as Robert, Diana's journalist boyfriend, John was firing off a terse memo to Raphael in which he asked for twelve specific rewrites that would give Robert more substance, "humanizing" him more, and in general giving the character more to do.

Raphael grew frustrated with the changes and the increased urgency to make them, later telling reporters that he thought the finished film "suffered badly from the pace imposed on it by the race to make it entertaining." The screenplay was, in fact, still not complete when shooting began in September 1964. To fix things up, John brought in Edna O'Brien, who'd written the screenplay for *The Girl With Green Eyes* for Woodfall Films, based on her novel.

The news of O'Brien's hiring was not received well by Raphael, who had taken off for Rome, frustrated with all the back and forth over the script. John promised Raphael that he would retain sole credit, but O'Brien was needed since they'd all gotten "too inside" the story over the past year. "I know your reaction might be to fear for the script," John wrote, "but nothing will be written that would damage what you, Jo and I have worked on for so long." Besides, John said, he needed a writer on the set; he had come to depend on having "a writer's mind over my shoulder" during shooting. Waterhouse and Hall had been around during the filming of *A Kind of Loving* and

Billy Liar; John would always prefer, throughout his career, to keep his writers close at hand. Eventually Raphael would return from Rome to make a series of last-minute adjustments to the script.

As it emerged, the story of *Darling* takes Diana Scott from an early, boring marriage to an affair with television journalist Robert Gold, during which Diana's desires and ambitions crystallize. There is nothing, she comes to believe, that she can't acquire with a little wile and flirtation. Like Billy Fisher, she dreams big dreams, but unlike Billy, she isn't afraid to go after them. She pursues a modeling career and moves in with Robert, who leaves his family for her. Taking up with advertising exec Miles Brand, Diana becomes the company's "Happiness Girl" and wins a part in a movie. When she finds herself pregnant, she blithely undergoes an abortion; she soon tires of Robert and heads off to Paris for a life of decadence with Miles. With a gay friend, Malcolm, Diana visits Italy and bewitches Prince Cesare Della Romita, whom she marries, but soon finds palace life boring. Returning to London, she assumes Robert will take her back, but he turns her down instead. She has no choice but to return to Italy and resume her life as a lonely, unhappy princess – a Princess Diana, in fact, a generation early.

"It was a very specific moment in time when we were changing from postwar Britain to mod Britain," Julie Christie said. Up until this time, "girls still looked, acted, and dressed like their mothers." Indeed, Ingrid in *A Kind of Loving* is demure and modest in crisp little suits, her hair swept back neatly. In *Billy Liar*, Barbara is supposed to be nineteen, but could pass for forty. True, Liz let her hair down, but Diana Scott let down a lot more than that. "Diana was a product of the new consumerist society," Christie said, a trend John had acknowledged with the supermarket opening in *Billy Liar*. "Life was suddenly about getting whatever you wanted," Christie observed, "and Diana fit that idea perfectly."

And seldom in the history of cinema had there been quite such a woman.

Once, early on, when I asked John about *Darling*, he whispered, "You can skip that one." I protested that it was a seminal film, that it launched a whole spate of "mod London" pictures, that it kicked off a Swinging Sixties mentality of good-time girls in miniskirts hopping from bed to bed with androgynous-looking boys. He nodded. Yes, it did all that; but still I could skip it.

"It also made you a star," I added. "You and Julie both. And it made an awful lot of money."

It wasn't something new, this disdain for his first international hit. "When it's being shown on television," he'd told a reporter a few years earlier, "I leave the room." The performances were good, he said, but the picture "seemed altogether too pleased with itself," a dated relic with "epigrammatic dialogue" that seemed too self-consciously hip.

"We thought we were very smart boys when we were doing it," John said. "It was our idea about how 'the other half' lives, [but we had] never really played such silly games . . . It was our fantasy, and, frankly, it rang false in time."

Even early on, while the film was still in the planning stages, John had wanted to rely less on dialogue and make the film more visual. Though he enjoyed the script's "clever, clever dialogue, which is sort of a hallmark of Frederic Raphael," he also found it "brittle and unreal." The classic example is the scene between Laurence Harvey and Georgina Cookson at the gambling club, where they trade biting banter that's quite funny yet very obviously scripted. "It seemed all so very smart then, but today, quite frankly, I cringe."

Harvey was one of the first to be cast after Christie. On 19 August 1964, Schlesinger went to see him as King Arthur in the musical *Camelot* at Drury Lane, taking Julie Christie along with him. "A pretty dressy but disastrous affair," John concluded in a letter to Frederic Raphael the next day. "How they hate him! [Bernard] Levin this morning was vitriolic. I must say I admire Larry for the way he takes it." John hoped that the star would be good in the film and "not 'act' too hard."

The biggest casting challenges concerned Robert, Diana's lover, who had become, with the script changes, the film's heart, and Malcolm, her gay chum, who had to be camp but not too camp. Nat Cohen was putting pressure on Janni to sign an American star for Robert; it would secure a U.S. distribution, he argued, and make the film more appealing to the American market. John set his sights high: Montgomery Clift, though by then in the twilight of his career, still possessed the right mix of sophistication and sincerity to bring Robert to life. Clift agreed to meet; Schlesinger remembered how tired and worn the star looked, the effects of his auto accident still apparent in his face. "You don't really want me for this film," Clift said, explaining he'd agreed to the interview simply because he'd wanted to meet the director of *A Kind of Loving*.

The part was next offered to Paul Newman, who politely declined. Raphael complained that he didn't want to waste any more time on American actors who were simply playing hard-to-get, and urged John to go along with his idea of making Robert an Englishman. Jo Janni remained unconvinced, pushing for Cliff Robertson, but John finally agreed with Raphael and persuaded Jo to cast Dirk Bogarde, then at the height of his fame in Britain after edgy roles in *Victim* and *The Servant*.

In the beginning, there was great rapport between Schlesinger and Bogarde. Right before filming began, John went out to Dirk's country house for the weekend; it was "enchanting," John wrote to Raphael, "the only way to describe it." Bogarde was "boyish and casual," John said, "but we have got to be careful how we dress him if he is not to look too camp. I think he knows this – he is very intelligent about himself."

There was a brief affair with Bogarde during the making of the film; John might have fallen for him had John Steiner still not been around. Steiner had a walk-on in *Darling*; his presence was surely part of the reason John recalled the shoot as one of the more pleasant and easygoing of his career. He got on well with all his actors, and with Edna O'Brien replacing the cranky Raphael, at least for a time, he was freed from bickering over the script. John was also pleased with his crew: Ray Simm, who'd been with him on both previous films, returned as art director; Jim Clark, introduced to him by Larry Kramer, came on board as editor, settling in for a long personal and professional friendship; and Ken Higgins, his cameraman on *Monitor* and for *Terminus*, was director of photography. John even hired Alan Cooke's brother Malcolm, who'd worked on *The Starfish*, for sound.

To the end of his life, however, Schlesinger remained puzzled over what eventually soured his friendship with Bogarde. "We rather fell out as friends, which is sad, but it happens," he said. They had a good deal in common, including belief in the cinema's potential as a great art form, which was shared by few British actors, most of whom tended to have a bias toward the theater. But Schlesinger and Bogarde also had much to divide them: Bogarde's biographer, Sheridan Morley, would describe Dirk's "clenched homosexuality," a mindset that insisted on referring to his lover of more than 30 years as the gardener or the handyman. This from the man who had played the screen's first sympathetic homosexual in *Victim*, a character notable for his integrity and authenticity. By contrast, according to Morley, Bogarde would end his life "an angry and lonely old ghost" – a condition John could neither understand nor sympathize with.

Casting Malcolm presented even more of a challenge than Robert. A number of names were suggested – Roddy McDowall, Brian Bedford, Gary Bond, Tony Tanner – but John wanted his chum Roland Curram. "He is very Malcolmish, warm, affectionate, slightly camp and rather childish," he wrote to Janni. After meeting with Roly, the producer agreed with John's assessment, and Curram was cast as the gay photographer.

I asked Curram if he had any concerns about taking such a breakthrough gay role. "It never occurred to me for an instant," he said, sitting opposite me at lunch at the British Academy of Film and Television Arts, where a wise-looking photograph of John stared down at us from the wall. "I just knew it was a jolly good part. I couldn't believe that work could be so much fun. We all couldn't wait to get to the set every day."

Of course, John was being a bit sly in casting Curram, who had moved in with him in Cornwall Gardens. John sensed something about Roly; he was forever teasing him about "coming over to the other side." It was only a matter of time,

John believed, before Roly acknowledged his gayness.

"Perhaps he thought giving me [the part of] Malcolm was a way of reinforcing that," Curram said, laughing. "I had a girlfriend and then I got married but still there was this perception about me. Of course, later on, I told John he was right. We were never lovers, though. It nearly came to it once or twice, but we never actually made it."

Roly also brought with him a connection to John's sister Susan, since he'd dated her in the late Fifties. "I knew a lot of *Darling* was based on Sue," Curram said. Specifically, the scene where Diana and Malcolm go to Capri and both end up sleeping with the same young man had been directly lifted from Susan's experience.

"John directed us with a lot of flair and style," Curram said. "He just carried on the way he would at home in our kitchen."

John had been itching to bring a gay character into his films for some time. Talking about the "homosexual overtones" of Dearden's *Victim*, he had told an interviewer in 1962: "I think that now the time is ripe for us to try and expand the range of subjects with which the cinema deals. The distributors have had a stranglehold on the film industry for many years. I believe that they have underestimated the level of intelligence of the average British audience. It is going to be possible in the next few years, I hope, to experiment with many more types of subject."

Indeed, while scouting locations in Manchester for *A Kind of Loving*, he had happened upon some gay pubs and considered adding a scene in which Vic stumbles into a drag show during his pub crawl. Janni overruled him, perhaps wisely; the scene would have run the risk of appearing sensationalist. Now, however, Schlesinger was working on a project where his impulse to make the gay world visible was appropriate: homo-sexuals were all through the fashion world. He directed Malcolm as both overtly gay and sympathetic, the one true, honest relationship Diana has in the entire film. The role became breakthrough in that, unlike *Victim* or even *A Taste of Honey*, Malcolm is neither adrift nor suffering. He may also have been the first unapologetically sexually active gay man on the screen.

John knew there would be some flak: in script revisions, he suggested to Raphael that they cut a number of specific references to a drag show since he was certain the censor would "have a good deal to say about Malcolm and that bit." In fact, a whole scene was excised in which Malcolm made specific reference to being homosexual. Still, what remains is extra-ordinary for 1965: Malcolm cruising the waiter at the outdoor cafe, hopping on the back of his motorbike while Diana watches from above. She knows what they're heading off to do – and so does the audience.

On the first day of shooting in September 1964, John was "excited and nervous, naturally," as he admitted in a letter to Frederic Raphael. He was also worried about Julie: "She seems incredibly young and childlike. How we shall ever make her sophisticated, I don't know." He brought in Vidal Sassoon to advise on her hair; costume designer Julie Harris was extremely selective in her clothes, making sure they bestowed sophistication and wouldn't date by the time the film came out a year later.

As shooting began, however, John was thrilled by the transformation he witnessed in Christie, writing in his diary,

"Julie is going to set the world on fire. She is pure magic. She will be everybody's Darling."

The very first shot of her in *Darling* recalls *Billy Liar*: there she is, sauntering down the street, swinging her purse, as if Diana is Liz, exulting in her new London life. The film is framed with the device of a magazine interview: Diana is telling the story of her life to a reporter from *Ideal Woman* magazine. Of course, the pun is that Diana's life is far from ideal – idealized, maybe, but not ideal. The problem with the device is that it is not consistent; Diana's narration disappears for long chunks of time, and because the voice of the interviewer (John himself) vanishes from the soundtrack early on, sometimes the irony of what Diana is saying is lost. As Gene Phillips has observed, viewers "lose sight of the fact that one is not supposed to be taken in by the spurious attempts at self-justification Diana makes" and are thus prone "to accept her specious explanations of her behaviour as valid, or at least sincerely meant." The interview contrivance loses all credibility when Diana's voiceover describes her abortion and the sex party in Paris, secrets she'd hardly be likely to divulge to *Ideal Woman*.

Throughout the film, John used montage to convey plot points: Diana and Miles are enjoying a little afternoon delight when the camera suddenly cuts to the parking meter flashing, "Penalty." It's an example of the kind of "obvious" filmmaking Pauline Kael so abhorred about Schlesinger, but here it seems to fit the sensibility of the film. Likewise, the fat woman at the charity fundraising event picking the meat out of her sandwich and discarding the bread is amusingly contrasted against a speaker railing against malnutrition. *Darling* is, after all, an obvious film; that's what made it such fun at the time. It's also why, years later, John would walk out of the room when he saw it on television.

His instinct for the obvious was challenged, however, with a *voyeur* scene set at a Parisian party. It's ironic, of course, given the kinds of jokes Schlesinger and Janni liked to tell about Trevelyan, but the BBFC was appalled by a scene in the original script where people gather to watch a man and woman having sex. One censor called it "vicious stuff," recommending it be completely deleted. Trevelyan, however, expressed confidence to Janni: "With you and John making this film, I would not expect any lapses in taste." Still, he insisted there be no overt message that the partygoers were there to watch the couple having sex, suggesting they obscure it in the way "Losey had done in the final scenes of *The Servant*."

Though Trevelyan had been acquiescent with *A Kind of Loving*, he proved intractable this time: the "obscuring" John managed of the scene was deemed hardly sufficient. In the revised script, John proposed a shot of a woman sitting on a bed, followed by a shot of a man entering the room. The woman is then seen from behind removing her clothes; the sequence would end with a shot of the partygoers lining up to watch. Trevelyan was aghast, ordering that the whole episode be cut. The Parisian party was thus left with only its strange mix of transvestites, Negroes and beady-eyed women – all the stereotypes middle-class suburban imaginations might conjure up for a decadent sex party.

For much of the rest of the film, however, John used his documentary eye, especially in the unscripted interviews Robert conducts on the street with passersby, but also for the justly famous ending: the camera pans from copies of *Ideal Woman* on a bookstall in Piccadilly Circus to a nearby homeless woman, singing opera in Italian. She was a real street person, familiar to many Londoners; John often walked past her on his way to the tube. "The awful isolation of this poor creature," he said, "singing her heart out in a language passersby do not understand," became for John "a symbol of Diana, who had failed to communicate with the people in her world." It was a brilliant finish; and in scrapping Raphael's original idea, a girl in a beauty shop mooning over Diana's glamorous life, John proved that he didn't always prefer knee-jerk obviousness.

Darling is not as enduring a film as either of John's first two, despite its reputation and the blockbuster commercial success it enjoyed. Yet neither should it be skipped, as John had suggested, with equal parts seriousness and cajolery. *Darling* is a highly entertaining, well-written, sharply directed film with a remarkable central performance by Julie Christie. It is of its time – yes – and, as such, it remains a fascinating document of a period. It is indeed a bellwether of the Swinging Sixties, evoking a world being recreated, rethought, reimagined. Everything in the film is new: from the fashions to the dialogue, from the streamlined modern architecture of Miles' building to the abstract modern sculpture outside it; from the eccentric modern artist at the gallery to the moves Diana and Miles make on the dance floor.

Newest of all was the sexual freedom. The ease with which characters move from bed to bed, the blithe way in which marriage vows are flouted, cannot help but recall for comparison that other great British film about the wages of adultery, *Brief Encounter* – a generation and a world away from *Darling*. How much distress and guilt, vexation and heartache, is expended in that earlier film, when in fact nothing sexual even transpires between the two leads. Here, by contrast, giddy lovers collaborate in deceiving their spouses, and we go along with them on their rendezvous.

Darling is remembered most for its social satire, surely part of the reason John retained so little affection for it. He'd always been more interested in the film's "personally haunting theme of loneliness and disenchantment." In exchanging the social realism of his earlier work for the psychological realism of *Darling*, Schlesinger brought himself far more in tune with his true sensibilities. Consider his work at the BBC, where his best films ("Benjamin Britten," "The Innocent Eye," "Private View," "The Class") were not so much about society and its ills as about individual people and their relationships, with each other or with their work.

Yet *Darling* does not always succeed as a psychological profile. Alexander Walker was correct when he said the ending didn't ring true: a woman like Diana, he argued, would never have stayed cooped up in her palace prison but, instead, would have had a spare Ferrari on the road within minutes, heading for Rome and a little *dolce vita*. In fact, the script tries to have it both ways: to make Diana cunning while keeping her sympathetic. Walker thought she should have been either "astringently moral or more defiantly immoral." As it is, we're never sure if we should admire Diana or loathe her.

What was the film trying to say? In the publicity materials prepared for the press at the time, both Schlesinger and Janni come off as moralizers. "Diana wants something for nothing," Janni was quoted as saying. "In the end she gets nothing for nothing."

John sounded equally judgmental. "Everyone knows girls like this," he said. "Society as it is now is only too ready to accommodate girls like her."

"Only too ready." "Girls like her." He sounds like Mary Whitehouse. In fact, at its heart, *Darling* is not so much about liberation as the *dangers* of liberation: it seems to be saying, especially to women, that if you're too ambitious, if you want too much, you'll wind up alone. But the sanctimonious tone of the press materials must be kept in perspective: critics of the cinema's "new morality" were making it increasingly difficult to sell pictures that dealt with sex and adult themes. One needed to subvert the criticism by positioning these films as cautionary tales. And while Diana does end up alone, it is not her ambition or desire that has defeated her, but rather her inability to integrate these things with a sense of humanity.

Raphael would, in fact, describe the theme of the film as "the destruction of the female principle," by which he meant the commodification of people, which was (and is) especially true for women: "It's a study of the wrap-up and throw-away relationships that people tend to have today." John wasn't suggesting that women "stay in their place" or sacrifice the pursuit of their dreams and ambitions; far from it, he was encouraging them to get out there and take their best shot, but with the implied warning that "the female principle" must become "the human principle."

Much of the frank sexuality that had been depicted in the social realist films up until this time had seemed liberating, yet in truth had been just the opposite, especially in relation to women. As the theorist John Hill has pointed out, women's interests in *A Kind of Loving* – television, clothes, status – were associated with the new consumerist obsessions of the middle class; while on the other hand, men's interests – brass bands, camaraderie, pub crawls – are decidedly working class. Women, then, are seen as enemies of the kind of social revolution these films were ostensibly calling for. Even *Billy Liar*, as Julie Christie herself has pointed out, offered the two stereotypical faces of woman: good girl and bitch. The one "liberated" woman, Liz, is a kind of fantasy creature, one who would be given fuller, if more cynical, expression in *Darling*.

That cynicism should not, however, be interpreted as sexism; it is, rather, an observation about the commodification of any relationship, about the need for greater humanity in charting one's ambitions. That's not to say Schlesinger was free of sexism, or that it didn't occasionally intrude into his work, as was apparent in *A Kind of Loving*. A look at his life is informative. Never would he have close female friends; while Julie Christie, Brenda Vaccaro, Natalie Wood, and Lily Tomlin all became family, they were more like his daughters than his peers.

"He would give cocktail parties that were so rigorously male you were almost embarrassed by it," said Alan Bennett. "Maybe Coral [Browne] would be there, or Eileen Atkins. But for John, it was an actual physical dislike of having women around. You could tell that to him and he'd be absolutely unrepentant about it."

Other friends acknowledged, under cover of anonymity, that they felt John resented female authority figures far more than he did male – Grace Wyndham Goldie, Penelope Gilliatt, Sherry Lansing come quickly to mind – though he certainly battled male executives, writers and producers as well.

"I think one of the reasons John and I became friends," said Ana Maria Quintana, who was in charge of continuity for several of his later films and became another of his unofficial daughters, "was that I understood how he saw women. I was raised in Chile to be a little deferential toward men, and that fit with John's English demeanor. I wasn't strident or demanding." John responded to Quintana, she felt, because of her subtle deference to him, not only as a director, but as a man.

Yet he was never condescending, Quintana added quickly: "Once that relationship was established, he treated me completely as an equal. I have a passion for my work and he recognized that, and respected me for what I did."

Indeed, John worked well with many women whose professionalism he admired: actors such as Glenda Jackson, Shirley MacLaine and Sally Field; costumers Ann Roth and Ruth Myers; casting directors Miriam Brickman, Marion Dougherty and Wallis Nicita; and others like designer Luciana Arrighi and choreographer Eleanor Fazan. Yet his close confidantes were always male; it was the company of men he preferred, and largely gay men at that.

What makes *Darling* so historically significant, and why it could never be "skipped", is the part it played in the cinematic sexual revolution, which in turn greatly affected the changing sexual habits and attitudes in much of the West. By the time *Darling* arrived, there was already a growing resistance to the new onscreen frankness. In the United States, the producer Ross Hunter, known for his lush, opulent films that harked back to a 1930s romantic melodrama sensibility, was leading a charge against realism: "T-shirts and psychology," as Hunter put it, had no place on the silver screen. For his own pictures, Hunter promised his audiences "real stars looking glamorous in beautiful gowns on beautiful sets. No kitchen sinks. No violence. No pores. No messages."

John raised his voice in opposition to the old guard. "We cannot continue to make movies to appeal to the lowest common denominator of society," he said shortly before

Darling's release. "We cannot keep making cowboy movies, or whodunits, or war pictures because they're full of action and spills and chills. We must have what is so very loosely referred to as 'culture' for the masses."

Of course he liked his "spills and chills," and "culture for the masses" sounds suspiciously like something those socialist Free Cinema types might have said. It's not that John didn't believe in what he was saying, or that he was merely offering lip service to the values of the new filmmakers, but rather that he was defending his right to make the types of film he wanted in the kind of language that would bring him the most support. At the Montreal Film Festival, where *Darling* was having its North American premiere, John was pressed over whether a "bedroom scene" might be considered culture. "Absolutely," he said; why not? "It simply must be viewed and appreciated in the light of the circumstances leading up to it," he added. "We must be frank and realistic. Life is life."

What *Darling* suggested, even more than his first two films, was that new ways of life were indeed possible. Moral ambiguities remained, as they would ever remain, but old paradigms of sexual "responsibility" and heterosexual hegemony no longer needed to be sacrosanct. Malcolm Boyd, writing in *Christian Century* magazine, noted the lack of "legal or sacred foolishness" in *Darling*, and it is this courageous and often innovative repudiation of the previous generation's values and guidelines that catapulted John Schlesinger to the forefront of British filmmakers and prepared the way for his embrace by the international community.

"We are finally at a point," he told his diary, "where the world is growing up."

While *Darling* was in post-production, John went back for his second season at the RSC, this time taking on Shakespeare with *Timon of Athens*. He would find much to criticize about Britain, especially in the next few years, but one thing he always loved about his country was the ease with which he could go back and forth between film, television and theater. In the United States, he'd encounter a "terrible stigma attached to any such crossover"; Americans assumed, because of their greater obsession with the cinema, that one only did plays and operas when no film work was available. It's true that in Schlesinger's later career he was often offered better opportunities outside the movies, especially in opera, but that wasn't always the case. It's important to remember that the crossover he so enjoyed began in 1963, and it continued straight through his peak cinema period.

Timon of Athens opened on 1 July 1965, at Stratford; Timon was played by Paul Scofield, then enjoying considerable celebrity for his performances as Sir Thomas More in *A Man for All Seasons*, first in the West End, then on Broadway (and soon in the Fred Zinnemann film). Tony Church, the star of *No Why*, returned in the part of Flavius. John hadn't directed Shakespeare since his days at Oxford, and Timon, one of the least known and least popular, was especially tough. "This is the play to end all claims that Shakespeare wrote simply to entertain the public," observed *The Times*.

Given that John was preparing to adapt Thomas Hardy's bleak vision of life in *Far from the Madding Crowd*, Shakespeare's message in *Timon* – that man is essentially a depraved animal and an insult to nature – must have been particularly intriguing. How does one survive being struck down by life? It was a theme that resonated for John, both creatively and personally.

John's direction received higher marks than Scofield's acting; *The Times* thought the star radiated "lofty magnanimity" in act one but never conveyed the emotional transition necessary to the play: "There is no single moment when one sees his world crack apart." John, however, by giving the production a cinematic visual style (the *Guardian* called it "splendour") delivered an almost "montage" feel. "The play bristles with difficulties," observed the *Financial Times*, but ultimately Schlesinger's direction "defeats them, or conceals them, by ensuring that it is constantly exciting to hear and to see."

After *Timon of Athens*, John headed to various film festivals where *Darling* was being given advance screenings. In Moscow, he encountered some hostile opinion among the British delegation who, uneasy about exhibiting such unsavory aspects of British life, were against showing the film. The Russians, however, thoroughly enjoyed the picture: "It was jolly difficult to tell if they were identifying with any of the characters or merely liked seeing Western decadence," John remembered.

As usual, the British critics were snide; *The Times* called the film "incomplete," dismissing it as "a caustic picture essay on London society's fags, hypocrites and well-heeled fashion setters." John's old Oxford chum Kenneth Tynan, at *The Observer*, was a bit more gentle, chiding the film's "stylistic dissonance" and the idea that the filmmakers were "sniggering" at their own characters; but he concluded that the best of the film "outweighs the worst."

Tynan asks a fair question: does the film celebrate or condemn Diana's life choices? John would concede later that the British critics "were probably right, though they're a nasty lot." There was even more venom than usual, he felt, since

Darling had opened simultaneously in New York and the Americans, by and large, had loved it. *Newsweek* called the film "delicious," *Time* said it was "irresistible," and the *New Yorker* pronounced it "shining and buoyant." Bosley Crowther in the *New York Times* quipped, "Schlesinger has made a film that will set tongues wagging . . . *Darling* should be pronounced the way Tallulah Bankhead pronounces it when she is raking her vocal claws over someone she heartily detests."

The only holdout was Pauline Kael, fast becoming for Schlesinger the American equivalent of Penelope Gilliatt, who said the film was "as empty of meaning and mind as the empty life it's exposing."

Still, the picture was a smash, even more in the United States than in Britain. Though many American distributors had initially balked at its frank sexuality (it was turned down by both MGM and Columbia), Joseph Levine stepped in and released it through his Embassy Pictures. "I think Joe knew exactly what a good wicket he was on," John said. In the United States alone, *Darling* made about four million dollars, putting it in the top 30 highest-grossing pictures of the year. What the exact final grosses were, particularly in Britain, John was never certain; Anglo-Amalgamated, perturbed over the fact that he'd gone considerably over budget, would keep the figures from him.

"Until *Darling*," John said, "I had never really known what true fame was. *Darling* taught me all I needed to know."

Suddenly he was feted around the world, sought after for interviews and deluged with scripts. By 1965 John Schlesinger had become Britain's leading cinematic export to the world. And if John sat atop the London filmmaking scene, London itself was suddenly and deliriously the hub of the filmmaking universe. It's true that much of this renaissance was funded by an infusion of American money into British production. By now, all of the Hollywood studios had major contracts with British producers; American money was, in fact, behind most of the big-budget British films of the 1960s, from *The Guns of Navarone* to *Lawrence of Arabia*, *Becket*, and *Dr. No* – the last of which kicked off the extremely successful James Bond series.

But the reality of American dollars didn't deflect the perception of British dominance, and films made in England were viewed as more mod and exciting than films that came from anywhere else. It was the period of Bryan Forbes' *Whistle Down the Wind* and *The L-Shaped Room*; Lindsay Anderson's *If . . .*; Sidney Furie's *The Ipcress File*; Clive Donner's *The Caretaker;* and Ken Russell's first big screen success, *Billion Dollar Brain*, a sequel to *The Ipcress File*. Foreign filmmakers suddenly found the U.K. an extremely desirable place to make movies: Kubrick's *Lolita* and *Dr. Strangelove* are British films; so are Robert Wise's *The Haunting*, Roger Corman's *The Masque of the Red Death*, Antonioni's *Blow-Up*, Truffaut's *Fahrenheit 451*, Polanksi's *Repulsion*, and Richard Lester's dazzling pair of Beatles films, *A Hard Day's Night* and *Help!*

American financing wasn't buttressing all of them: none of Schlesinger's pictures so far had depended on dollars, and neither did Tony Richardson's breakout smash, *Tom Jones*. There was a sense of possibility, of a real future for the British cinema, after doom and gloom for so long. "It was quite the heady time," Schlesinger observed. "The eyes of the world were on London." He never imagined, not in those thrilling months of 1965, that he'd ever have to go anywhere else to make his movies.

With the sudden prestige (and money) that flowed in from *Darling*, John set about presiding over the glittery London film scene, albeit in rather cramped conditions in his Peel Street house. Still, he was "terribly hospitable and flamboyant as a host," remembered Joanna Lumley, then a young actress just starting out. "He absolutely loved people, gossip, parties and gangs of gorgeousness."

Taken by a friend to one of Schlesinger's parties, Lumley was a bundle of nerves. "John was already one of the giants," she said, "like Steven Spielberg, of that stature, even then in the Sixties. I'll never forget, John himself opened the door, and I was so frightened, but he was so gracious and said, 'Come in, darling, come in.' I remember the house was wall-to-wall with stars. Julie Christie and Alan Bates and Tom Courtenay and James Fox and Maggie Smith. The gorgeous glitterati. I was so shocked at being there. I thought they all knew I shouldn't be there. But it was full of elegant, easy people, and John was right in the middle of them all."

For a man who once feared social gatherings, who had walked around the block to work up the nerve to join a party, this was quite a change. But his success with *Darling* had given him an adrenaline burst of self-confidence. The awards were piling up: in January the National Board of Review stunned many by giving John its Best Director award, a development that left him both thrilled and amused. "I thought it ludicrous that I won for *Darling*," he said, feeling his work on either previous film would have been more deserving. Julie also took home Best Actress from the NBR, and that spring she collected the award from the British Film Academy as well. Bogarde, Raphael and art director Ray Simm also won British Academy Awards; John's nomination was essentially the one for Best Picture, as there was no category for directors at this point. *Darling* lost to *The Ipcress File*.

The most telling sign of Schlesinger's standing, however, was the degree to which he and his colleagues had become such darlings of the American film industry. "Money talks in Hollywood, and when you have a success, they love you with everything they can," John would say, looking back, and not attempting to disguise the cynicism that had seeped into his voice after too many rides on the Tinseltown roller-coaster. When *Darling* was nominated for five Oscars, John was thunderstruck. "These were the years," he said, "where success simply seemed to pile upon success."

Joe Levine encouraged John to attend the Academy Awards ceremony in Los Angeles, but the director was reluctant to make the trip. "I really don't like the idea of coming all that way and sitting there while they open the envelopes, and risking returning empty-handed," he confessed in a letter to the American producer Jerome Hellman, with whom he was considering adapting James Leo Herlihy's novel *Midnight Cowboy*. "I really can't take it as seriously as all that."

Empty-handed he would have been: Robert Wise took the Best Director prize for *The Sound of Music*, a typically safe Academy choice, which also triumphed over *Darling* as Best Picture. But Julie won as Best Actress, with British headlines the next day blaring OCAR FOR JULIE; indeed, Christie was soon commanding a million dollars a picture, a staggering sum for 1966. The little girl John had discovered at the Central School was making out quite well indeed. Oscars also went to Frederic Raphael and costume designer Julie Harris; if *The Sound of Music* was the mainstream blockbuster of the year, *Darling* was the naughty favorite of the counter-culture and the avant-garde.

From Hollywood, Jerry Hellman wrote to tell John that his

"personal stock has never been higher here . . . the reaction to *Darling* has been just extraordinary." Indeed, Ray Stark was after him to direct Barbra Streisand in *Funny Girl* and Warren Beatty sent him the script for *Bonnie and Clyde* – though John would claim never to have received it. Radie Harris wrote in the *Hollywood Reporter* that, although John had directed just three films, he was "already in the enviable position of having every top actor eager to work with him."

And so the awkward boy from Uppingham, the too-eager young filmmaker who'd dragged down efficiency on the *Tonight* programme, found himself deluged with offers while, at home, he was entertaining the likes of Vanessa Redgrave, Ralph Richardson, and Lord Snowdon. "I found to my great pleasure," he said, "that there was, after all, plenty of room at the top."

Nine

1965–1967

"Tired of everything mod"

"I 'm not sure what I will end up doing with all of these," John Schlesinger mused in one of his tape-recorded diaries. "I suppose it's important that I record my thoughts now while they're fresh, though I can't imagine how I shall ever end up putting them all together."

I hit rewind, and went back to the beginning.

The sound of his voice had become important to me. His soft, measured tones, the slightly high pitch to his speech, the Oxford-educated accent that more than one American interviewer had described as "plummy." Listening to the tapes, I could get a sense of the laugh his friends had described for me, the way his voice deepened when he became a little naughty. He was usually even-tempered, a bit weary, when he'd sit down to record his thoughts; sometimes, Michael recalled, he'd be on the loo, the tape recorder in his lap. But there were moments when his particularly sharp enunciation would reveal lingering anger from the day, or when a rushed, breathless cadence signaled the excitement of a new project — as if he couldn't wait to get the words out and start the bloody thing already.

There were moments when I had to remind myself this was the same man with whom I regularly spent time in Palm Springs; the same man whose voice was now just a dusky whisper and whose thoughts had been condensed into the simplest, most enigmatic few words.

The tape clicked as it finished rewinding. There was a pause and then John's voice intoned, "It's about 5:30. I'm in the sauna again. These tapes are recorded in my bathroom invariably." He chuckled. "It's the only place which is really peaceful and quiet, as the house is noisy, and I like to be private when I'm recording these memoirs."

Later, meeting with David Kaminsky, one of John's doctors who had also become his good friend, I talked about how important these tapes were to my research. "I'm getting to know John through his tape-recorded diaries," I said, "as much as sitting with him in person."

Dr. Kaminsky nodded. "I think he's chosen to recede into himself. But I believe he's still comprehending. I've stopped saying, 'John, it's David,' when I walk into the room. He sees me. He knows who I am. What must it be like for him to endure everyone announcing the most obvious things? John is one of the great geniuses of our time, and I don't want to be demeaning to his intellect in any way."

"Yet he's stopped communicating even in the most basic ways," I said. "Is there any empirical way of determining what kind of consciousness might still be there?"

Kaminsky shook his head. "I had him evaluated by both a

speech pathologist and a clinical psychologist. The psychologist said there wasn't a lot she could do for him unless John wanted to interact. She did not say he lacked the capacity to do so, simply for that kind of therapy, you have to participate, and John wasn't. The speech pathologist said John did not need therapy, that there was no mechanical deficit. As for the whispering thing . . . John could speak louder if he chose to. I personally believe he's processing everything, that part of his retraction into himself is because he wasn't ready to quit when he had his stroke, that there was still more left in him in terms of creativity."

Back home, I sorted through the tapes. They were intended for his own use, for writing his own memoir; he hadn't expected anyone other than himself to hear them. Not for every film did John keep a detailed diary. There were gaps, but also some wonderful surprises: a rambling, intimate account of a holiday in South Africa with Michael; an on-the-set recording of rehearsals for *The Believers*; a tape left running after a radio interview had "officially" concluded. Not all of his diaries were tape-recorded: of his earlier work, he left mostly written records, often squeezed into the columns in his daily planners, a practice repeated again on his last film. Helpful and insightful as such written records were, however, they could not compare to the power of hearing his voice.

Small moments, like the morning he took a swim in his pool only to find a dead rat with its head stuck in the drain; or trying to figure out how best to barbecue vegetables on an outdoor grill; or going to a nightclub to hear Cleo Laine; or enjoying a respite in Palm Springs – the place where he would die – where, one Sunday at the height of his fame, he luxuriated with the warm sun on his face, following it up with an evening of

Schumann and Liszt on the piano, taking him back to the days of his youth. "We've all got so used to tape machines and gramophone records," he recorded, perched on the loo. "It's so rare that anyone sits down and plays at a piano. It's very pleasant."

This was the man whose story I was set on finding. The man who, another time, recounted a prank played on his good friend Paul Jabara, creeping up behind him in the dark when Jabara was already stoned out of his mind and shouting "Boo!" How John laughed on the tape recounting that tale, a deep-throated, hearty belly laugh. This man, as much as the man who crafted celluloid dreams, was who I was pledged to find.

What to do next? It's the eternal question an artist faces, and even as *Darling* wrapped, there was already banter on the set: what to do, what to do. John and Jo Janni had no clear idea in mind, only that it would star Julie Christie, and that it should be very different from anything they'd done before, something that would "surprise" the critics. During the final dub of *Darling*, sitting in the editing booth, Jim Clark suggested Thomas Hardy's *Tess of the d'Urbervilles*. It was a world away from what they had just done, but that very discordance intrigued John: he thought it might be interesting to do "something more romantic and about another age," when people weren't bed-hopping and going nude but were, instead, "buttoned up to the necks."

What was he *thinking?* The director who'd set London swinging adapting *Hardy?* "The thing to do," he said at the time, "is to be a one-of-a-kind director, to resist playing it safe." While that's well and good, the choice of Hardy (they'd eventually swap *Tess* for *Far from the Madding Crowd*) still boggles. Why not do an edgy thriller, the kind we know John always wanted to do, and *would* do later, quite stylishly, in *Marathon Man*? Or why not focus on the Herlihy book, which the American producer, Jerome Hellman, was ready and eager to start?

Part of it was Jo Janni, who would admit later to being dazzled by an offer MGM had put on the table, promising a four million-dollar budget for a "big roadshow" kind of picture. Rueful over their lack of courage in backing *Darling*, the studio was champing at the bit to sign up the film's creative team: Janni, Schlesinger, Raphael and Christie. "I will be the first to say I was corrupted by ambition," said Janni. "I gave in to the desire to make a big important picture."

But still, why Hardy? Why not some big modern spectacle, some avant-garde extravaganza, if they had that much money? The answer goes to the heart of how Schlesinger saw his career and his artistry. He was not a prickly, eccentric artist, obsessed with his own idiosyncratic view of the world; he was not Ingmar Bergman. He was fascinated by the huge possibilities of cinema, wanting to try every genre, every period, every color of the palette that he now held so securely in his hands. It went without saying that his new picture, no matter what it was, would be shot in color. He had *arrived*: John Schlesinger, as Janni said, was now going to make a Big Important Picture.

And that usually meant epic. And epic usually meant period, and period usually meant classic. And so the team that had been inspired by the doctrines of Free Cinema to make *A Kind of Loving* now embraced the very style of filmmaking that Lindsay Anderson had denounced in his letter to *The Times* back in 1958: "stale, dressed-up literary classics." Anderson told friends he wasn't surprised Schlesinger had sold out, just at how much he got for doing so. A budget of $4 million was enormous in those days – about what *Darling* had grossed in the United States!

At that point, John had read nothing of Hardy, so he took a copy of *Madding Crowd* along with him to read during the American publicity tour for *Darling*. He liked what he found in its pages: Hardy's brooding sense of doom, his pessimism and bleak faith in survival as man's best hope, was close to John's own worldview. "What a relief," Schlesinger said, "to get away from social comment films about life as it is now, and look at people who lived a hundred years ago."

No doubt that was a sincere assessment; it's tiring always trying to stay ahead of the curve, on top of the fads and fashions, always to be hip and mod and trendsetting. No doubt there was genuine relief in stepping away from all that. And it's also true that, in many ways, John found a soulmate in Hardy. Despite his success, there would always be that bleak part inside himself that made Hardy's "black mood," as John described it, very appealing – the way the author "would strike a character down and leave the pieces to gather themselves up and carry on." That was the kind of struggle which always fascinated John.

So perhaps it is unfair to judge Schlesinger and Janni as simply being dazzled by the dollars waved in their faces by MGM. In the fall and winter of 1966, John was already swung out on the Swinging Sixties, even if the rest of the world was just beginning to get in the groove. He was at the extreme other end of the cultural spectrum, ready to take on something completely different, to explore a bit of that dark side of himself that never seemed fully to go away.

The problem was, he chose the wrong property. As close as Hardy may have been to his soul, John Schlesinger and *Far from the Madding Crowd* were never going to be a suitable match. He would try, with varying success, to plumb the essential nature of the myriad relationships in the novel, to seek out the greater human truths; but in doing so in his previous films, even on a smaller scale, he had never forsaken *entertainment* — the thing that would entice people into the theaters to see what he had wrought.

There is very little entertainment in Hardy: *Madding Crowd* hardly resembles the other sweeping epics of the day — *Ben-Hur, Spartacus, Lawrence of Arabia, Doctor Zhivago* — except in scope and Panavision. The film lacked what the critic Penelope Houston called "kitchenmaid escapism"; Hardy was never one to provide rousing romance or crowd-pleasing adventure. Typically for the 19th century, his novel depends on coincidence and contrivance to tell its story, as profound as its heart might be. That left little room to maneuver if John were to attempt to understand the psychological motivations of these characters, especially since he and Frederic Raphael were treating their source as if it were holy scripture.

Indeed, working on the script with Raphael proved far more harmonious this time, because both of them approached it with the same attitude: reverence and awe. Later, John would acknowledge they were far "too slavish" to Hardy: "We didn't take enough liberty with the film because we were too worried about taking liberties with a classic," he said.

Far from the Madding Crowd would turn out to be John's least personal film. A month into the shoot he was already recognizing his blunder: "I wish I was enjoying it all more," he wrote to Jerry Hellman, with whom he was now aching to be doing *Midnight Cowboy*. "Somehow, working on this sort of movie where I am not very free to express myself makes everything very difficult."

He had, however, assembled a dream cast. Alan Bates was brought in, his rough-hewn features perfectly complementing Christie's beauty. Alan's eye was originally on the juicier, more villainous part of Sergeant Troy, but John persuaded him, after much coaxing, to settle for the upstanding Gabriel Oak. "I wanted to break the mold," Bates told me, "but I wasn't allowed to." John was insistent that Alan's "great inner quality" was more appropriate for Oak, who is really the moral center of the film.

Troy was eventually played by Terence Stamp, an actor of smoldering sexuality who had enchanted John with his performance in *Billy Budd*, and who'd just made a splash in another popular "mod London" film, *Modesty Blaise*. Finally, as Boldwood, there was Peter Finch, whom John had known and admired for years. Finch was going through "a very bad emotional patch at the time," John would remember, "and he wasn't a happy man." The dark, fatalistic attitude that emanates from Boldwood throughout the film may well have been at least partly a result of Finch's own personal relationship struggles.

If John's doubts about the project had begun even as they geared up for production, he also still had hope. "At least some of the characters learn to experience communication at the end of the story," he said, "which is more than can be said of the characters in *Darling*."

Before production could begin, however, John needed to attend to a few other commitments, not least of which was getting the project with Hellman off the ground and something for which he already seemed to have more fire than he did for *Madding Crowd*. He liked Jerry; he liked his brash, aggressive, American energy, and found his willingness to go head-to-head with the money people encouraging after five years of what he viewed as Janni's lack of interest in that department.

Lately, there had been some tough times with Jo, and not just the usual rough and tumble. John had originally presented *Midnight Cowboy* to Janni, and was deeply disappointed when his partner had refused to even consider it unless they turned it into a lad from Scotland making the journey to London. Its American setting may have disinclined Janni from the start, but it was also a novel about two losers in an extremely depressing setting – anti-heroes so "anti" they made Vic Brown and Billy Fisher (and even Diana Scott) look like upstanding citizens. Herlihy's novel, published in 1965, was given to John by a friend, model Kafe Fassett, later a well-known textile designer. "I saw it as a very visual piece," Fassett remembered, "and so I recommended it to John." He also recalled humorously John's initial response: "He said he couldn't get past page two, it was so boring."

Perhaps, then, if John's initial reaction was also negative, he should have understood Janni's reluctance; the novel is, after all, an unsparing piece of work, not easily recognizable as a movie. Yet Janni had, until then, supported his partner creatively, trusting in John's artistic sense. "Certain themes attract me," John said, "like the difficulty of finding oneself, the difficulty of finding happiness. I knew I wanted to make a film of *Midnight Cowboy* as soon as I read the novel. Even though I haven't the same sort of fantasies and illusions as Joe Buck, I could sympathize . . . I know what it's like to be lonely, and to be a failure."

If John believed this project could become an exciting film –

and after taking the book along with him on holiday to Morocco, his initial boredom quickly turned into passion – then he expected Jo to go along with him. Instead, Janni was infuriated by the idea. "He thought the idea was terrible," John said. "He said that I would ruin myself with it." Part of Janni's concern was that he considered the novel too gay, and that the undercurrent of homoeroticism between the would-be hustler Joe Buck and his tubercular friend Ratso Rizzo would stigmatize John, and, as a result, their partnership.

Balderdash, John thought. *Victim* hadn't tarred Basil Dearden; *A Taste of Honey* hadn't stigmatized Tony Richardson. Janni wasn't personally homophobic, despite all his "goddamn homosexual" rantings at John: it was simply that he felt, especially after the character of Malcolm in *Darling*, that John needed to proceed with caution. Never would Schlesinger concede this point: he would continue to incorporate homosexual elements into his films for the rest of his career. He recognized early on the homoeroticism inherent in Herlihy's novel; he acknowledged that it was, in effect, a love story between two men. But he also saw it was far more universal than that. *Midnight Cowboy* was for him an exciting property bursting with potential. Accordingly, when Janni proved intractable, John had packaged the book up with a note and shipped it off to Jerry Hellman in Hollywood.

Like Janni, Hellman was indefatigable in his devotion to the filmmaking process. John admired Jerry's passion and energy, and his brash American confidence was especially fascinating. One thing Schlesinger always admired about Americans was the sense of enterprise he perceived in them, the ethic for hard work and success. Jerry Hellman personified this American image for John. A New Yorker born and bred, Jerry was about

John's age (Janni was ten years older). After serving in the Marine Corps, he broke into showbiz as an agent and packager during the golden age of live television in New York. During that time, he worked with such stellar clients as Sidney Lumet, John Frankenheimer, Rod Serling, and George Roy Hill whose *Butch Cassidy and the Sundance Kid* would be pitted against Hellman's *Midnight Cowboy* at Oscar time.

With *The World of Henry Orient* (1964), Hellman took the leap into producing; it was directed by George Roy Hill and starred Peter Sellers in his first American film. He followed this up with *A Fine Madness* (1966), directed by Irvin Kershner, which gave Sean Connery his American debut.

John first met Jerry in London, when the American producer had paid him a courtesy call after *Billy Liar*. Under his arm, Hellman carried a script by Arnold Schulman that he was planning to produce for United Artists; it concerned a very mod girl who worked at the United Nations. "At this point, I didn't even know Jo Janni existed," Hellman told me. "I wasn't trying to invade his turf. I was just asking John if he might want to come to Hollywood to direct the picture. And John, by the way, never brought up that he had a partner who did the producing on his films. We just met at my hotel and from the get-go, we just really connected. We talked easily together and John said yes, he'd be interested, let's set this thing in motion."

John would later back out, however, claiming the script reminded him too much of *Darling*. It's likely he also didn't want to run afoul of Janni at that point. Hellman took it in stride: "That happens sometimes," he said. "I knew you couldn't get someone to do something if they didn't feel passionately about it. So I expressed my intense disappointment but also my hope that someday we would find another way to come together." The Schulman film was never made, but within a year Hellman had John's letter about *Midnight Cowboy*. "I knew this was it," he said. "This was going to be our picture."

An option was taken on Herlihy's book in March 1966, and Hellman immediately began hustling for financial backing. But the property, so squalid and depressing, wasn't an easy sell. One of the great stories John loved to tell party guests was how a reader's report at MGM had supposedly concluded that if *Cowboy* could be cleaned up and some songs added, it might make a splendid vehicle for Elvis Presley.

Jerry got to work right away. He pitched the idea to Joe Levine and Leonard Lightstone at Embassy, Ray Stark at Seven Arts, and Ely Landau, who worked with a number of distributors. Each time, however, he was met with less than enthusiasm. John was kept apprised of his progress, or lack thereof, reading Jerry's letters in the mud of Dorset as filming got underway on *Madding Crowd*. Hellman held out hope that Seven Arts or possibly Columbia might finance the film if he could guarantee them a negative cost between $750–850,000. That was quite the comedown from the four million of *Madding Crowd*.

Their saviour came in the person of David Picker, a former publicity man who was now an influential producer at United Artists. Picker had an eye for British talent and a commitment to British production; he'd made possible *Tom Jones* and the Beatles films. "The great thing about United Artists in those years," Picker said, "was that we dealt with creative talent differently than the studios did. We responded not so much to the property but to the beliefs of someone who creatively excited us." And John Schlesinger was reason for considerable excitement. "Jerry gave me *Midnight Cowboy* to read, but it wasn't the book that convinced me," said Picker. "It was John Schlesinger."

There were a few conditions UA set forth. The budget was one million dollars, up from the $750,000 but still a fraction of what MGM had given John for *Madding Crowd*. UA would also determine at some later point whether the film would be shot in Hollywood or New York (both John and Jerry were pushing for the latter). Finally, the film would be made in black-and-white – a financial stipulation Hellman, at least, felt was creatively correct. John still had some hankering to do it in color, excited by the experience of working with color on *Madding Crowd*.

Then there was the question of the Motion Picture Association of America. All the major producers and distributors were signatories to a contract dictating that any film released under their banner first required a seal of approval from the MPAA. Hellman made clear to Picker that they were planning to make *Midnight Cowboy* "in a most uncompromising fashion without regard to such approvals and endorsements." Picker agreed, saying it was not only an acceptable route to take but a necessary one, "since anything less would vitiate against the value of the film." They needed to be prepared, Hellman wrote to John, to release the film without a seal from the MPAA and possibly without the corporate name of UA; if the MPAA refused to approve the picture, Picker would still back the film, but release it under their Lopert banner, as they'd done with Billy Wilder's sex romp, *Kiss Me, Stupid*. The danger in this, as happened with the Wilder film, was that distribution could become spottier and publicity less comprehensive, and the film could wither away without ever finding an audience.

John was eager to move forward. The first step was to find a screenwriter, preferably an American living in London, so that a close working relationship could be arranged, of the kind he'd finally managed to hammer out with Frederic Raphael. Yet nowhere in the Schlesinger-Hellman correspondence was there a consideration of the Chicago-born Raphael. This isn't really surprising: Freddie had been educated at Cambridge and spent most of his life in Britain, and his finely cultured tastes would have been a poor match for Herlihy's urban cowboys and con-men.

Instead, the candidates Hellman had in mind were busy working in America: Charles Eastman, whose unproduced screenplay of Tony Richardson's *The Loved One* (the final script was written by Terry Southern) seemed "marvelously conceived visually"; and Tad Mosel, who had written the film *Dear Heart* (1964) and who was then adapting *Up the Down Staircase* for Alan Pakula. "All of [Mosel's] best work has dealt with strange and disoriented people," Hellman wrote to Schlesinger, "'losers' as you would call them, in an essentially hostile and terrifying world."

Such would be their conception for *Midnight Cowboy*. John replied that he was eager to talk to anyone Jerry thought competent, agreeing that their choice needed to be American if they were to get the feel for *place* that the screenplay absolutely needed. He suggested they should at least consider Herlihy doing it himself, but Jerry countered he'd prefer someone who'd had experience writing for film.

Hellman was busy on another front as well: after talk of John directing *Funny Girl* had gone nowhere, Jerry pitched Streisand the idea of adapting Richard Dowling's novel *All the Beautiful People* with her in the lead. John was quite eager to hear of Streisand's reaction, but admitted he found "the idea of even thinking about another project at this time almost unbearable. Why on earth do we do it!" (Streisand would eventually turn them down.)

As his excitement about working with Hellman grew, John still needed to complete one other major commitment before plunging into production of *Madding Crowd*: preparing for his third production for the Royal Shakespeare Company. This time it would be *Days in the Trees*, by Marguerite Duras, starring none other than Peggy Ashcroft – "a particularly talented and neurotic woman," John observed.

Indeed, Dame Peggy was insecure about performing in the very modern play, penned by one of France's leading intellectuals and a spectacular triumph for Madeleine Reynaud in Paris. Critics bantered back and forth as to Duras' meaning: the greedy mother (Ashcroft's part) represents France, they surmised, and the son she tries to entice back to run her factory is Algeria, or one of the other French colonies. John simply saw it as a fascinating take on love and hate; the prodigious notes he gave to Ashcroft, at her demand, were all about finding the fine line between the two extremes.

The script was translated by Sonia Orwell; George Baker played the gambling, pimping son. Ashcroft was a wreck for much of the rehearsals, convinced she was in over her head. Shakespeare was one thing, but a modern French intellectual . . . ! John, with whom she had a family connection through Roger, managed to allay some of her fears, but not all. He urged her to be *monstrous* in the part, not to strive for audience sympathy, something which she found terribly difficult to do.

"The last two weeks have been murder," John wrote to Jerry Hellman the night before the opening. "Hysteria, illness, tears and 'I can't-do-it-you'll-have-to-get-Edith-Evans' and the rest! So I've turned myself into as much Dunlopillo as possible, and played the psychiatrist at the moment when the worst part of the transference is taking place."

It remained to be seen if his coaching had worked. The play opened at the Aldwych on 9 June 1966. Waiting to make her entrance, Ashcroft sat frozen in fear. "Who's out there?" she asked John about the audience.

"Fuck them," he told her.

"Fuck them," she repeated, over and over, as she lifted her head and walked out onto the stage.

She was magnificent. Critics were impressed, and John was thrilled. "I could hear your sigh of relief all the way over the Arctic Circle," Jerry Hellman wrote to him. The play was filmed and transmitted the following year in the Wednesday Play slot on the BBC.

Shortly after the play's premiere, John returned his attention briefly to finding a writer for *Midnight Cowboy*. Nobody had really caught his fancy as yet. For a few weeks their hopes rested on Truman Capote; Hellman was urging they sign him right away. But Capote proved slippery, showing enthusiasm only to then back off. There would be no pinning him down, as he was currently riding quite high on the hoopla surrounding his book *In Cold Blood*. Instead, they turned to Capote's perennial rival, Gore Vidal, who proved equally hard to get. By May, they'd backed off Vidal as well, only to find their lack of inquiry boosted Vidal's interest and he was suddenly asking through his agent to meet with John and Jerry.

A meeting was held in New York that summer. "There's nothing new here," John remembered Vidal saying to him about *Midnight Cowboy*. "It's ridiculous, a silly book. I did it all before in *The City and the Pillar*." He smiled over at them. "Let's just have a nice amiable lunch, shall we?"

Outwardly John found Vidal charming and laughed about the experience, but privately he was enraged that he'd taken the time to meet with him only to be turned down. "An arrogant prick," he grumbled. John held no grudge however, and Vidal and his companion Howard Austen became occasional guests in his home.

What if, at this particular moment, John had continued to move ahead on *Cowboy*? Jerry Hellman had just finished his chores on *A Fine Madness*, and was now devoting *his* full attention to the project. The contracts with Herlihy and United Artists were in place; talks were underway with writers and actors. In July, John met Jerry in New York for several days of intense brainstorming; the encounter confirmed yet again their compatibility and mutual inspiration. Conceivably they could have started production by the end of the year; at the very latest, by the first quarter of 1967. What if John had never taken the Hardy detour, which came to be seen as an unnecessary deflection of his talents?

In so many ways *Far from the Madding Crowd* was an anomaly in Schlesinger's career; yet had he not done it, had he plowed straight ahead into *Midnight Cowboy*, we might not have ended up with the classic we did. It's possible Dustin Hoffman may still have been signed for it; Hellman was already tossing Hoffman's name around by the end of 1966. But if casting had had to be consolidated by that point, John was definitely not yet sold on him.

Certainly, Jon Voight would not have played Joe Buck if production had started by early 1967; the previous December, John was gung-ho on the actor Roger Ewing, an American he'd met in London through the playwright William Inge and who was currently playing a small part in the television series *Gunsmoke*. It's clear John was smitten with Ewing; it was the only letter in weeks that he would take the time to write to Hellman, so immersed had he become in filming *Madding Crowd*. On John's recommendation, Hellman met with Ewing; he reported back that, while he could understand what John found physically appealing about him, Ewing lacked what Jerry felt was necessary for Joe Buck: "the lithe, lean, unself-conscious, animal-like grace of Jimmy Dean, Steve McQueen or even Paul Newman."

So if that's what they were thinking about the character by early 1967, we'd never have seen Jon Voight in the part, even if, in fact, his name was on a shortlist compiled by Hellman in January. Some of the other names on the list fit Hellman's ideal better: Michael Parks, Alex Cord and Alan Alda. Yet somehow none of those actors, least of all Hawkeye Pierce, seem likely to have made *Midnight Cowboy* the enduring film it became.

There are reasons, then, one can be thankful for *Far from the Madding Crowd*.

Production began in late August 1966, shot entirely in Hardy's "Wessex" around Weymouth in Dorset. Seven hundred extras were drawn from local villagers for the crowd scenes. What was clear right from the start was that this was going to be a gorgeous production, and much of that is due to the extraordinary relationship John developed with his camera-man, Nicolas Roeg, who would, of course, go on to his own notable career as a director. Roeg considered it a "joy and privilege" to work with John, who gave him extraordinary freedom in composing the visual elements of a scene: "Just set it up and let's see what happens," Schlesinger would tell him. But so well had John set things up, so passionately had he communicated his desire to capture the English countryside, that Roeg was astounded to see the results. John had made the look of the film "so utterly his own that I hardly recognized it myself."

Indeed, that is *Madding Crowd*'s saving grace: it is a stunning pictorial achievement. Roeg's photography is brilliant, especially given that for the first time John was working in Panavision, a shape which the director considered "not a very comfortable one to compose in, except in the extreme long shots when it is lovely." Still, he was buoyed by Roeg's fearlessness with the form, and together they crafted an exquisite tableau. The lush, rolling hills of Dorset, the subtle colors of the trees and heathers, the dappled sunlight all combine to form one of the most evocative treatments of the English countryside ever put on celluloid.

Just as significant to the look of the film, and even more important in terms of Schlesinger's long-range career, was the relationship he established on this film with the production designer Richard MacDonald. MacDonald had been working with Joseph Losey, designing *The Servant* and *King and Country* and was just now coming off *Modesty Blaise*. "Richard taught me everything I know about color," John said, "the use of muted color, how to ration the use of primary colors like red. He was a wonderful man and a great artist."

This was, in fact, the first time John had shot a film in color; his only previous experience with it had been in home movies. He was ecstatic about the possibilities, and would indeed suggest to Hellman that perhaps they might still find a way to incorporate it into *Midnight Cowboy*, maybe just for certain sections.

It's tempting to speculate that the design and photography of the film were John's chief interests in the production, for the performances he managed to draw from his actors were in his own words, all in "different keys." For once the "actor's director" had lost his touch. Terence Stamp he found moody and belligerent, and they clashed almost from the first day of shooting. The result is a terribly uneven performance, not helped by a script that never properly determines what kind of a man Troy really is. Only Peter Finch, in John's opinion, really captured the "classic doom" of the novel.

He even expressed some worries about Julie Christie in a letter to Hellman: "Julie is her usual preoccupied and sweet self but gives us problems as she has got thinner and looks a bit peaky, which is not exactly right for a buxom country wench."

Already by October, John was becoming alarmed by the course the film was taking: a steady stretch of rain had gotten his spirits down since it prevented them from getting the shots they wanted and turned their bucolic hills into mud. Of course, his pessimism was something to be expected by now, but letters to Hellman and others document a longer-lasting depression than usual, hanging on through the winter months with even Christmas barely offering a respite. Clearly, the fact that John Steiner was not coming back into his life, that he was now unequivocally gone for good, had hit home; on New Year's Day, 1967, a few weeks shy of his forty-first birthday, John Schlesinger had rarely felt so alone.

Principal photography finished on 17 February. Much of his initial passion for the project was now gone and he was thrilled when it was over: "We threw our last dead sheep over a cliff yesterday lunchtime," he wrote to Jerry Hellman, "and I managed to drive back – God knows how – in the afternoon. It's so long since I have seen double-lane traffic – can you imagine!"

Post-production began at Shepperton studios in March. "We unfortunately have to do more than we wished," John wrote to Hellman. MGM was eager for the film; Hellman reported he'd spoken with executives there who thought the rushes they'd seen were brilliant, but John himself had serious reservations. "Some of our material is very exciting, and some well below the standards we set ourselves, but I hope when it's all put together it will make some sense."

To do that, they needed a new editor; poor Malcolm Cooke, just starting out in the field, was in over his head with so much footage. The film was running past three hours. Jim Clark took over – the first of many times, as John would say, that he "saved my bacon."

"It was a very long film," Clark said, "and I'm not convinced I ever actually sat through the whole movie. Most of what I did was in the center part of the film. We blew it up to 70 mm and it was beautiful, just a really lovely film." Especially noteworthy was Clark's assembly of the erotic swordplay scene between Troy and Bathsheba, a crisply-cut montage of phallic imagery and showmanship that ends in a climactic kiss. This is the scene that most people remember from the film.

With Clark, John enjoyed an instinctively trusting relationship; the director would say Clark was one of the few collaborators he could simply let go to do his own thing, because in the end he'd bring back something brilliant. "I called John 'Mother' while we were making a film," Clark said, laughing, "though never to his face. It would be to everyone else, 'Well, Mother wants this,' or I'd ask, 'How's Mother today?' If I heard, 'Oh, she's broody today,' I knew I'd better watch out.'" Clark would become John's most frequent editor: *Darling, Madding Crowd, The Day of the Locust, Marathon Man, Yanks, Honky Tonk Freeway* – plus "The Longest" segment of *Visions of Eight* and some last-minute salvaging of *Midnight Cowboy*.

"John never looked at what he had until he had finished filming," Clark said. "He was often too busy to look at stuff. Largely he and I worked together after I'd done a version so that the entire movie would be in one piece. I liked working with John because he cared about his material. Some directors were lazy. Many of the well-known American directors never saw their films being edited. John Ford used to say he never saw his films until they were previewed. But John Schlesinger was very interested in the editing process and was keen to be a part of it. We were honest with each other. He told me when he didn't like something and I told him when I thought he was going after something the wrong way."

By June, still trapped in the studio, John was itching to be done with it so he could start work with Jerry. He was also briefly distracted by the war in Israel, considering an idea for a television documentary with the producer Wolf Mankowitz. John flew to Israel and took considerable footage; it was the first time he'd been to the Jewish state, and the experience was quite moving for him, a sense of reclaiming his heritage. But the film, due to "creative differences" with the BBC, was never completed.

Back in London, he was increasingly irritable, especially with his producer. To Jerry Hellman he griped, "None of it is helped, I am here to tell you, by Jo Janni's deciding weeks after he should have made up his mind, that certain things still want experimenting with. The music timings are totally inaccurate, and we start the sessions this Wednesday, and dubbing in ten days! So God help us."

He wasn't so weary of Janni's volatility that he wanted to abandon the partnership, however. Despite the deal with Hellman, John was already planning for two more British films with Jo. Freddie Raphael was making notes for a script based on Iris Murdoch's *A Severed Head*, and Janni was casting about for a writer who might shape an original screenplay (suggested by John) based on a daring idea: the story of his relationship with John Steiner.

Those ventures felt very far-off, however, as *Far from the Madding Crowd* was being readied for release. John spent some time trying to prepare the critics for it, offering his own spin before others beat him to it; this wasn't going to be anything like *Darling*, after all. "People are tired of the flip side," John told *The Times* in August. "Contemporary" films were dated, he insisted, not Hardy. "People want something else," he said elsewhere. "They're tired of everything mod."

Of course, there was no evidence of this; in fact, if one considers the top box-office hits of 1967, dominated by *The Graduate, Bonnie and Clyde, You Only Live Twice*, and *To Sir With Love*, the opposite was true. A preview of the film was held for magazine critics in September: "The more intelligent adored it," Schlesinger wrote to Hellman, "but a few came to carp." Hellman assured him that in Hollywood there was "enormous optimism" for the film; MGM was expecting it to be a blockbuster.

The official British premiere was held on 16 October. The fact that the next day British newspaper critics were, by and large, disapproving did not immediately signal doom. After all, Schlesinger and Janni had come to expect such a reaction from them. Alexander Walker quipped that "only from the neckline down does this Bathsheba belong in Queen Victoria's reign," and Dilys Powell in the *Sunday Times* summed up the whole long epic as "faintly dull, faintly boring." Flying to New York that same day, John could only hope that, as they had with *Darling*, the American critics would prove his salvation.

He was met in New York by a gaggle of excited executives from MGM, who had big plans for him. A huge premiere party was scheduled for Hollywood on 19 October, and so great was the hype over the film that they were squeezing in a Washington premiere between those in New York and the West Coast. John was put up at the Plaza, and though he couldn't quite shake the sinking feeling in his gut, he allowed himself, for twenty-four hours, to hope for the best.

He knew, however, watching the audience shift in their seats at the Capitol Theater, that it was all over. Sure enough, in the morning, he got word that the Washington premiere was scrapped. Bosley Crowther in the *New York Times* had rung down the curtain on their plans, skewering the film for "antiquated narrative form and the dullness of its character revelations, which is most odd for Mr. Schlesinger." So great was Crowther's outrage that he would pen an essay for the *Times* headlined "Magnificence is No Longer Enough," taking epic films like *Madding Crowd* and *Camelot* to task for relying on elaborate production methods while ignoring human conflict: "How could John Schlesinger, who is one of the more brilliant of the group of young directors working in England, have let *Far from the Madding Crowd* become the pictorially excessive but dramatically barren film it is? Surely he knew that popular interest could not be held with simply lots of droll farm scenes."

The flight from New York to Los Angeles was one of the longest trips Schlesinger ever took. Seated across the aisle from him was the actor Lee J. Cobb, with whom he'd shared some pleasantries when they'd boarded. But when out of the corner of his eye John watched Cobb unfold his *New York Times* and begin reading Crowther's review, he wanted to melt into his seat. With him was an MGM publicity man, who whispered in his ear, "You know you're going to have to be really careful what you do next. What is this *Midnight Cowboy* idea?" Such concern about *Cowboy* would continue to be raised by his colleagues; John would later describe them as "Job's comforters."

"I arrived a jibbering wreck in Hollywood," John remembered, met by a handful of grey suits from MGM who put on false smiles and airs of solicitude and told him they'd taken the liberty of canceling the party that night, "since they knew how tired I must be." The actual premiere, however, could not be canceled; John had to go through with it, with the MGM reps either staying home or ignoring him. As he and Julie arrived in their limousine, John thought, "For months on end we were knee-deep in shit in Dorset, and here we are in an even bigger mess."

It was John's first visit to Hollywood. While the limousine waited to pull up to the theater, he listened as the stars' arrivals were announced: "Ladies and gentlemen, Mr. Edward G. Robinson!" Craning his neck when Julie nudged him, John spotted Hitchcock in the next car. But then they hurried down the red carpet to hide in the manager's office for the duration of the screening, unable to watch it again. It was an instructive introduction to Hollywood; he'd remember that premiere for the end of *The Day of the Locust* and, in truth, his lifelong relationship with the film colony never became much different than it was that night. He was always the edgy outsider, needing to prove himself over and over again, yet nonetheless endlessly fascinated by the glitz and, sometimes tawdry, glamor that surrounded him.

Later, at a reception, he met Ruth Gordon. "That'll teach you to leave those fucking classics alone," said the ancient, tiny actress, looking up at him. He laughed heartily, and they became friends.

Throughout his career, John Schlesinger was never on top long enough to really get used to it. All of the dazzle of the last two years evaporated with the disastrous premiere of *Far from the Madding Crowd*. It would barely be seen in America, no matter how hard John tried to sell it in a promotional campaign that MGM had suddenly lost all interest in supporting.

"You feel a failure in America," he observed, looking back. "My God, you do. The phone doesn't ring, people turn on their heel away from you. Because success is a god and failure is a disease. I think in Britain, it's rather the reverse. I think the British have a slightly nasty smell under their nose about anybody who's had a success, particularly elsewhere, and I find both [attitudes] equally reprehensible."

In Britain, the film eventually found an audience, but it wasn't Schlesinger's; it was an audience of matrons who appreciated the beauty of the costumes and the scenery. On television, while the film inevitably lost much of its scope and scale, it seemed more accessible and not as formidable as it had on the big screen; it became a Christmas staple for many years.

"It has its own sort of hypnosis, I think," Alan Bates told me, defending the film, which was virtually ignored by the British Film Academy. It gained just two nominations, one for

Nic Roeg's photography and another for Alan Barrett's costumes – really the two best things about the film.

Brendan Gill in the *New Yorker* suggested that the "Messrs. Janni and Schlesinger rush straight back to their rightful kingdom – that of *Billy Liar, Darling*, and the nervous, rootless, talkative urban present." Indeed, it was jarring to see the three stars, Christie, Bates and Stamp, who were so identified with modern styles and trends – so Swinging London – dressed in period costumes and acting with melodramatic postures. One almost expects at any moment that they'll burst into laughter and discard their funny voices, and Julie will tear off her long dress to reveal a miniskirt underneath. A film, no matter what its individual merits, is never seen in a vacuum. The contextual placement is significant; thus it was quite simply impossible for *Far from the Madding Crowd* not to remind one of *Darling* – "to its detriment," as Alexander Walker pointed out. That's not to suggest artists never vary their output; certainly what makes John Schlesinger's career dynamic is the number of genres and styles with which he experimented. But it is meant to offer the idea that timing is often everything; and if John had wanted to film a classic, he should have been more insightful about which classic to choose.

Andrew Sarris, as ever, brought his own eloquence to the debate, with his famous observation that any hopes of Julie Christie becoming the "British Karina for a British Godard" had now been dashed. Sarris took Schlesinger to task for his choice of projects, and for "*nouvelle vague* lyrical excesses like reiterated actions in slow motion" (Bathsheba in the grain market). But his major complaint was about the split he observed in the film between the actors and nature. If *Madding Crowd*'s most successful quality is its visual embrace of its bucolic setting, Schlesinger failed to integrate it with story and character: "Schlesinger's 'nature,'" Sarris wrote, "degenerates into a mere production value."

"Perhaps," Sarris went on to reflect, "we have been spoiled by Godard's fierce spirit of inquiry to expect too much of directors in less congenial environments. The British cinema has never been a stronghold of directorial style. The script is too sacred, the acting too overwhelming, the commercial pressures even more oppressive than Hollywood's."

John must have appreciated Sarris at least offering some context, even if the review was damning. The project was doomed before it even began. Penelope Mortimer in *The Observer* put her finger directly on the problem when she opined that "Hardy will not translate, he will only transfer." Even if Schlesinger and Raphael had not been less faithful in their adaptation, they would still likely have come up with an unworkable formula; Hardy was not meant for popular entertainment, which was what MGM wanted in *Far from the Madding Crowd*.

In the end, as Mortimer wrote, John probably made the film "as well as it could be done," but ultimately, what we are left with is "a beautifully illustrated edition of the book that, while harmless, seems curiously unnecessary."

"I was attracted to Hardy," John observed later, "because I was tired of presenting negative solutions to current problems. Hardy observed people's relationships very truly. He saw life as an endurance contest and felt that if Fate or Providence – call it what you will – knocks you down, you must pick yourself up and force yourself to go on. Here is a real affirmation of existence."

I read that quote of John's, given in 1975, as I sat opposite him in Palm Springs. Every day when he woke up now he forced himself to go on, but what kind of affirmation of existence was this? Sitting in his wheelchair, not speaking, not reading, no longer even able to feed himself?

"Here you go, sweetie," Michael said, fixing a bowl of strawberries and cream and placing it in front of John. "You want me to do it? Or do you want to try yourself?"

When I'd first started spending time with him, John never wanted me to see others feeding him. He would insist on doing it himself, his shaky hand bringing the spoon to his mouth, even if he sometimes made a bit of a mess. Now he didn't seem to care. Michael sat down in front of him. "Okay, sweetie," he said. "Open up."

They had met in Hollywood in those first terrible weeks after the disastrous American premiere of *Far from the Madding Crowd*. It had been a miserable John Schlesinger who stepped off that plane, but it would be a trip that changed his life.

I watched them. Such a simple gesture to feed someone. More than three decades of highs and lows, hits and misses, laughter and conflicts – so many movies and parties and friends and collaborators – and now, in the quiet of a Sunday morning, it was just the two of them.

"Taste good, John?" Michael asked quietly, as he wiped his partner's mouth. I saw the look that passed between them. Nothing mattered anymore but now.

Ten

1967–1969

"Things you see in America"

"Look, John," said Gary Shaw, his friend and assistant. "There's Ian, with a very hot boyfriend in tow."

We were watching the Academy Awards. John was riveted to the widescreen television as the camera swept over the stars assembled in the audience. There indeed was his old friend Ian McKellen, whose American stardom had been made possible by John through *Cold Comfort Farm*. Nominated that night for Best Supporting Actor for *Lord of the Rings*, McKellen was sitting beside his attractive, long-haired, 22-year-old lover, Nick Cuthell. John actually managed a smile.

"And over there, John," Gary said. "Maggie Smith! And there's Jon Voight. Three of your good friends right there."

Those past few days, John had been a bit more communicative. Maureen had even taken him to see *Gosford Park*, directed by his contemporary Robert Altman and produced by

Bob Balaban, who'd played the scared teenager in *Midnight Cowboy*. When I asked John if he'd liked the film, he said under his breath it was "all right." When I asked him if he thought it would win the Oscar, he shook his head no.

It was the first Academy Awards ceremony since the terrorist attacks on 11 September, so a tribute to the City of New York was planned, a montage of scenes from films set in Manhattan. I knew there had to be a clip from *Cowboy*. It had come to be regarded as a profound and iconic portrait of New York's seedy underbelly, and one of the great American classics. On its twenty-fifth anniversary in 1994, a documentary film had been made about it; on its thirtieth in 1999, a new DVD was issued and a host of screenings arranged. John and Jerry Hellman and Dustin Hoffman and Jon Voight and Brenda Vaccaro had gathered for retrospectives and photographs.

"Did you know you were making a classic?" I asked Jon Voight.

"You never know," he told me. "You just do the work. But I knew it was special. I knew I had a great director, an extraordinary project, great people I was working with. *Midnight Cowboy* was the beginning of a great period of American film. Bing! The bell was rung and we were into a serious group of extraordinary films."

I considered the films up for nomination in 2002. A good bunch, though few risk-takers: *Moulin Rouge!* was the only one to push at form and convention. *In the Bedroom* had some great acting; *Lord of the Rings* dazzled with awesome effects; *Gosford Park* showed a master at work but, in truth, not doing anything he hadn't already done before. John was right: it wouldn't win. In the end, it was *A Beautiful Mind*, the most formulaic of them all, that took the prize.

"I remember shooting the last scene in *Cowboy*," said Jon Voight. "We were running down this road in Texas chasing after this ambulance. And out in back behind the trailers I found John shaking – all by himself and shaking terribly. It was like he was having a heart attack. I said, 'John what's wrong?' And he looked at me, with such fear in his eyes, and he said, 'What will they think of this? It's about a dishwasher who goes to New York to fuck a lot of women. What will they *think*?'

"I grabbed him by the shoulders," Voight continued, not knowing John behaved like this at least once on all of his films. "I held him firm and I said, 'John. Listen to me. You and I will spend the rest of our lives in the shadow of this masterpiece.'"

He sat back in his chair and laughed. "I said the most extravagant thing I could think of to shake him from his fear. But I wasn't far off the mark."

"There it is, John!" Gary was shouting. "There's Jon Voight in *Cowboy*!"

It was just a brief clip, spliced into a gaggle of other films: Joe Buck sauntering down a Manhattan street, head and shoulders above the rest of the crowd.

John had seen it. His eyes were still on the screen. He began making that gesture with his hand again, rubbing his head in repetitive circles.

The camera panned across the audience again. "It's all Brits," Gary observed. "What do you think, John? A roomful of Brits. Ian, Maggie, Judi Dench, Jim Broadbent, Ben Kingsley, Helen Mirren."

He'd never been to the Oscars. Three times nominated, but never had John Schlesinger sat amongst the tuxedos and sequins for this yearly display of stuff and nonsense. He wasn't a part of them – not now, certainly, but never, really. Watching the Oscars in 1974 John had recorded in his diary how he was struck by the "awful feeling of how frightful the standards of success are and how dependent people seem to be on it." When a few years earlier the director Robert Aldrich had requested a print of *Midnight Cowboy* for a private screening, John wrote back: "It was decided some time ago that since David Picker, Jerry Hellman and I all despise the Bel Air circuit, the worst possible way for *Midnight Cowboy* to be seen, that we were going to make no exceptions whatsoever to private screenings in people's homes."

I looked over at him. John was now slumped down in his chair, his hand making ever more frantic circles on his head. Maureen jumped up and asked him if he wanted to leave. "Yes," he whispered.

Was it too much, seeing the clips, seeing his friends, feeling cut off, removed from the action? Or did he perhaps just not want to be reminded of a world he'd never wanted to be a part of, no matter how much he had helped to shape it?

During those depressing first weeks, as the enormity of the disaster of *Madding Crowd* settled down upon him, he took a place in Malibu. Maybe by the water, he hoped, with the sound of the Pacific in his ears, he could lick his wounds a little, and finally turn his full attention to *Midnight Cowboy*.

Welcome to America. And more specifically, to Hollywood: the "terribly vulgar" house he rented had garish pink walls and bright purple bedspreads. He felt as if he needed to wear sunglasses indoors.

Calls came in from MGM grumbling that *Madding Crowd* was too long. At 169 minutes, they were right, and John volunteered to "sweat some footage out of it." Instead, veteran film editor Margaret Booth, whose career stretched back to the silent cinema, was brought in to do the work. John was appalled at Booth's "hatchet job," most particularly at the way she had lopped off the ending. As originally filmed, after Bathsheba marries Gabriel, she is last seen fondling a music box given her by Troy, suggesting the happy ending has its qualifications. It was typically Schlesinger, but American audiences – the few who actually saw the film – were left with only the good cheer of the wedding scene. It was a producer-contrived happy ending, taken out of John's hands, that would echo 33 years later on *The Next Best Thing*.

And so, by the fall of 1967 John found himself alone and in a serious funk in Hollywood. Planning for *Cowboy* alone sustained him. At last they were moving ahead with a script, but getting to that point had not been easy. For the last several months, they had been laboring with the writer Jack Gelber, an edgy young playwright whose play about junkies, *The Connection*, had been made into an independent film by Shirley Clarke in 1961.

Before settling on Gelber, however, there had been a few other flirtations, one of the more tantalizing among them with a young unknown writer named Francis Ford Coppola. In June 1966, Hellman had written that Coppola was "a man of talent and imagination," but by August they had decided to go with Gelber, who agreed to deliver his first draft by January. He was paid $15,000 for the first draft, plus $5,000 for first revisions, then $7,500 if more substantial revisions were required after that.

John wrote to Gelber from the muddy fields of Dorset with some insights into the story: "What attracted me to the character of the Cowboy was his basic innocence and naiveté and need for love. The idea of a new look at the city is another reason for wanting to make the film." John encouraged Gelber to "throw caution to the winds and be bold."

Perhaps Gelber was too bold. In his first draft he refused to write Ratso as a cripple, calling it a clichéd device. Neither John nor Jerry were pleased with his take on the story. "We wanted to make a study of life both imagined and real in New York as it is today," John wrote to Hellman, "as experienced by a rather dumb lonely attractive character, who grows with an experience, and with a relationship with another human being. It is this element, the feeling of going through an experience with Joe Buck, that I find lacking in Jack's script."

Gelber did not respond well to such feedback, and John seemed unwilling to talk with him further. In April, Gelber traveled to London, hoping to meet with the director, but John was never able to find the time, so consumed was he by *Madding Crowd*. Yet to snub Gelber in such a way also indicates that he'd become fed up with the writer, who by this time had told Hellman he was considering dispensing with Ratso as a character altogether. "It seems to me," John wrote to Gelber in astonishment, "that their relationship [Joe's and Ratso's] is crucial to the reason for doing the story at all."

By the end of June, reading Gelber's second attempt, it was clear they needed a new writer. Jerry considered the television writers Loring Mandel and James Bridges, but the breakthrough came that summer. On 3 August, Hellman sent John the first 40 pages of a script about a draft dodger; it was written by a man named Waldo Salt. John immediately cabled him back saying he was impressed. "It was a pleasure to read something from a writer who really thinks filmically," John wrote later. "He certainly knows the 'hippy' scene alright."

Waldo Salt had been writing screenplays since the 1930s, and had been blacklisted in the 1950s for his membership of the Communist Party, but at the time John had never heard of him. "In came this disheveled, wonderful kind of amiable man," John remembered, "a man who'd obviously been through a great deal of personal pain." The loss of his career had left Salt disillusioned for many years, and by the early 1960s he found himself writing hack scripts for undistinguished movies. He insisted he would "never again write less than I was capable of," and began work on the script that his agent would show Jerry Hellman. "It was this street-savvy movie," Hellman remembered, "and even though its subject was different [from *Cowboy*] it was crazy, it was alive, it was exactly what we needed."

Born in 1914, Waldo was considerably older than both John and Jerry, older than any of the other writers they'd considered, and, indeed, older than they thought practical for writing such a modern story about modern times. But, as John recognized, Salt was conversant with the "hippy" scene; he was a man very much of the moment, with no allegiance to the past.

By the fall of 1967, as John was adjusting to his new life in California, the final script for *Midnight Cowboy* began taking shape under Salt's hand. It would concentrate on the second half of the novel, excising Joe's childhood in favor of his move to New York and his relationship with Ratso. Salt's notebooks reveal a brilliant creative process, words alternating with little images doodled in ink. Many television sets are sketched in the margins. TV, with its promise, its fantasy, its deception in American culture, was to be a major motif in *Midnight Cowboy*.

John would remember lying on his purple bed in his pink room with the remote control in his hand, "punching away at all this mass of television in America." It was the first time he'd ever had a remote control, "one of the most terrible tools," he thought, "because it makes all of us even lazier than we already are." Suddenly he came across an image so bizarre he had to sit up and make sure it was real: a wigmaker for poodles! He immediately leapt up off the bed and rang Waldo to shout, "Channel Seven! Look at it now, this minute! We could use it!"

And they did: Joe Buck sits in the bathtub and sees it, the man making wigs for poodles and offering them breath spray. "The fantasy, the offer," John said. "This is the madness of it all."

Later, at one a.m. at Canter's Deli on Fairfax Avenue, he spotted the woman and the child and the toy mouse. Strung out on drugs, it was the mother not the boy amusing herself with the toy, running it all over the table. "I was horrified but also attracted," John remembered, and this too Waldo incorporated into the film.

For the first time John really relished the experience of working with his writer. Not that there weren't problems. "They loved each other," said Waldo's daughter Jennifer Salt, who had a small part as Joe Buck's girlfriend in the flashbacks. "But I think my dad was frustrating to John because he was so slow. He was a 'putter-offer.' He would just ignore the script for a really long time because something had to be just right before he would sit down and write it. I don't know how conscious that was. The muse visits in some obscure secret way. But by the time he finally sat down, he would have it."

It was the kind of "what if" process John so loved. "Collaborating with all the creative people involved in making a movie is a real challenge," he'd say. "Everything is fine at the outset, but as work on the production progresses, egos assert themselves and tempers can flare. Nonetheless, this can mean a healthy conflict as you confront the people you are working with and make discoveries together."

"John in my memory was very emotional and intuitive and visual and visceral," said Jennifer Salt. "What he wasn't was a fancy-pants intellect. I think constructing a screenplay is really, really hard and if you're a good storyteller, which I think John was, you need a really good story to work from. I don't think that's what he does, invent the story. He looks to a strong writer for that.

"I remember that it was a big breakthrough when John and my dad made the decision that the flashbacks were insights into Joe Buck's mind," she continued. "And that the flashbacks had to come when something in the present would trigger them, so that there was a relationship. The flashbacks would be an illumination of the present. Once they came up with that, it kind of unlocked the story."

It was an approach similar to the one taken with *Billy Liar*, when the fantasies grew out of specific events that connected them to the narrative. The specific problem with *Midnight Cowboy* had been how to squeeze in all the exposition that was needed to explain Joe's past: where he'd come from, how his dreams had been formed. Characters and situations from the book would either have to be dropped or radically condensed; neither John nor Waldo wanted to spend too much time cluttering up the main story. Flashbacks — quick, abstract, mostly visual — were seen as the way to go. There would be plenty of rethinking that decision, but for the moment it allowed them to move ahead.

Reading Salt's script, both John and Jerry realized they'd need much more than the $1 million budgeted. Hellman showed the script to David Picker, who loved it, finagling an increase that more than doubled the film's budget. It wasn't quite the $2.8 million Hellman was asking for, but a reasonable compromise of $2.2. There was a condition, though: John, Jerry and Waldo all had to agree to defer much of their salaries in lieu of a percentage of the profits. "I was able to keep increasing our percentages because they didn't think this film would make as much money as it did," Hellman would say, looking back, eminently pleased with his negotiating skills. In the end, their salaries were modest: John got $50,000 in cash, Jerry $25,000. But by splitting 60 percent of the profits, both Schlesinger and Hellman would get rich. "At the time, United Artists would rather give us an extra 10 percent than an extra $10,000," Hellman said, enjoying a good long laugh over the memory.

Yet as much as John enjoyed the process of creating the *Cowboy* script, he felt adrift living in Los Angeles. He knew few people and missed his circle of friends in London. The failure of *Madding Crowd* meant he wasn't invited to Hollywood parties; one of the few kind words sent his way came from Jack Lemmon ("bless him") who offered him a job directing *The April Fools*.

"John was terribly, terribly lonely," said Kaye Ballard, who invited him out to her house in Palm Springs. They had met a few years before during all the hoopla over *Darling*, when he'd come to see her in *The Decline and Fall of the Entire World as Seen Through the Eyes of Cole Porter* at the Square East Theatre in New York. John had enjoyed Ballard's rollicking sense of humor, and looked forward to seeing her again in Palm Springs.

But gone was the buoyant personality Ballard remembered

from New York. "He didn't have anyone in his life, not a soul," she said. Later, John would call her the "Dolly Levi of the desert," for Kaye took it upon herself to engineer a little match-making. Ringing her press agent, Jay Allen, Ballard asked, "Who can we fix John Schlesinger up with?" The very first name from Allen's lips was "Michael Childers."

"Oh, my, Michael was a cute little fella!" Ballard laughed as she recounted the tale for me. "So I arranged for them to meet. But I kept thinking, what have I gotten John into? He's so *young!*"

"I was 22 years old, with long blonde hair," Michael remembered, sitting on the couch, gesturing over to a picture of himself with John, taken not long after they met. He was indeed stunning. "I was a cinema major at UCLA, and *Darling* was my favorite film. I mean, Julie Christie in Swinging London! I wanted to hop on the next plane over there!"

So he was thrilled to be set up as a blind date for John Schlesinger, but a bit wary, too. Nearly twenty years separated them, after all, and Childers had just read an article that called John "mercurial." "So I took an actor friend with me for safety," he said. "One kick meant we go, two kicks meant I could handle the situation."

They met at the Beverly Wilshire Hotel. "After a couple glasses of wine," Michael said, "I gave my friend two kicks. John was absolutely charming. And the rest is history."

A film buff from the time he was a young boy, Childers, the son of a Marine Corps colonel, was born in North Carolina. He grew up in various places around the country as his father was transferred from post to post. Like John, he'd been a "different" child: while his athletic brothers papered their walls with posters of sports stars, the young Michael cut clippings from

Vogue and *Paris Match*. "I had Richard Avedon and Irving Penn and Suzy Parker and Audrey Hepburn all over my bedroom," he said. "I was the only kid on the block who read the *New York Times* Sunday Arts and Leisure section." He was already dreaming glamorous dreams. Enrolling at UCLA as a business administration major, he soon switched to theater and cinema arts.

It was a time of change in Hollywood, but some of the old glamor lingered. While still in college, Michael took a job as assistant to the legendary Hollywood designer Jimmy Pendleton. "Jimmy would say, 'Don't you have a shirt and tie? I want you to go pick up Norma.' And I'd say, 'Norma who?' And he'd shout, 'Norma Shearer, you fool! And on the way back, stop and pick up Agnes Moorehead. I'm throwing a party for Claudette.'"

Michael laughed, remembering how very young and starstruck he was. "I mean, Claudette Colbert! You can imagine the thrill. The pool parties at Pendleton's – Clifton Webb, Edward G. Robinson. And George Cukor! I just loved George."

Meeting John Schlesinger, however, offered access into a new Hollywood that complemented the old. "I was still living in my hippy student house up in Beverly Glen, and we were giving a dinner party for our friend, the French film director Jacques Demy," Michael remembered. "I invited John, and asked him if there was any way he could bring Natalie Wood, because I knew they were friendly. And he did! Can you imagine? When Natalie Wood walked in, my friends went ape shit! Pretty heady stuff for twenty-year-old film students at UCLA."

Smitten, John would've done anything to impress Michael.

Bringing Natalie was a snap: she was one of the few Hollywood stars he liked, down-to-earth, unassuming, and very glad to accompany him to Michael's soiree. Within a year she'd marry John's agent Richard Gregson; after their divorce, it was Natalie, not Gregson, who stayed on in John's life.

"John fell head-over-heels for Michael," said Stewart Grimshaw. "That was very obvious."

In some ways, the initial fascination for Michael Childers resembled his earlier love affairs: absolute intoxication with another person who was physically more attractive than he was, more outgoing, more confident. Growing up, John had dealt with his sense of difference by drawing into himself; Michael had done the opposite. He was gregarious and social, boisterous and emphatic. Even at this point in John's life, with all his success, Schlesinger still found it awkward entering a room full of people he didn't know. Childers, by contrast, plunged in with gusto, charming everyone in the room within minutes.

So it wasn't just his physical beauty that attracted John, far from it: the physical alone was never enough to hold his passion for long. He was also enraptured by Michael's energy, his sense of purpose, and indeed his talent: the young man's photography included unique, penetrating portraits of his friends and associates, artists just blossoming onto the scene. One of these was Rod McKuen, who chose a Childers photograph as the cover of an album.

Yet for all the seeming echoes of past relationships, Michael also offered John something new and different: unlike John's past lovers, Michael was *available*. There was nothing bisexual about Childers, nothing to keep John at arm's length, no excuses, no prevarication. A child of the American Sixties, Michael was very grounded in his gay identity, unapologetic and politically liberal – in his own words a "hippy," and in many ways an activist for change. This time, John saw dangling before him the chance at a real relationship, a thrilling new experience.

"It took a couple of months to get serious," Childers said. Obviously flattered by the attention he was getting from a bigtime film director, he nonetheless remained cautious, a bit detached. That is, until his twenty-third birthday on 11 November, when John treated him to a weekend in Carmel. They stayed at the Tickle Pink Inn, a romantic hideaway recommended by Natalie Wood, perched atop rugged cliffs overlooking the Pacific and the lush Carmel Highlands.

"We were sitting there, drinking too much chardonnay, looking out at the sea," Childers remembered. "I looked into John's eyes and started to cry. 'This is very special,' I told him. 'I want you to know that I feel something very special.' We were falling in love."

For the first time in his life, John's affections were being returned as equally as he was giving them. For the first time he was experiencing the exhilaration of falling mutually in love, with the object of his desire responding to him with equal ardor and passion. Forty-one years it had taken to arrive at this point, forty-one years of heartache and disappointment, of being "afraid to love." Whatever growth had taken place, whatever strength had been acquired through those difficulties, now enabled John, for once, to fall in love with someone for whom it was possible to love him back. It changed his life.

"Of course I knew all along that John was gay," said Jerry Hellman. "But you know, he was very reserved about it, didn't talk about it much. When he came here [to Los Angeles] he was hiding it from people. He talked to me about his fears, how he was afraid an American crew, if they found out, would turn on him, make fag jokes behind his back. I said, 'John, we're the bosses here. If someone's stupid enough to do that, we'll fire them.' But the fear was very real."

Meeting Childers galvanized him, Hellman said. "Sparks were flying. I could see that very clearly. He was entranced with Michael. Who wouldn't be? Mike was a beautiful young guy, and no dope, either. He was a brilliant photographer and made wonderful suggestions about what we could do on *Midnight Cowboy*."

So helpful was he that John wanted to hire him as his assistant for the film, but was worried what Jerry might think. "I told him, 'This is our picture. Let's ride this tiger. Let's put Michael on the movie and fuck anyone who doesn't like it.'"

Childers remembered the moment with affection. "John asked me if I might be interested in working on this little movie he was making in New York. Hah! Little movie! He gave me the book to read and I said, 'This is incredible! What an opportunity!'" He still had six months until graduation, he recalled, but figured the opportunity John was offering could promise him much more than a diploma. "I mean, for a film student to start with *Midnight Cowboy* as his first movie . . . My God!"

"John was dazzled by him, honey," Brenda Vaccaro said. "I was there! I saw! And Michael was so gorgeous, just a baby, and he was taking pictures of everything. So cute and so much fun. He's got that Scorpio charm and when he was young, he was even more dazzling. Michael's always had the desire to be the handsomest boy in the room, you know what I mean? He could have been a movie star himself. And together, he and John – oh, my God, what tremendous communion they had together as partners. They were going to conquer the world, the two of them; equally talented, equally ambitious."

Hellman said the relationship with Michael served as a tremendous creative catalyst for Schlesinger. The depression which had marked John's first months in America was replaced with an exuberant passion by the time filming began. "He was on fire during *Cowboy*," Hellman said. "It was thrilling to watch. He just came alive."

Soon after Christmas, 1967, Childers went with John to see *The Graduate*. "We were looking at this guy, Dustin Hoffman, to see if he was right for *Midnight Cowboy*," he said. But John felt Hoffman all wrong: Benjamin Braddock, the earnest young college student seduced by Mrs. Robinson, was as far away as possible from how he envisioned the slovenly, straggly Ratso Rizzo.

Jerry Hellman had been pushing Hoffman for almost a year, having seen him Off-Broadway in the play Eh by Henry Livings. In February 1967, Jerry had written to John that Mike Nichols had signed Hoffman to do *The Graduate*, but that Dustin was "so high on *Midnight Cowboy*" that he wouldn't have accepted the part if it had meant losing his chance with them. Hellman urged John to meet Hoffman, who was passing through London en route from Spain back to America. Swift action was needed, Jerry urged: he'd heard that Nichols was trying to sign Hoffman for his fall production of *The Little Foxes*. But once again Dustin promised he'd decline if it interfered with his getting the part in *Cowboy*.

John, exhausted from *Madding Crowd*, chose not to meet with Hoffman in London. It wasn't until late that year, when he caught his performance in *The Graduate*, that he would have any sense of who this Dustin Hoffman was. And then he thought Jerry was out of his mind for suggesting him.

Hoffman wasn't typical movie star material. He was part of that late Sixties insurgence of oddball, eccentric-looking stars: Streisand, Walter Matthau, Lee Marvin, Elliott Gould, Donald Sutherland. But neither was he a repulsive slimeball of the Ratso Rizzo sort: in *The Graduate* he had looked downright wholesome.

Determined to win the role, Hoffman met Schlesinger soon after the New Year in Times Square. He dressed the part: unshaven, greasy hair, frayed shoes, a dirty old raincoat. He took John to Giordano's, an Italian restaurant in Hell's Kitchen, where the head waiter was always snatching up coins and tips. "I wanted John to see this guy," Hoffman remembered, "because I thought he was who Ratso would want to be." Head waiter in a Hell's Kitchen restaurant, pocketing tips: that was Ratso's idea of success, and John was pleased to see he and Hoffman shared similar insights into the character. "We sat there and we talked the same language," Hoffman said. "We had an immediate aesthetic marriage."

They walked the city until late that night, visiting poolhouses and automats and all-night cafes. "Hoffman blended in so incredibly," John said, "that the Benjamin from *The Graduate* disappeared."

They didn't just discuss Ratso. A conversation with a man who seemed sweet but possessed "killer eyes" prompted a conversation about the film's other lead role, that of Joe Buck: "We discussed the idea that we needed an actor for the Cowboy who was innocent but also had the possibility of violence in him," John said.

Now that Ratso had been cast, the more complicated task of finding Joe Buck took center stage. Warren Beatty, then in the midst of his much-hyped romance with Julie Christie, got word to John that he was interested in the part, but John rejected the idea out of hand. "Somehow," he would later record in his diary, "seeing Warren Beatty fail as a hustler on 42nd Street would seem ludicrous." Robert Redford, too, expressed interest; in October 1966, Hellman had written John that while he considered Redford a "terribly exciting screen personality," he wasn't right for Joe Buck. John heartily agreed.

The final candidates included Kiel Martin, a television actor who'd appeared in *The Virginian* and *Ironside,* and Keir Dullea, who'd just made a splash in *The Fox* and who would, in a short time, appear in Kubrick's *2001.* Hoffman took the trouble to rehearse with all of the Joe Buck candidates, a wonderful gesture which John appreciated. By March of 1968 it had come down to two: Jon Voight and Michael Sarrazin, with both Schlesinger and Hellman leaning toward Sarrazin. A handsome, intense actor just on the crest of fame, Sarrazin seemed to have a lock on the part when suddenly Universal, which had him under contract, upped his price and refused to provide a firm start date.

"With John in the room, I called Universal and said, 'Good news, Mr. Schlesinger has decided Michael is the actor for this part,'" Hellman remembered. "So Universal said, 'Okay, let's make a deal.' I said, 'We made a deal weeks ago.' John looked at me and said, 'Is what I think is happening really happening?' I nodded yes and John said, 'Do what you want to do,' so I slammed the phone down."

They went back to the tests. Hellman was already in Voight's camp, loving his "elk in the headlights" eyes, but John had some real doubts. Casting director Marion Dougherty had first sent in his shots, and they hadn't matched John's conception of Joe Buck at all. He looked too blond, "too Dutch," John thought; in his mind, the Cowboy was dark, brooding, not so big. But Dougherty had insisted John see him, and then Voight had charmed him by gushing about *A Kind of Loving*.

"I think John saw that I was enthusiastic about his art and not just somebody looking for a job," Voight said. Still, Schlesinger discouraged the young actor by hardly acknowledging even why he was there, going on and on about Kiel Martin, about how he thought he was perfect. "I don't know why he did that," Voight said. "I don't think it was trying to prepare me for defeat. He was just being open, but he was acting as if I didn't even have a shot."

It seems cruel, and indeed there would be stories of John, increasingly from this time, being insensitive, even belittling, to actors and others on the set. "He could go from being so kind and courteous to being absolutely brutal," said one person who asked to remain nameless. "It was as if he was determined to show he was in charge, he was the god of the movie, he could do anything he wanted."

Despite his apparent indifference, Schlesinger ordered a screen test for Voight. It remains a fascinating artifact: Voight, done up in tacky purple Western garb, stands awkwardly in front of the camera, responding as best he can to a volley of rapid-fire questions from Waldo Salt.

"How long since you been on a horse, cowboy?"

He stammers, seeming not sure how to answer. "Now you're gettin' personal," he finally says.

His accent isn't right. He keeps saying "shee-it" when he can't think of anything else to say.

"You ever make it with a man?" Salt asks.

"You do what you can." He thinks of a better answer. "I make it with fuckin' *sheep*."

"What about the kids in Vietnam?"

The cowboy fumbles. He can't answer that one.

"What will women like about you?"

He smirks. "I got somethin' in my pants they'll like."

"No, no, no," John said when he first saw it. This cowboy was too angry, too defensive. Voight came across hostile, and Joe Buck was anything but – not at first anyway, and certainly not on the surface. The rage was buried deep down inside; it would not be so easily enticed forward by a few simple questions.

Yet when he went back to the screen test after it was clear they'd lost Sarrazin, John saw something else. In Voight's very awkwardness, in his very inability to come back with quick-witted replies, he saw Joe Buck's vulnerability. His innocence. This was a boy not ready for the bigtime, which was precisely what the part needed. "I think," John told Hellman, "Universal may have kept us from making a terrible mistake." Voight was informed the role was his.

Dustin Hoffman knew and liked Voight – they had worked together off-Broadway in Arthur Miller's *A View to the Bridge* – so the chemistry was already in place. Whatever doubts John might have had about his two actors quickly disappeared as they began rehearsals; soon their chemistry had rubbed off on him as well. "We worked very well together, the three of us," Voight remembered. "John really enjoyed Dusty. He was like enter-tainment for John. Me, I was his pal going through the mud. He shared stuff with me, confidences. Dusty also had a surer hand in his character. I knew there were still lots of doubts about me."

Not as many as he thought, however: in another pattern that would repeat itself on future films, John had started withholding praise from his actors in fear they might become complacent. "I overheard a conversation in which John said he didn't want to show me rushes because he didn't want me to know how good I was doing," Voight said. "He thought it would turn my head or something."

The rest of the cast was complete by April except for a few small roles which would be filled by Texas locals that summer. Sylvia Miles, as the brassy Park Avenue hooker who gives Joe his first taste – literally – of the Big Apple, was ordered by contract to put on weight; Cass was meant to be over-fed and over-ripe. Bob Balaban, the young nephew of Barney Balaban, chairman of the board at Paramount, was signed for the teenaged homosexual who propositions Joe in the theater. For Shirley, the sexy society girl Joe meets slumming it at the loft party, Ann Wedgeworth and Eileen Brennan were considered, but John seemed most taken by Janice Rule, who'd been making films since the 1950s and was then enjoying a bit of a vogue after playing the party girl in Arthur Penn's *The Chase* (1966).

"Janice Rule was a formidable competitor," said Brenda Vaccaro, who ended up with the part. "John had his eye on her. I think if he'd been straight, he would have hired her, no question. Because he was mad for her. She was beautiful, she was mesmerizing. Take a look at her with Brando in *The Chase* and listen to that voice and you'll see what John [originally] had in mind for the part. He thought I was too nice. That I wouldn't convey enough of that Madison Avenue, very crisp, unpleasant person – you know, sexy but ball-cutting. He had me come and read maybe six or seven times. I was worn out. I hated it. And then he made me wait two weeks which drove me mad. He was taking his time with it because Shirley's the only bit of glamor he had in the movie."

Glamor. A subjective word. For one could argue there's glamor in Joe Buck riding that bus from Texas to New York to the catchy, upbeat, hopeful tempo of Nilsson's "Everybody's Talkin'". There's glamor in that sense of discovery, in the feeling of newness and cinematic risk-taking that pervades the film. Glamor not of the old kind, which esteemed beauty at the expense of truth and never challenged the old bromides, but rather a new, original glamor, based on youth, rebellion, and change. Looking back now after 30-plus years, there is definitely a glamor to *Midnight Cowboy*: to the fresh, young appearances of Hoffman and Voight, and the boldness of Waldo Salt's script, in which he often traded dialogue for visuals — something John had been desperate to do on *Darling* and which stunned and excited many cineastes here. Watching the film today, with an understanding of its context and how it ripped a hole down the center of cinematic propriety, gives it a counter-culture mystique that is still dazzling to behold.

The film's story is breathtakingly simple: Joe Buck, small-town Texas stud, figures he can make it rich in the big city by pimping himself out to wealthy women. But his dreams are shattered when he finds the streets of New York are paved with grime and vomit instead of gold, and that his quest isn't so much about fame and fortune as it is simply a search for his own humanity. Alone, adrift, there is nowhere for him to go — not back, certainly, and not forward, either, for there is no one in this enormous, uncaring city who shows him any kindness, any concern, any love. Except, that is, for a sniveling little vermin named Ratso Rizzo who, despite pulling some cons on Joe, becomes the only one to offer him a home. The story of *Midnight Cowboy* is then profoundly transformed: it is a love story from that point on, about the redeeming, transcendent power of love. A love that eventually allows Joe to see through his fantasies and to devote himself for the first time to another person, risking everything to fulfill Ratso's dream to go to Miami. He gets him there, too, even though, in the final scene, Ratso dies before he can get off the bus.

And so, in that spring of 1968, a time of huge and tumultuous upheaval in American society, *Midnight Cowboy* began shooting on the streets of New York. It was an enterprise the historian Paul Buhle would call "the most daring film of the moment and arguably of any moment in Hollywood history."

Actual production began in May. It would, finally, be a color film: Hellman had been so impressed after seeing the natural color effects in the independent film *You're a Big Boy Now*, made by his young maverick friend Francis Ford Coppola, that he convinced United Artists to let them try something similar. It was part of the reason for the increased budget.

"I'm glad in the end I made *Cowboy* in color," John said. "We needed all those garish lights." Color usually glamorized things, but working with Richard MacDonald had taught Schlesinger how to mute colors and make them work to give the right effect. The grimy, flashing neon of the city became an indispensable part of the look of the film.

New York was a huge experience for John. "It's the one city in the world where I've seen things that leave me feeling that I can't believe my eyes. So New York would indeed be a character in *Midnight Cowboy*. It can't help being so."

"We were walking up 42nd Street one day, looking for places to shoot," Jerry Hellman recalled. "We were coming around a corner and someone dropped in front of us. Just fell face-forward. And John said, 'That's got to be in the movie.' That's where the dead man in front of Tiffany's came from. That is a typical example of how things happened on this film."

Much would be made of the fact that the British Schlesinger was making a film about this most American of cities. "I didn't know what the reaction would be," he said, "a British director 'discovering' the South and 42nd Street in a story that is essentially sordid with no love story in the accepted sense." Elsewhere, John said, "There were probably things I noticed that an American director wouldn't have seen. Everything was grist to the mill. There are things you see in America on the street that you see much less of in Britain, where things go on behind closed doors."

Jerry fulfilled his promise to keep John insulated from money issues, especially as it became clear they were exceeding their $2.2 million budget (the final film would end up costing $3.6 million). "My primary goal," Hellman said, "was to keep the world away from John so he could let his vision come through."

As grateful as he was for Hellman's support, John would remember most of the actual production of *Midnight Cowboy* as terribly unhappy. Part of it was simply being in a foreign place: "It was like coming into a totally new world," John said. "I didn't know any of the people or who to ask for."

But he was also faced with an unsympathetic crew, who he felt were hostile toward the material. Worse, he considered them riddled with graft: "There were people who were bringing in their own people and equipment and robbing the production."

Their lack of camaraderie, "which you don't find in a really good British unit", was very dispiriting for Schlesinger. "On *Madding Crowd*, for six months we'd been working as a community, really, in Dorset, with people who were totally committed to what they were doing," he said. But in New York the camera operators wanted to be paid overtime to come in and see the rushes. "It depressed me, and finally angered me considerably, because I didn't think their work was of a high enough standard to warrant that kind of high-handed attitude."

In Britain, John had been able to assemble freelance crews where "you can handpick the best of the bunch." This, on the other hand, was a studio crew put together by UA. John fought with cameraman Adam Holender; despite some impressive cinematographic results, their relationship was difficult and tense. Likewise he never gelled with editor Hugh Robertson. After such easy and close collaboration with Jim Clark on his British films, John felt stymied in his lack of connection with his *Cowboy* editor. Behind closed doors he fulminated over his inability to fire him: because Robertson was black, John feared being called a racist.

It's possible that some of this unease with his first American crew may have stemmed less from any hostility on their part than from John's own fears, expressed to Hellman, of being perceived as homosexual. With Childers running around as Boy Friday, there was surely going to be some talk, and despite John's reluctance to let it be known, the director's gayness was soon common knowledge on the set.

"I remember sitting there with John, early on," Dustin Hoffman remembered, "and saying to him, 'Are you married? Do you have a girlfriend?'" He laughed as he recounted the tale for me. "John said, 'Oh, no, no, no, dear boy.' I'm clueless —

this is 1968, remember, when no one was out [about being gay] – so I said, 'How come?' John looked at me, and this sentence is imprinted in my memory. He said, 'I just couldn't bear the idea of waking up in the morning with a woman next to me.' I just looked back at him and said, 'I see.' I thought it was marvelously courageous."

It's a story that hardly fits with the idea of a man beset by fear; clearly, as the movie progressed, John figured to hell with keeping secrets. One of the crew was a man named Burtt Harris, a second unit director who John came to appreciate for his irreverence. "Burtt was a character," Hoffman said, "very heterosexual, and he and John had a great rapport. They'd tease each other. When they were ready to shoot, Burtt would always say, 'We're ready my queen,' and John would laugh as hard as anyone. And then after a few weeks John had a comeback response: 'Won't be long for you, my boy.' In my opinion, John was not just open but brave."

With the "artistic" side of the crew, he tended to have better relations. Hellman had hired his costume designer from *The World of Henry Orient*, a young woman named Ann Roth. John immediately adored her. It was Roth who assembled what would become the iconic look of the film's costumes, sewing fringe onto the Cowboy's suede jacket and finding the right "throwaways" for Ratso.

"The invention for Dustin was the most creative of everything," Roth said. "It was a suit that I found on 42nd Street. It was dark red and I overdyed it green and then white. I pretended that it came out of the trash can and that some high school kid had thrown up on it after his graduation party or prom. And the pants came from this shop called Robin's next to Port Authority, where they had a table out front with pants for five bucks each, with a dirty ridge where they'd been folded. They were white because I imagined that since Ratso was Italian, he'd fantasized about a kind of Marcello Mastroianni look."

With John, Roth worked more through symbiosis than any actual discussions. "I'm not good at talking about it," she said. "Neither was John. The idea is that you've got to have the same sense of humor. It's humor whether it's tragedy or not. John and I had the same sense of humor. We could walk into a room and our eyes would go to the same thing. That's what it is. That's all that is needed with a director."

With his actors, too, John found a creative give-and-take; American actors, he said, were "free-wheeling" in a way they weren't in England. "We're more reserved and kind of held-in," he said.

Voight, still shaky in his accent, spent weeks touring around the back roads of west Texas with Michael Childers and a tape recorder in order to absorb the sounds and atmosphere. "Man, did Voight ever work hard on that accent," Childers said. "We were together 24 hours a day. We'd find people in the street and take them to a greasy spoon café and talk to them all afternoon, so Voight was really doing his stuff."

Driving around with Voight, Michael also chanced upon the film's famous opening shot. The shoot was well underway and still they hadn't determined the right opening; a big hole existed in early drafts of the script. But Michael's photographer's eye had spotted a drive-in movie screen, forlorn, forgotten, tumbleweeds rolling past. He hurried back to John and Waldo: "What if our opening image was a deserted drive-in movie theater in the middle of nowhere?" They thought it was brilliant – an empty screen because all the dreams are gone, dried up, abandoned. Over time, the image of little Joe Buck on the creaking rocking horse was added, and the opening few pages of the script were finally banged out one hot August night in a stuffy motel room near Big Spring, Texas.

Much of the filming took place on the street. In Texas, they shot in and around a little town called Stanton; in New York, they were everywhere, Times Square, Madison Avenue, the East Village – a nod back to Schlesinger's social realist, location-heavy roots. Interiors were done at the Filmways Studio in East Harlem, where designer John Robert Lloyd re-created a flat they'd inspected in a real condemned building, even taking the doors from the rooms to use in the studio.

Rehearsals were improvisational rather than plotted out, with John's goal being to discover "just how far beyond the scripted material the actors could go." They had to be "as near the knuckle as possible," John said, "in order to investigate various aspects of [the characters'] lives."

Fascinating, spontaneous role-play followed. What, John wanted to know, did Joe and Ratso talk about after they started living together? What thoughts were shared in that condemned tenement, late at night, or when they woke up shivering next to each other in the morning? Did they talk about girls, fantasies, dreams? Did they ever masturbate? Wouldn't Joe be appalled when he saw that Ratso never changed his underwear?

"Go ahead," John encouraged Hoffman and Voight. "Talk to each other." Waldo crouched beside him with a tape-recorder. Little snippets of what they said were incorporated into the script: the underwear, the last time they got laid, Ratso's disdain for the "dumb cowboy crap." Small moments that caught John's eye were remembered and used once the cameras were rolling.

"I remember we were rehearsing the scene in the stairwell at the party," Hoffman said. Joe sees how profusely Ratso is sweating and untucks his shirt to pat down his friend's hair. Ratso, not used to such tenderness, holds onto him, his eyes closed in a stolen moment of bliss. "Somehow I just let my head fall on Voight's chest and Schlesinger, as an artist, saw that moment," Hoffman said. The director kept the moment in the film. It's one of the most poignant and loving images in a film otherwise unrelentingly bleak; indeed, John considered the moment "very dear" and would always be grateful to the actors for finding it.

"Then there was the scene where Joe comes back," Voight remembered, "all full of himself, after finally scoring with Brenda Vaccaro. He finds that Ratso can't walk. We rehearsed that many times and John didn't like it. He calls Waldo in finally because he says we're doing it too sentimental, no depth. Waldo gets there and just says plainly, 'Joe is going to leave Ratso.' It was like a light went off for me. Joe wasn't there to celebrate or share his victory, he was there to tell Ratso, 'See you later.' He figured he could make it without this guy now. Now he was going to be stuck with him. That made the scene work for me. John had known there was something wrong with how we were playing it and he wouldn't let it go until we had got it right."

Hoffman's immersion into the role allowed him to solve the problem identified by Jack Gelber way back in early script discussions: how to deal with Ratso's disability without being clichéd or sentimental. In one scene where Ratso pulls down the blinds, John watched in wonder as Hoffman, instinctively in character, lifted his lame leg with his hand in order to get up on a chair to reach the blinds. A small, telling touch which John found perfect.

In those play-acting rehearsals, in those imagined conversations between Joe and Ratso, John was exploring the very essence of their relationship. "What did he want to find out about them?" I asked both Hoffman and Voight. "What truth was he trying to get at?"

"There was one point," Hoffman responded, "when Voight and I both approached John and said, 'We're not just roommates, we're lovers.' It was a scene where John had said, 'All right, Dustin's going to be on the floor and Voight's going to be on the bed,' and I said, 'Why aren't we in bed together, they're lovers,' and John's response was, 'I'm sure they are but you try and get this film financed.'"

I laughed. "So in your mind, then, you saw them as physically lovers?"

Hoffman paused. "That's a good question. No, we didn't. We didn't think of it sexually. What we thought about was: this is the story of Joe Buck, who sells love but doesn't know what love really is, and at the end of the movie he finds out. It's like any love story really."

"Here's the deal," Voight said. "There was a lot of talk about the homosexual element at that time. How to deal with it, where was it. But it was a love story, not a sex story. It was two people who couldn't live without each other. It was a classical tale. Joe was lost. He was looking for love and he doesn't know how to get it."

When the film was first released, John would spend a lot of time denying that the relationship between Joe and Ratso was homosexual, indeed that the film itself was "homosexually themed." His frustration was obvious in several interviews: "We filmed two homosexual sequences which are explicit in the novel," he said, "and this is the only question that the press seemed interested in when we were making the film. There was hostility. They felt it was going to be a sex-exploitation thing, which it absolutely isn't. The majority of people, when they come out, do not feel they have seen a sexy film."

Yet there was no getting away from the fact that the central love story was between Joe and Ratso; indeed, it was a time when many American films were exploring the male bond, from *Easy Rider* to *Butch Cassidy and the Sundance Kid*. At one point, Brenda Vaccaro as Shirley asks the question that's been on the audience's mind all throughout the film: "Don't tell me you two are a couple?" They huff and puff in protest ("We ain't no fags," in Ratso's nasal whine) but of course, they *are* a couple: that little moment when Ratso takes refuge against Joe's chest tells us all we need to know.

Ratso, of course, as John seemed to enjoy pointing out, would have had sex with anyone who found him attractive, man, woman or dog. In that rather crude assessment there is truth: defining the relationship, or indeed the film, as "gay" isn't so much wrong as it is insufficient, and whether or not Joe and Ratso ever had sex is, in the end, irrelevant. Later, when the climate became less hysterical to discuss such things, when words like "homoerotic" or "homosocial" could be used as distinct from homosexual, John would feel more comfortable answering, "Absolutely, that's true," when asked if *Midnight Cowboy* was in fact a love story between two men.

For all the spontaneity and ad-libbing, John would insist that the one scene that has gone down into legend as improvisation really wasn't: the moment where Hoffman, staggering out into traffic, is nearly hit by a taxicab and hollers, "I'm walkin' here!" This became a catch phrase which would soon be repeated endlessly in every major city of the world.

"We got an extra inside a cab and did it," John said. "That was not improvised."

There would be a few minor clashes with Hoffman, but nothing like the earth-shaking battles to come during *Marathon Man*. There would also be some frustration with Voight, whose leftist, lofty political diatribes John sometimes found "maddening."

The main battle, however, involved Brenda Vaccaro, who announced after shooting began that she wouldn't perform nude. A few days before her much-anticipated bedroom tussle with Voight, Vaccaro insisted on a clause in her contract stating her nipples would not be seen in the finished film. Jerry Hellman asked John to get her to reconsider. In one of the more whimsical memos in John's files, Jerry wrote: "Please remember to have a private meeting with Brenda Vaccaro about her nipples."

The memory made Vaccaro laugh when I reminded her of it, sitting with her on the terrace of her home in Encino. "I knew going into the film there was a nude scene called for," she said. "But I just couldn't! I thought I was overweight but John kept saying, 'No, darling, you're perfect.' He said, 'Oh, my dear, Julie did it and it was fine, she had the pasties and then she just whipped them off because they were a pain in the ass.' But still, I couldn't do it. So I went to Ann Roth and said, 'Annie, save my ass here. I need something.' And Annie said, 'What about that fox fur there?' And I said yes, I could cover myself. I was nude underneath, no pasties, but the fox would cover me. And John said, 'Well, you know, I rather like it. Let's do it. Fucked in fox!'"

Vaccaro laughed uproariously remembering it all. It remains an incredibly sexy scene, she and Voight rolling around each other, the fox fur always strategically placed. "Sexy! Hah! I was like falling off the bed," she said, "the tits going this way, Jon's weight so heavy on me, and John has the camera on me the whole time saying, 'Breathe now, darling, breathe now. Now come, darling, come now.'

"That's how we did it," she said, trying to catch her breath. "And ever since then, John and I, we'd say to each other, 'Hello, darling. *Fucked in fox!*' "

Principal photography wrapped on *Midnight Cowboy* in September. John set out for London, for the first time in almost a year. And Michael went with him.

"I was like his little war bride being brought home to meet the family," Childers said. "It terrified me. I knew I was on show to all his friends. I was this brash little American, not a terribly sophisticated traveler. I'd never been to Europe before. I knew there were people saying, 'This will never last.'"

Three decades later, we're sitting in their Palm Springs home. It was a happily-ever-after fairy tale; there would be arguments, separations, mistakes, heartache. John's friends would recall Michael, even as a young man, being gruff with John, not sufficiently deferential. Michael's friends tell of the rages John would direct at Michael, especially as he got older.

"They were never a touchy-feely couple," said Stewart Grimshaw, "and so I think John's friends here [in London] thought there wasn't any caring, but there definitely was."

Michael knew that the London clique viewed him with suspicion. "Too much age difference," Michael said they felt. "And too American. There was a sense that I was taking John away from them, keeping him in America."

Grimshaw, who was Michael's age, got to know him best, going to the movies and the theater with him. "I always saw a strong bond between Michael and John," he said, "and I think it showed itself, because it lasted."

John's parents kept expecting Michael to go the way of John Steiner or Peter Buckley. But every time John came home, Michael was still at his side. Eventually Bernard and Win warmed to Michael "when they realized I wasn't going away," he said, that twinkle in his eye.

To *Midnight Cowboy*, Michael brought a very necessary component, and it's really what he brought to John Schlesinger's life as well: a connection to the moment, to the times. John was, after all, 42 years old. Michael, twenty years younger, was an active player within the youth movement, in tune with the shifting, turbulent sensibilities of the new generation in a way John could never be. Once in New York, Michael started photographing for *Dance* magazine and for the hot new gay-tinged publication, *After Dark*, which gave him entrée into all sorts of arts and theatrical circles. He also landed a job as official photographer for the New York production of Kenneth Tynan's *Oh, Calcutta!*

With such high-profile activity, Michael was easily welcomed into the Andy Warhol scene, the epitome of New York counter-culture; he was soon an important contributor to Warhol's newest project, *Interview* magazine. John found himself brought along to soirees at The Factory, Warhol's famous studio complex. Together, he and Michael attended all the fashionable art openings, partied at all the trendiest supper clubs, and sometimes even paid late-night visits to the underground gay clubs of Greenwich Village.

Through Michael, they also rented a weekend house on Fire

Island, where expressions of gay culture and identity were more overt and undisguised than anywhere else in the country at that time: dance parties, drag shows and, especially, the easy, casual, anonymous sex of the "Meat Rack" — bushy areas where, day or night, sexual partners could always be found. It was a world completely alien to anything John had ever experienced, and he found it absolutely intoxicating.

For all of John's gay adventures on Fire Island, however, the most memorable encounter was with a woman. "One night," Michael remembered, "we were out there with some of Warhol's crowd, and Viva got John stoned on grass, and she was saying, 'Oh, John, you're so fascinating, will you fuck me?'" Michael hooted. "And so he did! I turned around and saw John was gone and I thought, 'He's in there cheating on me with some hot stud.' But when I went in and saw it was Viva, it just blew my mind! Viva went around telling everyone, 'Absolutely one of the three best fucks I've ever had in my life.'"

It's not surprising that the famous East Village loft marijuana party scene in *Cowboy* was Michael's idea. "I said, wouldn't it be great if they went to a really psychedelic party? We could just see the possibilities." The darkroom in which Voight and Vaccaro make out was actually Childers' own. "It was a real party we threw," he remembered.

Indeed, Jerry Hellman said the party went on for three days, with the filming running straight through it. "It started in the morning after everyone had makeup, and there was a lot of dope smoked," Hellman said. "The crew would go in and film the specific parts. There's the macrocosm of the party, and then the microcosm moments — for instance, Hansel and Gretel filming with the 16 mm camera — that were all carefully designed. And then the party was set in motion, music played, and people were encouraged to do their thing. As spontaneous things happened they were identified and would be filmed."

Michael himself can be spotted in the party scene running the movie projector with Joe D'allesandro, Warhol's discovery and the stunning star of his films *Flesh* and *Lonesome Cowboys*, which some critics would claim as a forerunner to *Midnight Cowboy*, although John never saw it. "I got all of the Warhol crowd to appear in the film," Childers said. "Paul Morrissey, Viva, International Velvet, Ultra Violet." In fact, on 3 June, Viva rang the Warhol studio with the announcement that she'd been cast, and heard gunshots on the other end of the line: Warhol had just been shot by Valerie Solanas. "It's true," Childers said. "She was on the phone the moment Andy was shot."

Additional extras for the party scene were rounded up by Childers at Max's Kansas City, the legendary Park Avenue café and pre-eminent salon of the psychedelic era, and where Warhol and Janis Joplin and a dazzling assortment of stars, speed freaks and transvestites could be found.

"I think I was able to show John an America he wouldn't have seen otherwise and he was fascinated by it," Michael said. "Whether it was Warhol or Reno or Vegas, I opened up that world of America to him. I like to think I helped John get a grasp on this country.

"It was a trade-off, though," he added. "We helped each other. I didn't know about classical music, had never been to an opera or ballet. I didn't know that much about classical theater. And then John brings me to London and the Royal Shakespeare Company and I go backstage with Peggy Ashcroft and Paul Scofield. So we challenged each other. I loved modern dance and art, but John knew nothing about any of it, so I could do that for him. I mean, we opened each other's eyes to different things."

Early on, like many gay couples, they abandoned the heterosexual paradigm of strict sexual monogamy. "We'd call each other when we were away," Michael recalled, twinkling, "and we'd ask each other, 'How are things in *your* department?'"

There was, however, always the ground rule of commitment to each other. "There were lines that were not to be crossed because it would hurt," Michael said. "I was always concerned that if John was seeing someone, they had to treat him right. I didn't want it to be some Hollywood hooker trying to use him to get a movie part or something like that."

They called them "the mistresses." In London, John's friends used a different name, "the understudies." No matter what they were called, these men came and went, some lasting longer than others; a few blossomed into friends after the initial sexual attraction wore off. But none ever dislodged either John or Michael from their primary place in each other's lives. Some observers would never understand. They would assume things they shouldn't have assumed, judge John and Michael for a lifestyle they couldn't ever imagine living themselves. Of course, their formula of non-monogamy would be tested, sometimes to the breaking point, but in the late 1960s, in the heady throes of new love, there seemed only promise on the horizon.

"When John got uncertain, which was often, when he started to doubt what he was doing [on *Midnight Cowboy*], I told him he was mistaken," Michael said. "I told him it was going to be a hit. I *knew*. I had my finger on the pulse in a way he didn't. I said it was going to be huge. I said, 'You just watch, John. You just watch.'"

Eleven

1969–1970

"The need to feel for another human being"

I f one were to discover a man by the books he kept in his bedroom, a fairly accurate picture of John Schlesinger might emerge. Staying in his room, I perused the titles on his bookshelves. *Classics of Italian Cooking*. *The Joys of Wine*. Books on music: a Stravinsky primer, *The Wagner Companion*. About a dozen biographies: Buñuel, Benjamin Britten, Frida Kahlo, Tennessee Williams, David O. Selznick, my own book on William Haines. Memoirs: Peggy Guggenheim's *Out of this Century*, Alan Bennett's *Writing Home*. Books that spoke to him as a gay man: two from Edmund White, *The Beautiful Room is Empty* and *The Farewell Symphony*, and a compendium of stories from the AIDS Memorial Quilt. And books of humor: funny picture books, collections of irreverent jokes, a darkly ironic account of the Nazi propaganda machine.

It offered the picture of a literate and civilized man; a man supremely interested in art, in food, in life, in the lives of others. And a man who liked to laugh, often at things people told him he shouldn't be laughing about.

"John loved stuff associated with death," said John's friend Pat Crowley, who worked with him as an assistant director on *The Falcon and the Snowman* and *The Believers*. "He had a real morbid sense of humor. When we were doing *The Believers*, during a scene in a morgue in Toronto, there was a giant metal cabinet in the center of the room that had unidentified cases kept in cold storage. And there was this unidentified leg, found in Niagara Falls, and John was obsessed with that leg, with what could've happened to it, who it belonged to.

"So we took an actor and tied his leg behind him and had him run in during shooting, hollering, 'Where is it, where is my fucking leg, someone told me that my leg is in here!' And John was shocked and we all just laughed because he was always playing jokes on everybody else, and you were always looking for ways to get back at him."

I was finding his story, bit by bit, and humor and laughter informed so much of it. In his files, he kept a letter he'd received from an Arizona college student soon after the American release of *Midnight Cowboy*. The student had been quite offended when the audience laughed at Ratso's complaint, late in the film, that he has wet his pants. Moved by the story, near tears at the plight of the dying Ratso, the student wondered how, as the director of the film, John might have responded to such insensitive amusement.

"Thank you for your very interesting letter," John replied. "I take a rather different point of view. I think much that is tragic is also comic at the same moment. The point about audience reaction is that one wants them to feel something, and laughter at this particular moment, when one is so near tragedy, only says to me how tremendously involved the audience was with the film and with the characters. On the occasions I have been in the theater with the film and watched the audience reaction, it is amazing to see how quickly the laughter is changed to total silence at the moment of Ratso's death, and this is exactly what I as the filmmaker intended."

Much that is tragic is also comic. I thought again of John's gag of pretending to have had a stroke long before he actually did.

"You know, I think he sometimes enjoys this," said Gary Shaw, nodding over at John in the wheelchair. "He always enjoyed making people squirm. I think he finds some humor in their discomfort when they come to see him now, when they try to get him to talk. I wouldn't be surprised if he's having a little fun with all of this."

Comedy or tragedy? I remembered what he had said in his diary: "I like to think it's always about both."

Post-production began on *Midnight Cowboy* in September 1968, soon after John and Michael had returned from London. What became immediately apparent was that the problems with editor Hugh Robertson had only become worse; he was cutting the film with none of the style John felt was necessary for such a modern film. If it was radical in content, it had to be radical in form as well. Once again, John called in Jim Clark.

"I thought it was extraordinary," Clark said, "especially in terms of performance. But it had problems with the fantasies, mostly in the opening twenty minutes, basically a construction problem. It was too long, overdone. It took forever to get Joe to New York. I was there for three months and all I did was cut the dreams, the fantasies, and the party. The rest is Hugh Robertson's."

The flashbacks were the biggest problem. They had been a problem in writing the script, in the acting, and now in the editing. "Well, you know, the book had all these rape scenes that were linear but could not be linear in the film," Clark said. "I remember one which was a nightmare that Joe Buck has. It was shot in black and white and we slowed it down. Then, as the nightmare is reaching its peak, we put it into red. It was a very stylistic thing to go from black and white into this stabbing red moment, and then he wakes up. There were lots of things I did experimentally that we kept in the film.

"There was material everywhere, that's what the problem was," Clark said. "They didn't know what they had. The film was being completely mismanaged. I kept finding material shot by some second unit director that was just sitting on a bench. It had never been seen or used but it was good.

"The situation was very awkward," Clark continued, "because Hugh Robertson was still there. He was still the editor but he never liked the film. Hugh was very tall, always smoking big cigars, and he owned the cutting room. I was in the room next door and I could hear John approach. He'd be in there trying to talk with Hugh, his voice getting louder and louder, and eventually he was screaming at Hugh. Then John would be standing at my door, sweating and angry, and he'd yell, 'You've got to get that film away from him, he's ruining it!' He'd disappear and I'd be left in an awkward situation. You see, everybody thought I was one of John's boyfriends and that's why I was there. And I didn't have a work permit. I was illegal and everybody knew it. So it was difficult."

When the film was finally cut there were more chunks of Hoffman left on the floor than of Voight. "I was angry because a lot of the stuff we had shot wasn't in the film," Hoffman admitted. "While he was cutting it, John realized he could not cut it equally. This was Voight's story. And so there was stuff that got cut that I had loved and seen in the rushes – a whole Chaplinesque scene by Ratso at the party."

Then came the task of placing a score onto the film. John Barry had composed a beautiful, haunting theme which remains familiar to moviegoers even three decades later. Barry had made his name with the scores for *Dr. No*, *Born Free* and *The Lion in Winter*, and would win a Grammy for *Midnight Cowboy*.

But something more was needed: an opening theme that would set the mood and spirit of the film. In September Jerry Hellman spoke to Bob Dylan, who agreed to write something but then kept them hanging for so long they had to look elsewhere. It was Michael, once again, who found the eventual choice, Harry Nilsson, who began writing a song expressly for the film. Meanwhile, to use in rough-cut screenings, Michael gave John one of Nilsson's other tracks, "Everybody's Talkin'", from his *Aerial Ballet* album. While they waited to see what Nilsson came up with, John got used to the song they had, discovering resonance in its lyrics: "*People stopping staring/ I can't see their faces/ Only the shadows of their eyes . . .*" And, as a harbinger of the final, pitiful bus ride to Miami, in which Joe Buck removes Ratso's filthy, urine-soaked New York clothes and replaces them with bright, colorful tropical wear: "*I'm going where the sun keeps shining/ Thru' the pouring rain/ Going where the weather suits my clothes . . .*"

"We knew we had to have it," Childers remembered. "We had to keep it." The irony was that Nilsson hadn't written

"Everybody's Talkin'" – Fred Neil was the songwriter – and the piece Nilsson actually composed for the film, "I Guess the Lord Must be in New York City," would be rather buried in the overall soundtrack. Bob Dylan, too, finally came through with a composition, but too late for inclusion: Michael remembered opening up a package from Dylan and popping in the track. It was "Lay, Lady, Lay."

But one cannot imagine *Midnight Cowboy* now without "Everybody's Talkin'". It is one of the great movie openings of all time, with a song that evokes not only the story of the film but the legacy of the times. It is the perfect theme song for the final culmination of the adventurous, rebellious, scary, exciting, heartbreaking Sixties.

It was a time of rapid change and conflict. Just prior to filming, Martin Luther King had been assassinated; during production, Robert Kennedy was killed. John had to call off filming for a day when police blocked the streets for Kennedy's funeral at St. Patrick's Cathedral. By the time *Midnight Cowboy* had wrapped, the number of American soldiers sent to Vietnam had passed the half-million mark. The violence at the Democratic National Convention that August had further seared the nation's conscience.

It wasn't just conflict, but out-and-out rebellion in the air. All throughout the summer, the crew had heard daily exhortations from Abbie Hoffman inciting civil unrest; just before the picture was released, drugged-out students staged "Freak-Ins" across New York. In April, members of the Black Panthers in the Bronx were indicted on conspiracy charges, galvanizing a movement. *Midnight Cowboy* was still playing in theaters when, in June, patrons fought back against police harassment at the Stonewall, a gay bar in Greenwich Village, thus kicking off Gay Liberation. And that summer, just before the film's gala premiere in London, the legendary rock concert was held at Woodstock, New York.

Midnight Cowboy cannot be understood outside its times. It was part of the zeitgeist, part of the worldwide cultural shift, the conflict caused by colliding generations. It became a symbol, a rallying point in many ways: like *Easy Rider, Medium Cool* and *Alice's Restaurant*, it was required viewing for the youth movement, part of the currency exchanged by the new generation.

Studio executives weren't sure what Schlesinger had wrought. An advance screening was held for the United Artists brass at the West 54th Street movie lab. "We were getting out of the taxi," Jerry Hellman said, "and John turned to me to say, 'Do you honestly believe anyone in their right mind is going to pay to see this rubbish?'"

David Picker was feeling more optimistic. "I brought everyone to that first screening," he said – all of his bosses, the marketing people, his entire family. "I knew I was taking a chance, because we hadn't seen anything yet. But I trusted what John was doing, and I was right, because the reaction from everyone was stunning."

Appropriately so: even within the increasingly permissive cinema of the 1960s, *Midnight Cowboy* went boldly where few films had gone before. With the abolition of the Production Code, a new ratings system had been set up by the Motion Picture Association of America. The board decreed that *Midnight Cowboy*, with its nudity, homosexuality, and four-letter words, would receive the "Adult" classification, or "X." John concurred with their decision. "We felt the X was the correct rating for it," he said. "We had made the film for adults, not for children. I had no problem with the X initially."

Of course, in those days, X did not carry the baggage it would even just a few years later; it was not yet associated with explicit pornography. Yet it soon became apparent that an X on a film was going to prove problematic regardless – "the filmic equivalent of a Scarlet Woman," Hellman would say. What the X did was to severely limit not only where they could exhibit the picture but also where they could advertise it. "It also dashed hopes for network television revenue," Hellman said, as he and John refused to alter the film in any way. Happily, not only David Picker but Arthur Krim, the head of UA, backed them up firmly in this decision.

Once *Midnight Cowboy* was nominated for an Academy Award as Best Picture, the X became even more troublesome. The Academy didn't want an X among its nominees, so the MPAA offered to change the rating to "R" if John would simply slice a single frame from the theater blowjob scene. Again Schlesinger refused, again backed up by United Artists. After the film won, the situation simply could not be allowed to stand: the Academy would never tolerate an X-rated film being advertised as "Best Picture of the Year." So, without a single cut made, the MPAA reversed itself and changed the rating of *Midnight Cowboy* from an X to an R.

Yet it's important to remember that, as first released, *Midnight Cowboy* was rated X, and *still* it was a blockbuster, *still* it had people lining up around the block to see it. Its official New York premiere was held on 25 May at the Coronet Theater on Third Avenue with a glittering array of celebrities in attendance. "Everybody from Henry Kissinger to Jane Fonda and Roger Vadim," Michael said. "People were coming up to us, grabbing us, speechless, or they were crying, 'This is the most devastating, moving, wonderful movie.' That kept happening, all around the world."

Two nights later, Michael went out to gauge the reaction of the general public, to see if the masses had as much enthusiasm for the picture as the A-list celebrities had shown. What he saw stopped him in his tracks. "I ran to a pay phone to call John," he said. "I was screaming that the lines were ten blocks long and they went all the way back to the bridge! And it was still only three o'clock in the afternoon! John said, 'Stand on the corner in front of Bloomingdale's across the street. I'm coming down. I've got to see this!'"

"There is nothing, absolutely nothing, like having a huge blockbuster success," Michael said. "Your whole world changes."

From being ignored and invisible following the flop of *Madding Crowd*, John was now the hottest property in Hollywood, appearing on television on *The Today Show* and with Dick Cavett, being interviewed, debated, discussed, and fawned over. The best table at Sardi's was now reserved for him whenever he wanted to drop by. At industry gatherings, executives from Paramount and MGM made it a point to drape their arms around his shoulders. Every actress wanted her picture taken with him. The success of *Darling* had been nothing compared to this; John Schlesinger was now the toast of the world.

His files from these heady few months bulged with all sorts of good wishes: Joe Levine, Lew Wasserman, Bob Rafelson, Warren Beatty, Joan Crawford. "We simply can't stop thinking or talking about your film," wrote Peter Allen and Liza Minnelli. Author Shel Silverstein telegraphed: "You've given me one of the few great movie experiences of my life."

Yet, like many pictures that have gone down as classics, the reviews weren't unanimously good. While Stanley Kauffman in the *New Republic* adored the film, using adjectives like "dexterity," "intelligence" and "perception" to describe John's direction, and Gene Shalit in *Look* proclaimed it a "reeking masterpiece," most American critics were qualified or outright hostile. Andrew Sarris thought the performances intelligent but had reservations about John's direction. In what would become a growing chorus, Jacob Brackman in *Esquire* singled out the flashbacks as chaotic and heavy-handed, rechristening the director "John Sledgehammer." Richard Schickel, making his prejudices plain, simply couldn't abide the "faggery" he insisted the film was trying to foist upon an unsuspecting public. And Pauline Kael tossed her usual brickbat, finding the satire "offensively inhumane and inaccurate."

Perhaps it's not surprising that the reviews were as negative as all that, since *Cowboy* was so startlingly new and different. What to make of a film that celebrated the love of losers? That glorified failure? The suggestion of homosexuality, no matter how implicit, was enough to cause some critics, like Schickel, to hurl invective. Even the more liberal reviewers found it easy to dismiss the film as cynical and exploitative, two words that would forever make John bristle. "I don't think the movie is cynical," he insisted late in his life, when the question clearly still rankled. "The reality is [Joe has made] the discovery of the need for a relationship, however peculiar and odd . . . The Dustin Hoffman character has a real need. Joe Buck gets him on a bus and rejects the opportunity to realize his own cockamamie fantasy. So I don't call that cynical."

Yet some critics would detect a vein of cynicism running through much of John's work. Tim Rhys would link *Billy Liar* to *Darling*, to *Midnight Cowboy*, and even to parts of *Cold Comfort Farm*. John responded to the idea with bemused consideration: "A wry look in amusement," he offered, "is not necessarily cynical. I like humor and I like wit, but I don't know that I'd call that cynical."

For all his personal struggle with the idea of failure, John emphatically did not see Joe as one. "I don't think the Cowboy fails. I think he succeeds in bettering the possibilities of Ratso. I'm much more optimistic than you give me credit for."

Indeed, in the aftermath of the box-office success of the film, and, perhaps even more importantly, with the deepening relationship with Michael, John was in a rare frame of mind. "I am for the first time in my life really secure in the knowledge of what I have done," he wrote to a friend, "and can't be bothered to read word for word everything that is written about the movie. That must sound very superior but I mean it merely to be confident."

It was, in fact, a confident time. There was the Oscar, of course, not only for John but also for the picture and, most poignantly, for Waldo Salt, a telling triumph over the infamous blacklist. In many ways, *Midnight Cowboy* was the clarion call of a new Hollywood that rejected the prejudices and predilections of the past, although the fight was still not yet won. Thanking Dustin Hoffman for his telegram of congratulations, John referred to Dustin's own loss of an Oscar to John Wayne by saying, "I am only sorry they are still paying lip service to an old regime in Hollywood."

Awards came not only from the Academy, but also from the Directors' Guild and the Golden Globes, as well as from the Berlin Film Festival and the Italian National Syndicate of Film Journalists. And *Cowboy* pulled off a complete sweep of the

British Academy Awards, winning Best Picture, Best Director, Best Screenplay, Best Actor for Hoffman and Most Promising Newcomer for Voight.

Sailing for London on the *Queen Elizabeth II*, however, John was not at all eager to go home. Flushed with his American success, he had entered into one of his recurring England-bashing periods. A strike at Southampton caused "appalling delays" in reclaiming his and Michael's baggage; as he wrote to Jerry Hellman, he was "bitching England already . . . Quite clearly the sorting-out period for both of us is going to be very prolonged."

He was immediately confronted with further antagonism from his countrymen when, despite John Trevelyan having approved the film on 8 July, *Cowboy*'s British distributor, Rank, expressed worries about its content. "I thought I would be received with open arms by Wardour Street," John said, "but of course not. What was I thinking?" Frantically, he called David Picker, who sent a representative from United Artists over to London to give the distributors a pep talk. "I've often thought that Wardour Street really would be happier one street over," John griped, "selling cauliflowers, perhaps."

Yet, for the first time in his film career, the British critics were nearly unanimous in their praise for him: John Russell Taylor in *The Times* headlined his review, "Schlesinger's Best Film," and credited *Cowboy*'s success to John's "immediate and intense response to an unfamiliar scene, a new milieu." Penelope Mortimer in *The Observer* was the most prescient: "Schlesinger's triumphant film," she wrote, "will go into the archives to remind future generations of the very best that the 1960s could produce."

There is clearly much sociology to be uncovered behind the

fact that British critics had, up to this point, tended to dismiss John's British pictures, while they warmly embraced his first American one; while American critics who had adored his British films were nitpicking over *Midnight Cowboy*. John often commented on this dichotomy, and it was part of the general enjoyment he felt at the gala British premiere in September at the London Pavilion. All of John's family and close friends attended, including Alan Cooke, Roland Curram, Peter Hall, and Glenda Jackson, as well as colleagues with whom he was now on a first-name basis: Joseph Losey, Roddy McDowall, Ava Gardner, Sir Ian and Lady Fraser, Harold Pinter.

Both John Schlesinger and Jerry Hellman became millionaires as a result of *Midnight Cowboy*'s huge worldwide box office success. It was the seventh top-grossing American film in 1969, eventually piling up a total of $44.8 million. John could be a bit indulgent with his sudden fortune; Michael recalled him splurging on $20,000 worth of Indian baskets, which he had developed a passion for collecting. He could be impulsively generous as well: when he observed that his friend Roly Curram's new home had no central heating system, he had state-of-the-art equipment installed the next day, leaving Curram stunned and grateful.

But he could also be stingy. Stewart Grimshaw recalled around this time John getting quite upset when someone in the household spent what he felt was too much on biscuits. "He could be like that," Grimshaw said, "very tight about money." He had been through lean times, of course; always in the back of John's mind was the nagging little voice warning this might not last.

"Let me tell you one other story," Hellman said, leaning across his desk as we were nearing the end of our interview, "because it reflects on the money we made and the incredible people at UA at the time. By their standards, we had gone half a million over budget, and they could have taken away percentage points from us for every $10,000 we went over budget. By now, they could see this was going to be a giant hit, that our 60 percent shares were going to be worth millions. So they had a meeting, Arthur Krim, Bob Benjamin, David Picker, some others, and it was asked, 'Does anyone feel we should take points back from John and Jerry?' No one raised their hand. Not one of them! This was a generation of integrity. You could shake hands with these guys, make a deal and trust it."

He glanced off sadly out his window, shaking his head. He didn't have to say anymore.

As the British critics would eventually reclaim *Billy Liar*, so too would the Americans finally get around to embracing *Midnight Cowboy*. On the occasion of its twenty-fifth anniversary, Siskel and Ebert said the film stood "the test of time"; the *New York Observer* called it "still heartbreaking and timeless." In 1998, the American Film Institute placed *Midnight Cowboy* at number 36 in its list of the 100 greatest American films.

More than any other film of the era, *Midnight Cowboy* redefined the idea of the Hollywood blockbuster. By all conventional wisdom, it should not have done as well as it did; it should have played a few weeks along the art house circuit then disappeared. After all, it was rated X; its lead gets a blowjob from another guy; it's violent and sordid and filled with fags and druggies. But in that defiant period, it was those very things that enticed the film's audience; *Midnight Cowboy* had such appeal because it was rejecting the same convention and tradition that had the campuses in revolt. It also had Dustin Hoffman, of course, whose popularity was at a peak following *The Graduate*, and whose presence at that point, as the writer Paul Buhle has written, embodied the spirit of rebellion that the times demanded. *Midnight Cowboy* proved that films which overthrew convention, that dared embrace radical form and content, could also make money; the flowering of American cinema would not be long behind.

Beyond all its social implications, all of its impact on American culture and the evolution of American cinema, *Midnight Cowboy* is also one very good movie. But what about the flashbacks? For decades, they have been a sticking point for critics. *Time* magazine called them a "haze of stylistic tics and baroque decorations," handled by John with the "primitivity of a comic book." True, the flashbacks can be maddeningly cryptic; they raise more questions, in fact, than they provide answers. The ones with grandmother Sally Buck seem clear enough: she was a kind but negligent guardian with a bad sense of boundaries, allowing the young Joe Buck to climb into bed with her and her lover. The flashbacks involving Joe's girl-friend Crazy Annie, however, are less clear in their meaning: she gets raped, and he apparently does, too, though (unless one has read Herlihy's book) one is never quite certain why.

By 1979, John would come to feel that the film was filled with too many "gimmicks." Not only the flashbacks, he said, but other scenes as well, like the subway scene that tumbles over into a cacophony of sound and images, some in black-and-white, others in exaggerated color. "I think there's just a little bit too much jump-cutting and razzmatazz," John would say, during a time when his filmmaking style had become much more sober (*Yanks, The Falcon and the Snowman*.)

But, in truth it's that very "razzmatazz" that stamps *Cowboy* with such a personal imprimatur, that gave audiences in 1969 such a psychedelic trip, and today provides the film with its otherworldly, dreamlike feel. From the first flashbacks while Joe is riding the bus to New York – a cowboy who breaks convention by going east instead of west – we must consider the place where dreams intersect with reality. That the flashbacks do not ultimately reveal everything we might wish is, in fact, part of the brilliance of the film. Few of the great movies of the period gave us all the answers; John would say many times he wanted his audiences left asking questions. Joe's is, after all, a fragmented life, and so we are given only fragments to assemble as best we can. It's a discordant, chaotic world in which he lives, and so the psychedelic rock music on the soundtrack, the jump cuts, the razzmatazz, is appropriate. And maybe "the primitivity of a comic book" wasn't so far removed from how the film-makers saw their efforts: Joe looks across the aisle on the bus to smile at a little girl reading an issue of *Wonder Woman*. Its cover proclaims "Forget the Old, the New is Here," as Wonder Woman steps out of her old star-spangled costume and into mod 1960s clothes.

In the end, what makes the film so lasting is its testament to human friendship, devotion, and love. "*Midnight Cowboy* is about the emergence of some sort of human dignity from degradation," John said, "and the need to feel for another human being." At one point, Joe literally gives his blood for Ratso in order to make a few dollars and buy him medicine. In the final fadeout, he has placed his arm around his dead friend, the only overt gesture of affection between them in the entire picture, and we are left with that image of the transforming power of love.

For all that, the film would still be thrashed as hateful and self-loathing by the emerging gay movement, by the very community of which John and Michael felt so much a part. John would sit at his house on Fire Island and read the blistering reviews of the film in the gay weeklies. He endured the condemnation of such activists as Vito Russo, who, in the groundbreaking *The Celluloid Closet*, wrote that *Midnight Cowboy* endeavored to depict homosexuals ("real homosexuals" as separate from Joe and Ratso) as contemptible and pathetic creatures.

It's hard to argue against that charge. The "real homosexuals" in the film are indeed pathetic: the nelly Times Square queen who taunts Ratso, the student in the movie theater, the mother-fixated traveling salesman Joe beats at the end of the film to get money for bus tickets for Florida. (The scene with O'Daniel, while definitely imbued with a gay read, does not seem to be necessarily a homosexual sequence.) As Russo pointed out, the script is filled with examples of Joe and Ratso distancing themselves from "fags," assuring the audience that, no matter how many other rules are broken here, our two "heroes" are free of that particular stain. Is it a fault of Salt's screenplay, written by a heterosexual man a generation older than John? Many liberals, after all, were late in coming to the gay cause, finding it difficult to reconcile a commitment to social justice with a lifetime of conditioning against the evils of perversion.

Dustin Hoffman would recall suggesting to Schlesinger that Ratso call a black man a nigger, rationalizing Ratso was probably a racist, but the director was aghast. "My God, we're trying to get people to *like* Joe and Ratso," John said. "We'll lose every liberal in the audience." But he would justify his characters' vociferously anti-gay attitudes with the "realism" defense – an argument that only goes so far. Ratso and Joe would utter homophobic epithets; it was part of their characters. But the fact that John specifically chose *not* to show another side to them – the fact that they were undoubtedly racists as well – shows there were still certain barriers he hadn't yet crossed and connections he hadn't yet made.

Andrew Sarris' observation that Britain had never been a stronghold of directorial style was right on the mark, part of the reason why John was so enthused about making films in America. Pauline Kael accurately called the cinema America's "national theater"; John had finally found a place that shared his passion for cinema and what might be done with it. As 1969 turned over into 1970, even as he returned to England to make a new film, he felt very much a part of the new movement in America where, for a brief and glorious moment, directors would reign and individual style and statement would come to define the cinema.

"The climate in America seems to me to be now right for a little more honesty," John told reporters. "There is less interference [from front offices] than there used to be, and I think people are just saying, 'Well, get on with the job and we'll see whether it works or not.'" With the social and political ferment going on in America, he predicted "a lot of interesting [films] are going to come out of it."

Over the next decade the American cinema would astound audiences with daring, innovative pictures that changed the syntax of filmmaking. "We were going to be the new Godards and Kurosawas," John Milius said. Bogdanovich, Coppola,

Kubrick, Hopper, Nichols – and not just Americans, either. Like London just a few years before, Hollywood became a magnet for filmmakers from all over the world: Polanski, Bertolucci, Milos Forman, Louis Malle, Sergio Leone. And while John may have led the pack (Tony Richardson, who'd made *The Loved One* a few years earlier, hadn't had nearly Schlesinger's success), other British directors soon followed: Ken Russell, John Boorman, Nicolas Roeg.

"It was the last great time for pictures that expanded the idea of what could be done with movies," said Peter Bart, then at Paramount, who would later, at John Schlesinger's Hollywood memorial service, call him the greatest of all English directors, a man who had blazed a path that everyone in that room had followed.

"What's happening in America is very interesting," John observed to a fellow Englishman shortly after he'd won the Academy Award. "There has been an enormous movement away from the traditional. People are saying, 'Enough bullshit.' This has been largely produced both by domestic conditions and by the Vietnam War, which has affected the whole country one way or another. A great number of people are now saying, 'Look, we will no longer tolerate these values.' And I think what has happened is that people, almost willy-nilly, have grasped on to films that are in any way anti-establishment. Suddenly a lot of very direct and honest films about conditions in America are being made, and that, tied with the demise of Hollywood as we used to know it, and the rise of the independents, is making a climate that is very healthy."

First, however, he had a film to make in England, where the climate, as ever, was very different.

Twelve

1970–1971

"I can get away with anything now"

"It had never really occurred to me," Glenda Jackson said, as we sat in the cafeteria of the House of Commons, "that directors could be as frightened as actors. I was startled to observe how insecure John could be. I thought only actors felt that way. But he would go on and on about making 'this piece of shit,' when, of course, the film was so beautiful. It was quite something to witness."

John Schlesinger is eulogized as the man who made *Midnight Cowboy*, but *Sunday, Bloody Sunday* is his masterpiece, and Glenda Jackson was his star.

"It was his own personal experience," she said. "He knew when things weren't working because he'd been through it. He was so in tune with life. You see, bad directors know what they want but good directors know what they *don't* want, and that's a big, important difference. John knew this couldn't be sensationalist."

It is one of the great British films; indeed, a universal cinema classic, a unique gem of that most exciting period of filmmaking, the 1970s.

"I've been making noise about getting him a knighthood," Jackson told me, as we neared the end of our interview. "Alan Bates rang me a while back, and of course it's something we both still hope can happen. You'll let John know that, won't you?"

I did, of course, though when I told him, he made no response. Not that he was responding to much at that point, but he'd long ago given up any hope for a knighthood. Early on, after the success of *Darling*, friends had told him it was inevitable. But then his greatest success turned out to be an American film, and the British one that followed, which should have clinched the title for him, became most famous for its massive close-up of a male-to-male liplock. "That fucking homo kiss," he'd report wryly to his diary, "will keep me from a knighthood."

In those heady months after *Midnight Cowboy*'s premiere, he *was* invested with a CBE (Commander of the British Empire), an honor for which he was grateful yet always considered something of a consolation prize. Even then he believed, in his usual pessimistic way, that he would remain Mr. John Schlesinger while so many of those he'd guide along on their careers would get to add a Sir in front of their names. On that much, anyway, he was proven correct: Ian McKellen, Antony Sher, Alan Bates, Tom Courtenay.

At first, he would have believed that his increasingly obvious homosexuality stood as a barrier; even Noël Coward, infirm and aged, had been made to wait until it was almost too late. Memories still lingered, too, about the John Gielgud scandal seventeen years back, when the great actor had been arrested for soliciting sex only months after being knighted by the Queen.

But as the years went on and such openly gay figures as McKellen, Sher and others were so honored, it became evident that the denial of a knighthood was due less to John's gayness than to the perception that he had become an American director – a perception that was, quite simply, wrong: the eighteen films he made after *Midnight Cowboy* would be evenly divided between Britain and the United States. Still, John would tamp down any speculation about a knighthood among his friends: "They're not going to give it to an old faggot now."

It was so like him to see it in those terms. "John was so aware of his sexuality," said Alan Bennett, "that he contrived to find a corresponding awareness in the unlikeliest of places." He recalled John's story of his investiture with the CBE in June 1970. There was a moment when the Queen had some difficulty getting the ribbon around John's neck.

"Now, Mr. Schlesinger," she said. "Let us see. We must try and get this straight."

"Which," Bennett said, laughing heartily, "John chose to take as both a coded acknowledgement *and* a seal of approval."

John always believed that if the Queen, who he loved, had her way, he'd have been knighted; it was everybody else in Her Majesty's government who stood in opposition. And in 2003, as Glenda Jackson, now a Member of Parliament, was prominent in the charge against Tony Blair's war on Iraq, she was hardly in a position of much clout to change anybody's mind.

Consolation prize it may have turned out to be, but the CBE

was nevertheless an honor which seemed to prove, if any proof was still needed, that Bernard Schlesinger's physician friend had been right: his son would indeed grow up to make him very, very proud.

In just three years, the British cinema had plummeted from the giddy heights of the Swinging Sixties to the near-inactivity of the Somber Seventies. Inflation and a sterling crisis had put the brakes on the domestic film industry, and American money had dried up, too; preoccupied with their own crises – by 1970 every U.S. studio was deep in debt – American producers lost interest (and incentive) in keeping British movies afloat. Much hand-wringing took place in London: Alexander Walker compared the British cinema at this point to a "kept woman" resentful of her benefactor's sudden impoverishment, and taking it, in fact, as a personal slur.

Things were made worse by a decline in audience attendance: the number of cinemas in Britain dropped from 1,971 in 1965 to 1,529 in 1970. A corresponding decline in admissions, from 327 million to 193 million, was also charted. Consequently, British filmmakers found it impossible to make back their costs in the domestic market alone. Raising finance in Britain, never an easy task, now became a Herculean struggle.

"I do feel a little depressed at the moment," John admitted after arriving back in London in the spring of 1970. "When I started making films, the British film industry was having a renaissance and people were making films about people in England. I think that movement has switched to the States. I think we're going to be looking to what's going on in America.

We've had our revolution; what's going on here now is, in a sense, a backwash of what's going on in America."

In looking for money for *Sunday, Bloody Sunday*, the script of which was still taking shape, John found his success in America mattered little in London: he would be dragged along by Jo Janni to any number of potential financiers, and forced into "being a salesman on my right knee singing 'Mammy' to different people," he grumbled. "There were moments I said, 'Fuck this, I'll do something else.'"

But there was no way he could abandon this project: it was the most personal film he had ever planned. He knew if he didn't do it then, it might never happen. The story of his relationship with John Steiner was a bold follow-up to *Midnight Cowboy*, but he was feeling cocky. "It was a film I wanted to make," he said, "and the opportunity was there to do it. After the commercial success of *Cowboy* there was nothing to stop me doing anything I wanted." To his diary he bragged, "I can get away with anything now."

A sea change had also occurred in British society: in 1967, homosexuality between consenting adults in private had been legalized by the Sexual Offences Act, resulting in a shift toward tolerance and even a measure of curiosity. With pop stars flirting with the idea of bisexuality, same-sex desire acquired a certain chic; the line in the rock musical *Hair*, in which an otherwise straight boy admits he wouldn't kick Mick Jagger out of bed, seemed to sum up a new societal attitude.

Still, Schlesinger knew all along his idea was "a piece of chamber music," unlikely to reap great profits — at least according to conventional wisdom. But that same wisdom had predicted failure for *Midnight Cowboy*, and a new audience, emboldened by the changing times, had made that film a global phenomenon.

Never before had anything like *Sunday, Bloody Sunday* been so explicitly attempted by a director; gay life and experience, as previously treated by gay directors, usually appeared in coded form. The American films of the British director James Whale in the 1930s are infused with his own idiosyncratic, "queer" take on the world; likewise the films of Anthony Asquith, George Cukor, Edmund Goulding, and Dorothy Arzner. Yet few examples of actual homosexuality crop up in their work, and the trend was not evident until the 1960s, when Tony Richardson and John Schlesinger introduced characters and small moments from real life.

But now Schlesinger was taking a significant step forward: the homosexual would be the lead character, his story the movie's essential narrative. John knew the implications of what he was doing, and so did his associates. In his files, John kept a clipping a friend had sent him from the *Evening Standard*, a gossip-column remark made by Princess Luciana Pignatelli. "Many of my best friends are homosexuals," the Princess said. "Every woman over 30 should have at least one homosexual friend in her life. They are very refined and have marvelous taste." The friend had added his own postscript to the quote: "It's going to be a great year for Jewish homosexuals."

When John told his family what he was doing, they listened with polite interest. Later, Bernard asked his son, with a degree of levity, "On top of everything else, John, does the doctor have to be *Jewish*, too?"

But of course he did. This was John's story, after all, and he understood both the conflict and correspondence between Jewishness and homosexuality. Orthodox Judaism condemned homosexuals; indeed, one rabbi would renege on his promise to allow John to film a scene at his synagogue after he found out the picture's subject matter. But there is also a sympathetic connection between the two experiences: both Jewishness and homosexuality can "disappear" into the larger culture. Both the Jew and the homosexual can, if they choose, "pass" – for Christian, for heterosexual, and sometimes both. This duality of identity forms much of the background interest of *Sunday, Bloody Sunday*, as indeed it did John's life.

Early drafts of the script called the film simply *Bloody Sunday*, referring to a British expression describing a quiet weekend, "Oh, God, it's bloody Sunday again." And it was often on bloody Sundays that John had felt his most alone, while Steiner was off with his other lover.

Bloody Sunday, however, made too many people think of a St. Valentine Day-type massacre, and United Artists told John that Americans would assume it was a gangster picture. Mulling over the problem with the writer Charles Wood, with whom he was already in talks about the script for *Hadrian VII*, John was loathe to lose the title, which he'd come to love. Wood suggested *Sunday . . . Sunday*; inspired, John stuck the "bloody" back in between, ignoring advice that "bloody" didn't carry the same connotation in the United States. "I'm the filmmaker here," he told them.

It was a claim of auteurship he felt more intensely on this than any other picture. Usually eager to acknowledge collaboration, John would find that he had to fight for recognition of his creative imprimatur on this, his most personal film. The critics, never in his corner, would be all too eager to assign credit not to him but to the film's writer, Penelope Gilliatt, who was, of course, one of them. Until now, John had always shrunk back from any head-to-head confrontation with intellectuals, fearful he'd inevitably lose; but now, in taking on Penelope Gilliatt, he'd be fighting for his artistic soul.

"The first concept of *Sunday, Bloody Sunday*," Jo Janni would spell out in a letter, "was originated by John some time before we started *Far from the Madding Crowd*, and it was while we were in Weymouth that John first started to discuss the subject with me. We had some discussions about it and then considered possible writers to develop the story into a film."

A letter dated 22 November 1966 expressed Gilliatt's desire to work on a script with John and Janni; a curious request, given the devastating reviews she'd given *A Kind of Loving* and *Billy Liar*. But Gilliatt wanted a screenwriting career, and she wanted it badly; after *Darling*, she knew the Janni-Schlesinger team meant good box office. For their part, John and Jo considered that hitching up with an intellectual critic might work to their benefit and give them a leg up when it came time for reviews. Accordingly, the three of them met in late 1966 or early 1967, John describing his idea and providing details of his life with John Steiner. Gilliatt was enthusiastic, having written a novel, *A State of Change*, which also featured a two men-one woman relationship. Many months of conversations followed, with Penelope taking copious notes about John's feelings and experiences. "This is going to be a great story," John remembered her telling him.

By October of 1968 he was writing to Janni from New York, where he was still in the midst of editing *Cowboy*, urging that a deal be finalized with Gilliatt so they could start writing as soon as possible. "I had lunch with her the other day," John wrote, "and she seemed in good form and anxious to start."

Actually, she already had, with a rough script shown to Janni that March being deemed as heading in the right direction. At that point, discussions about the two leads centered on Paul Scofield for Daniel Hirsh, the doctor based on John, and Vanessa Redgrave for Alex Greville, the woman at the other end of the love triangle. "The part was written with Vanessa very much in mind," John said, although he also tossed around the idea of Maggie Smith and would later become excited about Zoe Caldwell. Janni's suggestion of Glenda Jackson, however, received a curt dismissal from John, who remembered her from the Royal Shakespeare Company as being "terribly strident."

He wasn't sold on Scofield either: "I doubt if Scofield would really want to play the doctor, but he might," John wrote to Janni in the spring of 1968. "My only reservation is that he might appear too saintly." When Janni suggested they consider Dirk Bogarde, John once again demurred: "He is marvelous at playing long-suffering lovers and indeed has already done so for us. [But] the casting is so obvious that I think it would seriously rob the film of some of its originality."

Already he was considering Peter Finch, calling him a "better idea" than Scofield, but Janni and Gilliatt, enthused by the very saintliness John felt instinctively was wrong, were determined that Sir Thomas More play their homosexual. When Scofield at last declined, attention turned to Harold Pinter; all of them, particularly Gilliatt (who idolized the actor-playwright) thought Pinter would be perfect.

Relations with Gilliatt remained cordial throughout 1968, though there was always an undercurrent of tension. "She was a critic and I don't like critics," John said. "I think it's impossible to have a friendship with a critic." By this time Gilliatt was working in New York, for the *New Yorker*, and John would find time during post-production on *Cowboy* to meet with her, talking "very freely" about his personal life. Despite this, they never became close, and their relationship was always marked by insincerity. John would describe each meeting with Gilliatt as starting "slightly acidly" then ending "with definite improvements and kissy-poohs all round."

"We didn't like each other much," he said another time. "She was an intellectual snob and I resented that. There was a kind of tension between us but I think perhaps out of that tension came a very good film."

Collaboration became even more difficult after John returned to England. Just as *Midnight Cowboy* opened in London, *The Times* ran a piece announcing he was working with Gilliatt on *Bloody Sunday*, now in its third draft. At first John kept mum to the press about the bisexual angle, saying only that it would pose the question: "Is half a loaf better than no bread to two people who are involved emotionally, not with each other, but somebody else? It's a very truthful film about people's emotions."

Going through the letters between Schlesinger, Janni and Gilliatt in these months, an increasing antagonism quickly becomes obvious. Gone were the "Dearest Penelopes" and "Darling Johns." In June 1969, Janni wrote that he was seriously alarmed about the pace of revisions, especially in terms of dialogue, which, in his opinion, was "too involved." By the following month open hostility had broken through the surface, with John dropping out of communication altogether and leaving it to Janni to fire off a letter saying how "very perturbed and unhappy" they were about the dialogue. Adding insult to injury, Janni told Gilliatt that they'd shown the script to Harold Pinter, who'd declared her dialogue impossible to speak. "Although we have accepted the style of the film," Janni wrote, "we also want the people to talk as people do and this is not the case in the present script."

He issued an ultimatum: Gilliatt needed to return to London so that John could be more directly involved in shaping the screenplay or she was off the film. "This is very usual," Janni told her, "and the only way we know how to work." Gilliatt agreed to sail to London within the month.

John didn't trust her, however, and wanted her gone. He set up a meeting with his old army friend, Peter Nichols, now a successful playwright, who described John as "fatter, greyer, but otherwise just as he was in 1947." To Nichols, John argued passionately that this was *his* story and Gilliatt was making a mess of it. "Penelope's brilliant and I'm not," John said, "but her brand of superior upper-middle-class left-wing humbug rubs me up the wrong way. All the characters know themselves so well and they're all buttoned up and in control and sit there smiling like Cheshire cats and discussing pre-Columbian art until I want to take my knickers down and fart!"

Nichols sympathized but expressed an inability to know what to do with the material. He advised John to take charge of the script, and not to be intimidated by Gilliatt and her "humbug."

Reluctantly, John gave her another chance, and after some face-to-face meetings in the autumn of 1969, he felt some improvement was being made. He loved the ending, for example: that daring deconstruction of the fourth wall when Daniel directly addresses the camera. It was an innovation for which John always made sure Gilliatt got credit: "I thought since the film ends this beautifully," he said, "we've got to make all the rest live up to it."

Gilliatt returned to New York after a series of script conferences, promising to have the final draft to them within a few months. Soon after, John received a letter from a United Artists representative, who related how she had run into Gilliatt and found her "loaded." When the rep mentioned how delighted UA was to have John doing another film for them, Penelope started to scream, demanding to know what John was saying about her behind her back. John took a certain glee in the report. "All writers think they have created a script solo handed," he wrote to the UA rep. "She may possibly have felt you ought to have been more pleased to have *her*."

The budget for *Sunday, Bloody Sunday* was set at £1.5 million. "It needs a fairly long schedule," John explained, "not because it's an involved film, but because it needs very beautiful playing. It will work only if the finer grading of shades of people's emotions and the subtleties of the scenes are brought out. It's got to be very carefully made, or otherwise it will be a disaster."

By this time, Vanessa Redgrave had officially declined the part. Devastated, John and Janni had begun considering Jean Simmons. But their attendance at a crew screening of Ken Russell's film *Women in Love*, written by John's old lover Larry Kramer and starring Alan Bates and Glenda Jackson, changed their minds. "We were absolutely bowled over," John wrote to Gilliatt. "The idea of Jean Simmons paled by the impact of Glenda's face and personality. The hardness that I was frightened of has mellowed and although she comes across as pretty tough, is still utterly feminine. I think the whole personality might work in a strangely marvelous way to our advantage."

Still, he remained a bit nervous about working with the star, whose reputation for stridency was now emphasized by her casting as the Virgin Queen in the BBC series *Elizabeth R*; her Mary Stuart from that production, Vivian Pickles, would also play in *Sunday, Bloody Sunday* as Alva Hodson. Yet John's trepidation dissipated on the first day of shooting, when he made a rather rude joke about his anatomy and Glenda howled in laughter. "We did nothing but giggle the whole way through," John recalled. "We had a whale of a time because she's actually got a great sense of humor and a fairly, in those days, dirty mind – which measured up to mine!" Jackson wore a wig for the duration of *Sunday, Bloody Sunday*, her hair still not grown back from the Russell film.

Glenda wasn't the only one John snatched from *Women in Love*; he also hired the film's cameraman, Billy Williams, who he remembered from making television commercials, as well as Luciana Arrighi, a young designer who had started with Russell at the BBC. "I was quite untried," Arrighi said, "and it was a big movie, so John was risking quite a bit."

The whole film was about taking risks. To play the part of the boy, John went with the 24-year-old Murray Head, known more as a singer than an actor; he'd released a few singles for Norrie Paramor and, at the same time as *Sunday, Bloody Sunday* was in production, was recording the role of Judas for the soundtrack of Andrew Lloyd Webber's *Jesus Christ Superstar*. Yet from the moment Head sauntered into the audition, cowboy hat on his head and guitar slung over his shoulder, John was entranced. Head was just his type – young, soft, and pretty; had Michael not been in London with him, friends said, John might have become even more entranced with his new discovery.

The role of Daniel was finally settled on the Scottish actor Ian Bannen, another connection from the Royal Shakespeare Company who, with his aristocratic, bemused air, seemed to embody the right mix of humor and nobility. Production began in good spirits. Despite the casting problems which would arise and the ongoing struggle with Gilliatt, John would look back on this shoot as a happy one, especially after the battles with his crew in New York on *Midnight Cowboy*. He was thrilled to be working with a British crew again, with people he knew and respected.

His style had, however, changed dramatically. From the somewhat self-effacing director of his early films he had become, according to William Hall, film columnist for the *London Evening News*, "fearsome to a lot of people." On the set, he was increasingly volatile; not autocratic, for he still welcomed collaboration, but far more difficult to please and accommodate. "When he makes a point," Hall observed, "he punches it home with a pungency that seems to relegate anyone else's ideas to second-best. It is a mark of authority or ego, or both. With Schlesinger it isn't easy to determine which."

Some saw it as a mark of greater self-confidence, yet while John clearly was much more sure of what he wanted, he remained, as ever, desperately insecure. That insecurity would boil over, with increasing frequency, into great fits of temper, and many a crew member would be reduced to tears on the set of a John Schlesinger film. "He could be terribly belittling, even sometimes cruel, in order to get his way," one said, asking not to be named. "If you had a thin skin, you'd never last on a Schlesinger film."

Ann Skinner said getting along with John was easy if one knew the trick. "When I told him I thought continuity would be a difficult job, he said, 'All you have to do, my dear, is remember what I say about takes and always laugh at my jokes.'"

He loved Annie Skinner, and he loved Luciana Arrighi, whose design for the film fit his image for it perfectly: simple and naturalistic. "I would sit there with Penelope, John, and Jo Janni and they'd be working through the script," Arrighi said, "so by the time that finished, I knew the characters. I didn't have to do any more homework than that. I think that's why in a way *Sunday, Bloody Sunday* is one of the best things I have ever designed, because it had nothing to do with just pretty pictures, but rather with *people*."

Likewise, John told Billy Williams that the cinematography had to be understated. "It was flamboyant in *Women in Love*," Williams said, "and John wanted the exact opposite here. The cinematography made a statement in *Women in Love*. For this, John wanted it to disappear."

Accordingly, Williams used soft lighting and stationary cameras; very few handheld cameras would be employed. Hard lighting would have left more shadows, spoiling the film with a studio look. In many ways it was back to the old realist school, preferring location over studio work: although some interiors were shot at Bray studios, where Hammer made its horror films, much of the film was shot in an actual house in London. Williams remembered the place being very cramped, and that many takes were ruined by the sound of planes flying overhead.

Within the first few weeks, however, a more serious

problem had emerged. Ian Bannen, having filmed a few early scenes, was "just not hacking it," John said. The decision was made to fire him and bring in Peter Finch. John felt terrible breaking the news to Bannen, whom he considered a friend, "But I knew the film would fail if we continued with him."

Finch arrived within days and plunged right in without any rehearsals. "There was no time to talk it over with him," John said. "He knew the character in some way without, I think, ever having experienced any of it." After watching Finch work that first day, John's faith in him was confirmed. "That's exactly what I wanted for the part," he said, "a pair of open arms."

To Gilliatt he wrote, "Peter is really finding the measure of Daniel," but it was Finch's very astuteness that led to the final rift between director and screenwriter. Almost immediately, Finch put his finger on a problem in the script which, in all fairness, had probably contributed to John's dissatisfaction with Bannen. It's the first scene in the picture, in which Daniel is interacting with a patient who's worried about a cancer diagnosis. The doctor's mind is on something else, however: an impending phone call from his lover, Bob. The scene is supposed to show Daniel's attempt to remain present and compassionate for his patient while his mind is elsewhere, yet Finch felt it failed in that regard.

"He couldn't play it," John said, "and in fact the scene just hadn't been written correctly. I had never noticed it. The emphasis was wrong. The scene was not about a doctor waiting for a phone call. It was about a character who is neurotic talking to a doctor, and it wasn't until we discovered that that it went right."

Gilliatt, however, could see no other way to write it. Suggesting, as they had to Freddie Raphael on *Madding Crowd*, that perhaps she was just too close to the subject after working on it for so long, Janni and Schlesinger brought in another writer, Ken Levison, to fix the scene. On 15 May, Levison, who'd been script editor for the sci-fi television programme *R3*, turned in an analysis of the scene which, in a few simple sentences, solved the problem in a way that had eluded Gilliatt. "There is more tension and conflict in the scene if it is made more obviously a triangle between Daniel, the Patient and the Phone," Levison wrote. Daniel's most important relationship in the scene, Levison instructed them, is not with the patient but with the phone. "It would also seem advantageous to establish very firmly right at the start something that runs so strongly throughout the whole picture [the use of the telephone as a device]."

Gilliatt was not happy about the Levison rewrite, and "came to blows" with John over the telephone a few weeks later. He had rung wanting yet another rewrite, this time of the final scene between Alex and Bob. It was filled with veiled inferences and lacked any emotional power, John felt, but Gilliatt adamantly refused to change a word. That she wasn't fired on the spot can only be attributed to her status as a critic and her connections to that world. Jack Gelber had certainly not been indulged this long. In the spring of 1970, John was still treating Gilliatt with kid gloves, almost suppliant in his letters to her: "These are just a few seeds to plant in your mind for when we get together on Sunday. I hope it won't be too harrowing an afternoon for you and that you will feel that we are all basically on the same side."

Yet what he was doing was teaching her some very basic lessons in plotting out a screenplay. "I think Bob's reactions in this scene are too repetitive once he's said, 'Nothing's changed,'" John wrote, concerning the problematic final scene between Bob and Alex. "If we haven't suggested his coolness by this time, then the movie's had it."

It was soon after this that the script was at last taken away from Gilliatt. It was nothing official and certainly not announced; she would retain sole screenplay credit. But John was at the point where he needed, as ever, a writer over his shoulder as he shot the film, and Gilliatt refused to come to London. It was just as well, John felt, for he needed a writer who could give him everyday dialogue, not one who was limited by an intellectual myopia. "If he couldn't laugh with somebody," said Luciana Arrighi, "John didn't want to work with them." And he certainly could never laugh with Penelope Gilliatt.

Her replacement was David Sherwin, who had written the script on which Lindsay Anderson had based *If . . .* (1968). In his diary for the spring of 1970, Sherwin remembered Schlesinger telling him Gilliatt's script was "unshootable"; Jo Janni called him in "to rewrite the whole film."

Not the whole film, but a good portion of it. Much of the dialogue is Sherwin's; almost every scene Gilliatt had written needed to be tweaked and snipped by the new writer. "Jo teaches me everything about working in a crisis," Sherwin wrote in his diary. "Whatever the chaos, he insists on making a 'scalata' every day – a little ladder, a kind of memo-cum-script outline."

Sherwin was never more than a day ahead in the rewrites. "Glenda Jackson and Peter Finch eye me warily as I approach each morning across the jumble of wires and brute lights with their latest lines," Sherwin recorded in his diary. The weeks dragged into months, with everyone reaching a "snapping point," especially the director. On a location shoot at a café on Oxford Street, Schlesinger and Sherwin got into a terrible row, both of them calling each other's work "absolute shit." Sherwin walked off the film, only to return when Janni begged him to reconsider.

By now, with Gilliatt gone, John was staking his claim as the film's chief auteur. It had been on his insistence that Gilliatt had written the scene where Daniel attends a family bar mitzvah; one more stamp of personal experience John succeeded in placing onto the picture. "I've been to that kind of bar mitzvah," he said, "where I'm faced with that business of cousins asking when I'm going to get married because otherwise I'll be very lonely and all that shit, and I've always wanted to use it."

Originally, there was to be even more of that scene than there was. John wanted a moment included when someone disrupted the gathering with an anti-Semitic remark, an event he remembered from one of his own visits to the synagogue in St. John's Wood. Richard Marden, who'd cut *The Starfish* and gone on to become a highly regarded editor on such films as *Anne of the Thousand Days*, returned to John's cutting room for *Sunday, Bloody Sunday*. He recalled that the anti-Semitic disruption scene was, in fact, filmed, but they ended up snipping it out, Marden said, "because it wasn't really relevant."

What quickly did become relevant was the film's music, discovered almost by chance in the editing room as John and Marden were putting together rushes. Today *Sunday, Bloody Sunday* is identified as strongly with "Terzettino," from Mozart's opera *Cosi Fan Tutte*, as *Midnight Cowboy* is with "Everybody's Talkin'." A trio for mixed voices, the piece is both joyous and melancholy, and its placement against both relationships equalized, through music, the homosexual and heterosexual experience.

"It's about waving goodbye," John said, admitting that the actual translation is imprecise. "It's about having a calm and safe trip. It has a sort of overtone which I thought was right for the film, as well as the music being so very beautiful and soulful, the kind of thing that one would play, I think, late at night."

It was shaping up to be a profoundly literate and intelligent production, with the performances of its two stars plainly transcendent. Soon into production, however, it became obvious that Murray Head was being far outshone by Jackson and Finch. Richard Marden remembered that John, increasingly frustrated, was very hard on the young actor, blowing up at him whenever he muffed a line. "I don't think [John's temper] helped very much," Marden said.

"I think you will find Murray is a personality rather than an actor," John wrote to Gilliatt while relations were still cordial. "He isn't quite the Bob you had thought of."

In later years, John would say he cast the wrong person for the part; Head was too inexperienced an actor to convey the depth of personality that such a character, who bewitches the two leads, must demonstrate. "In real life," John said, "the boy who was the basis for the character was enchanting – funny, outrageous in many ways, a thoroughly entertaining, intelligent human being. I don't think that's what we got from either the script or the performance of Murray Head."

Glenda Jackson didn't agree. "I don't think it's hard to realize why he's so attractive to these two people," she said. "The only people who know what's in a relationship are the people who are in it. Murray was young and inexperienced, yes, but he was a very hard worker and I thought quite good."

For his part, Head told Elaine Dundy, Peter Finch's biographer, that he was aware of John's displeasure. Conflicted about the character he was playing, Head was, however, very supportive of the famous kiss: "To me," he said, "it was an infinitely simple gesture which caused eruptions right, left and centre." On the day the kiss was to be filmed, Head remembered tension on the set, especially among "the grips and the sparks." Lots of cigarette smoking, grumbling behind the camera. It's a memory quite different from the one held by Luciana Arrighi, who recalled no discomfort from anybody. "You know the English technicians," she said. "Seen everything, been everywhere."

Yet Billy Williams acknowledged that some of his men did, in fact, make some noise, and Head recalled someone asking John, just before the cameras started rolling, "Is this really necessary?"

"Of course it is!" John shot back.

The actors, however, took it in stride. John would love to tell the story – and it may have been just that, one of his stories – that Peter Finch said he'd gotten through it by closing his eyes and "thinking of England." What seems more likely is the account given by Head of watching the kiss during rushes, with technicians nervously crossing and uncrossing their legs, and smoking cigarette after cigarette.

"Camera operators as a race are pretty square," John would observe. "They say, 'You can't do this,' or 'Never heard of that on film.'"

Billy Williams had to face his own discomfort, he admitted to me. "When I learned what the subject matter was to be on the film," he said, "I was quite concerned, because it had never been done before. John had to convince me that it was going to be done well, and that's why I agreed to do it. Many years later I thanked him for it, because it had been such an extraordinary experience."

Production wrapped in the autumn of 1970. It was a period of highs and lows for John: the exhilaration of finishing the film was tempered by the loss of a second sister, Wendy, who died of cancer. Wendy had married and was living with her family in Holland; John left the set at one point to visit her in hospital. Her death was a terrible blow to the family, especially coming so soon after Susan's.

At the same time, John had enjoyed sharing London with Michael, who was blossoming in his own career as a photographer. Remembering Childers' work on *Oh, Calcutta!*, Kenneth Tynan had been instrumental in getting Michael a job at the National Theatre, the first and only American to hold an official position of photographer there. "Young and cheeky," Michael described himself. "I had Gielgud one day, and Olivier the next, and oh my God, Edith Evans! And then some nude shots for an experimental play with some young actor I'd never heard of, Anthony Hopkins."

Sitting with me in his Palm Springs living room, remembering those days, Childers laughed. "I knew how great these people were, of course, but I was so young. If I'd fully realized their legendary heights, I would have been terrified. I *should* have been terrified! But I wasn't. I just rolled along with it."

John was supportive and proud. "He wanted me to have a career on my own," Michael said, looking out at his partner sitting in his wheelchair on the terrace. "He never wanted me to be just Mrs. John Schlesinger."

With principal photography on *Sunday, Bloody Sunday* complete, the two of them took off on a three-month Asian holiday that included India, Bali, Nepal, Thailand, Hong Kong, and Japan. John loved Bali and hated Hong Kong ("Fifth Avenue, Saks and Disneyland," he called it). As always, food was an abiding passion for him, and he enjoyed discovering new cuisines. In Japan, where he had his memorable meeting with Kurosawa, he partook of an elaborate lunch of sushi and octopus at a restaurant in the shadow of Mount Fuji. Friends recalled him after the meal, fully sated, sitting in the corner, the corners of his mouth turned down, looking very much like the Buddha.

Unlike the tense post-production of *Midnight Cowboy*, the editing of *Sunday, Bloody Sunday* went smoothly in the capable hands of Dickie Marden. No troubles, either, from the censor; John Trevelyan regarded it as a "beautiful and sensitive film." In fact, for a film that broke ground by showing not only a male-to-male kiss, but later had the two of them in bed together, there was surprisingly little butchering. Only a few countries, Mexico, Singapore, South Africa among them, ordered the explicitly homosexual scenes excised (though shots of Glenda Jackson's bare breasts were approved). Schlesinger and Janni lodged protests, saying such cuts made "mincemeat of what we were trying to do," but recognized they couldn't fight (and win) all of the battles.

The London premiere at the Leicester Square Theatre on 1 July 1971, was a dazzling occasion in the presence of HRH, with Princess Margaret and Lord Snowdon. Mr and Mrs Richard Attenborough, Sir Laurence and Lady Olivier, Elizabeth Taylor and Richard Burton were all in attendance. Afterward, Princess Margaret, despite being an old friend of Penelope

Gilliatt, registered her definite disapproval. "I thought it was horrific," she said, in full earshot of both John and Michael. "Men in bed kissing!"

Hers was a decidedly minority opinion. Already the reviews were in, the best of Schlesinger's career, before or since. George Melly in the *Observer* said it was "as near flawless as we have any right to expect." Richard Mallett in *Punch* called it "first-rate . . . every scene is beautifully, perceptively done." John Coleman in the *New Statesman* opined, "Its method is the mask of art."

Such near-unanimity of opinion had occurred before among British critics about John's work, but always in opposition; this time, with an uninterrupted stream of praise, John was stunned, "and a little overwhelmed by it," he wrote to Gene Phillips. Making things even sweeter, the film, boosted by its critical reception, was pulling in spectacular box office at the Leicester Square Theatre. When it opened the next month at various other theaters in metropolitan London, its appeal seemed only to increase. By the late summer John had every reason to believe that his latest picture was going to be another *Midnight Cowboy*: an offbeat, risky, art house picture that had somehow turned into a blockbuster commercial success.

Of course, things were done so differently then: opening a picture in just one theater in one city and letting it play there for a month, building an audience, racking up positive reviews, is no longer even imaginable in today's cinema. And part of the reason things are no longer done that way, movie execs would argue, is because of the example of films like *Sunday, Bloody Sunday*. It wasn't until the autumn of 1971 that United Artists understood that, contrary to the reviews and good box office in the city, John Schlesinger's film was going to lose money. Nowadays, these things need to be discovered right away, so the studios can pull the film, cut their losses, and cancel any contracts with the filmmaker.

We can be glad, then, that this was 1971, that *Sunday, Bloody Sunday* was given a chance to seep into the consciousness of the world. "It was a city film obviously," John said, but he would accuse his distributors, Rank Leisure Services, of not making a serious attempt to market it beyond the city limits, claiming he was told, "There isn't a thinking audience outside London." Certainly there were "thinking audiences" in the university towns, John said, but he would bluster about "idiotic distributors" who premiered the film before the term started. "Not a student in sight!" he bellowed.

The records tell a slightly different story: *Sunday, Bloody Sunday* was, in fact, given a fairly widespread release throughout England and Wales in the early autumn of 1971. Just a partial list: Brighton, Blackpool, and Hove on 2 September; Bristol, Cardiff, Bath, Manchester, Liverpool, and Grimsby on 5 September; Bournemouth and Plymouth on 9 September; Oxford, Cambridge, Exeter, Birmingham, Derby, and Lincoln on 12 September; and Northampton, Peterborough, and Reading on 19 September. John had a point in decrying the month-too-early release in the university towns, but the fact that business could not be sustained in any of these provincial areas was not a fault of the distributor, but rather a reflection of social realities. Urban audiences were willing – indeed, often eager – to sit through a literate play-on-film which challenged their notions of sexual and gender roles. Provincial audiences simply were not.

A similar pattern would develop in the United States after the film's American release in September. Smashing reviews: the *New York Times* called the picture "nearly perfect," John's "wisest, least sentimental film," and even Pauline Kael declared it "instantly recognizable as a classic." Playing at the Coronet – the same, good-luck-charm theater that had premiered *Midnight Cowboy* – *Sunday, Bloody Sunday* pulled in steady New York crowds, and indeed would do well in other American urban centers. UA executives were thrilled, and John was treated like a king during his promotional tour of America. A blue Mustang was waiting for his use in the garage of the Beverly Hills Hotel; flowers and liquor were provided in the suites of all the members of his party. John Schlesinger, Academy Award winner, was a star director, and he would be treated as such.

But the American heartland, like its British counterpart, stayed away from the film, and by the late autumn the studio knew they would not be making back their costs. They would have to content themselves with the critical acclaim; it was the first time John had experienced the critics' approval, only to have audiences turn their backs. At the Venice Film Festival in August he was received as a true *artiste* by his peers; Visconti made it a point to come over to him, shake his hand, and tell him rather grandly, "I now pass onto you my mantle of international film director." Stewart Grimshaw remembered John being thrilled and flattered, but also overwhelmed by all the attention; the expectations now being settled upon him were truly daunting.

Schlesinger and Janni may not have been able to prevail over the Mexican censors, but one battle they did win was with the French. UA's distribution arm in Paris, under the direction of Jean Nachbaur, had devised a poster for the film which horrified John: superimposed over the image of Daniel and Bob kissing was a shot of Glenda Jackson screaming, snipped from the sequence in the film in which she sees a dog being hit by a truck. It looks, of course, as if she's screaming about the kiss.

John fired off a letter that sums up quite succinctly all that is wrong with the poster as well as what is *right* about his approach to the film. "Both Jo Janni and I react pretty violently to your proposed poster," he wrote to Nachbaur. "Not because you wish to overtly state that the film is about homosexuality, though that is not the point of the film. What we both find inaccurate and old-fashioned is that you have chosen a still of Glenda Jackson suggesting that the woman involved in the film is shocked by what happens. This is so against the nature of the picture that we cannot in any way support you on this proposed advertisement. By all means sell the picture to the public but for heaven's sake let the advertising represent accurately what is in the film, which is: love, tenderness, affection, honesty, loneliness, and so forth. The poster that you suggest looks like the cover of an old Fifties novel on the subject."

Nachbaur initially defended the poster, writing back that "New York-developed" advertising approaches might work in England but not in France. From UA, John called in reinforcements to apply pressure; by 18 August Nachbaur was singing a different song, replacing the image of a screaming Jackson with a smiling one, telling John, "Believe it or not, we had not realized how much we were missing the point with the first photo."

What *Sunday, Bloody Sunday* was asking people to do — whether they were critics, audiences or advertising executives — was take a light-year leap into the future in the way they viewed and considered homosexuality. A woman screaming at the sight of two men kissing would not have seemed so outrageous to most people; it's what they would have done if they witnessed such a thing. Nachbaur's defense of the original poster was based on people being able to *understand* it; he had a film to sell, he argued, a film about homosexuality, so he had to make that point "as directly and precisely as possible." By contrast, a shot of a woman looking serenely at two men kissing evokes confusion instead of clarity: what *is* this film about? Why is she smiling at such a thing? It's that subversion, that subtle reconsideration of the way things are, that makes *Sunday, Bloody Sunday* so revolutionary.

"Although it was by no means a Gay Lib film," John would say, looking back, "I thought at that moment in time it was fairly advanced. Homosexuality had been treated seriously earlier in *Victim*, but that, for me, didn't go far enough."

Those are the words of an activist. Of a political man, which John always insisted he was not. Much would be made to me by people close to Schlesinger that he was never a "gay director" making "gay films." Indeed, such constructs emerged from a later period, the queer cinema of the 1980s which produced such people as Derek Jarman, Bill Sherwood, and Gus Van Sant. Yet from the time John began making short independent films, he endeavored to capture gay life on celluloid, to equalize his experience with the lives of others. To a *New York Times* reporter he lambasted the supposedly revolutionary gay film *The Boys in the Band* (1970) because of its perpetuation of self-loathing stereotypes: "This business of 'Show me a happy homosexual and I'll show you a gay corpse' isn't the way it really is," John insisted. "That's the exception, not the rule." *Sunday, Bloody Sunday*, then, becomes political by its sheer apoliticality: John was not asking for tolerance, he was assuming that among people of intelligence it was already there.

"Ahead of its times" is a clichéd phrase, but in 1971 there was not yet the language for a public discourse on what the film was really setting forth, which was a complete overhaul of social restrictions on sexual expression and sexual identity. Couching it in educational terms, as filmmakers of break-through films usually do, John said, "I thought the film would enable people to understand a little bit more about the subject." Yet it was hardly "a little bit" he was asking people to understand: the film's presumption, which critics largely bought and the public largely rejected, was that the way life was presented onscreen was in fact the way life should be.

A few critics managed to grasp at least partially the film's radical break with the past. The *New York Times* said "the sobs and sorrows" of *The Boys in the Band* were now as "up-to-date as the fox-trot." Stefan Kanfer in *Time* rather famously observed that Daniel's "affliction is not homosexuality but the tradition that abhors it." Most astute of all, however, was the *Guardian*, which stated: "What was previously unmentionable is now not considered worth mentioning. The film's supreme aplomb lies in the fact that the subject just doesn't come up."

There is no preaching. In that elegant, eloquent, daring last scene, Daniel is telling us he may be wistful but he is not broken; he is strong, he is healthy. Many critics have observed that in this scene the doctor has become the patient, the audience placed into the role of the physician. Yet Daniel is still the one to determine his own diagnosis: he will be fine, indeed, *is* fine, just as he is. Schlesinger would explain that last speech by rephrasing it: "It was worth going through this experience, though you might not think so. Our relationship was not pointless. You may not understand it, but don't judge me for it." After all, as Daniel says in the film's final, slightly enigmatic line, "I only came about my cough."

There is no apology, no "explanation" needed: his sexuality just *is*, and it is equal with Alex's. In the original script Daniel was also to say, "You've no right to call me to account," but Schlesinger deleted it, wanting no defensiveness on Daniel's part. By making the loss of Bob something shared by Alex and Daniel, the conflict of the film became the universal one of love and loneliness, thereby frustrating any attempt to marginalize the story's homosexuality or to turn it into something "other," something separate from the mainstream of life. Tellingly, one of the advertising catchphrases for the film was: "*Sunday, Bloody Sunday* is about three decent people. They will break your heart."

"*Sunday, Bloody Sunday* saved my life," said Michael Cunningham, the Pulitzer Prize-winning author of *The Hours*. "When I was growing up, beginning to understand that I was gay, all I could imagine for myself was a life of furtive sorrow which involved, to my young mind, skulking around with a lapdog in my arms looking for love in the men's room of the Greyhound station, with guys who would probably beat me up afterward. Then I saw Peter Finch play a complicated, honorable gay man, simply and fully human. It was revelatory. I began to believe, after seeing that movie, that I could have a future as neither more nor less than myself, and that being myself was more than enough to be."

The film also received praise even from critics who had been unable in the past to disguise a streak of homophobia. Richard Schickel in *Life* magazine attempted to opt out altogether by claiming not to have strong feelings about characters who, "for better or worse, have solved their problems of sexual identity."

Yet he had to admit that once he'd "registered appropriate culture shock," he considered the kiss "so much better than the variously prissy, poetical, metaphorical and melodramatic ways people since T. Williams have been dealing with this subject." And Pauline Kael, who'd once despaired over the tendency to treat homosexuals "seriously, with sympathy and respect, like Negroes and Jews," was now obliged, in addition to naming it a classic, to call it "one of a kind" and salute Daniel Hirsh as "one of the most simply and completely created characters in recent films."

Both Finch and Jackson are superb. The truth is found in small moments: the way Alex watches Bob with the children, the controlled anger Daniel expresses when he realizes the trip to Italy with his lover has always been a pipe dream. The encounter between Daniel and Alex, their only meeting in the entire film, is a brilliant, understated acknowledgement of both the honesty and the discomfort in their lives. The smile Jackson gives Finch as she crosses the street; the gesture he makes of offering her a cigarette; these are the moments that make up their superlative, heartbreaking performances.

Murray Head was doomed from the start to be almost eclipsed by this pair. In truth, despite all the bitching by some reviewers that they couldn't understand the attraction, Head manages to convey an essential decency behind his youthful energy and resistance to commitment. John struggled with adding material to make Bob more believable as a love object obsessed over by two interesting, introspective people; the scenes with his artist friends, and with the children after the death of the dog, are intended to do just that. John would go so far as to blame the character for the film's financial failure "because I think some people who didn't like it couldn't understand the predicament. If they had found the boy interesting and entertaining, perhaps they would have understood it more.'

Yet he would also agree – and here is why the performance, in the end, is exactly right – that "people do waste time over the most unlikely people whom others deem to be valueless but in whom they have found something they need or want." Bob's youth and his unwritten, uncharted future are all that either Daniel or Alex need in order to find him fascinating. Onto his unlined face they project all of their hopes, wishes, and might-have-beens.

The rest of the cast is also first-rate. John enticed Peggy Ashcroft to play Alex's mother, in a sharp, brilliant scene that shows why Alex decides not to settle for half a loaf; why, at times, "nothing has to be better than anything." Bessie Love, who'd been a star of the silent screen dating back to *The Birth of a Nation*, delivers a memorably comic turn as the busybody answering service lady. Vivian Pickles as the outrageous liberal mother – beaming her sly, knowing grin while her kids smoke pot – warranted a film all of her own, along with the talented Kimi Tallmadge as her obnoxious eldest daughter Lucy. A younger daughter was played by John's niece Emma.

As always, place is a vital element in Schlesinger's films; Jo Janni would say that their intention in this film was to capture "a weary, self-doubting England." Indeed, Gilliatt's early notes on the script offer specific background in this area: "Sterling is rocking and the Pound is being devalued. The economic situation glints through the private behavior of our characters." Long gone was the confident swagger of *Darling*; in various places in *Sunday, Bloody Sunday*, one can see the uncertainty of life that Britons were facing in the early 1970s, from news bulletins that drone on about the economic crisis to the surrealistic, out-of-kilter moment when "an ex-opera singer reduced to being a doorman" (Schlesinger's words) suddenly launches into an aria. It was one of those moments the director had observed in real life and filed away to use on film. To drive the point home, a woman is seen carrying a newspaper with the headline, "Eight Million Jobs Threatened."

The film is also a comment on how technology, even with the telephone's "vast network of wires and connections", hadn't helped humankind all that much in its ability to communicate. Being "at the mercy of the telephone" was something John loathed; his abhorrence of technology would persist throughout his life, extending to fax machines, computers and mobile phones. Though assistants would set up email accounts for him, he found the whole idea absurd.

Flaws in the film are few. Perhaps a couple of the fantasy shots have a little too much razzmatazz, as John called them in *Midnight Cowboy*: for example, Daniel imagining Bob dying, or a dreamy hallucinatory scene of junkies at a chemist shop that goes on too long. Length, too, is the primary objection to the bar mitzvah scene; while some critics felt it was irrelevant and indulgent, akin to the party scene in *Cowboy*, it clearly has a dual function in the film, to place Daniel in the context of his life and to underscore his loneliness.

And, as in *Darling*, there's a slight problem with a framing device. The film opens with a title announcing "Friday," then moves to Saturday and then Sunday, on which, because of the main title, we assume the main action is about to take place. But when we move on to Monday, we are left momentarily confused, and the later titles building back up to the following Sunday lose their impact.

Pauline Kael, in her review, compared the film to a novel; indeed, it is an internal film, with its most visceral moment occurring when the dog is hit by the truck, and does in fact give one the sense of reading rather than watching; it is this experience that prompted many critics to assume Gilliatt had left a greater artistic imprint on the picture than Schlesinger. "I have no idea who suggested what to whom while Miss Gilliatt was writing the screenplay," said Vincent Canby in the *New York Times*, "but because I'm familiar with her fiction, as well as with Schlesinger's other films, it does seem to me as if she supplied the director with the most rigorous material he's ever worked with, material that more or less precluded the kind of romantic, sentimental touches that kept both *Darling* and *Midnight Cowboy* from being quite as great as they originally looked."

In other words, *Sunday, Bloody Sunday* was as good as it was not because of John but because of Penelope – a reversal of the critics' usual conceit that a director is the ultimate auteur of a picture. Canby even acknowledged this apparent contradiction by saying he, and others, would no doubt be accused of "having discovered screenwriting is an art" through their colleague, "especially those of us who identify films as the works of their directors." But there were some screenplays, Canby wrote, "that simply cannot be mistaken as the works of anyone except the people who wrote them."

John was enraged. The final screenplay of *Sunday, Bloody Sunday* was *not* the sole work of Gilliatt, though he was prevented from publicly naming Ken either Levison or, more significantly, David Sherwin. He would insist that he and Jo Janni had had to twist and reshape the screenplay several times, but few critics cared much about that process. John was left having to bite back his temper whenever they gushed over their colleague's "superbly natural, fluid dialogue" (Kathleen Carroll of the New York *Daily News)*. John fumed to Michael: "She *didn't* write natural dialogue! That was the whole god-damn problem!"

It was Pauline Kael who, as ever, proved the most egregious. Given Schlesinger's "hideously obvious" direction in the past, Kael – Gilliat's writing partner at the *New Yorker* – wrote that she could only assume that this new film (remember she called it a "classic") had been inspired "by the delicate substance of Penelope Gilliatt's screenplay."

There appeared to be a concerted effort to dislodge John from any claim to authorship. And Gilliatt was determined to ride the good words of the critics straight into a screenwriting career, even if it meant she had to use the ideas of John Schlesinger and the words of David Sherwin to do so. When she negotiated a deal with Bantam to publish the script in book form, she included in her biography that the idea for *Sunday, Bloody Sunday* had come to her on a train in Switzerland as she was going to see Vladimir Nabokov. John went apoplectic. "How's *that* for intellectual pretension," he wrote. "And a lie!"

In outrage, Janni wrote to Gilliatt soon before the film's American premiere. "You have gone out of your way to create in everybody's mind the impression that a script entirely con-ceived and written by you was delivered to John Schlesinger and myself to be made into a film. Every time you read or hear things that do not corroborate this idea, you get very annoyed. I am afraid more irritation is bound to be caused if you persist in an attitude which does not reflect the facts."

Janni went on: "At all times we have been extremely careful not to give the impression that the help [Levison and Sherwin] gave us was any more than assistance [or] that they had made any substantial contribution to your screenplay. I want to be very clear that we do not want to take away from you any glory or fail to recognize the marvelous work you have done. Once again, I am asking you to stick to the truth and to the facts as we all know occurred."

By November the quarrel had been leaked, probably by Janni, to the press; columnist Robin Adams Sloan called it "the biggest feud in the cinema world," and said John was threatening to produce Gilliatt's original script "to prove how little it's like the finished hit product."

Still, Gilliatt won best screenplay from the National Society for Film Critics, the New York Film Critics and the Screenwriters Guild. She was also nominated, along with John for Best Director and Finch and Jackson for acting awards, by the Academy of Motion Picture Arts and Sciences, but Oscars wouldn't go to any of them that year. John did win a British Academy Award, as did the picture, Jackson, Finch, and Richard Marden as editor. Gilliatt, though nominated, was the one major player not to take home a BFA prize, a fact which pleased John no end.

Certainly, much of Gilliatt remains in the picture; it would not be the film it is without her. But the influence of the other writers, and the creative stamp of its director, should not be overshadowed by her contribution. "Such good writing," John would say, "but such a sad woman." Her dreams of a screenwriting career were not to be; no other screenplay by Penelope Gilliatt ever made it to the screen.

By the time I tried talking to him about *Sunday, Bloody Sunday*, John wasn't saying much anymore, but mention of Gilliatt's name still prompted a glance up from his wheelchair, where his eyes usually remained downcast.

"Tell him what you thought of Penelope, John," Michael goaded him.

I bent down so I could look up into his eyes. They were alert and shining.

"She was a *cunt*," John whispered, hardly audible, but still delivered with a tremendous amount of passion.

Thirteen

1972–1975

"Waterloo collapsed spectacularly"

W hat keeps a man alive? Is it hope? Is it fear? Is it the simple enjoyment of a warm, sunny afternoon, looking at the mountains, Puccini playing on the CD?

In the beginning, when I'd begun this project, there had been at least the few scattered conversations, the good days when I might get John talking a bit, pry from him a few thoughts, opinions, memories. But now there was nothing, and as I got to know him through his friends, through his archives, through his letters, through his films, I began to wonder just why he was hanging on, what kept him alive, when all of the things he once loved to do so much – eat, laugh, have sex, make movies – were now impossible.

"I'm trying to understand, John," I said to him. "What keeps you here?"

There was, of course, no answer.

"I wouldn't get too sentimental about it," his nephew, Ian Buruma, cautioned me. "He's physically extremely strong, which gave him so much energy all his life. One doesn't always have control [over when one dies]. My grandmother lived longer than she wanted to. I certainly don't think [John's hanging on] reflects a great lust for life. He's not enjoying himself, and ever since he was unable to go on making films, I think he's lost interest in living."

Did he want to die then? Did he wake up in the morning disappointed to endure yet another day of seeing the mountains, feeling the sun, hearing his music?

Did he think of God? All his life he'd professed a wish that he'd been brought up more Jewish, but his words were cultural, not spiritual. He'd never professed any kind of deep belief, yet neither had he ever called himself an atheist.

"Once, sitting at his bedside, I asked him if he wanted me to recite some Jewish prayers," said his sister Hilary. "He didn't answer so I did. I read him Psalm 138, and suddenly I saw he was responding, engaged with what he was hearing."

Part of the psalm reads: "Though I walk in the midst of trouble, you preserve me against the wrath of my enemies; you stretch out your hand, and your right hand delivers me. The Lord will fulfill his purpose for me; your steadfast love, O Lord, endures forever. Do not forsake the work of your hands."

To her surprise, Hilary found her brother had begun stroking her arm.

"I believe John's connection to spirit played a big part in the subconscious of his mind, though within this secular realm, he did dismiss it," said his friend Ilo Orleans, a Buddhist, who became close to Schlesinger in the last years of his life. "John obviously had amazing karma and rode the wave of spirit without having to practice any religion formally."

"I used to tease him," said Shirley MacLaine, known for her belief in metaphysics. "I'd say, 'John, you're interested in things spiritual, but only from the dark side.' You look at a film like *The Believers* and you'll see where his interests were. He found the dark side more artistic, intriguing, complicated, whereas he considered the light and some of the things I was talking about unprovable.

"But he was *interested*," she continued. "There was a part of him that wanted to learn, wanted to hear, and maybe believe. We'd have these conversations and he'd listen to me, but then all of a sudden he'd say, 'Enough!' and want the dish on who my brother [Warren Beatty] was bedding down."

Was he depressed sitting there, not speaking? Maureen, his faithful nurse, spelled out the various anti-depressant medications he was on. "He wouldn't smile if he was depressed," she said. "And John's always smiling."

What kept him going then?

What keeps a man alive?

Was it just his heart, as strong as an ox since his bypass?

Or was there, possibly, something more?

In 1973, John and Michael moved into a house in Victoria Road, a much bigger, grander place than the Peel Street flat. "Tailored brown and beige flank a log fireplace," one reporter described it. "Plate glass windows reveal sunken green terraces, hidden speakers sound string quartets. He's got it just the way he wants it."

Friends remembered the house with great fondness. "John

and Michael knew how to entertain," said Brenda Vaccaro. "Such wonderful dinner parties. Everything was always so precise. The best food, the best champagne, the most beautiful table arrangements. It was a gorgeous house and John loved to sit there at the table, encouraging people to talk and carry on."

As much as he loved his new home, John would describe the year after *Sunday, Bloody Sunday* as his "worst ever." Of course, he made this assessment at a time when *Honky Tonk Freeway*, *The Next Best Thing* and his stroke were all well in his future but still, 1972–1973 was definitely a down period for the whore's drawers (remembering John's comment about how often his career went up and down.) He made a few commercials, something he would do periodically to keep cash in his pocket. The ones best remembered from this period were for After Eight chocolates.

Michael, meanwhile, had returned to America to pursue his photography, feeling professionally stalled in England. Alone, and without a confirmed project, John became involved in a "rebound love affair" with a young man; the open relationship with Michael permitted such dalliance, yet John was unprepared for the depression that ensued once the young man left him. Missing Michael, he implored his partner to return to London, but Childers was by now becoming increasingly in demand as a celebrity photographer in the States.

Michael's professional upswing contrasted with a series of setbacks for John. With the completion of *Sunday, Bloody Sunday*, Schlesinger had been gearing up to start casting *Hadrian VII* when Dustin Hoffman, his top choice as star, backed out; soon afterward Columbia, with whom he had a contract to do the film, also withdrew support. United Artists, saddled with the financial wreck of *Sunday, Bloody Sunday*, wasn't about to bail him out either, and so *Hadrian* was shelved. "Charles Wood wrote a brilliant script which they didn't understand because it didn't have the cosiness of the play," John said. He promised Wood that he wasn't abandoning the project, that he would get the film made one day "by hook or by crook."

It was a period of might-have-beens. In January 1972 the producer Si Litvinoff (*A Clockwork Orange*) signed John to direct and co-write the film adaptation of Luke Rhinehart's novel *The Dice Man*. By March, John was juggling *Dice Man* with a possible American adaptation of Nathanael West's *The Day of the Locust* as well as renewed discussions over *Hadrian*. "I always have two or three projects cooking at the same time," John would say. "It's the only way to be assured of having work."

He also approached Peter Nichols again, trying to develop an original screenplay about two brothers and their relationships with their parents, stretching from World War II to the present day. Clearly an early manifestation of the film he'd want to make about his own family, the script was to be "funny and a rather touching comment on the British middle-class way of life." John stressed to Jo Janni that, due to the "complications over our last original film," he wanted a joint screenplay or story credit with Nichols; never again was he going to allow someone else to lay claim to a story drawn from his own life.

But the problem, as ever, was money; none of these projects got the green light. The one that came closest was an adaptation of Evelyn Waugh's novel *A Handful of Dust*. John asked the playwright Alan Bennett to adapt it, and the two forged a friendship in the spring and summer of 1973, working together on the project at Victoria Road. John even put up a chunk of his own money to try to get things moving, but to no avail.

It's important to understand that, contrary to conventional wisdom, John did not abandon Britain following his success with *Midnight Cowboy*. For three years after *Sunday, Bloody Sunday*, he and Jo Janni attempted to get another British picture off the ground, but the money men had decreed British subjects uncommercial. John would rail in his diary against Frank Yablans, the head of Paramount, who was quoted as saying he was turning his back on films like *This Sporting Life* and *Sunday, Bloody Sunday* – "choosing two critical successes that made no money," John wrote. "But on the other hand, if you faced him with *Saturday Night and Sunday Morning* or *Darling*, both of which were highly commercially successful, they would immediately be thought of as 'international' films. That's one of the stupidities of this business."

If the American producers remained intransigent, the problem at home was there was simply no money to be had. "The central weakness of the British film industry," wrote Alexander Walker, "was the fact that the home market simply would not support a film industry." It had less to do with numbers – certainly France, with five million fewer people than the United Kingdom in 1971, had always managed to support a thriving film tradition. It was more a reflection of one of John's most frequent gripes: the indifference with which most of his countrymen viewed their national cinema.

It's perhaps not surprising, then, that in early 1972 John returned his attention to a much more English enterprise: the theater. This time it was not Shakespeare, or any brittle, modern, avant-garde play that commanded his attention: rather, in another one of his quirky career moves – even more unlikely than his choice of Hardy and *Madding Crowd* – John decided to take a shot at a musical. Originally entitled

"H.R.H.," it would tell the story of Queen Victoria, from young girl to old woman. The book was written by Jay Allen, the well-known playwright (*The Prime of Miss Jean Brodie*) who'd helped play cupid between John and Michael; this latest brainstorm, however, would prove neither as fitting nor as durable.

At the same time, John also accepted an assignment from the American producer David L. Wolper (*The Hellstrom Chronicle*) to film a documentary segment for a proposed film about the upcoming Olympics Games in Munich. Other international filmmakers signed for the project were Milos Forman, Kon Ichikawa, Claude Lelouch, Yuri Ozerov, Arthur Penn, Michael Phleghar, and Mai Zetterling. John represented Britain; originally Ousmane Sembene of Senegal was also included, but his piece was cut from the final print. Each director was given the freedom to choose his or her own cameraman, crew and subject; John chose to focus on Ron Hill, a chemist from Lancashire who'd been training for the Olympic marathon since his teens. Along with cameraman Arthur Wooster, John ventured back to the north country of his first films to shoot footage of Hill training for the event. It was his first return to documentary since the aborted 1967 film about Israel; ironically, the ghost of that earlier film would return before this one was completed.

Meanwhile, the title of the proposed musical had been changed to "Ma'am," and producer Richard Pilbrow had secured financial backing from Paramount, which had its eye on an eventual film of the property. With music by Charles Strouse and lyrics by Lee Adams, there was considerable excitement about the show; Childers returned from America to help with the research and experts were brought in to advise on everything from costumes to language to dance. Richard Barstow and Donald Sadler were both considered for the choreography; the job eventually went to Patricia Birch, the wife of John's old Oxford chum William Becker, who'd just scored a huge success choreographing *Grease* on Broadway.

"What made John think of me for this after *Grease*, I have no idea," Birch said. But he did, and she arrived in London to find the director "thoroughly at home on the stage." Birch was impressed by his command of the material, even if John would call the experience "agonizing," and muse that, in truth, directing a musical was "really a choreographer's job." He relied a great deal on Birch; even her American *faux pas* of starting the British army on the right foot instead of the left didn't rattle his trust.

Polly James, best known for her performance as Beryl Hennessey on the BBC's *The Liver Birds*, was signed to play Victoria. By now the show had been rechristened yet again with the awkward moniker *I and Albert* – misleading, since Albert disappeared, as he did from Victoria's reign, halfway through. Sven-Bertil Taube played the part of the Prince with nobility and authority, but it was Lewis Fiander as Disraeli who proved most memorable, leading a doddering Gladstone (Aubrey Wood) across the stage in a lively tango.

I and Albert premiered on 6 November at the Piccadilly Theatre. In a letter to Gene Phillips, John wrote that, although the previous weeks had been nightmarish, "we managed to get it into pretty good shape for the opening night, which went well." Audiences seemed to enjoy the production, but the critics were predictably savage: "Action but no plot," said *The Times*. "Everything is there except a good basic idea for lack of which the show comes over as an exhibition of animated shortbread tins and jubilee mugs." The extravagant sets and lighting by Luciana Arrighi garnered the most praise, particularly the magic-lantern projection of various contemporary prints and royal cameos.

"We were dealt a number of pretty severe body blows," John observed to Gene Phillips. "It's early to tell how long we can survive. If it had happened in New York, we would have closed the same week."

As it was, the show lasted until 10 February, but lost more than $329,000. "The music wasn't good enough," said Stewart Grimshaw. "There were some wonderful tricks in it but it didn't quite work."

Patricia Birch thought the problem lay in a lack of unity. "John kept trying to solve the book and the music," she said, "but never to his satisfaction." They consoled each other over the musical's failure. "It was sad, of course, but in time we learned to laugh about it."

By the time the show had opened, however, John's main interest was elsewhere.

On 5 September 1972, five Palestinian terrorists hopped the fence surrounding the Olympic Village in Munich, killing two Israeli athletes and taking nine hostage. After a day of tense stand-offs, the hostages were killed in a firefight; some observers, including John, would blame bungling by German police as part of the cause. The drama riveted Schlesinger's attention; he was outraged that the Olympics were not canceled, agreeing with Jim Murray of the *Los Angeles Times* who wrote, "It's almost like having a dance at Dachau."

No way could John now produce an innocuous little film

about a marathon runner. His sense of his Jewishness — or, at least, his *yearning* for his Jewishness — compelled him to find a way to include some kind of reference to the massacre in the film. Wolper expressed some initial opposition; John responded that if he wasn't allowed to include it, he'd withdraw his participation. Wolper finally consented, and Schlesinger flew to Munich.

As determined as he was, however, John still had no clear idea how to incorporate the tragedy. His answer came from Ron Hill, who, when asked on camera what he felt about the massacre, replied, "I don't want to know about it. I'm here to run a marathon race, and that's what I'm going to do. Anything that is going to distract me I don't want to know about." The tragedy affected him, he said, only in that it put off his race for a day.

John was taken aback by his answer, but it also provided the vision for the piece: "That's the tack we will take," he said, "the irony of this athlete completely dismissing this terrible event."

Hill doesn't really dismiss it; like any athlete in training, he cannot allow his emotions to get in the way of his performance. Yet he comes across as detached, unfeeling, which would be the point of John's segment, called "The Longest," which attempts to showcase the hypocrisy and exploitation of the Olympics. Fifty cameramen under the direction of editor Jim Clark were stationed along the 26-mile route of the race; together they amassed some 90,000 feet of film, later chopped down to about 1,400.

There are some powerful shots: the steely determination of Hill running over the Lancashire hills on a quiet Sunday morning; the somber profundity of the murdered athletes' coffins; the pluck of the last man to finish the marathon, who's still running even as it starts to rain and no one is paying attention anymore.

Yet the problem with the segment is there is no center: certainly not Hill, who's positioned as somewhat callous and self-absorbed, thus preventing our identification with him; and not the Israelis either, who we never see and whose fate we can only understand through texts outside the film. As contemporary newsreel, it may have worked; but 30 years on, without any historical perspective, it seems rudderless. Schlesinger was well aware of that danger. "We've got to be very careful how we handle the Israeli incident," he said during the editing of the film, "so that it's meaningful, in a sense, for all time." His impulse to incorporate the tragedy was heartfelt and appropriate, but the material does not easily harmonize. John seemed to recognize this, too; writing to Gene Phillips, he admitted he was "trying to bend somewhat intractable material to include the Israeli tragedy."

The omnibus film, entitled *Visions of Eight*, was first shown at Cannes in May 1973, then put into general release in August. What had begun as an interesting idea had devolved into an awkward casualty of war. Although Gene Siskel of the *Chicago Tribune* considered "The Longest" such a distinguished film that it recommended the whole picture, Charles Champlin felt it was "a rather uneasy compromise," and took Schlesinger to task for "downplaying" the massacre. Given how John had had to fight to include even a reference, it was an unfair criticism, but simply by raising the topic the director had left himself open for brickbats from all sides. *Time* wrote that the footage of the tragedy was a "tasteless, last-minute paste-in," implying John shouldn't have made any attempt to include it at all.

It was almost as unpleasant an experience as *I and Albert*. "I found it interesting to return temporarily to documentary filmmaking," John said, "but I prefer to direct fiction films in which I can tell a strong story and manipulate characters according to their individual motivations."

The time had come to get back to making movies. And thankfully, Jerry Hellman was on the line.

When *The Day of the Locust* was shown at the Palm Springs International Film Festival in January 2003, it was hailed as "John Schlesinger's dark masterpiece." Its cinematographer, Conrad Hall, had died the previous day, but not before overseeing a complete remastering of the film, restoring its deep, muted colors and sharp, contrasting lighting. When the festival audience realized the restored version wasn't the one to be shown that day, there was palpable dismay. "This is one of the great film classics of all time," one woman sitting behind me fumed. "How can they show it in such a compromised form?"

Today it's taught in film schools, but when *The Day of the Locust* was released in 1975, Hollywood shuddered. Reviews were decidedly mixed; no one thought then that it would ever be described as a "classic" or a "masterpiece."

No one except John Schlesinger. "Of all my ugly ducklings," he said, "it's the one I've got the most affection for."

Indeed, one of his stars, William Atherton, remembered John striding about the set saying, "This is my *Greed*" — referring, of course, to Eric Von Stroheim's unwieldy, controversial, personally driven silent masterpiece.

It was around the time of *Darling* that Schlesinger had first considered filming Nathanael West's novel: "To me it seemed like the best piece of writing about a place and period, with the best allegorical references, that I had ever read." It was as much an evocation of Hollywood in the 1930s as *Darling* was of London in the 1960s, so it needed to be an American film, made in America with an American cast. But with *Midnight Cowboy* still a few years in the future, no American studio would take a risk on John Schlesinger.

After *Cowboy*, however, it seemed only natural that the Englishman who'd taken such a keen eye to New York should now turn his gaze to the other Coast; the producer Ronald Shedlo (*The Whisperers*) signed on to do *Locust* and set about trying to find a studio to back it. But given the financial disaster of *Sunday, Bloody Sunday*, it was two years before Shedlo arranged a development deal with Warner Bros., although the studio's terms were never good. They insisted on a short, twelve-week schedule and balked at the kind of money John thought was necessary to make the film.

By late 1972 it was clear that Warners was having second thoughts. "My calls weren't being answered quite so readily," John said. "The usual shit." Reading the handwriting on the wall, he told Waldo Salt to chuck the script: "What's the point? They're dumping us. I can smell it all over."

Fifteen years later, remembering the experience, John snapped at an interviewer, "You know this town is full of two-faced, disloyal people." He was feeling bitter, facing the same battle again, trying once more to get *Hadrian* off the ground after the twin flops of *The Believers* and *Madame Sousatzka*. "All the conversation is, 'Does he have a hit? He hasn't had anything in years. He's out. He's in.' "

The difference in 1972 was that John had a writer who could

fight shoulder-to-shoulder alongside him, and indeed he'd credit Salt with snapping him out of his doldrums: "You're not playing fair by me," the writer charged, demanding that John not give up. "I want the same determination I remember from *Cowboy*. You owe me that much."

So John agreed to give it another shot; Waldo came to London and they settled down to writing the script. "I knew that to get a page of script out of Waldo was like pulling teeth," John said, "and that I'd have to nurse him along, but once I started to work, and saw things coming together, I got hooked."

The development deal with Warners did, as John suspected, finally collapse, though there was never anything official about it. John would love to tell people that, years later, he still had never gotten a call or letter from Warner Bros. telling him they weren't interested. "Maybe they're still waiting for the film," he said, laughing.

With no backing now for a picture he suddenly felt passionately about, John rang Jerry Hellman, who had been taking a sabbatical from movie making. He enlisted Hellman's involvement, and the *Midnight Cowboy* team was reunited. Trying to raise money, however, Hellman was quickly frustrated. No matter that just three years before, the *Cowboy* triumvirate of Schlesinger, Salt and Hellman had been kings of the hill; three years was an eternity to go without a box office hit. Finally, soon after the new year of 1973, John got the call that Jerry had lined up five million dollars from a group of Canadian investors, primarily dentists, and that Paramount would put in another two as well as allow them to film on their lot.

But first, John had to go into the front office and act out the film's climactic riot scene for an assembly of Paramount's top brass: Frank Yablans, Charles Bluhdorn, Peter Bart, Robert Evans, Barry Diller. John screeched and cried, writhing about in the middle of the room as he interpreted Homer's death throes in the riot. Evans would remain unconvinced by the director's theatrics, but Diller was enthusiastic, swaying the others, and by March 1973 the deal was clinched.

Except at the last minute, the Canadian investors pulled out. Jerry Hellman had to shuffle back into Yablans' office with his tail between his legs, expecting the worst. John was already setting up on the Paramount lot, auditions were taking place, crews were being chosen. Yablans' response stunned Hellman: "Fuck the dentists," he said. "Let's go." Paramount would finance the entire $7 million.

"*Seven million*," Hellman said to me, articulating the words carefully. "You look at that film today and there's no way you would think it cost just seven million. Today they'd insist on staging the whole riot downtown on Hollywood Boulevard and that alone would cost fifty million. We made the whole picture for seven."

The economics could be partially explained by the fact that they took very little money themselves; Jerry said he got no more than $50,000 while John probably didn't make much more than $75,000. "I wasn't hungry for success at that point," said Hellman. "I just thought this was a masterpiece. Were people going to flock to see it? Maybe not, but who gives a shit? We wanted to do it."

John had higher hopes, telling his diary early on, "If we can get sufficient humanity into the performances and the script, I think people will want to know what happens to the inmates of the San Berdoo."

West's story was always idiosyncratic: a tale of the false promise of Hollywood as seen through the eyes of Tod Hackett, an aspiring film designer who gets a job at a big studio and comes face to face with the corruption of the American dream. He finds an apartment at the San Bernadino Arms, called the San Berdoo by its residents, which include a midget, Abe Kusich; a monstrous stage mother, Mrs. Loomis, and her obnoxious son, Adore; and a former vaudevillian, Harry Greener. It is Harry's daughter Faye who sets the story, such as it is, in motion; Faye hooks up with (and subsequently ruins the life of) a lonely studio bookkeeper, Homer Simpson (contemporary audiences never fail to laugh when he announces his name, connecting him to the cartoon character). In the end, a browbeaten Homer is taunted by the hateful Adore at a movie premiere on Hollywood Boulevard; Homer, a man of almost preternatural calm up until now, finally explodes, stomping the child to death. The discovery of this causes a riot, with throngs of people overturning cars and setting buildings afire. Tod Hackett, twisted by his own impossible love for Faye, imagines the whole of Los Angeles burning; indeed, in Waldo Salt's script, he has predicted such a cataclysm in a series of surreal images he draws throughout the film.

There would be a significant difference in approach between novelist and filmmaker. "I think West regarded his characters with a certain amount of real dislike," Schlesinger said. "I liked the characters. They fascinated me."

Yet *The Day of the Locust* is about more than just the plights of its individual characters. Here Schlesinger was making his grandest, most expansive observations about life — not just about the corruption of people but the absolute decline of civilization. John knew, of course, what Nathanael West could only have surmised, that the world he was writing about would soon be at war, embroiled in the twentieth century's great battle of good versus evil. Thus Schlesinger layered onto West's story the coming of war: throughout the film we are given glimpses of the impending conflict through newsreels and newspaper headlines. In the final scene, the announcer at the movie premiere, with his small black moustache, grows more Hitleresque with each cut back to him, exhorting the rioters to greater fits of passion. The spectre of war becomes itself a metaphor for the dangers faced by a civilization grown too indulgent and self-absorbed.

Not for nothing had the Hollywood studios given a cold shoulder to the property ever since its publication in 1939. That John and Jerry were actually on the lot of Paramount, one of the oldest of the great Hollywood studios, turning West's novel into a film was miraculous. "I don't think I would have enjoyed making *Locust* quite as much if it hadn't been such a battle," John said. "The fact that we were in Hollywood making something that everyone said would never happen was a couple of fingers up to them all."

That was the kind of attitude with which Schlesinger had invaded Hollywood in 1968, the "fuck you" worldview he represented, even in absentia, the night he won the Oscar for *Midnight Cowboy*. Now, with *Locust*, he was mounting an even more direct challenge to Hollywood's Golden Age, at a time when some of the great moguls were, in fact, still living: Darryl Zanuck, Jack Warner, even Adolph Zukor, Paramount's chairman of the board emeritus at the age of 101.

Hollywood movies and Hollywood history had never really held much fascination for Schlesinger; he could never understand why Michael was so starstruck, for example, meeting Joan

Crawford on the QE2, or having Bette Davis corner them and demand a part for her in one of John's films ("What you did for Julie Christie, Willy Wyler did for *me!*"). But what *did* fascinate John was the culture of Hollywood, the behind-the-scenes reality of America's dream factory. The Los Angeles premiere of *Far from the Madding Crowd* remained vivid in his mind, the cameras, the klieg lights, the pushing, shoving throngs of people. As an outsider, he brought his own insights: "It's the foreigners who grew up on the dreams while the people here in Hollywood were living them. They tore down every historic monument in this town and built parking lots and supermarkets where they used to be. The era vanished while everyone looked the other way. It's the outsiders who remember what it was like, so as an outsider, I'm probably better qualified than anyone else to bring it back to life."

Working on the Paramount lot, John couldn't help but get a sense of the old Hollywood. His studio masseur had been there for 30 years, and while giving John rubdowns would regale him with tales of Cecil B. DeMille. Through Childers, Schlesinger had also befriended George Cukor, who was often a guest at the house they were renting in the Hollywood hills. Cukor told it like it was: the glamor of the studio system had been offset by the rigid parameters in which he, as a gay man, had been forced to live. John's new film, then, would evoke that glamor while also seeking to expose the truth behind it.

Cukor was, in fact, offered a cameo in the film, as the director who watches in horror as the scaffolding holding up his set, a re-enactment of the Battle of Waterloo, collapses into pandemonium. Cukor turned the role down, telling Joyce Haber: "I've never acted, you know. I think I would be a blight on the picture. I can only tell actors what to do. I don't think I could do it myself." Instead, William Castle, the famed horror film producer-director (*House on Haunted Hill, Rosemary's Baby*), took the part.

Cukor did, however, secure a job for his old friend Madge Kennedy, the latest silent film actress — first Ena Evans in *Black Legend*, then Bessie Love — John would bring back to the screen. Kennedy played another neighbor at the San Berdoo, but proved nothing like the crisp, efficient Love; John had to redo several takes because "the poor old thing" kept forgetting her lines.

Indeed, much of the film's advance promotion played up the connections to Old Hollywood. In March 1974, when shooting was nearly complete, Gloria Swanson visited the set, courtesy of the Paramount publicity machine. "I think she didn't really know what it was all about, what was going on around her, but she was very charming," John recorded in his diary. "I never realized how small she was, nor that the beauty mark that has been so much her trademark was in fact a rather ugly, raised black mole, quite hideous on close inspection. I'm amazed a film star of such magnitude would have clung to it for so long, that it never registered what it really was."

Swanson settled in, rather enjoying the experience of being back on a movie set. Childers remembered it was like a scene out of *Sunset Boulevard*, with old-time lighting men shouting out "Hello, Miss Swanson!" and the great star turning with the obligatory, "Is that you, Whitey?" or whatever the name was. She had finally to be asked to leave, which John feared was "churlish," but in fact they were behind schedule and, after all, accommodating Old Hollywood was hardly his purpose in making this film.

One name from the old days shared at least some sympathies

with Schlesinger and the New Hollywood: Mae West, who was driven up through the Paramount gates in another publicity coup during the shooting of the final riot scene. Asked to pose in front of some burnt-out cars, the legendarily image-conscious West demurred, but pointed a finger at John and said, "But I'll pose with *you*, boy." Later, he accompanied her to a screening of *Sunday, Bloody Sunday*. Afterward, she turned to Schlesinger and purred, "That's sure a breakthrough for the gay boys."

Casting for *Locust* was an exhausting process: 30 speaking parts and 2,000 extras. The biggest problem of the script was the character of Tod. In Waldo's notes to John, he pointed out that Tod had been a literary device in the novel, "little more than a cipher, without motivation or dramatic thrust," a function that would be next to impossible to translate to the screen. "The poetic vision and compassion expressed in Tod's observations in the novel are lost in a literal translation of the Tod Hackett character," Salt wrote, "leaving only the fragmented, freaky and fascinating but peripheral characters and events of the book." It would be necessary, Salt believed, to turn Tod from "an observer to a participant – or further even – not only to make Tod a participant in the various scenes and dramatic action but to make the incidents and characters participants in Tod's story."

Salt's final script made attempts in that direction, but while Tod was placed centrally in the narrative the character still felt peripheral. Any actor given the part was going to have a difficult job putting flesh on Tod's bones.

"I wanted that part," Jon Voight told me. "I was up for that challenge. I know I could've done it." But when he expressed his interest to Schlesinger, the director looked at him askance, "almost as if he hadn't worked with me before," Voight said. Instead, John offered the actor the minor role of the dimwitted cowboy who is Tod's rival for Faye Greener's affections. He surely knew Voight would turn it down.

John wanted an unknown. His track record had always been to introduce new faces to the screen: Alan Bates, Tom Courtenay, Julie Christie, Voight himself. Michael cautioned him, however, reminding him that Murray Head hadn't exactly set the world on fire. But John persisted, drawn to a young man he'd seen in a couple of advance reels of *The Sugarland Express*, a film by a young director named Steven Spielberg. The actor's name was William Atherton.

"It was a big event that I was in the movie because I wasn't anybody at the time," Atherton remembered. "I was surprised I got the part because I didn't think I was particularly right for it." John, however, saw something in him, something innocent, unformed, not unlike the quality he had seen in Jon Voight five years before. "They prettied me up a lot," Atherton said. "They gave me a cosmetic tooth because my teeth were crooked. [Costume designer] Ann Roth gave Tod all these great clothes. I got a tan and I just didn't recognize myself."

More vexing was the casting of Faye Greener. Nathanael West had written Faye as a beautiful, alluring teenager. Many teen actresses were brought in, but John felt none possessed the kind of gravity he wanted, "the sheer feel for play-acting." Faye was maddening, coquettish, cruel, ambitious, but audiences had to retain some sympathy for her. "It demands a certain amount of sophistication to be able to be that affected without seeming just silly and childish," John said.

Jerry Hellman was pushing for Goldie Hawn; John was leaning more toward Tuesday Weld. He spent a day with Raquel Welch and came away very impressed. "We nearly went with her," John remembered, "but something made us say she's too good to be true. She would succeed."

"What we needed was a girl who was a little off," Hellman said, "someone who you knew couldn't make it in a hundred years, but was desperate and had the passion."

In came Sally Struthers, straight off her Emmy win as Gloria Stivic on the television series *All in the Family*. John adored her, feeling she brought the right "funkiness" to the part, but Jerry feared her identification with the popular TV show might be too great. "Sally Struthers was begging to do it, but she was totally wrong," Hellman said. By now the producer was firmly behind Karen Black, the eccentric star of such cult favorites as *The Pyx* and the television film *Trilogy of Terror*; she had also just distinguished herself in another period piece for Paramount, Jack Clayton's *The Great Gatsby*.

John would soon be as enthralled with Black as Jerry was, calling her a cross between ZaSu Pitts and Jean Arthur. "There's something about Karen Black," he said, "excellent actress though she is, that convinces you she wouldn't succeed." Slightly cross-eyed and quirky, Black was an unlikely, offbeat star, exactly the qualities they wanted for Faye.

With none of his *Locust* actors did he become close in the way he had on other films, though he admired all of them a great deal. Donald Sutherland, who played Homer Simpson, was "a tower of strength"; Geraldine Page, who brought the Aimee Semple McPherson-like evangelist to life, was a "consummate professional." Billy Barty, who played Abe, charmed John from the start with his ease in performance. For

Adore Loomis, Michael Childers discovered little Jackie Haley, a precocious child who could do imitations of Mae West and James Cagney; the kid would go on to greater fame as Jackie Earle Haley in *The Bad News Bears* movies. John's closest connection among the cast was probably with Lelia Goldoni, who played Mary Dove; she'd first made a name for herself in John Cassavetes' improvisational film *Shadows* (1959). "Lelia photographs wonderfully," John told his diary. "She looks very good and has the sort of toughness and a certain dykeyness in her appearance which is right for the role."

To play Harry Greener, Faye's father, John first cast Paul Hartman, a veteran character actor best known as Emmett on *The Andy Griffith Show*. But when Hartman dropped dead of a heart attack on the first day of rehearsals, the press buzzed about the film being "cursed," made worse later when a couple of crew members also died unexpectedly. To replace Hartman, John auditioned William Demarest, another familiar TV face (Uncle Charlie on *My Three Sons*), and Ray Bolger, who'd been immortalized as the Scarecrow in *The Wizard of Oz*. But the final choice was Burgess Meredith, best known then as the Penguin from the *Batman* television series but who, after *Locust*, would enjoy a resurgence as a major character player in feature films.

"He does a wonderful series of improvisations," John told his diary about Meredith. "I know we can get both the coarseness of the part and the tragedy from it." A previous encounter with the actor lingered in John's memory: at London's Wyndham's Theatre in 1969, watching *Oh! What a Lovely War*, John had been interrupted "all the way through by terrible noises coming from a few rows behind — Burgess Meredith, drunk and noisy." Meredith had been asked to leave, but John retained the image, drawing on it (without telling Meredith) as he directed the actor, searching for the same sloppy, tragic, pathetic behaviour he had witnessed in the theater.

Just as important as finding the right actors was finding the right *look* for the film. To choreograph the dance numbers, John brought in Marge Champion, who, with her husband Gower, had been a star choreographer-dancer in some of the great MGM musicals of the 1940s and 1950s. For the design of the film, John insisted on hiring Richard MacDonald, who took one look at Los Angeles and became as fascinated by the city as John was: "Bizarre architecture," he opined, "tied together by telegraph wires."

Too many films set in the 1930s had striven for a glossy glamor instead of true period accuracy. "I did not want the movie to strike a kind of art deco fist at you," Schlesinger remembered. "We were careful to be as accurate as we could but I didn't want it to look chic." Considerable research was done to ensure authenticity; when some of the Paramount brass complained the rushes didn't resemble Polanski's *Chinatown*, another 1930s film being shot at the studio, John replied: "Neither Polanski, nor Bob Evans, nor any of the *Chinatown* crowd, have done their homework, while we have prepared ours as carefully as possible." Later, John learned Evans was showing rushes of *Locust* to his crew because he wanted to copy the look.

MacDonald's set of the San Berdoo was particularly satisfying for John. On Sunset Boulevard, they had found exactly the kind of complex they wanted – only to copy it, nearly brick for brick, on the Paramount lot. "Miraculously, every detail is there," John said, "down to the marks that the rain gutters make when the rain drips down the sides of the buildings." The set was dressed by one of Hollywood's ancient decorators, George James Hopkins, who'd started with Theda Bara in 1916.

For a movie shot in Hollywood about Hollywood, it's notable that most of the filming was actually done on the studio backlot. On the few location shoots, John said, "We had to be very careful not to move the camera to the left or to the right because everything interesting that has survived demolition in Hollywood is surrounded by hideous glass monstrosities. If you move the camera a fraction of an inch, you destroy the illusion."

Destroying the illusion was, however, the point of it all. "We were out to show the less-than-glamorous life in Hollywood," said costume designer Ann Roth, another of the *Midnight Cowboy* team reunited on this film. "It was important that we all understood what we were doing. We all got it – myself, John, Richard MacDonald. No one had to explain to me what we were going after. The word is trust. During the course of it, I'd say to Richard, 'Come on over and look at this pale green rickrack I found to put on her nightgown' and he'd say, 'Come over and look at the crack on the wall and the plaster and the floors and the rotten plumbing . . .' We were all just working together."

Camaraderie, in fact, extended from the grips and the technicians right up to the top. John liked his second American crew much better than his first: "This is not at all the Hollywood experience that I had somehow expected," he recorded in his diary. "I had expected bullshit. I had expected union problems. I had expected a kind of blaséness and I've found none of that. I suppose it's the executives and the agents that sometimes turn me off the place, but I must say, working with these people has been an eye-opener."

He especially adored working with cameraman Conrad Hall. Early on, John took Hall to see Bertolucci's *The Conformist*, which has a brilliant yet muted use of color that John wanted to emulate. "We wanted the camerawork to look sheeny but not glossy," John said. "We wanted the color to be very well controlled."

Hall was just the man to give him what he wanted, the kind of expert collaborator John adored. "Connie is probably the best artist in that field I have ever worked with," John said. "He's an instinctual cameraman, as I believe I'm an instinctual director, and will suddenly do something because it occurs to him."

When Hall suggested that during the campfire scene they try a close-up of Karen Black's lips as she drinks from a bottle, John thought it might look over the top, but he was thrilled with the results. Hall was bringing something out in Black that surprised them all. "I think she's slouched around realistically so often in films made on location that nobody has ever bothered about wanting to make her look glamorous," John said, "and Connie, great cameraman that he is, uses any means to do it. A plastic cup jammed into an inky dink is his method of lighting her eyes, so that soft light will drift onto them through the bottom of the cup. Extraordinary."

Hall felt the same about Schlesinger. "You don't find directors like John anymore," the cameraman told me, standing in the courtyard of the Egyptian Theatre the night of Schlesinger's BAFTA Lifetime Achievement award. "He was such an inspiration. He wasn't afraid. We just believed in what we were doing, and we did it."

Rehearsals began on 1 October, 1973, with actual shooting kicking off on the 15th. Unable to film on the precarious hills around the actual Hollywood sign – and because, in the 1930s, the sign had actually read "Hollywood*land*" – the decision was made to erect a facsimile. Just the two letters were enough, however, because John would pan brilliantly from a shot of a postcard of the original sign to the group of people, Bill Atherton and Karen Black among them, standing at the foot of the H.

But Atherton proved to be the film's first headache. "Obviously very nervous and untechnical," John told his diary. "He doesn't seem to be able to do anything the same twice – a problem." By the end of October John was wondering whether they had made "a most terrible error" in casting him. "Everyone else seems to be free and within their parts but he is having tremendous difficulty. Jerry and I decided that we were very foolish to turn down Jon Voight."

Upon further consideration, however, John realized they had chosen Atherton "very carefully and with good reason," so he and Hellman decided to be up front with the actor about the problems. Behind closed doors, Atherton broke down and admitted his fears. "Panic had totally gotten hold of him," John noted. "We sat in my office until it got dark. I think he opened up a good deal and it was rather like a boil being lanced. I think the pus came out. Whether the wound can ever heal, I don't yet know."

Days later, the wound was still festering, and John was losing patience: "Atherton does seem to be ruining our chances of making a good film if he stays in the cast." Inquiries were sent out to Voight to see if he might be available after all. In his diary, John recorded that Childers was pushing him to cut his losses and fire Atherton, telling him: "It's Ian Bannen time again!"

Thirty years later, Atherton was upfront about the difficulties he faced with the character of Tod. "All I was doing was standing there trying to look profound," he said. "After a while, I kind of felt like a model. Because there's Karen and she can scream and cry, and Donald can scream and cry, and Burgess can go over the top and be wonderful – and I'm just kind of looking on interested. It was tough."

Yet, by the end of the month, John had changed his mind about Atherton. "His intensity on the screen is working for us," he told his diary. "Indeed, cut together, I think he is going to be a very interesting Tod."

"John was quite smart," Atherton recalled. "Less is always more. Waldo had written reams of pages and at first I was like, 'I must say every word that the writer of *Midnight Cowboy* has written.' But finally I started to tell John, 'It's not sayable,' and begged to cut the lines. After a while, John seemed to know that I was right. Waldo would still overwrite but we would simply pare it down every day."

John never mentioned anything about paring down the script in his diary, but he did record a growing satisfaction with Atherton's performance. By November, he wrote that even Michael was convinced after seeing the rushes. By the end of the year, John would go so far as to say, "The amazing thing is that Bill Atherton, whom we wanted to get rid of after two weeks of shooting, is to me the finest thing in the picture at the moment."

Rather the reverse happened with Karen Black. Early in the shoot, John was completely taken by her: "Really brilliant, so obviously free as an actress." But her personal quirks – changing her makeup and hair, delaying the shoot because of conflicts over costumes – began to infuriate him. "She's a strange, dotty girl, not very disciplined in terms of punctuality but extremely disciplined in her performance," John reported in November. "Sometimes I feel sadistic toward her because she's so maddening. Not sadistic for the sake of it but just angry about the way she behaves. Other times she responds with such sweetness and such ability, such talent, that you forgive her everything."

By the end of the shoot, however, he had nearly lost his objectivity: "I can't even judge her performance. Every time I see her on the screen I can't disassociate the Karen Black I have come to know and rather dislike from the brilliant actress that she is capable of being."

Almost immediately, Black had clashed with Donald. Atherton recalled telling Sutherland, "You want her to drop dead over the glory of Donald Sutherland and she wants you to drop dead over the glory of Karen Black, and you know what? It's just not going to happen."

John's diary confirmed "quite a tussle" in attempting to keep peace between Donald and Karen. "I'm frankly bored," the director said, "with the idea of having to deal with them for the rest of the picture."

Yet through it all he maintained a respect for Black's talent. "I must say, I take my hat off to her. She holds her ground and she listens till my outburst is over. She's a pro, she doesn't take it amiss." At the end, he'd muse, "She really does give an extraordinary performance. I don't regret for a minute that we cast her."

The Day of the Locust is filled with memorable set pieces. There's the scene at the bordello run by Audrey Jennings, played with aplomb by Natalie Schafer, in which a pornographic film, *Le Prédicament de Chérie*, is screened. The film-within-a-film was shot in a nearby house with French wallpaper and French furniture; a couple of girls were rounded up who, John said, "didn't care what they did." It was an amusing experience. "I suppose if we had wanted to," he reported in his diary, "we could have made a truly pornographic film, which might have been rather interesting."

Then there's the cock fight, almost unbearable to watch, with Billy Barty licking blood out of the rooster's eye and suckling its beak. Letters from groups opposed to cruelty to animals were found among John's files, along with carbons of his responses. He insisted the cocks wore rubber gaffs on their beaks and that the bird that supposedly dies was actually doped to simulate its death throes.

The studio accident scene – the "Battle of Waterloo" – was shot toward the end of January. MacDonald rigged up an awesome set: fake hills and trees atop a massive scaffolding of balsa wood that was designed to buckle and fall on cue. With Napoleonic soldiers scampering across the platforms carrying muskets and bayonets, John gave the signal for it all to come tumbling down, and controlled pandemonium ensued. "Waterloo collapsed spectacularly last week," John wrote to Gene Phillips, although, in an example of life imitating art, there *were* a few injuries. Eight extras were taken away in ambulances, though all but two returned the next day."

Even less orderly was the faith-healing sequence. Several hundred extras were bussed in to act as Geraldine Page's faithful followers. "Old-age pensioners," John reported, "many of whom had come from Jewish old people's homes and who were confronted by three neon crosses saying, 'Give to Jesus.'" Up on stage, the choir mistress was trying to rouse the extras by urging them to pray to the Saviour. Some in the crowd didn't understand they were to be in a movie and were terribly offended; some stormed back to the bus, complaining loudly. "Looking back on it," John said, "it was really very funny."

After seeing the rushes, Page was thrilled, but John had second thoughts. "I don't know why," he said, "but every time someone says something looks splendid, when I look at it again it never seems the same. I thought Geraldine Page was rather shrill. I think I misdirected her. I should have asked her to be more mystical perhaps. She was using bags of energy, poor woman, to try and top the din the choir was making." With all the flashing "Give to Jesus" signs, John wondered if maybe he hadn't "gilded the lily" overmuch. "It's a tendency I have," he admitted.

He had doubts, too, over the famous final scene, when the riot on Hollywood Boulevard turns surreal, with extras wearing Edvard Munch-like masks to evoke the sense of Tod's drawings coming to life. "I hope the idea will work," John said. "It's odd, dangerous, possibly pretentious. It may work and yet may not."

The sequence was storyboarded with great precision. "There was a great deal of input from the designer, the writer, the cameraman, and myself," John said. "And certain images like those silhouette figures streaking across the searchlight – my favorite images in the whole thing – were an accident. We just happened to see it on the set and we shot it, and when we saw it in rushes it was terrific. The masks evolved from a need we felt to have something half human and half drawn."

The surrealism of the sequence is a striking departure from the rest of the film. "Did John say this was a fantasy in Tod's mind?" I asked Atherton. "Did he say the riot tips over into a dream, that Los Angeles doesn't really burn, that Tod's just imagining it? That it's really his dreams going up in smoke? That it's an allusion to the conflagration of war that loomed on the horizon in 1939?"

"We played it absolutely real," Atherton replied. "He had us play it as if it was really happening, because you can't play a figment."

It was shot at the end of production in February and took ten days to complete. Three stages were linked together with black plastic, with the facades of Hollywood Boulevard recreated with exacting accuracy. Fumes from the cars driven onto the soundstage made the nine hundred extras choke and wheeze. An extra had been found who bore an uncanny resemblance to Ginger Rogers; Dick Powell, Jr. played his father. John presided over the whole scene in a hydraulic lift.

"Donald Sutherland was very brave in allowing himself, not a double, to be used for the lynching scene," John told his diary. "I think we have a very graphic and quite horrific image." In the novel, Homer had simply disappeared into the mob, but for the film, John indulged his love of the macabre, an impulse kept in check since *The Starfish*.

Columnist Rex Reed was there to watch the filming. He described Donald Sutherland staggering out of the mob of extras, his suit torn to shreds, prop blood all over his face, plastic eyeball dangling from his face. "He looked like the Frankenstein monster," Reed reported.

From his perch, John called, "Let's do it again. I want more screaming from Ginger Rogers! You are *disgusted* when you see him bleeding, dear."

Back into the mob went Sutherland. "Now lift his body up from the crowd," John shouted through his megaphone. "Rip his face with your fingernails! Turn him to the camera so we can see the blood!"

"Another Disney epic hits the screen, folks," Conrad Hall quipped.

Sutherland was licking the blood (raspberry-flavoured corn syrup) from his hands. "Don't eat the blood!" John roared. "I want it to look horrifying, not delicious!" He sent his actor into the crowd once more. "Do it again! Make it more stylized, like a crucifixion. The last two images I want to see are his useless, flopping hands covered with blood!"

A bit player confided to Reed, "There's a feeling among the extras that we're on the verge of a classic."

Indeed, as word filtered out what Schlesinger was doing on the Paramount lot, there was huge interest in the film. John recorded in his diary getting notes from Peter Bart, saying how much he liked the rushes. At one point, Frank Yablans sent word that he was "overjoyed" about the footage he'd seen. "He thinks the film is beyond his wildest expectations and has the possibility of being an immense blockbuster," John said. "They always go overboard but it's nice to have that kind of reaction."

Production was completed without a final shot: everything seemed anti-climactic after the destruction of Los Angeles. It was a "much-vexed question" that had been debated for weeks. Waldo's original draft ended with a shot of Tod being consumed by the flames, but John felt they needed to suggest he survives: "Perhaps by a close-up where he is looking at [the audience] or smiling at them, [suggesting the riot] could have been a fantasy but might happen." Doubts about Atherton's ability to convey such a complex set of truths in one simple shot eventually led John to dismiss that idea. "Without this solved," John wrote with despair, "we really have no satisfactory picture."

Once again, it was Childers who offered the magic bullet. With principal photography complete, John and Michael spent a Saturday morning brainstorming, with Childers finally coming up with the idea to end the film with Faye going back to the San Berdoo, "flitting around like a kind of nervous and hysterical butterfly." John would call Karen Black in for one last scene, but instead of nerves, Faye exhibits a certain acceptance, even maturity, when she sees that Tod is gone, though the paper rose he stuck in the crack in the wall is still there. It was just enough of an implication of his survival to give the film its final punctuation.

John had hoped to go home to England by March but didn't make it until May, when he and Jim Clark began editing the film at Twickenham studios. It was held longer because Paramount wanted some distance between it and *The Great Gatsby*, the failure of which had made the studio anxious. "All the problems over *Gatsby* has taken the heat off us," John said, "as all the VIPs at Paramount have been in New York worrying about their overblown publicity. From the costume and the fashion designers and promoting a certain line of dinner wear – I've never heard such nonsense. Poor Jack Clayton, my heart really bleeds for him."

Looking at the rough cut of *Locust*, John wasn't sure his film was going to do much better. "It has been the most difficult film ever," he wrote to assistant director Tim Zimmermann. "I know it cannot, by its nature, please everyone. I simply hope it pleases enough."

"I remember at the premiere," Jerry Hellman said, "I got up to use the men's room and coming back into the theater,

I saw Cher on her way out. Not knowing who I was, she gave me the thumbs-down sign and said, 'Don't bother.'" He shook his head, laughing wryly. "It played to dead silence. But now, you show that film at festivals, and people are riveted. They laugh and cheer, and at the end they stand up and applaud."

The Day of the Locust was one of the biggest flops of 1975, grossing just $2,300,000, about a third of its cost. "Now you've got to remember," Bill Atherton said, "that this was the time when all those Cines 1 and 2 began, with their little screens and shitty sound systems. This film needed to be artistically shown, and suddenly there were very few venues for that. The only other picture made at that time which demanded that kind of care and presentation was *Chinatown*, and *Day of the Locust* didn't have huge stars like *Chinatown*, so the studio started putting all its money into *Chinatown*. I'm not saying that *Chinatown* killed *Day of the Locust* but it was very hard to take care of a picture on the road in those days."

All that's true, but *Locust*'s problems went deeper than that. Hollywood was, quite frankly, appalled; many took the film as a personal affront. John was told that at a screening at a movie executive's home in Bel Air, the exec's wife stood up halfway through and apologized to her guests for making them sit through such an outrage. Even some who seemingly shared John's spirit of challenge found the film too hard on the industry. Sidney Lumet, director of *Serpico* and *Dog Day Afternoon*, was bashing *Locust* all around town, reportedly asking, "How can Schlesinger shit where he eats?" Word got back to John, who was furious, prompting a four-page hand-written apology from Lumet.

Many critics, despite their usual antagonism toward Hollywood, seemed to share Lumet's impulse to defend the industry; Hollywood may not be perfect, the sentiment seemed to suggest, but it's *ours*. Brendan Gill thought the opulence of the set pieces destroyed any authority Schlesinger had to criticize Hollywood, abandoning as he had the novel's "intimate scale and coolness of tone." Others found the ending pretentious, as John had feared, berating the attempt to parallel West's apocalyptic vision with the onset of World War II. *Time* magazine called the idea "perfectly in order for a movie so far out of control." From Pauline Kael came little more than her usual Schlesinger bashing ("his direction seems to grow worse in direct ratio to the number of people on the screen"), but Andrew Sarris, equally as critical, did offer a useful observation: "Perhaps one must have more feeling for Hollywood before one can be emotionally equipped to destroy it. Killing the thing one loves is poetry; killing the thing one hates is rhetoric."

Yet John didn't hate Hollywood; growing up, he had been largely indifferent to it, and as his diary revealed, he'd actually come to admire both the work ethic and the eccentricities of the place during the making of *Locust*. Already by the end of the film he was considering buying a house there and making Hollywood his home. While he may not have loved the place, he certainly didn't hate it: Hollywood fascinated him, and some reviewers caught that fascination. Judith Crist was bowled over by Schlesinger's "consideration of the American dream by way of the factory town that dispensed it . . . To call it the finest film of the past several years is to belittle it. It stands beyond comparison."

Such extremes defined the reception of *Locust*. If John could not take the kind of critical solace from box-office disaster that he had with *Sunday, Bloody Sunday*, when the praise had been nearly unanimous, he was at least boosted by the fact that those who admired the film did so with enormous passion. He wasn't terribly surprised by the stark dichotomy in reactions; the material was, after all, the most unsparing he'd ever committed to the screen, more challenging and raw than even *Midnight Cowboy*. "Electric and frightening and dangerous" was *The Nation*'s assessment of the film; Clive Barnes in *The Times* opined that "its cold heart beats strongly . . . Of course, the whole film is a cliché. But then so is 'Hamlet.'"

The Day of the Locust was the last of John Schlesinger's "great" films. It was the last time he would so completely immerse himself in an attempt to create something monumental, in which he and a group of brilliant, trusted collaborators truly sought to find an original, artistic interpretation of the material they were putting on the screen. That should not imply that his later work lacks interest or merit. Instead, it is a measure of the crisis being faced by the industry that John was so skewering; by the time he mounted his next film, Hollywood would already be a very different place. If the craft of filmmaking had been fraught with compromise in the past, John would now come to understand that the making of these last five features had been his glory years, when his own creativity matched opportunities within the industry that would soon be extinct.

The Day of the Locust is, as critics charged, a film whose parts are more powerful than its whole, a picture without a clear and cohesive unity. The first half of the film seems to belong to Tod, the second to Homer, but through neither's eyes do we ever really see. The film failed at the box office because there is no one with whom we can easily identify, and mass audiences tend to need that identification, that link to themselves. Unlike the characters in Schlesinger's earlier films, the people of *The Day of the Locust* don't cope, don't find a way to survive. Only Faye is left standing at the end; we assume Tod has escaped, but escaping isn't coping. Their stories are metaphors for something much bigger, more expansive. All of the pain and debasement of the film are like trails of gunpowder leading into the ending, where they are at last ignited; all of the self-absorption and corruption of the world leads to a cataclysm like World War II. Never again would John Schlesinger attempt so lofty, so sweeping an observation. *The Day of the Locust* would remain his grandest, most ambitious expression as an artist.

Fourteen

1975–1978

"A rare pang for England"

I didn't expect him to be awake, much less talkative, but I popped my head into John's room anyway, to let him know I was back from London.

"Were the daffodils in bloom?" he asked, startling me.

I sat down next to the bed. He hadn't spoken so directly to me in months.

"Yes," I told him. "Everywhere you looked. There were daffodils all over the place at Strawberry Hole. It was beautiful."

"Very beautiful," John agreed.

Strawberry Hole was his country house in East Sussex, near Robertsbridge, a tranquil, converted oast house beside a stream, surrounded by a thick wood. He had bought it as a retreat with Geoffrey Sharp, eventually taking over Sharp's share and generously opening up the place to his family. His brother Roger had invited me to spend the weekend, a gloriously sunny couple of days when the spring sunshine was thawing the earth and popping the buds on the trees. And, yes indeed, the daffodils that John and Michael had planted a decade earlier were blooming all across the grounds.

"I know how much you would like to see it again," I offered to John.

"Yes, I would," he said.

The fact that he was talking was nothing short of miraculous. Nobody had told me that he'd started talking again. In fact, as I'd learn, this was an anomaly: by morning he'd be back to silence. I sensed this was an opportunity not to be squandered.

"Do you miss England?" I asked. "Are you still hoping you can go back?"

"Yes," he said, but he wasn't interested in sentimental speculation. "Who did you see?" he asked.

He wanted gossip, so I complied. "I saw Joanna Lumley, who sends her love. And Eleanor Fazan . . ."

"Fizzie," he said.

"And, of course, Roly Curram . . ."

His eyes sparkled. "Was Roly in rare form?"

I laughed. "Yes, he was. We had lunch. He was saying how much he wished you were with us."

John smiled. What he wanted to know, lying there in the dark, was where we ate, what we ordered, what places I'd explored in his old neighborhood of South Kensington. I tried to tell him about the films I'd seen at the BFI, the early television documentaries, but he was less interested in hearing about any of that than he was the simple things: what kind of jokes Roly made, if I'd met any cute boys, how the daffodils looked at Strawberry Hole.

That was our conversation, the last one we ever had: about simple things, ordinary things, things that had nothing to do with movies or art or ambition or glamor or career.

"Find the story," he had said.

I felt as if I just had.

For the rest of his life after *The Day of the Locust*, John Schlesinger would become, in his words, "a mid-Atlantic" director, dividing his time between Britain and America. "I think Los Angeles is the most seductive place I've ever lived," he said. "It's a comfortable kind of place, except for the smog. It's sexy and full of pretty people. It holds out the apparent promise of everything – beautiful weather, oranges falling on the ground. It's instant gratification: instant sex, instant promise, instant stardom, instant failure."

Soon after the completion of *Locust*, John bought the house he'd been renting in the Hollywood hills, a place he'd come to love. "When I first came here to Los Angeles," he said, remembering back to the terrible days after the flop of *Madding Crowd*, "I couldn't wait to get out of town. Now I'm so happy living here, I never want to leave the house."

It was a great house. Perched on the crest of the hill, the Schlesinger domicile offered a wide-angle lens on Tinseltown, one of those great big movie-star views of the city. Producer and publicist Andy Kuehn remembered "parties that went on for days," with paths that led down the hill to his house and to actress Beverly D'Angelo's, spreading out the festivities. Built on two acres of land with the requisite swimming pool, mirrors, and lots of glass, the house was Schlesinger's castle. "Burgundy lacquered walls and 16-foot ceilings!" Childers exclaimed. "Did we have a life!"

The first time he and John had seen the place had been as guests while it was still owned by Michael Butler, the producer of *Hair*. "It was so outrageous and extravagant and of the period," said Childers. "It had the smell of rich hippies: hashish and pachouilly." Decorated by legendary Hollywood designer Tony Duquette, there wasn't one chair in the entire house. "It was supposed to be Moroccan. Camel cushions and rugs, and the Rolling Stones were living in the guest house. Everybody was getting stoned. It was really wild."

After buying the place, John kept most of the Duquette furniture, but felt maybe a few chairs and sofas might come in handy – so he gave a young designer named Waldo Fernandez his first big break. Fernandez would become a top designer to the stars, later doing the homes of Goldie Hawn, Burt Bacharach, Michael York, and Merv Griffin. "The house had everything," Childers said. "Everything you wanted – a sauna, a studio, great views, everything."

Returning to London, John felt like a foreigner – like an American, in fact, missing the little luxuries that had yet to infiltrate everyday British life. "I've come back to find the showers don't work," John griped, "and the telephone system is appalling."

His cousin Andrew Raeburn, who had joined him in America during *Locust*, understood his feelings exactly. "I think what John and I both liked so much about America was its convenience," he said. "In the States, everything was done so efficiently." Going back to England, John felt, was like stepping back in time.

In early 1975, however, he was obliged to return to London to direct George Bernard Shaw's *Heartbreak House* at the

National Theatre. Michael stayed behind in Los Angeles, which left John very lonely. He wrote to Brenda Vaccaro, "I can't keep making apologies for the state of this country to Michael, but he is clearly avoiding it for as long as he can."

It was more than just showers and telephones. "What John and I both loathed more than anything else about England," said Andrew Raeburn, "was the 'Little-Do' syndrome – the idea that you do as little as you can to get by."

"I think it's the lack of enthusiasm," John said, reflecting on the malaise that seemed to have crept over Britain by the mid-Seventies. "It's the lack of energy, the apathy, which worries me. In America, apathy doesn't really exist. People are either hell-bent on getting somewhere or they've dropped out, and even then it's not the sort of apathy, the 'we don't care' attitude, that I find so distressing about England."

It would be a lifelong complaint. In 1985, judging the Best Sound category for the BAFTA awards, John had found the quality of the film *Greystoke, The Legend of Tarzan* "a fucking scandal . . . scratched, bumps, awful." He was so incensed he wanted it removed from the list of nominations, but no one seemed to share his outrage. "Make a fuss," he fumed. "Create a stir. Not very British, I'm afraid. I can't bear it actually. It makes me very hot under the collar. It goes back to nappy days."

Later in life, he lamented: "I don't know why we sit on this island and look at each other with such great suspicion. It may have something to do with how we're brought up from the cradle with words like 'Don't get excited' and 'Don't get above yourself.' And people who do get off their asses and do things, like Kenneth Branagh, are unpopular because of it."

There was more than a little bitterness in John's attitude

toward his home country. "I don't miss England very much," he recorded in his diary during his heyday on Rising Glen. "The film industry there is collapsing totally now. They weren't ever really prepared to go out on a limb and support filmmakers who had something to say. When I was in real trouble with an interesting project [*Hadrian VII*], nobody came to the rescue there, so I don't really feel any loyalty. I'm English and I'm proud to be English, but I can see my future probably lies – as does Mike's – both here [the U.S.] and in England."

The love-hate relationship he had with both countries colored the last third of his life. He came to feel more at home in America than in Britain, but never entirely. "John liked the possibilities America offered," mused Michael York, who became close to Schlesinger around this time. "I think if you're raised in an old culture you very often flourish in a place where things are new and everything is possible. But then again you get nostalgic for the very things that are British."

Indeed, John would often long for the British countryside; no matter how much he enjoyed the California sunshine, it never seemed quite to take the place of a tranquil weekend at Strawberry Hole. Even a trip to the Tickle Pink Inn with Michael for one of their anniversary celebrations could leave him blue for England, with the rocky coastline of Carmel reminding him of Cornwall.

In November 1973 he watched from his home in Los Angeles the televised wedding of Princess Anne and Captain Mark Phillips. "I had a pang, a rare pang, for England," John recorded in his diary. "Green leaves, the Mall, sunshine, trumpets. It's something that we do very well. The dignity of the occasion, whatever one's feelings about the ballyhoo of the wedding, was something unique and traditional and not found anywhere else but in England."

Watching Alan Bridges' film *The Hireling*, with a script by Wolf Mankowitz, he also felt "homesick." Musing to his diary, John wrote: "I felt once again a sense of terrible loss about the British cinema because when we do it well, we do it well. Much better, I think, than the average film made here."

Especially as he got older, he would miss the way of life of England, where civility and manners and graciousness had their place, so unlike the wild and woolly frontier of Los Angeles. Even during the peak of his love affair with America, John preferred to stay home in his house and let people come to him, rather than venture out himself into the crassness of Tinseltown. "I don't like the world of the movie colony," he said. "It makes me insecure, and I'm not asked anywhere because I don't return invitations. I don't want to be part of the whole gang-bang of Hollywood. I'm very happy to go down to the studios and do my job . . . and then come back up here and be with my friends."

The admiration he had for the American sense of "get up and go" was tempered by a contempt for the boorishness with which so many Americans got up and went. He despaired of the self-absorption, the dearth of culture, the lack of historical or global perspective. In *Yanks*, the American officer played by William Devane certainly reflects Schlesinger's own view of America when he says: "I come from a simple, primitive people. We're mongrels. We have no traditions."

Or manners. For John, every outing to the cinema was fraught with annoyance. "Audiences talk incessantly," he complained. "They run up and down and eat all the time, because that is what they are used to doing at home." He was appalled by the "political correctness" of America, the fear of committing a major *faux pas* like calling a woman a "girl" or an African-American a "Negro." American hypocrisy infuriated him more: the way the media seemed indifferent to violence yet "embarrassed and self-righteous about sex."

The chasm between the two cultures both fascinated and confounded him. "We're different people," the American soldier played by Richard Gere tells the British girl played by Lisa Eichhorn in *Yanks*. "We look the same, we talk the same, but we're not the same."

Even as he adored basking in the sun by his pool, John knew his life in America was illusory; he understood the danger to the lure of Los Angeles: "You get up," he said, "you have a little swim, a little dinner, a little sleep, a little cocktail – and suddenly you're 60."

Never would be completely sever his ties with England. Never was there a thought of becoming an American citizen; even official residency status was avoided, making his tax situation forever chaotic. "I always intend to keep one foot in England," John said. "My heart will never really be anywhere else."

As part of this connection to his homeland, Schlesinger was one of the RSC associates brought to the National Theatre by Peter Hall, who had succeeded Laurence Olivier as director a few years earlier. It was with some trepidation that John anticipated his first production there, as the disaster of *I and Albert* still loomed in recent memory. After some talk about adapting Chekhov – a fascinating prospect to consider– he settled on *Heartbreak House*, which is, after all, the most Chekhovian of Shaw's plays. Carry-over themes from *Locust* could be spotted: "It is a play of moods," John said. "There is an atmosphere. Everyone has an objective, and the pose of each is to reveal the pose underneath. It's a play of extremes."

Shaw's use of the country house as a frame had allowed him to offer an exposé of Britain's leisured class, with the play's moments of comedy shadowed always by a looming sense of destruction. Fresh from directing Nathanael West's take on the decline of civilization, John was now helming Shaw's interpretation. With its unhappy love affairs and the apparent death wish that hangs over the household, the play's themes were close to John's heart, offering one of his favorite lines in dramatic literature: "Do you think the laws of God will be suspended in favor of England because you were born in it?"

Strong actors were needed to pull it off, and John got them: Graham Crowden as the boisterous, blustery Hector Hushabye; Paul Rogers as the conniving capitalist Boss Mangan; Anna Massey as the regal Ariadne; Colin Blakely as the crusty Captain Shotover; Kate Nelligan as the noble Ellie; and Eileen Atkins as the shrewd Hesione Hushabye.

"John wanted me for the part but I said no, that I didn't want to play the kind of woman who calls somebody 'pettikins,'" Atkins told me. "But John kept after me, and we were both in Los Angeles, so we had lunch. Truth was, neither of us had read the play yet and we were both trying to keep that fact from the other one. So it was a very funny meal. Then later, in London, I heard who John was going to cast and it was somebody who I did not think was a very good actress, so I rang him and asked if it was true and he said yes. Well, I might have thought I wasn't right for the part, but I was much better for it than she was! Literally by the bell I did it. In fact it turned out to be a terrific success. It was one of the most prestigious productions for the National."

As good as the actors were, they didn't have a smooth ride. "John could get quite bored with rehearsals," Atkins said. "He would start shouting at us." When the young, relatively inexperienced Kate Nelligan dared to shout back, John exploded; it would be Nelligan who'd bear the brunt of the director's wrath all through production.

Part of the problem for John was the boredom. "Working in the theater left him very impatient, because, unlike film, it's a very slow process," said Atkins, who was in a good position to compare, since she would also act in John's film *Cold Comfort Farm*. "He got bored terribly quickly sitting there. If you didn't want him to fall asleep you did something different to wake him up."

So why did he take on the play? "I'm comparatively inexperienced in the theater," John said at the time of *Heartbreak House*. "I want to do more on stage." Peter Hall's invitation to become an associate at the National had given him "a London foothold," as well as the "opportunity to be a part of a team, something I've never really experienced outside the group of people I work with regularly in the cinema."

It also afforded him a degree of legitimacy, giving him credibility as more than just a movie director – although he'd admit to his diary that he didn't think he'd "ever get the satisfaction from directing in the theater" that he got from the cinema. "The scissors are the real difference," he said. "You can get away with murder in film. In theater there is a fixed vantage point and you can't cheat that. In theater text is God while in cinema the script is merely the blueprint."

Yet, given how precarious his movie career always seemed to be, John was wisely investing time and commitment elsewhere lest he should find cinematic opportunities diminishing.

The success of *Heartbreak House* proved he could have a career in the theater if he ever wanted it.

"The instant merit of John Schlesinger's production," wrote Irving Wardle in *The Times*, "is that it couples the feverish, sickening atmosphere of the house with the unfailing resilience of its inmates." Once again, it would be John's deft handling of actors that boosted the script: "This kind of theatrical poetry, far removed from the usual Shavian fine writing, is something new to me in productions of this author," Wardle continued.

When the play premiered on 25 February 1975, the release of *The Day of the Locust* was still more than two months away, so John was not yet as pessimistic about his cinematic future as he would be shortly. Certainly, however, the bravura notices for *Heartbreak House* would sustain him even after *Locust*'s critical reception, and went a long way toward erasing memories of the debacle of *I and Albert*. The success of the production was also a boost to the National, which had endured a few rocky years of controversy after Olivier's retirement and Hall's succession. "Heartbreak House," Irving Wardle said, was "clear evidence that the National is back on form again."

For all the accolades and good will he enjoyed in London during that spring of 1975 – and no matter how brutal many of the American reviews of *Locust* – John was anxious to get back to Los Angeles and his new home in the Hollywood hills. He had a movie to do, and he was never happier than when he was starting a new picture.

There were actually two pictures in the works: a "light-hearted" romp Jerry Hellman was pursuing with Liza Minnelli, and William Goldman's script of his novel, *Marathon*

Man, which Robert Evans was producing at Paramount. The deal with Liza fell through, but *Marathon Man* was easy to raise financing for, the first Schlesinger film ever to enjoy that distinction. It wasn't so much John's reputation, still battered by *Locust*, that excited investors; it was the fact that the script contained sure-fire audience-pleasers like car chases, kidnappings, action and suspense. For the first time in his fifteen-year feature film career, John was finally getting the chance to direct a thriller.

Robert Evans told me that with *Marathon Man* he got everything he wanted: "I wanted John as director, I wanted Dustin Hoffman, and I wanted Laurence Olivier." John was stunned when Evans requested him; considerable animosity had existed between the two of them during the making of *The Day of the Locust*, which Evans never liked. "But he told me at the premiere that he thought I had directed it well," John remembered. "Then he asked if there was anything I had cut out that I would like to put back. That was the first time I knew how much he respected directors."

It was the first project since *Billy Liar* that John hadn't developed himself, and that he agreed to it left both Jerry Hellman and Jo Janni surprised and disappointed. But John, despite his reputation, was itching to do a thriller: "Up to now," he said, "all of my films have been about small people and real relationships, but I wanted a change. I admire Hitchcock, but I don't know how he's been able to make the same movie over and over again without feeling the need to change."

He also smelled box-office success, something he hadn't known in the five years since *Midnight Cowboy*. There was another draw as well: the story concerns a young Jewish graduate student, Thomas "Babe" Levy, who innocently gets caught in his brother's involvement with a diamond-smuggling Nazi fugitive, Christian Szell. In the end, Babe must out-maneuver, through his marathon-running strength as well as his wits, the diabolical Szell, known as the "White Angel of Auschwitz." Not for nothing did John call *Marathon Man* his "Jewish thriller" to friends; Pauline Kael would not be far off the mark when she called it a "Jewish revenge fantasy." As with gay subjects, anything Jewish always piqued John's interest.

John did not share Evans' enthusiasm for Hoffman, how-ever. Dustin was nearing 40; Babe was in his early twenties. Besides, as was his custom, John wanted to discover an unknown. But the days of building a major motion picture around an untried actor were coming to an end. Evans wanted a big box-office star, so Dustin got the part, jumping at the chance to work with John again.

The third part of Evans' wish list didn't appear to be so easy. Lord Olivier had been ill, some said near death, though John had heard rumors that the great man was well enough – and eager – to go back to work. Accordingly he wrote to Olivier on 6 June 1975: "I am so delighted to hear that you are getting better, and I am wondering if there is any chance of tempting you to play a really flashy part in my new film for Paramount." Olivier responded with a quick yes, providing John could "finagle the insurance for a very sick man." Evans coaxed Lloyd's of London into a six-week insurance policy – *six weeks*, nothing more, so certain was everyone that Olivier, then 69 but appearing twenty years older, wouldn't live much longer than that.

Roy Scheider, straight off the blockbuster of *Jaws*, took on the part of Babe's brother Doc, whose diamond doublecross of Szell sets the plot in motion and ensnares his innocent brother.

William Devane played Janeway, Doc's cohort in crime – and lover, in Goldman's book. John chose not to make the relationship between the two men explicit in the film, but it's there, subtly, in the way Doc speaks to "Janie" on the telephone. It was the first time a Schlesinger film had obscured rather than heightened a gay element in the material; plot-wise the obscuring made sense, as the script stays very tight on Babe and his story. This would not be a film that had much room to explore interpersonal relationships, another Schlesinger first.

That's not to suggest that it's simply a mindless thriller, all plot and action and no characterization. "It's wrong to call *Marathon Man* just a thriller," said Marthe Keller, the Swiss actress who played Babe's conniving love interest, Elsa. "It is much more than that. Mixing up the Jewish and Nazi situation for an entertainment movie was usually done in such a superficial way, but this movie was making some very profound statements."

Keller was recommended to John by Michael York, who had seen her onstage in Paris in Peter Nichols' *A Day in the Death of Joe Egg*. The entire team flew over to check her out – John, Bob Evans, other Paramount execs – and Keller, then barely speaking any English, met them all in a hotel suite. "Nobody introduced themselves," Keller said, "so I didn't know which one was John Schlesinger. So I lit up a cigarette and said 'I loved *Midnight Cowboy*,' knowing the one who said thank you would be John."

Working with Evans proved an adjustment for Schlesinger. With Janni and Hellman, he had had producers who were in sync with his vision and methods, who shared with him a desire to create something "more" than just an entertaining movie. Always that first, of course – entertainment *always* came first –

but the showbiz side of making movies (calculating audience reaction, making decisions with an eye on the box office) was never a significant part of their creative process. Rather, choices were made in pursuit of an artist's vision. This was the way John's films had always been shaped, from *A Kind of Loving* to *The Day of the Locust*.

Bob Evans was a very different animal. He was a Hollywood playboy, a mover and shaker, a flashy operator with a canny sixth sense for box-office potential. A former model and actor, he'd awakened one morning to find himself head of production at Paramount, one of the milestones by which chroniclers document the arrival of the New Hollywood. The force behind such slick packages as *Rosemary's Baby*, *Love Story*, *The Godfather* and *Chinatown*, Evans was a maverick and an iconoclast, but he was also one of the most powerful men in Hollywood. Until now, John and his producers had always been the outsiders. Now he was working with the Big Man, the Man in Charge.

John enjoyed Evans' larger-than-life style, but found he had to fight for an artistic vision to be layered onto the picture. He had his creative team (Conrad Hall, Richard MacDonald, Jim Clark) with him, but the new producer set a different tone than what they were used to. Evans was impatient with discussions about character, and the little directorial touches so typical of John completely befuddled him. "Bob couldn't understand why I wanted a lot of garbage littering the streets of Paris," John said. "Jerry Hellman or Jo Janni would simply have taken that in stride."

There was, at least initially, a more simpatico relationship with William Goldman. "I wanted more texture to the script," John said, and Goldman was largely receptive to his ideas.

Setting the car crash that opens the film on Yom Kippur was a brainstorm of John's. He came up with another as they scouted locations in Paris: after observing people on their balconies watching a street demonstration, John decided to have Doc attacked from behind as he stands on a similar balcony. It added an element of surprise and offered a chance for Doc to show off his fighting prowess. "It's little things like that that make films different," John said.

The logistics of the plot, however, gave him some trouble; action scenes were hardly his forte. Fretting over whether certain scenes were believable finally led Goldman to shout, "It's a thriller, for God's sake! You just have to believe it!"

John laughed as he remembered the moment for his diary. "That's when I decided it would only work if we treated it just as seriously as Chekhov," he said.

Yet Goldman wasn't Chekhov, and John would finally reach a creative impasse with the writer over how to the end the film. "I realize that the final scene is not as terrific as it must be," John confessed to Olivier in September. In the book, Babe kills Szell, but Hoffman admitted that, as a Jew, he was uncomfortable playing such a revenge-soaked scene. John also felt it simply too pat, asking Goldman give them something more. The screenwriter, however, couldn't see beyond what he'd already written, so Robert Towne (*The Last Detail, Chinatown, Shampoo*) was brought in to give them an appropriate killer of an ending. Towne devised a brilliant set piece in the pump house of a New York reservoir, where the final, ironic confrontation between the two adversaries occurs. Szell, at gunpoint, is forced to swallow the diamonds he has risked so much for, then scramble for them as Babe tosses handful after handful over the railing. He finally falls on his own protruding wrist knife and ends up floating face down in the water.

Goldman called the new ending "horseshit," but John was thrilled with it, feeling that the intensity of the film needed to be balanced with an equally intense ending. It also gave Olivier a whole range of emotions to play other than simply cruel, steely determination.

Rehearsals began in September 1975 at the New York Cultural Center. Right away John saw that working with Hoffman was going to be very different this time, that the actor, now one of Hollywood's top stars, had become increasingly intractable in the demands he made in pursuit of his art. "It's no secret that Dustin Hoffman, who I regard as an absolutely splendid and inventive actor," John said, "is a packet of trouble, because he's got 60 answers for every question and he's never content to settle for one simple solution. Even when he's got it, he wants to try something else, just in case. That can be exhausting. It's like dealing with a child prodigy."

Once actual filming began, John brought in Howard "Hawk" Koch as assistant director. "The picture was terribly disorganized," Koch remembered. "My first day was the scene where Hoffman and Marthe Keller drive up to the house. Every angle was being considered. Conrad Hall had the house in focus, then not in focus. Then he wants to try shooting from the backseat over their shoulders. It's 9:30 in the morning now and still we don't have a set-up!

"Then Hoffman arrives and says he can't shoot the scene this way. He and John go off into the trailer to argue it out. I'm looking at my watch. Finally I knock on the trailer door and say, 'It's just a car drive-up!' John just looks at me. I say, 'Connie is a brilliant cinematographer but if you try all his ideas

The iconic image of Schlesinger's most famous achievement: Dustin Hoffman and Jon Voight in *Midnight Cowboy*.

When Brenda Vaccaro announced suddenly that she would not do a nude scene, John wrapped her in a fox fur for her bedroom romp with Jon Voight.

Crafting his masterpiece: John gives direction to Murray Head and Peter Finch in *Sunday Bloody Sunday*.

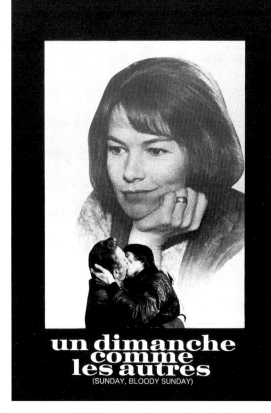

The French advertising campaign tried to use the image on the left to market *Sunday Bloody Sunday*. After John's fierce objections, the image of the right was substituted.

The climactic scene of John's most ambitious work: Donald Sutherland consumed by the crowd in *The Day of the Locust*.

A staged scene for *Yanks*: in the film, the lovers never get the chance for such a tender goodbye. (*Right to left*) Richard Gere, Lisa Eichhorn, Chick Vennara, Wendy Morgan.

Fifteen years and counting: John met Michael Childers in 1967 and the relationship endured. By the 1980s Childers was serving as producer on a number of Schlesinger's films.

From 1975 into the 1990s, John's homes in London and Los Angeles became salons for the famous and fascinating. Here he poses with one eclectic cast of guests, including Liza Minnelli, Tim Curry, Barry Humphries, Dennis Hopper, Doris Roberts, and Dominick Dunne. (*Left*) John watches Mick Jagger sleep off a particularly rowdy party, gets cosy with Bianca (*below left*), and (*below*) warbles with Dustin Hoffman and Bette Midler (who was there to serenade Lord Olivier).

During filming of *The Falcon and the Snowman*, Schlesinger often felt he was running a kindergarten trying to keep the peace between Timothy Hutton and Sean Penn. But the result is a fascinating, complex film.

A close second for cinema was John's passion for opera: Here he is directing Placido Domingo and Luciana Serra in *The Tales of Hoffmann* in 1981.

All smiles here, but directing his last film, *The Next Best Thing*, with Rupert Everett (pictured) and Madonna turned out to be an agonizing nightmare.

The best of Schlesinger's latter work was done with playwright Alan Bennett (left). On *An Englishman Abroad* and *A Question of Attribution*, John saw eye-to-eye with Bennett.

John in an atmospheric pose on the set of *The Believers*.

John and Michael, in a portrait by Greg Gorman.
In 1995, John was finally to admit to the press: 'I'm happy to have a companion of 28 years, and we enjoy each other's company, and that's quite wonderful to have.'

we're here all day. *Pick one*!' Then Dustin starts to protest. He was exasperating John. So I turn to Dustin and say, 'You have every right to want to know how a shoot will be set up but not on the day of the shoot!'"

John's battles with Hoffman on the set have become legendary. "There was a lot of yelling," said Marthe Keller. "But it was creative tension. In America, I have found that you have to be in a good movie and in Europe you have to be good in a movie. From the very beginning, I saw that Dustin wanted everyone to be good. He wanted a good movie. He worked very hard with everybody. I saw it as a productive thing. I never saw it as a negative. So I think that all the tension and yelling was on purpose."

"It was an unhappy experience," Hoffman acknowledged. "It was a terrible part in my life and John said to me, 'You've changed.' It was a drug time for everybody. As Nicholson said, it was recreational. People smoked pot and tried cocaine, whatever. I think that probably added to the irrationality."

But Hoffman was adamant that what Goldman wrote in his memoir, that the actor bullied and badgered a sick and frail Lord Olivier, was simply not true.

"It's an outright lie," Hoffman said. "That never happened. I did ask Olivier to improvise and he said, 'My dear boy, I don't know how to improvise.'"

John agreed that Goldman's account of the Hoffman-Olivier relationship was not entirely accurate. "I do think there was a certain flexing of muscles on the part of Dustin," John said. "But they became good friends. Olivier came from a totally different theatrical tradition and Dustin was very keen on improvisation. Olivier liked to learn the lines and didn't want too many changes because he was afraid he'd forget them

... They did have a sort of slightly competitive spirit which was not necessarily bad for the movie."

Watching films of the rehearsals, with Hoffman, Keller and Scheider finding their characters through improvised dialogue, offers a fascinating window into their creative process. John occasionally enters the frame to position them differently or to make hand gestures speeding things up or slowing them down. It must have been very difficult for Hoffman then to throw himself into a scene with Olivier who could do none of that, who simply carried the words of the script around in his head.

Of course, the film's most famous legend has Hoffman, in an earnest attempt to inhabit his character, coming onto the set one morning, weak and bleary-eyed from staying out all night. Olivier, so the story goes, took one look at him and uttered the immortal line, "Why doesn't he just try *acting*?" The anecdote has been told and retold in so many different versions that it's become impossible to pin down now. Everyone from Bob Evans to Conrad Hall to Hawk Koch would claim to have been there when it was said, and each of their accounts were different. John himself would tell the story in a variety of ways, sometimes insisting Olivier made the remark to him in the cutting room, other times that he spoke it directly to Dustin. Hoffman, for his part, said Olivier uttered the line as a laugh between the two of them, when Dustin staggered onto the set after a night of partying, weakly joking to "his lordship" that it had been his way of preparing for the part.

No matter its actual genesis, the quip summed up the difference between the two actors, which was enormous. Yet their playing together is some of the most dynamic acting in any John Schlesinger film. The most memorable scene, of course, is the torturing of Babe in the dentist's chair. Szell, a former dentist, had extracted gold from Jewish prisoners' teeth before they were shipped to the camps. Now he would use the same instruments – so universal in their connotation of childhood terror – to pry from Babe information he believes the young man has: whether it's safe for him to reclaim his diamonds. The line, "Is it safe?" repeated over and over by Szell as he pokes and scrapes inside Babe's mouth, became a catchphrase of 1976.

Olivier would claim that watching a gardener tenderly trim his roses gave him the insight on how to play the scene, with precision and care. But much of the rest of the time he had a tendency to overact, to add flourishes to the smallest of moments. John was loathe to inform the great Laurence Olivier that he was going over the top. One of Schlesinger's favorite stories concerned the time he'd haltingly suggested that Olivier make a scene "more intimate", to which the great actor supposedly replied, "You mean cut off the ham fat, dear boy?"

More often, John's strategy would be simply to ask him to pause between sentences "so I would have a place to get the scissors in later." However he managed it, John elicited a finely tuned, chilling performance from Olivier, one of his latter-day finest.

"The best thing I remember from the film," John said, "was this great stage and screen actor, who'd been very sick for quite a long time, getting better with every day he worked. The relish he had for the role and for working was quite moving." Indeed, instead of six weeks, which is all the insurance people thought Olivier had left to live, he'd go on for another fourteen years. In his memoir, he'd single out *Marathon Man* from his later pictures as "particularly good."

As ever, John enjoyed the post-production period far more than the chaotic shoot, especially as it afforded him a greater connection with Evans. "Not until we were in the cutting room," he said, "did I realize what a remarkable, tasteful man Robert Evans is. I was deceived by the eye-catching glamorous lifestyle he likes to advertise." Together with Jim Clark, they shaped the leanest, tightest, most technically agile film in John's canon. *Marathon Man* unspools like a lunging cheetah: fierce, strong, its every muscle taut and hard.

Too hard for some: at a preview of the film in San Francisco, the audience, apparently populated by a few too many of John's despised "politically correct" types, began booing the film's violent scenes. During a sequence in which Roy Scheider kills two people, someone stood and shouted, "Sadistic shit!" John was startled, turning around in his seat as the audience got angrier and angrier; finally he and Dustin Hoffman took refuge in the manager's office.

"I guess it was the politics of the people of San Francisco coupled with the fact that the air conditioning had broken down," Jim Clark recalled. "It was hot as hell in there and whenever there was violence on the screen people were shouting, 'Fascist rubbish!' and things like that."

The next day, fearing similar reactions from a general release, Schlesinger and Clark reconsidered the film shot by shot, trimming as much violence as they could. Scheider's scene was cut, and the dental scene, originally much more intense, was shortened. Clark told me he thought the excised footage might still exist somewhere in the vault at Paramount, and hoped someday a restored version of the film might be released on DVD.

"It was some strong stuff we cut out," Clark said. "When we

were shooting it I said to John that I'd really like some close shots of the drill in the tooth so I can cut them in to the final sequence. John said, 'Oh, you're a sadist.' I just thought it could be very dramatic. So he gave me a unit and let me shoot all this footage and I cut it in. The truth is if you look at the film as it is now, you never see anything. It's all in the soundtrack."

Controversy over the film's violence would not be stemmed by the cuts. Already by the time of its premiere on 6 October, the buzz that preceded the film deemed it one of the most violent American films ever made – a ridiculous charge, but one which escalated as stories grew of patrons running out of theaters or covering their eyes until the infamous "dentist scene" was over. Of course, such scuttlebutt attracted as many moviegoers as it kept away, and *Marathon Man* became a huge blockbuster success, John's first since *Midnight Cowboy*. The movie made more than $21 million in domestic returns alone, ending up the twentieth highest-grossing film in the United States for 1976. In New York, it broke the opening weekend record set by *The Godfather*.

The film did even better business in Europe, where controversy over the violence wasn't as great as it was in the States. It was one more example of the kind of American hypocrisy that infuriated John. He would write to Gene Phillips: "How anybody can [complain about the film's violence] in a country where judges in Texas are advocating executions on the network – and the whole grisly business of the shooting of Gary Gilmore can be perpetuated by T-shirts with targets painted over the heart, and the words 'Let's do it' as the slogan – beats me."

To the press, John defended the violence in *Marathon Man*. "I don't like slow-motion blood and Peckinpah violence at all," he said – though the film had Doc dying in Babe's arms, his blood slowly seeping into the carpet. Still, the scene could hardly be called gratuitous since it serves as a powerful, emotional counterbalance to the brothers' happy, boisterous first scene together. In fact, none of the violence in the film is without a purpose. "*Marathon Man* was a film about fear and paranoia using violence as a means to find something out," John said. "There is in fact very little graphic violence shown. More is implied and the audience is made to feel the violence strongly."

It is a tribute to his filmmaking, in fact, that protests over the violence occurred at all. John was right in asserting that the violence is more implied than visible; the fear he invoked from his audience was so strong, so palpable, that many were left with the impression of having seen a much more violent film than they had. The dentist scene is truly a modern masterpiece of horror: Babe's refusal to open his mouth and Szell's patient tapping of the probe against his lips set the scene with a perfect pitch of terror.

Even more disturbing is the kidnapping of Babe. He sits in his bathtub – Schlesinger's version of Hitchcock's shower scene from *Psycho* – his face covered with a cloth. He hears something, or does he? We are as innocent and vulnerable as he is, sitting there, naked in the bathtub. A shadow in the outer room is enough to convey the depths of fear. Babe jumps up and slams the door, but its flimsy lock is no good. We are as trapped as he is. No dialogue – the sequence is nearly silent – as we watch the hinges of the door begin to loosen. A knife slices through the doorframe. The only window is too small to pass through. Babe breaks the silence by screaming for help. The sequence is brilliantly acted, directed and cut, a textbook example of cinematic suspense.

For the rest of his life it would be the experience of *Marathon Man* that John tried to recapture, from its ease in financing to its box-office reception. As thrilling as the artistic laurels of *Midnight Cowboy* and *Sunday, Bloody Sunday* had been, there was no beating the fulfillment he got from scaring the pants off his audience; this was, after all, the man who'd gotten his start in movies making *Black Legend*. "It was thrilling," he'd say after attending a regular screening of the film. "This was the first time I'd made a genre picture of that kind, and to see the audience reacting exactly as they should have done was terrific."

He was hooked. "I'd like to go back and forth between making thrillers and more personal pictures," he announced; the formula of "one for them, one for me." But in truth, they were *both* for him. He knew one offered financial gain and career security, the other gave artistic acknowledgement, and rarely would the twain meet. *Midnight Cowboy* had been an anomaly; although there was considerable talk that John would be nominated for an Academy Award for *Marathon Man*, when the nominations were announced in early 1977, only Olivier received a nomination.

"We are obviously not popular," John remarked after seeing the list of nominees. "I wonder if Hollywood will ever forgive me for *Day of the Locust?*"

John was also ignored by the British Academy, which at least gave nods to Hoffman and Jim Clark. In the end, the only award John would pick up for *Marathon Man* was the David di Donatello Award from Italy for Best Foreign Film.

Like the awards committees, reviewers tended to judge the material as "beneath" Schlesinger. Russell Davies in the *Observer* thought the violence and bloodshed was merely John's way of proving he could be "as ostentatiously hard-boiled as any Fuller or Frankenheimer." Jay Cocks in *Time* thought the "ideas" of the film were pretentious and tacked-on; Stanley Kauffman in *The New Republic* said Schlesinger had "surrendered his previous interest in style." Vincent Canby liked the film, calling it an "elegant, bizarre, rococo melodrama," but agreed it was a step down from John's previous filmmaking goals: with *Marathon Man*, Canby said, the director "just wants to scare the hell out of you."

Within the industry, there was an attitude that John had somehow cheapened himself by making a thriller. The snub from the Academy reflected what many people were thinking: Jerry Hellman told me he never thought *Marathon Man* was worthy of John's talents. For his part, John would grumble he was "damned if he did, damned if he didn't," adding, "First there were those who bitched that I was making inaccessible, uncommercial pictures. Then others said I'd lowered my standards and sold out for the box office."

John firmly believed *Marathon Man*'s success was not simply due to its escapism, but because Babe Levy was a character with whom the audience could identify. "*Day of the Locust* did not find wider acceptance because there was no one in it that the audience could root for," he said. "Babe Levy is definitely someone that you can root for. The film is about his survival in a grim and hostile world. In our present age of anxiety we can all identify with characters who are not trying to get ahead but simply to survive."

The film is not, of course, a deeply probing character study like John's earlier films, yet neither is it the simple actioner some critics tried to label it. When Szell is recognized by former concentration camp prisoners in New York's jewelry district, it is a moment of raw political and emotional power. Jack Kroll in

Newsweek was one of the few critics not to be blindsided by prejudice toward the genre. He found the film intelligent, with a dash of "Graham Greene's quality of metaphysics-made-melodrama."

John's post-*Marathon Man* career would be consumed by his desire to once again find a vehicle that would unite the two experiences (box-office success and critical acclaim), but his efforts turned out to be little more than tilting at windmills. Did he sense what was happening? Did he look around and see the huge marketing campaigns for *Jaws* and *Star Wars* and wonder where he might fit in this *new* "New Hollywood"? Even with *Marathon Man*'s blockbuster success, he was, as usual, more than a little pessimistic. "Studio executives are trying to break through with offers that go ignored," Rex Reed observed after an interview. "Schlesinger is king of the mountain. There's nothing like lines around the block to ensure self-confidence. Yet he seems nervous."

He was nervous because he knew the relationship with Evans, as satisfying as it was, would never match what he had shared with Hellman or Janni. "I don't think Bob Evans is prepared to take the same kind of risk I am with material," he told Reed. "He would never have made *Sunday, Bloody Sunday*. He only wants to make films that are big commercial blockbusters. I am glad we have a commercial blockbuster with *Marathon Man*. But in the final analysis, I don't think that's the way to make pictures."

The ambivalence he felt upon the completion of *Marathon Man* would affect the course of the rest of his career. But for the moment there was no question that he was savoring the picture's success. John was indeed the king of the mountain – a Hollywood hill called Rising Glen.

Bathhouse Betty was serenading Lord Olivier: "You made me love you . . . I didn't wanna do it . . ."

Residents of the quiet Rising Glen enclave in the green hills above Hollywood had gotten used to free shows like this one. Tickets to see Bette Midler were hard to come by, but all that John Schlesinger's neighbors had to do was walk outside and listen. The voice belting through the night was unmistakable.

"It was one of those magical Hollywood moments, the kind they said never happened anymore," said Michael Childers, reflecting back more than two decades later. "But there was Bette Midler, in our living room, singing to Laurence Olivier, with Dustin Hoffman on piano, and Natalie Wood and Lily Tomlin and Roddy McDowall gathered around listening."

It was shortly after New Year's, 1977. In the spotlight of *Marathon Man*'s success, John Schlesinger was white hot in Tinseltown again. Unlike the period after *Midnight Cowboy*, when he turned a cold shoulder to Hollywood and hurried back to London, this time he stuck around to bask in the glory. The house he and Michael shared on Rising Glen quickly became the watering hole for the "in crowd," the court at which visiting celebrities paid homage: Midler. Hoffman. Wood and Tomlin and their respective Wagners, Robert and Jane. Plus Mick Jagger, Tennessee Williams, Liza Minnelli, Paul McCartney, Stefanie Powers, Placido Domingo, Anjelica Huston, Ali MacGraw, Michael York, Shirley MacLaine, John Travolta.

"I was totally dazzled the first time I ever went to John's house," said Tomlin. "Warren Beatty was there. Jack Nicholson was there. I was so carried away I stole a soap from his bathroom so I could take it home and show my mother."

"We kept Michael Butler's Japanese bed," Childers said. "Fourteen feet wide, custom sheets, custom day-glo, with a mirror above the bed. Hah! If that mirror could talk, it would make *Confidential* magazine look like a Disney tale! And not only from when we had it, but from all the others who would stay at the house when we'd be in London. Sean Connery stayed there, and Richard Gere, Stevie Nicks, David Geffen. It's a pretty good cast of characters who stayed on that bed."

For gossip columnists, a Schlesinger soirée meant good copy; leafing through the yellowed newspaper pages, I was treated to a panorama of life on Rising Glen. Natalie and R.J. Christopher Isherwood and Don Bachardy. Rex Reed. Candy Bergen. For a "chase-those-January-blues away" party, a contingent of Brits showed up: Tony Richardson, Anne Heywood, Malcolm McDowell. Columnist George Christy reported seeing super-agent Maggie Abbott strutting around the place, "a white fox boa dripping from her shoulders, answering to the nickname of Foxy."

For Natalie Wood's fortieth birthday party, Cat Stevens led the singing. Charlotte Rampling showed up in a black velvet pantsuit and was promptly pronounced the height of fashion by Liz Smith, who added parenthetically that "the fit and the fashionable always seem to find their way to Schlesinger's."

Another time Elton John arrived wearing pink sneakers, green satin pants and enormous white-framed eyeglasses, and sang songs from his "Blue Moves" album. Allan Carr buzzed about the place, talking nonstop about his new film, *Can't Stop the Music*, starring the Village People. At a dinner for Jacqueline Bisset, actor Jack Larson and his partner, director James Bridges (*The China Syndrome* and *Urban Cowboy*), were quoted as complimenting Schlesinger on his choice of Verdicchio.

It wasn't always so kiss-kiss. There was the time Bob Fosse

showed up, Dyan Cannon on his arm, only to run smack into Isherwood. Fosse had, of course, directed *Cabaret*, based on Isherwood's *Berlin Stories*, and though several years had passed, Childers said Isherwood had never told Fosse how he felt about the film. A few cocktails, however, had put him in the mood to do so. "You fucked up my book, my classic!" he shouted. "You ruined the integrity of my piece, turned it all into surface!"

Schlesinger burned with embarrassment, but Fosse handled the moment. "I'm sorry you feel that way, Mr. Isherwood," he said, "but I do hope all the royalties you're getting because my film was such a hit might help assuage those feelings a little bit."

Another time Schlesinger grabbed Allan Carr by his purple velvet lapels and practically threw him out of the house. John had told Carr he wanted to make a film of Piers Paul Read's book, *Alive*, about the Andes plane crash survivors who were forced to cannibalize each other. It was perfect fodder for John's macabre sensibility, but Carr had stolen the idea, importing a poorly dubbed Mexican ripoff called *Survive!* to present under the Robert Stigwood banner. "He was off our list after that," Childers said. "Never darkened our doorway again."

Happier moments were shared with John's great friend, the songwriter Paul Jabara. Those I interviewed for this book often had more stories to tell about Jabara than they did about John. A notorious raconteur, Jabara had demanded a part in *The Day of the Locust*, and John agreed, saying only that Paul would have to accept whatever part he was given. Jabara, eager to be seen onscreen, agreed, and was promptly cast as the drag queen in the "Hot Voodoo" sequence. Forever struggling with drug addictions, Jabara was famous for collecting money from friends so he could enter rehab and then taking off on holiday. Some say it was at Schlesinger's house that Jabara locked

Donna Summer in the bathroom and forced her to listen to a song he'd written, "Last Dance" – which went on to win Grammy Awards for both of them.

Another night Tennessee Williams was in great spirits, egged on by John's "beyond gorgeous" butler. The butler kept pouring the martinis all night long, flirting outrageously as Williams sat with John and Gore Vidal discussing the difficulties of being an artist in America. "It was a real salon moment," Childers says, "listening to them all talk about survival and keeping their integrity, the fight, the fight, the fight. Simply electrifying." But Williams, polishing off his last martini, had the last word. "Oh, fuck it all," he suddenly declared, and jumped, fully dressed, into the pool.

George Cukor was another frequent guest, bestowing upon John his coveted mantle of pre-eminent Hollywood host. "John's parties weren't your typical Bel Air Hollywood-insider kind of thing," said Brenda Vaccaro. "He was never comfortable with that world." Instead, he "attracted the best from around the world."

Like Cukor had done in the 1930s and 1940s, Schlesinger distinguished himself by playing host to a wide cultural spectrum: not just movie people, but theater, opera, music and literary greats as well. Attending a soiree on Rising Glen became *de rigueur* for visiting celebrities; it was a mark of recognition. On any one Saturday it was not unusual to sit among such a diverse assembly as Joan Plowright, Dennis Hopper, Alan Bennett, David Hockney, Donna Summer, Helmut Newton. One night Vincent Price and Coral Browne arrived with Joan Rivers and Edgar Rosenberg. "Now *there* was a fascinating foursome," cracked the comedian and writer Bruce Vilanch, another frequent guest.

"John always enjoyed mixing it up," said the actor Hart Bochner. "The whole London artsy fartsy crowd mixed with New York and L.A. to create this interesting soup. He loved to be surrounded by that energy. He became joyous."

But no mix was quite so memorable as the pairing of Midler and Olivier, which has slipped into Hollywood legend. Schlesinger and Childers had taken Olivier to see the Divine Miss M in her "Depression Tour" show. "He was absolutely bowled over," Childers recalled. "He said she was the greatest performer he'd seen in the last fifty years." This from a man who'd known Bea Lillie and Gertrude Lawrence.

Backstage Midler mirrored Olivier's admiration: "Oh my God, it's a Lord! I'm meeting a Lord!" Inspired by their chemistry, John hosted an after-show supper for Midler, where she sang and Dusty Hoffman played the piano.

Michael added his own sparkle to the household. Discovered by agent Marysa Maslansky, he'd been signed by the prestigious Sygma agency and was shooting for *Vogue*, *Interview* and a host of others. The most beautiful people of the era were trotted out to his studio behind the house: Natalie Wood, Jacqueline Bisset, Richard Gere, John Travolta, a young Demi Moore.

He was also in demand as a stills photographer, working on films from *Saturday Night Fever* to *American Gigolo* to *The Year of Living Dangerously*. He developed an eye for spotting a star in the making: to one party he brought along a young Mel Gibson, announcing, "Mark my words. This one is going to be a big star."

"All terribly glamorous," said Bruce Vilanch. "But what made it even better was the minute anyone showed up at one of John and Michael's parties, they quickly realized, if they hadn't known it before, that these were two gay men. In movies about Hollywood, there's always the party scene: wild dancing with all these bimbos in tight skirts and big boobs running around. I used to find it funny to watch straight people arriving at John's and looking around at all these incredibly gorgeous guys. It was the one Hollywood party where there weren't any bimbos."

People often assume that life for gay men and women in Hollywood became easier after Stonewall, after a political movement existed to supposedly "liberate" homosexuals from oppression. But in many ways, the 1970s and 1980s were even more difficult for gay men and lesbians in the industry than in the pre-Stonewall days. The old studio system had offered a degree of protection, even refuge, for its gay workers. Whole departments (wardrobe, set decoration) were often exclusively gay enclaves, and with much of the studio publicity in gay and lesbian hands, even same-sex-loving stars enjoyed a degree of freedom in their private lives. No respectable publication in those days was willing to go the *Confidential* magazine route, so there was no threat of a public "outing." Of course, in this system, no one was really "out" in a modern definition, but without the construct of "openly gay," one wasn't necessarily "in the closet" either.

With the dissolution of the studio system and the rise of the gay liberation movement, however, the once-tolerated open secret of a George Cukor or Dorothy Arzner or James Whale became less manageable for the studios. Homosexuality had been named; it was a bogeyman that might visit anyone too indiscreet. The supposed "liberation" of Hollywood movies in the late 1960s had the opposite effect on its gay workers. For many gays working in the film industry, the activists marching with placards in the streets didn't offer liberation but rather a threat to their careers. Most found it better to play the game and keep their heads low.

Most, but not all. "I don't suppose I could ever have lived that way," John said. He knew the ruses perpetuated by people like producer Frank McCarthy and his lover, the publicist Rupert Allan, who'd arrive at parties separately with women and then act surprised to run into each other. Like the rest of Hollywood, Schlesinger was amused by the farce of producer Ross Hunter (*Imitation of Life, Airport*) pretending to be engaged to Nancy Sinatra when everyone knew he'd been living with set decorator Jacque Mapes for twenty years.

Schlesinger and Childers attended premieres together. They hosted together at their home. The press, unaccustomed to such openness, was unsure how to respond. The *Village Voice* came closest to stating the obvious in 1975: Schlesinger was "a gifted director who's in touch with gay sensibilities."

"Michael and John were rather pioneers in being an openly gay couple," said Michael York. "There was never any pretense about it." They pronounced themselves "this generation's Isherwood and Bachardy", which annoyed Isherwood who still saw himself as part of the "now" generation.

"John was one of the few people I knew who didn't make any bones about his sexuality," said Stewart Grimshaw. "He wasn't militant but he recognized in his avid way that there was change about. I think he felt [by the mid-Seventies] that it wasn't enough just to *be* out, but now he had to be *seen* as being out. He wanted to be overt."

George Cukor stood in awe and admiration. "I envy you, John and Michael," he once told them, "because you can do what I never could. You do everything right out in the open. I could never have done that."

For all the sexual adventures they pursued, both together and apart, it was obvious to everyone that John was still very much in love with Michael. During production of *Locust*, he recorded in his diary how they had snuck away to Carmel and the Tickle Pink Inn to mark their sixth anniversary: "It's nice to be back," he said. "We've lit a log fire and we overlook the sea beating on the rocks. It's been a beautiful weekend, very good for Michael and myself to have been alone like this together."

But with the freedom of the era came excess – easy drugs and even easier sex, one last hurrah before the age of AIDS. "There wasn't a party you could go to in Hollywood, unless it was Cukor's or Rosalind Russell's, that you wouldn't find eighty lines of cocaine out on the table," Childers said. "Or else the butler was carrying it around on a tray. Dom Perignon, caviar, and coke."

He remembered attending Halston's Christmas party at Studio 54 in New York with John, accompanied by Bianca Jagger and Liza Minnelli. "We were given little Tiffany bags when we walked in," Childers said. "We opened them up to find little sterling silver coke-snorting spoons with our initials engraved on them. How thoughtful. As we got closer to the table we realized it was not Christmas decoration snow we were seeing but rather $20,000 worth of cocaine. And all these famous divas were there shoveling it into their purses."

Although Michael would battle, and finally courageously overcome, his own addiction problems, John didn't partake much in the drug scene. Never more than a moderate social drinker, he'd sip a vodka with grapefruit juice or maybe a couple glasses of wine. Harder drugs held little appeal, though he enjoyed pot; several friends recalled many happy times being blissfully stoned with John.

"At his parties," said Vilanch, "John was on his way to a Buddha status. He would find a place to sit and everyone would come to him. He'd sit there quietly conversing with people while Michael ran around being the partymeister."

Often, John's partner in conversation would just so happen to be the most gorgeous, most spectacular specimen in the room. "John would be talking in very hushed tones to some beauty," Vilanch said, laughing, "and only with much reluctance turn away to say hello to Sidney Poitier or Elizabeth Taylor."

Fifteen

1978–1981

"Americans just didn't get the joke"

"John could either have made *Yanks* or *Coming Home*,"
Childers told me, sitting at his dining room table, going
through piles of scrapbooks and photos. "He chose
Yanks."

I thought it was a curious choice. "*Coming Home* would
have reunited him with Waldo Salt, Jerry Hellman and Jon
Voight," I offered. "He would have done a beautiful job with
that film."

Childers sighed. "He didn't think he could." He leaned
across the table to make his point. "This is a good story because
it tells you something about John. He didn't have such a great
big Hollywood ego that he had to make some picture just
because it was prestigious. He turned down *Coming Home*
because he felt he couldn't relate to the story. It was about
disabled Vietnam war veterans, a very American story. He

didn't feel he was the right man for the job and he had the courage and integrity to say no."

That night I watched *Midnight Cowboy* again. Another very American story, and John had done pretty well with that one.

"Of *course* he could have done it," said Jerry Hellman when I asked him about *Coming Home*. "But he was worried that the film would collapse. Jane Fonda had come to us with the project and she was still box-office poison then, you know, Hanoi Jane and all that. John read the script and I think he just felt he wasn't the right guy to deal with a bunch of crippled veterans. He said to me, 'Let's face it, my dear. The last thing in this world you need on this picture is a broke English faggot.'"

Hellman laughed, then thought of something else. "It also didn't help that Michael didn't like the project much. He never hid that. It was a low-budget picture without much chance of being a hit."

Of course, *Coming Home* would go on to win Academy Awards for Jane Fonda and Jon Voight, as well as receiving a nomination for Best Picture. *Yanks*, released the following year, was ignored by the Academy, making $1.5 million domestically to *Coming Home*'s $32.6 million.

John Schlesinger's career after *Marathon Man* would be studded with "if onlys." If only he had made *Coming Home*. If only he hadn't gone back to England. If only he had *stayed* in England and not returned to America to make *Honky Tonk Freeway*. If only he had continued making brilliant television dramas for the BBC instead of always hoping for a big, fat movie comeback. If only he had accepted offers to direct *The Firm* or *In and Out*, instead of *The Innocent* or *Eye for an Eye*.

If only Hollywood had not changed irrevocably. If only there had been money to make films in Britain. If only the film industry had continued to allow its artists to experiment, to take risks, to try and fail, the way it had during the brief and glorious period when John Schlesinger made his greatest films.

"If John had chosen a more stringent path in life," Jerry Hellman said, "I think he would have been happier with his career. Speaking with complete honesty here, I was very unhappy with the direction John's career took. What if he'd continued to live in London, occasionally finding that piece of material like *Sunday, Bloody Sunday* that lived close to his heart? He'd come to America, make it, then go back home. No big houses, no hobnobbing with Bob Evans and the stars. But John wanted that world. He and Michael were entranced with it. And he spent the rest of his life trying to find a way to maintain that."

"But why shouldn't he want to make popular movies?" countered Wallis Nicita, casting director on *The Falcon and the Snowman*. "John was a great director. An artist. Of course he wanted to keep making movies. He had something to say."

The problem, beginning in 1979, was getting people to listen.

Eight years had passed since John Schlesinger and Joseph Janni had worked on a film together. To mollify the critics who'd looked down their noses at *Marathon Man*, Schlesinger announced, "I'm not making any more adventure thrillers. I'm going back to my roots" – which, of course, was a lot of baloney. Nonetheless, he was eager to prove he was still an artist, and Colin Welland's gentle, thoughtful script about American soldiers stationed in Britain during World War II seemed just the right antidote to *Marathon Man*'s violence and excess. "It made me very nostalgic," John said, "to go home to England to make another film."

"One of the reasons I wanted to make the film so badly was that I'd been looking for a subject which expressed my own dichotomy," he said elsewhere. "I am divided. I'm an English director who loves working in England but who also loves working in the States where I've been given a lot of opportunities."

But first there was another play to direct for Peter Hall: *Julius Caesar*, in Edwardian costume and starring John Gielgud. Schlesinger's second turn at Shakespeare, however, did not prove as satisfying as his first tryst with Shaw. "I will think twice again about doing a well-known classic," he wrote to Brenda Vaccaro. "It always seems to be a mistake for me e.g. *Madding Crowd* and *Day of the Locust*." To Gene Phillips he quipped about the play, "It looks like being a painful birth, and I think in the future I shall remain firmly on the pill!"

Gielgud, however, he found a joy. "He was the perfect pro," John said. "When he was murdered, I used to say, 'Do you mind dying in this scene?' Then he would lie this great actor on the stage, as a kind of threat to all the rest: 'Get on with it and do it properly.' He would lie there motionless and never say, 'May I have a mattress?' or 'Can't you get a dummy?' Never ever."

Brian Cox, who played Brutus, was less agreeable. When the play opened at the Olivier on 22 March 1977, John would grumble about "that wretched Brian Cox slowing the pace down to such an extent that six minutes were added to the running time." Critics were very hard on the production, giving Gielgud high marks but dismissing the rest. "Climax after climax slides by in a continuum of monotonous anxiety," wrote Irving Wardle in *The Times*, who also thought the Edwardian garb sorted "oddly with the forum, where the black-coated conspirators huddle round Brutus' door like Conrad's anarchists."

Despite the disappointment of *Julius Caesar*, Peter Hall retained a great deal of affection for Schlesinger, and hoped he would continue directing productions for the National every couple of years. Indeed, John took his role as associate director quite seriously, showing up regularly to directors' meetings, which Hall described as "a sort of cabinet" that numbered Harold Pinter, David Hare and Harrison Birtwistle, among its members. It would be John who made the first move in defending Hall when some in the cabinet threatened a coup. "I made the mistake when I went to the National of keeping Olivier's two chief lieutenants, Michael Blakemore and Jonathan Miller," Hall said. "It was clearly a tactical mistake because both of them thought they should have had my job." When Blakemore passed around a paper to the associates, outlining grievances, John was the first to pass his copy back. The others followed suit, indicating their support of Hall, and any intended rebellion was dissipated.

Had John wished it, Peter Hall would have given him a regular home at the National; already there was talk of him directing Diana Rigg in *Cat on a Hot Tin Roof*. But it simply would not have worked. "If I was prepared to come back and work in television and the theater, I could make my life here," John said. "But I'm not. I really enjoy theater, it's a purer way of dealing with actors, but I can't pretend that it could ever supplant filmmaking."

At the time of *Julius Caesar*, he told Sheridan Morley: "Occasionally I wake up in the night and wonder what I'm doing up here on Beachy Head risking my neck again. I'm already nostalgic for the cinema, even after only a few months away. I love the final control which can never be the director's in a theater." He loved something else, too, as he wrote to Gene Phillips: once production had moved to the cutting room, "the actors cannot talk back to you – although Dustin Hoffman did his best at every preview of *Marathon Man*."

Back in England, away from movie sets and his Hollywood hills palace, John felt out of his element, no longer at home. Had he stayed in America, he'd have been on the set with Jerry Hellman and Jon Voight making *Coming Home*. But, determined to make a picture in his native land, he found himself instead banging on doors with Jo Janni, trying to raise the money for *Yanks*.

No one answered, not Rank, not EMI, not even Lord Grade. "You know how studio executives think today," Janni wrote to John. "A story must be, in their opinion, commercially sound, and that means thrillers, adventure stories, best sellers and especially stories with parts for big stars. Into not one of these categories *Yanks* falls. It is an excellent subject but not the type that studio executives consider easy to exploit."

It is amazing to realize that Janni penned that letter in 1976, that the climate was already so hardened against risk by then. Even with the success of *Marathon Man*, Paramount was insisting that Janni pay for all "overhead" costs in exchange for their financing the film; as a result, John found himself back with United Artists, though still in need of additional money if they were to do it right. In the end, *Yanks* received its major funding through German tax-shelter cash. As John said wryly, "Dollars and deutschmarks made possible a film about the British home front during World War II."

Yanks was perceived as a small film, with a budget of three million in pounds sterling. Colin Welland, a young British actor and playwright (who had appeared with Dustin Hoffman in *Straw Dogs*), had drafted a thoughtful story about three very different couples who meet, fall in love, and face uncertain futures because of the war. Thousands of American soldiers had crammed into Britain during World War II, provoking a vital and passionate culture clash; the Yanks were, in the jargon of the day, "over-paid, over-sexed, and over here." Indeed, at the end of the war, more than 100,000 British women left the country to join their G.I.s in America.

Onto the script John layered much of his own experience, giving expression finally to the ideas he and Peter Nichols had explored in making a film based on the Schlesinger family. A sentimental journey was had all around: much of the film was shot in Stockport, where *A Kind of Loving* had been filmed.

"I have a very strong feeling that whatever the outcome of this picture," John recorded in his diary, "whether it's commercially successful or not, I'm making the right move at this moment of my career." Certainly, he was now enjoying being back in England, defying the odds in mounting a major film there – even if none of the money was British. "There is sheer pleasure in having won all our financial battles in getting the thing off the ground after an extremely depressing summer, when I really felt that it would never see the light of day."

Some last-minute reworking of the script was done by Walter Bernstein, John's second collaboration with a black-listed American screenwriter. "I must say an American point of view is what we have badly needed for sometime," the director said. He was determined to balance the experiences of the two cultures as best he could.

A first-rate cast was assembled. Vanessa Redgrave played Helen, the upper-middle-class wife and mother who becomes involved with an American officer (William Devane, in his second Schlesinger film.) At the opposite end of the social scale, Wendy Morgan played Molly, a bus conductress who gets pregnant by (and marries) Danny, a Brooklyn boxer brought to life with considerable "dese" and "dose" by Chick Vennera. Rachel Roberts, connecting John back to his New Wave roots by association with her performance in *Saturday Night and Sunday Morning*, took the part of the stoic, cancer-ridden Mrs. Moreton.

The film was carried, however, by its two central characters, the English girl Jean and the American G.I. Matt. From the start John wanted Richard Gere for Matt; he had seen him in *Looking for Mr. Goodbar* and been entranced. "There was a complexity in him that hadn't been tapped in his previous films, a sensitivity and beauty," John said.

For much of the filming, Gere kept to himself, taking off on long solitary treks through the Yorkshire countryside on his motorbike. Moody and handsome, Gere was being groomed for stardom, and fan magazines made quite a fuss over his every move. Reports of his "misbehavior" on the set began popping up in gossip columns, though John said they were exaggerated. "He's had a tough time hanging about with not much to do, because we have had to concentrate on the sequences with Vanessa, Bill Devane and Rachel Roberts," John wrote to a friend. "It is also a logistically big picture, which is not much fun for a young actor. We have had only one difficult day, and the rest of the time he has been tremendously patient and good."

To his diary, however, he admitted a bit more: "We had a bit of drama today with Richard who suddenly expressed a desire to throw chairs out of windows, which was really rather boring. He calmed down by evening."

If Gere was his new American male star, John wanted to discover a female English counterpart. Enter Lisa Eichhorn, a young actress recently graduated from the Royal Academy of Dramatic Art. She was beautiful, poised, and exactly what John envisioned as the high-minded north country girl who wins Matt's cocky American heart. There was only one problem: Eichhorn was born in Glens Falls, New York.

"My agent said John Schlesinger was looking for a new English star," Eichhorn remembered. "I had never lied to get a part before but my agent stressed that John wanted to discover a new British star like he did with Julie Christie."

Noel Davis, now working as a casting agent, arranged an audition for Eichhorn at John's house on Victoria Road. "I really hadn't decided how I was going to handle it," Eichhorn said, "but when Noel opened the door, I said 'Hello' in a British accent." Noel led her downstairs where John, Michael Childers and Colin Welland were waiting.

"You're Lisa Eichhorn and you're British," John said, standing up to greet her.

"Yes," she said, trembling all the while.

"What part of England are you from?"

"London."

He looked at her oddly. "Hmm," he said. "I detect a bit of north country in your accent."

"Well, yes," Lisa said, "my best friend at RADA was from Yorkshire."

John was smitten. Although Jo Janni was leaning toward Jane Seymour or Cherie Lunghi, John was insistent on Eichhorn. "In typical John fashion," Eichhorn said, "he informed me that Cherie Lunghi did the best test but that my eyes were my fortune. It was all a dream for me. I was euphoric."

Of course, euphoria was rather quickly followed by pangs of guilt. "Afterward, I went round to Victoria Road and said, 'John, I have to talk to you,'" Eichhorn recalled. "He absolutely exploded and said, 'You don't have a fucking equity card!' I said, 'I have an equity card, but I'm American.'"

"*Half* American," he said, narrowing his eyes at her.

"No," Eichhorn admitted. "All American."

John bluffed that he'd known it all the time, but she had fooled him. So enamoured of her did he remain, however, that he forgot his dream of finding a new English star. Now his only concern was about her name. "How can I make a movie about the Americans coming to England," he asked, "with an actress with a German name!"

His enchantment with Eichhorn did not last, however. Once shooting began, he complained to his diary that she was stiff and nervous – William Atherton all over again. "She tenses up every time the camera starts to turn," John said. "She'll be in repose before the take and suddenly the muscles in her face will tense up and she'll allow nothing to come through."

Eichhorn would remember how hard John drove her, the deep feelings of inadequacy that overcame her, the sinking sense that she was disappointing him. His anger, his rages, his doom and gloom confused her. Who was this man who could move between such extremes in so short a span of time? Was she the reason he would throw his hands in the air and declare all of this, the entire film, one big pile of shit?

"I learned something," Eichhorn wrote me after attending John's memorial service in London. "I learned something about

John that I couldn't have known until that night. I learned that he was always the way he was with me. I learned that that was how he worked on the set of all his projects. To hear everyone speak about his temper and his rages and his often wicked humor was a kind of benediction. I suppose if *Yanks* had been an unqualified success or I had risen to greater heights, I might have still retained John in the orbit of my life and learned some of these things over the years. I don't know. It doesn't matter. What matters is that he chose me, I did the best I could, he was pleased with my effort, and I received a life-forming lesson on the way to do the work I love."

Indeed, John would come to view Eichhorn's performance as nearly pitch-perfect. "I rang Lisa to tell her we are now working from a position of strength," he recorded in his diary. Jo Janni agreed, sending a private memo to John on 1 June saying, "Lisa gets better and better. I have absolutely no doubts about her."

No such conflict over Vanessa Redgrave, however: from the start, there had only been awe. "Vanessa is without question one of the best actresses I've ever worked with," John told his diary. "She is the consummate actress, able to take direction, really a wonderful musical instrument, so to speak, for a director to play."

Like Glenda Jackson, however, Redgrave brought out John's fear of intellectual women: "I was worried about working with her," he admitted, "because of the political animal which has loomed rather large." Her socialism and support of the Palestinian cause seemed to him "very strange ideas," and he watched warily as she distributed a "newspaper of the workers' revolutionary party" to the crew. "Her political activities we agreed somehow tacitly we would never mention," John said.

Indeed, in the midst of shooting, Redgrave flew to Los Angeles for the Academy Award ceremony where she won Best Supporting Actress for *Julia*. Collecting her Oscar amid protests against her nomination, she famously thanked the Academy for not bending to "Zionist hoodlums," prompting a cacophony of boos and cheers. Paddy Chayefsky rebuked her from the stage and editorial writers around the world took her to task. "Yet she came straight back to us and plunged into rehearsal as if nothing ever happened," John said. "I thought her politics would get mixed up with the work. It never has for one second."

After successfully previewing the film in London, John mused in his diary about how best to sell the film at a time when the American market was glutted with Vietnam war films (*Coming Home, Apocalypse Now, The Deer Hunter*). "I have a feeling that there is still a problem awaiting us as to how best to advertise the film so that we can sell it as a love story and not just as a war story."

His gut was telling him the timing for *Yanks* was wrong; indeed, Peter Hyams' *Hanover Street*, another British-American romance set during World War II, had bombed earlier that year. When *Yanks* opened in America in September, a disappointing first week led UA and Universal, which had signed on for distribution, to brand it a flop; John went on the offensive, telling interviewers that the picture needed time to build, that it wasn't an easy sell. But Hollywood had little patience left these days; if a film didn't start making money right away, it wasn't worth waiting around and hoping. In Britain, *Yanks* did considerably better business; it would be there, and in Europe, that the film eventually turned a profit.

With *Yanks*, the second tier of John Schlesinger's film

career begins. A beautiful film, some lovely performances, some interesting moments, but nothing, really, that he hadn't done before. Nothing, really, that was so important that he would do it again. Reviewers reacted similarly to the way they'd greeted *Far from the Madding Crowd*, praising the atmosphere and photography but finding little worthwhile drama in the story. *Variety* called it "lovely but listless"; Vincent Canby agreed it was "beautifully realized" but had "the look of someone who's fat without being well-fed."

More telling, as usual, was the review by Andrew Sarris who called it "surprisingly conventional." That's really the problem with *Yanks*. If his decision to make the film was to offer an antidote to criticism of his popular, genre success with *Marathon Man*, John should have injected something *more* into the narrative, some twist, some upset of the status quo. His return to "intimate, personal filmmaking" emerges as yet another exercise in genre, this time a romance instead of a thriller. And as romance, it's perfectly lovely, especially with the magnificent score by Richard Rodney Bennett, but critics were left scratching their heads and wondering what Schlesinger's point was.

A valentine to his homeland, perhaps? At least five times American characters comment on how beautiful England is. As photographed by Dick Bush, it certainly *is* beautiful, one more flashback to *Madding Crowd* as we gaze upon rolling green pastures, foggy mornings along the riverbank, gently winding country lanes. The attention to detail in recreating a 1940s northern English village makes for a powerfully evocative piece of cinema, but it's almost as if John was so enamored of the scenery he couldn't bear to authorize a single cut. Long stretches of Gere and Eichhorn bicycling and walking could have been trimmed without surrendering atmosphere. At 139 minutes, the movie is about twenty minutes too long.

Curiously, David Thomson, so averse to all of John's other films, loved *Yanks*: "John Schlesinger has never done anything so touching, natural, or well worked-out in screen space before," Thomson wrote. "How many films are there today that can treat effacing self-sacrifice without a threnody of strings and lockjaw ennoblement?"

The ending, in which Jean and Molly push their way through the crowd to catch a glimpse of Matt and Danny leaving on the train, is classic Hollywood hokum; Andrew Sarris said it was straight out of King Vidor's *The Big Parade*. But, for all that, it works. The film ends with the four laughing and waving to each other, ecstatic to have made one last connection – a seeming repudiation of Schlesinger's penchant for unhappy, or at least ambiguous, endings. Yet in truth, Matt and Danny are going off to war; there is no guarantee they will come home or, even if they do, whether Jean and Matt will have a future. What that exuberant, transcendent final scene suggests – and this is pure Schlesinger – is that all we have is the moment, and if we can find some joy, however fleeting, in moments like these, it will be enough.

Although the American Academy turned a blind eye to *Yanks*, the film was highly honored by its British counterpart with several nominations. John, nominated as Best Director, lost to Francis Ford Coppola for *Apocalypse Now*, but Rachel Roberts took the prize for Best Supporting Actress and Shirley Russell won for her costumes. John did win Best Director from the National Board of Review, an honor he'd last achieved for *Darling*. And, once again, he received the David di Donatello award from Italy.

All of this was bittersweet, given the debilitating stroke suffered by Jo Janni during post-production. Hurrying to Jo's hospital bedside, John was distraught: it was clear that Janni was never going to recover sufficiently to work again. In his diary, John had said his decision to make *Yanks* was the right one; now he was tremendously grateful he had done so, for it had allowed him one last chance to work with his old friend.

Later, sitting with Jim Clark, John was shattered. "I only hope," he managed to say, "I don't go the same way as poor Jo."

By the early 1980s, no matter that *Yanks* had under-performed, John was still perceived as vitally engaged in the making of major, A-list motion pictures, something which could not be said about his former New Wave colleagues. Jack Clayton hadn't made a film since the disaster of *The Great Gatsby*. Mediocre response to Karel Reisz's *Who'll Stop the Rain* kept him off the screen until 1985. Lindsay Anderson and Tony Richardson supplemented their film work with television assignments, something Schlesinger – no doubt remembering Anderson's earlier cutting remarks – insisted he would not do. He was especially peeved, according to his diary, over a remark of Anderson's which had gotten back to him that *Sunday, Bloody Sunday* "was a film that could be seen any day on television."

It was enough to keep Schlesinger far away from the small screen. "Television holds no interest for me," he said in 1980. "It is generally so bad – better here in England than in America – but still surrounded by so much junk I don't want any part of it."

Yet the lifestyle at the summit of Rising Glen was costly to maintain, so other sources of income needed to be found when it was clear he wouldn't be reaping much financial reward from *Yanks*. In 1980 John realized a long-held dream: to direct an opera. As host to the glitterati in both Hollywood and London, John had become good friends with Placido Domingo, and the tenor was determined to snare John as a director. First it was *Salome*, then it was *Carmen*, but both projects fell through as movie commitments took precedence. Finally, accepting "Placido's dare," John agreed to stage Offenbach's *Tales of Hoffman* for the Royal Opera House at Covent Garden.

"I'm a devoted opera fan," Schlesinger told an interviewer, "a much greater fan of certain singers than of any film actor. I have been since I first started going to the opera in my early adolescence." Yet elsewhere he admitted: "All my friends warned me not to do *Hoffmann*. They wanted me to do *La Boheme* or *Tosca*, but those have been done so terribly well, and this is open to a lot of interpretations."

In learning to swim, John was diving into the deep end of the pool: *The Tales of Hoffmann* is a difficult opera, and one which courts some controversy among purists. A new edition of Offenbach's unfinished score had recently been published, eliminating the spoken dialogue of the traditional Choudens version. John would find himself immediately embroiled in a battle with the conductor, Carlos Kleiber, who insisted, against John's wishes, on sticking to tradition and using Choudens; Kleiber also rejected John's idea to cast a single singer in the part of Hoffman's three loves. It made for a quick lesson in the peculiarities of directing an opera: it is the conductor, not the director, who is the *maestro*, whose word is the ultimate law. For a man so desirous of final authority, John had some adjusting to do.

"Opera works in strange ways," said Eleanor Fazan, who'd choreographed the dance hall scene in *Yanks* and then arranged movement for *Hoffmann*. "What happens is that the director is in charge for the first two weeks. Then the maestro takes over and if he's in the mood and he's going to be horrid, he can come in and change everything. This has happened. With the maestro there's nothing you can do. He is number one."

In the power struggle that ensued, Kleiber eventually withdrew, and was replaced by Georges Prêtre, but he left his mark. Choudens was kept and the roles were indeed sung by different singers. Nevertheless, John managed to exert his own influence: he prevailed in cutting most of the spoken dialogue, an element of opera he frequently disliked. He also brought a very cinematic style to the production: several critics noticed the pastiche of Fellini's *Satyricon* in the Venice act, an allusion John acknowledged. But there was more, too: "You'll see a bit of Lotte Reiniger, a touch of *Caligari* perhaps, and one or two other silent films," John promised his audience. What he consciously stayed away from, he said, was the film version of *The Tales of Hoffman* by Michael Powell and Emerich Pressburger. "I'm one of their greatest admirers," he said, exaggerating a bit, "but *Hoffman* is the exception. It was hideously designed and equally hideously camped up."

Designing the production was something on which John spent considerable time and effort. "I worked with John on three operas, and we always planned out everything ahead of time," Eleanor Fazan said. "Nobody works like that in opera. With John, we had the model of the set, and we'd go through literally bit by bit. It was a surprise to some people in the cast because they were suddenly being given little things to do. Very few people notice this but you'd be amazed how in fact it adds to the whole. A little blind man going across the stage, tiny little things like that, that John had thought up."

Indeed, as I watched the videotape of *Hoffmann*, I was struck by all the bits of business going on among the people on stage. In the opening scene in the alehouse, waiters move about with platters; the patrons turn to each other, reacting to the leads. Clearly this is the stamp of a movie director. "I wanted to treat the chorus as individuals," John said, a viewpoint he had toward his film extras as well.

John knew enough to defer to Domingo: appropriately, when Domingo is on stage, all eyes are on him. He is the star. Having sung in two other *Hoffmann* productions that year, the tenor could have come across weary and bored, but John was successful in reinvigorating the work. Bernard Levin in *The Times* found Schlesinger's interpretation was "more interesting and coherent" than Jean-Pierre Ponnelle's production at the Salzburg Festival that summer, calling it "a dark, almost bitter reading that could fairly be described as more Hoffmann than Offenbach."

Or more Schlesinger. Hoffmann was, in fact, a soulmate in a shared love of the macabre, his nightmarish tales anticipating those of Edgar Allan Poe. "Those stories are fascinating," John said, "and they gave us a lot of ideas on how to approach the opera. So we've examined it a little more from Hoffmann's point of view than is normal."

The production was a spectacular triumph for all concerned, from its rich, sumptuous look, courtesy of William Dudley's sets and Maria Bjornson's costumes, to its stellar performances. "John brought so much to me, gave me such a gift," Domingo said, and indeed the notices he received following this production exalted him to new levels. "Surely he is the greatest lyric tenor now living," pronounced Bernard Levin. "Even Pavarotti seems to me, for all the caressing beauty of his voice, to lack the drama that Domingo's adds."

That the star would credit John as helping him achieve such drama is testament to how highly Schlesinger was held in esteem after the opera's premiere on 15 December. On the night of 2 January 1981, *The Tales of Hoffmann* was carried on a BBC live broadcast throughout Britain. Even more than his associate directorship at the National Theatre, John's association with the Royal Opera gave him a critical and artistic standing beyond the more garish world of the cinema. Again, had he wanted to, he could easily have had a distinguished career directing theater and opera in London, perhaps making the occasional film in America. But although he considered his work on *Hoffmann* to be an "extreme pleasure," the reviews were barely in before he was heading back to Hollywood to start *Honky Tonk Freeway*.

How does one begin to describe a movie featuring a nymphomaniac, a drive-through mortuary, crooked politicians, a pimp, a disco soundtrack and a water-skiing elephant?

"People were murmuring, 'Why is John Schlesinger making a film like this?'" remembered Jim Clark. "What they did not understand was that John's serious side was only one aspect of him. He had a wicked, impish, outrageous, naughty sense of humor. He thrived on the eccentricities of others. Give him an old woman and he'd put her on a walker or with a dog that required a leak."

"I like to laugh," John said, by way of explanation for choosing *Honky Tonk Freeway*. The script had been sent to him by the "very go-ahead" British producer Don Boyd, who'd made a name for himself with youth-oriented films but had also produced Derek Jarman's *The Tempest*. Boyd had the right combination of offbeat sensibility and artistic purpose that John enjoyed.

"I read the script twice and just said yes," John recalled. "I usually make snap decisions like that. It doesn't take me long to reject a script and it doesn't take me long to jump at something. I think you know instinctively when you've found something you like."

He'd always wanted to try a comedy. He once said he wanted to get around to every genre eventually in his career. It was part of him, that urge to explore, never to be typecast. But it seems to have been something more than that, too, an insight that only truly becomes apparent in retrospect: after the lukewarm response to *Yanks*, John began to fear he'd never top *Midnight Cowboy* or *Sunday, Bloody Sunday*. Nothing he could do would ever measure up. He'd tried, after all, with *The Day of the Locust*, and again with *Yanks*, and the critics had cut him down cold. His old internal voice, the one that told him he was a failure, that he couldn't compete with the intellectuals and the true artists, grew louder and more persistent. *Don't even try*, the voice was telling him. Stick to the commercial films, the crowd-pleasers like *Marathon Man*. You're judged by a different standard when you do them.

His friends defended John against such a charge when I suggested it to them. Many pointed out, quite truthfully, that the film industry by 1980 was no longer financing risky little intimate films like *Cowboy*. To stay in the game, John was forced to find projects that a studio would back. He himself would say that "after all the *sturm und drang* of trying to set up *Yanks*, it was such a relief to find something [*Honky Tonk Freeway*] that a company [EMI] was actually enthusiastic about."

Indeed, in 1980, six of the top ten films were comedies. It was the era of *Animal House, Airplane!, Porky's, Caddyshack* – wild, wacky farces with scatological humor and dumb sex jokes that John felt, with a little twist of his subversive British sensibility, he could do so much better. After all, American audiences liked the winking, mocking comedy of Monty Python and Benny Hill; why not jump into the fray and make a comedy that would finally show the world the naughty, playful side of John Schlesinger?

And it would also save him from any comparisons to his masterpieces. In his diaries he'd lament especially those reviews that asked "What happened?" to the man who made *Midnight Cowboy* and *Sunday, Bloody Sunday*. The reviews of *Locust* – a film, after all, into which he had poured his blood, sweat and tears – were more devastating to him than many people realized. They had sapped what little confidence he'd been able to amass during those peak years of 1969–1971. Now, in the aftermath, he'd rather try for commercial success than artistic greatness. Box office gold was precarious enough, but in 1980 it still felt easier to achieve than the critical acclaim of his earlier films.

The script of *Honky Tonk Freeway* was written by a young American playwright named Edward Clinton. His satirical take on the fits and foibles of American culture, from a couple of wisecracking nuns to a bickering family of four in a shag-carpeted trailer, appealed greatly to John. "I was in the cutting room during *Yanks*," Jim Clark recalled, "and John came in and said, 'I've found it! I've found my next film! It's an off-the-wall comedy.' We sat there and read the script and we just thought it was very, very funny."

A couple of Englishmen laughing at America. That would be the image, the perception around Hollywood. And where *Yanks* had been an American-subsidized film made in Britain, *Honky Tonk Freeway* was, in essence, a British film being made in America, thanks to Boyd's arrangement of financial backing from EMI. Its far-flung locations and enormous cast would rack up a cost of $24 million.

Hawk Koch came on board as an American co-producer. "John thought the script was very funny," he said. I asked him if he agreed. Koch paused. "I trusted John's vision."

"When John gave me the script to read," Childers remembered, "I asked him, 'Is this meant to be a comedy?' If so, there was absolutely nothing that was funny to me."

They got a terrific cast anyway: William Devane, in his third consecutive Schlesinger film; Beverly D'Angelo, who became a great friend; Hume Cronyn and Jessica Tandy; Beau Bridges; Teri Garr; Howard Hesseman. John even lured Geraldine Page into playing Sister Clarissa, and gave his chum Paul Jabara a more substantial part this time around, that of the songwriting cowboy who hauls a rhinoceros cross-country to Florida. Jabara also wrote several songs for the picture, including "Faster, Faster," the upbeat disco tune to which the final multiple-vehicle car crash on the Florida freeway is choreographed.

"It was a gas to make," Koch said. With locations ranging from New York to Arizona to Chicago to the long flat expanse of central Florida, with a cast of hundreds that included a rhino, an elephant and a lion, and with filming being done in all kinds of weather, the experience was bound to be, at the very least, memorable.

"We had so much fun out there," said Beau Bridges. "It wasn't easy. We were sitting in cars on the freeways in the blazing hot sun, but John turned it all into a party. What I remember most from the shoot is his full-bellied laugh."

"We had such a good time making that film," said Jim Clark. "Everyone was always having parties. That should have told us something was wrong. Filmmaking should be very intense. If making the film is a nightmare and you can't wait to be done, it's usually a brilliant film. On the other hand, if you're having so much fun making it . . ." His voice trailed off and he shrugged his shoulders.

In October 1980, nearing completion, John told a reporter: "I've never really enjoyed the shooting period of my films, and I was beginning to feel guilty that I was enjoying this one too much." Blowing up a portion of the Florida freeway added enough discomfort and nerves to put an end to the fun and games, however: "Now it's become more difficult," John said with a laugh, "and I feel better."

Here, as best as can be managed, is a description of the, er, plot: the town of Ticlaw, Florida, has bribed a state official for an exit off the new freeway, but the exit is never built. Fearful they'll miss out on the tourist trade, the residents of Ticlaw, led by their mayor-preacher-innkeeper William Devane, attempt all sorts of shenanigans to obtain their off-ramp, finally dynamiting the freeway and building one themselves. That stunt detours everyone into Ticlaw (and Devane's hotel), where the motley crew of characters we've been introduced to along the road finally converge and play out their parts. These include the alcoholic Tandy, the would-be children's writer Bridges, the nympho D'Angelo (carting an urn of her mother's ashes), and the henpecked husband Hesseman.

"I wanted to show the indomitability of a small town," said Schlesinger, attempting to give the farce some serious spin, "that determination to survive and keep itself on the map and not be obliterated. That's one of the things I admire about this country, even if it means bribery and corruption."

Comments before the film's release show John anticipated some negative reaction. "This is an affectionate comedy, remember," he told Rex Reed a year before the film premiered, while he was still sweltering on the highways of Florida. Elsewhere, he insisted, "It's not a snide look at anything. The dilemma of Ticlaw is perfectly universal. The faster that life goes, the more we bulldoze our way through."

Jim Clark said he should have known something was wrong when he showed rushes to his American crew in Sarasota and no one so much as cracked a smile. "They'd ask me why I was laughing," Clark said, "and I'd tell them, 'Because I think it's funny.'"

It was a gap that would not be bridged. In post-production, EMI was struck by a major financial crisis, which forced John to turn to Universal for distribution. Never having approved the original script nor seen any footage, executives at Universal were worried. To allay their concerns, Schlesinger and Clark screened some rushes for them; Clark said the execs weren't all that impressed, but John made assurances that the finished film would be hilarious. Ned Tanen, the brash young head of production at Universal, was John's friend and an occasional guest at Rising Glen. He told Schlesinger he had his trust.

"What happened next I'll never forget," Jim Clark said,

literally shuddering. "It was the most ghastly experience of my entire profession. No director of John's stature should ever be treated the way he was by those nervy suits."

The final print of *Honky Tonk Freeway* was screened in Universal's Hitchcock Theater for the entire studio brass. "Of course, nobody laughed," Clark said. "We went through the entire movie in silence, and in the end, people didn't know what to say. Everyone just walked out except for a few of the executives and their wives. They gathered around John, who was still sitting in the front row. And suddenly they began screaming at him. It was unbelievable, horrible. They were saying things like, 'This is anti-American, anti-religious. How could you have made such a thing?'"

Clark was sitting in back, watching all of this in horror. "I could see John's bald head, covered in perspiration," he said. "He just sat there. He couldn't move."

Clark's wife Laurence, an assistant editor on the film, was also present that day. "It was the first and only time I'd ever seen John totally defenseless, totally demolished," she said. "He was just so overcome. He didn't fight back." She remembered especially Kitty Hawks, Ned Tanen's wife, standing over John and berating him. "The ferocity of the attacks was really unbelievable."

Finally Tanen drew himself up tall and shouted that John was "disallowed" a preview of the film, which was scheduled for the next night. Schlesinger could manage no words in response. He just slunk off the lot as fast as he could.

At home, however, the rage finally kicked in. Tanen was a "fucking Nazi," John said, for canceling the previews. "Fuck 'em all," he told Jim Clark. "We'll have our own preview."

A screening was arranged in Seattle without Universal's

permission, with all of them checking into hotels under assumed names. John chose a theater where they'd get a large number of university students, who seemed to enjoy the film's more outrageous humor — Bridges walking barefeet through the spilled ashes of D'Angelo's mother, the elephant on waterskis — but not enough to relay raves back to the studio. The lukewarm response convinced John that maybe Universal was right, that the film needed to be fixed, so he consented to Clark working with a studio-appointed editor to recut the footage. A few weeks later, another preview was held in Phoenix, where it was booed off the screen. More editing, another preview in Dallas, and the boos were even louder. "The original film had actually gotten a better reaction," Clark said, "so we went back to that one."

Universal was forced to release the film in August, but "buried it as fast as it could," John said. Not fast enough, however, for the critics to miss getting their claws into it. "Sylvia Miles' poodle is alive and well," wrote Janet Maslin in the *New York Times*, "the one that appeared in *Midnight Cowboy* wearing false eyelashes and yapping nastily at everything in sight. Not that particular dog, perhaps, but certainly its attitude. John Schlesinger still thinks America is a crass, foolish, disagreeable place." Despite its anti-Americanism and rip-offs of *Nashville*, Maslin said the film had "gumption," but its structure was "a mess."

That was a good review. *Variety* asked why anyone would want to make a film so "devoid of human appeal." The *New York Post* blamed "too many cooks, some of them British," for diffusing the effect, and asked, "Besides, what's so funny about a small town in Florida ruined when an Interstate refuses to place an exit within 35 miles?"

"Americans just didn't get the joke," John said. The film was a flop of monumental proportions: it earned just $600,000 against its negative cost of $24 million.

It fared only a little better in Britain, where John hoped its humor might find a more receptive audience. Before its release, EMI chief Barry Spikings had found it amusing, John complained, but afterward he'd washed his hands of it. Making things worse, British reviewers seemed more interested in writing about the film's colossal failure in America than in critiquing it on its own merits. John wasn't surprised by the "bloodbath," given that "the film cost so much and the British industry is in such doldrums. 'Why, therefore,' they say, 'are so many millions being poured into a film that didn't even work in America?'"

Comparisons to *Nashville*, with its musical soundtrack and parallel storylines, were perhaps inevitable, but in truth *Honky Tonk Freeway* was more Schlesinger's *Heaven's Gate* – the legendary flop of the previous year that had effectively destroyed director Michael Cimino's career. John's career wasn't destroyed, but it was never the same again. Around Hollywood, *Honky Tonk* was viewed in much the same way as *Heaven's Gate* had been: a terrible betrayal of the industry. Schlesinger had betrayed them before, of course, but this was far worse than *The Day of the Locust*. For one thing, this new film wasn't merely attacking Hollywood, but America itself; for another – and surely this was what *really* offended the suits – *Honky Tonk Freeway* lost a whole load more money than *Locust* ever did.

After such legendarily bad reviews, it's hard to view *Honky Tonk Freeway* with any kind of objective eye, but in truth, it's not as bad as all that. John would, in fact, make worse films. The script isn't as terrible as critics made out (poor Edward Clinton never had another shot at a film) and actually contains some very funny lines: when, for example, Beverly D'Angelo, the buxom sexpot who hooks up with Beau Bridges, muses about her life, she says, "The International House of Pancakes has been the one consistent thing in my life." When a waitress carrying a platter of seafood asks, "Who gets the crabs?," she's answered by a group of gay men (the buff boys in the Jeep), who sing out, "We all do, sooner or later!"

The film's various narrative threads don't really lead to much of a payoff, hard as Schlesinger and Clinton tried to find one with the car crash and the stolen money going flying and the wild animals getting loose. But the real reason for the film's failure to find an audience lies in its defiance of social convention. Beau Bridges leaves his wife and kids for D'Angelo with nary a compunction. The young nun doffs her habit to become a hooker. Politicians bribe and swindle with impunity, and the traditional American family is literally blown apart in the end. With Ronald Reagan the new occupant of the Oval Office, such subversion was definitely not America's idea of commercial fare.

The man who, a decade before, had ridden the moment, who had walked in the center of his times, who had transformed the British cinema and helped bring the revolution to American shores, was now dramatically out of step. He would spend the rest of his life trying to catch up.

Sixteen

1981–1988

"Frightened of extraordinary passions and enthusiasms"

I was fast-forwarding through the videos of several of John's films, trying to determine in which ones he'd made his Hitchcockian walk-ons. Michael had named a handful, and I was trying to spot the scenes: there he was in *Darling*, the director sitting in the audience during the audition sequence. And there – I had to rewind just to be sure – he was in *Honky Tonk Freeway*, walking down a New York City street. In *Pacific Heights* he actually had a function, appearing for a moment as a possible villain until we realize he's just a guy in the elevator. He's easy to miss in *Billy Liar* as an Ambrosian officer and in *Far from the Madding Crowd* as a Wessex shepherd, but he popped right out at me in *Marathon Man*, as he climbed aboard a bus.

John Schlesinger had a good time making movies.

Watching his walk-ons is evidence of that. He liked to grumble about the production process, the struggles with his actors, the battles with the money men, but when he wasn't making a picture, he was miserable. And in the early 1980s, he spent a lot of time being miserable.

"Well, you don't have a flop the size and intensity of *Honky Tonk Freeway* and just roll with it," Childers said. "It was colossal. It became legendary in its failure."

But it wasn't just *Honky Tonk Freeway* that kept John off the screen for four years. Hollywood was metamorphosing into something different, something John, and many of his contemporaries, could not recognize. "Now here we are, twenty years after *Heaven's Gate*," Francis Ford Coppola told Peter Biskind (he might have said *Honky Tonk Freeway*). "Directors don't have much power anymore, the executives make unheard of amounts of money, and budgets are more out of control than they ever were. And there hasn't been a classic in ten years."

In his study of the decline of the Age of the Director, Biskind points out that much of it had to do with the personal excess of so many of its key players: "It would take a couple of years," he wrote, "for the topography of the post-New Hollywood landscape to emerge from the blizzard of coke." But the decline these auteurs faced in the 1980s was also due to factors far beyond any personal misbehavior of the Coppola-Friedkin-Polanski crowd. Hollywood, as ever, was about money, and the studios, for all their indulgence of a brilliant, risk-taking director's cinema, would stay committed only so long as it turned a profit. Stephen Spielberg might have stayed the course of small, edgy films like *Sugarland Express*, and George Lucas might have continued making dark, quirky pictures like *THX*. But instead they proved, with *Jaws* and *Star*

Wars, how much money the industry could *really* make if movies were sold not as films but as packages, as franchises, as merchandise.

"The mentality of the industry shifted," Bruce Vilanch said. "It became the era of the blockbuster. The only way to make big money was to make big pictures that opened wide and brought in a lot of money to justify what was spent on television advertising. The kind of picture John made best, adult dramas, became far less prized than an outer space franchise. It was pretty clear John was going to be doing *La Traviata* soon."

Maybe not *La Traviata*, but thank God for those operas. While so many directors crashed and burned, John had something to fall back upon, and his would be one of the few voices left sober enough to chide the industry on its increasing cravenness. "You've got to take risks," he said. "Only by taking risks do you make pictures like *Shampoo, Easy Rider, Midnight Cowboy*. When you make *Towering Inferno* and *Earthquake* . . ." His voice trailed off. "I don't want to say anything against them."

He didn't need to. And if he thought things were bad in 1976, a decade later the industry had undergone a complete transformation from the ground floor up. A new breed of blow-dried execs were now running the show, reading the *Wall Street Journal* ahead of *Variety*. "Hollywood has fallen into the hands of tough MBAs who are only concerned with the bottom line," said Andy Keuhn. "Not that the business didn't always care about the bottom line, but there's caring about it and not caring about anything but. You can care about the money and still care about films. Even Louis B. Mayer cared about the movies. You have a whole new generation of people running the studios who just don't care about film, who don't even go to the movies."

"The new executive breed are frightened of extraordinary passions and enthusiasms," John lamented. "The conglomerates — Gulf+Western, Coca-Cola, Trans-American — have now taken over so many of the companies that one's no longer dealing with those extraordinary crazy moguls who believed in the artist, but with frightened committees who are terrified of their own position."

"Like so much else in our culture," said Jerry Hellman, "movie-making became a feeding frenzy for fame and recognition." The studio execs "became less and less those creative passionate individuals" — the Nat Cohens, the Joe Levines, the David Pickers, the Arthur Krims, the Barry Dillers, the Bob Evanses — "who, however peculiar they were, really had an investment in film and a passion for the process."

John found himself more sympathetic to the idea of the old studio system as described to him by George Cukor. "Not that I ever knew the old days," he would muse, "but I feel that I would have preferred them infinitely to the Hollywood that now exists."

In the wake of the disaster of *Honky Tonk Freeway*, John retreated to London to lick his wounds. "I am so happy to be back in Europe and away from that malicious town," he wrote to a friend. And it was suddenly even more malicious: he was outraged by the scandalous coverage and speculation about the death by drowning, in November 1981, of his good friend Natalie Wood. Photographs Michael had taken of her were illegally acquired by the tabloids. "One of the last of the truly transcendent movie stars," John wrote in his diary.

He kept busy by remounting *The Tales of Hoffmann*, while

at the same time directing his third production for the National, Sam Shepard's *True West*. For Antony Sher, one of the play's stars, working with John was a childhood dream come true. "He was one of the reasons I wanted to come to London," the South African-born actor told me. "I confessed to him how important *Darling* and *Sunday, Bloody Sunday* had been in my adolescence in beckoning me towards England. Both are bleak but also foxy and attractive, playing a double game with you, which is absolutely John."

Such were attributes of *True West* as well: "It was not a surprise to me that John's theater was as good as his film," Sher said, "because his films were never just the pyrotechnics of film. They were always about the humanity of what was going on. *True West* is a violent, bleak story, but John trusted in the humanity, and really brought it out."

Schlesinger admired Shepard's hard-hitting play, a morality tale about two very different brothers: Austin, a Hollywood screenwriter, and Lee, a small-time criminal. The plot explores the duality of human nature and the instinctual capacity for violence. Sher played Austin; in preparation for the part, he spent time in Los Angeles, staying with Michael on Rising Glen (John was still keeping his distance from the film capital), and soaking up Hollywood ambience. The original choice for Lee was Michael Gambon, but the actor, according to John's diary, "walked out" after several rehearsals. It was much to the play's "eternal advantage," John opined, as Gambon's exit made room for Bob Hoskins, who, with Sher, made "the perfect team."

"Bob Hoskins and I came from such different places as actors," Sher said. "At that time, I was terribly technical and researched. Bob was much more instinctive. Animal. So different were we that, although everything was there, something wasn't. A certain chemistry. Now any other director would've accepted it. Technically we were doing it all. We were already in preview. The play was going fine. People were enjoying it. But John knew it could be better. At a certain preview he said to us, 'When I direct a film, sometimes I ask the actors to throw away the script once they know it, and to kind of improvise. So tonight will you play as if you've thrown away the script and are improvising it?' "

It was an extraordinary request: throw away the script without really throwing it away. "I'd describe it like free-falling," Sher said. "We did just what John asked and it was one of the most extraordinary nights I've ever had. We just threw away all the preconceptions and line readings and just redis-covered – which is what the best theater experience will do and the hardest thing to do when repeating something."

Audiences loved the play when it opened on 10 December 1981; it ran for nearly four months. The critics loved it, too, but the National seemed indifferent: John complained in his diary that the play was reconfigured in the schedule to end a week earlier than planned. "The lack of enthusiasm is extraordinary, though not totally unexpected," John said, blaming it on the fact that his cast wasn't an official National Theatre company. *True West* would be his last work for the National.

He seemed to be fighting everybody these days. In January he flew to Cape Town with Michael for a retrospective of his work, where he found the press more interested in asking him political questions – why he had agreed to come to South Africa when so many refused – than in talking to him about his films. He ended up feeling like a "political pawn" of the organizers, "overexposed and exploited." It was with great relief that he and Michael boarded the QE2, only to find all of his films had been packed in barely fastened cardboard boxes, and some of his belongings were lost.

They sailed to Singapore via Mauritania and Madras, with John revisiting some of the sites he remembered from his army days. With him was a script by a young writer named Steven Zaillian, an adaptation of Robert Lindsey's book, *The Falcon and the Snowman*. On the QE2, John read about Christopher Boyce and Daulton Lee, the American spies who'd gone to prison for selling secrets to the Soviet Union. Michael had been the one to turn him onto the project, and by February of 1982 John had come to agree that it was a fascinating prospect for a film. "It could be as exciting as *Marathon Man*," he said.

It would be the first project John produced himself. After *Honky Tonk*, few of the Hollywood money men were eager to get involved with a John Schlesinger film. "If we couldn't get anyone else," John said, "we'd do it ourselves." With Michael as associate producer, they began working with Zaillian, and found, much to their pleasant surprise, some preliminary interest from Fox. There was also an overture from Barry Spikings from EMI, all of which relieved John: "There was a moment," he admitted to a friend at the time, "when I thought I might never work [in film] again."

Michael would play an increasingly influential role in John's film career during the next several years. Some of John's friends questioned the wisdom of Michael's influence, judging that he steered Schlesinger away from smaller ideas toward riskier, big-budget projects with an eye chiefly on recapturing box-office success. But what Michael was actually doing was stepping into the void left by the Hollywood execs who, after *Honky Tonk*, couldn't run away from John fast enough. The wide-eyed youth who'd played Boy Friday on *Midnight Cowboy* was now a 37-year-old seasoned insider who had as many, if not more, contacts in the industry as John. He also had his lover's complete trust. After all, hadn't it been Childers who had found the solutions to so many problems on films in the past? The opening of *Midnight Cowboy* for one, the ending of *Day of the Locust* for another. "He is one of the few whose criticism I really take," John told his diary. "He's known me for so many years and seen me through thick and thin."

Two camps emerged: one, largely based in London and led by Noel Davis, who wanted John to work in the theater and on small British films, and the other, led by Childers, who weren't quite so ready to surrender John's place in a rapidly changing Hollywood film industry. By late 1982, these two forces were competing in a tug of war, with Schlesinger the rope, and that struggle would be represented by the work he'd do over the next couple of years. Despite all his grand pronouncements about never wanting to work in television, he accepted (on Noel's encouragement) an assignment to direct a small-screen version of Terence Rattigan's successful stage play *Separate Tables* for HTV, the independent television licensee for Wales and the west of England. It was a joint production with the American cable television company Home Box Office (HBO) and would be presented by the veteran producers Ely and Edie Landau.

What finally persuaded John, other than a lack of big-screen projects, to take on the television play was the coup of casting Julie Christie and Alan Bates in the lead roles. If the London contingent needed any evidence for their side of the argument, this film was it: John had returned to his roots in a quality project that, even if it didn't mean big money, was virtually assured of helping rebuild his critical reputation.

Separate Tables also featured Claire Bloom and Irene Worth and, if the production comes across as a little stagebound, the performances are so extraordinary they make up for it. Christie, first as the brittle, vain ex-model who comes to the Bournemouth inn in search of her former husband (Bates), and then, in the second part, as Worth's mousy, browbeaten daughter, is absolutely transcendent. Bates, too, is superb, as the down-and-out alcoholic in the first half and the pompous fraud in the second. Clearly, the old magic between John, Julie and Alan was still there. "Mr. Schlesinger's direction keeps a firm but unobtrusive grip on the play," wrote John O'Connor in the *New York Times*. "Mr. Rattigan and his reputation have been served well."

"It was a great joy to be reunited, after fifteen years, with Julie and Alan, who are both wonderful," John wrote. "It was my first attempt to do anything on videotape and interesting to have had the experience under my belt. We edited it at home in four weeks, which was quite tough to do, but in the final analysis I enjoyed it a lot."

Buoyed by this experience, John began work in December 1982 on another film for television, this time with a script by Alan Bennett, which marked his return to the BBC after 21 years. "It was like a time capsule going back to the BBC," he said. "Nothing had really changed."

The producer was Innes Lloyd, revered by colleagues as one of the fairest and most decent men in the television business. Lloyd was deeply committed and always judicious, with a roguish sense of humor that complemented John's own. Known as a mentor of writers, Lloyd had nurtured the careers of Andrew Davies, Don Shaw and Roger Milner, not to mention Bennett, who'd first worked with him in 1974 on *Sunset*

Across the Bay. He was that rare producer who understood the elements of good storytelling, disinclined to sentiment and impatient with ideology. Genial in person but ruthless with a script, Lloyd was remembered by Alan Bennett as the one person he could never recall ever being cross. "Conservative, clubbable, at ease with himself and the world," Lloyd was also, Bennett wrote, "tolerant, gentle, and lacking in any respect for the forms of things."

After being ground into hamburger by people for whom form – or formula – was sacrosanct, John was reborn under Lloyd. Indeed, their film together would be the first time since *Locust* that John re-experienced a simpatico three-way relationship between director, producer and writer.

The film was *An Englishman Abroad*. It had started life as a story Coral Browne had told, separately, to both Schlesinger and Bennett. In 1958, as a member of the Shakespeare Memorial Company (later the RSC), she had toured Moscow and met the exiled British spy Guy Burgess. An insightful, provocative dinner followed, during which they discussed ideas of loyalty, loneliness, and isolation. "The picture of the elegant actress and the seedy exile sitting in a dingy Moscow flat listening again and again to Jack Buchanan singing 'Who Stole My Heart Away?' seemed to me funny and sad," Bennett said – not to mention fodder for brilliant drama. With its small, intimate scope, John had immediately seen the encounter as a television film; Bennett was likewise inspired to adapt it as a play. With memories of their happy association trying to get *A Hatful of Rain* off the ground, John and Alan decided to make the film together, with Innes Lloyd signing on as an enthusiastic booster.

"Then we started talking about casting," Bennett said. "It was kind of funny because Coral at that time was in her [late] sixties and in the film she'd be in her late thirties, but neither John nor I dared to suggest anyone else play the part."

John was insistent that age didn't matter, and he was right: whether Coral was 30 or 60 when she met Burgess is irrelevant to the story. This was a meeting of minds and souls, not a love story: and besides, Burgess was homosexual. "I couldn't see anyone other than Coral playing the part," John said. "It would have been pointless."

Burgess presented a bit more of a difficulty, however. "He's very much an upper-class figure," Bennett said, "and I felt the actor we chose ought to be from that social sphere. It's a thing that would be more noticeable in England than America. John didn't feel as strongly about that and wanted to offer the part to Alan Bates. I came around to thinking that he was quite right in saying you should go for the actor not the class."

Bennett's script was one of "the best and wittiest" John had ever come across, he told friends. The playwright's words he regarded almost as gospel; there would be much less changing of the script than on his other films. Instead, the director concentrated on the visuals. Glasgow and Dundee stood in for Moscow and proved remarkably authentic. The town hall of Glasgow doubled very convincingly as the British embassy, and the bleak, gray textile mills of Dundee gave the film a genuinely Soviet industrial feel. John found a local community of Ukrainians who had the right looks and accent to play Russian characters. It broke the rules of Scottish Equity, but the director was insistent. "The most important thing to me was to get the detail right," John said.

Walking about Dundee with both Alans, falling into fits of laughter, John had an enormously happy time making the film, a critical healing experience after five years of Hollywood brutality. No quarrels with his crew, either, because they numbered so few; no one was jockeying for position or authority. "The crew were brilliantly organized," John recalled. "We had just three weeks and there was still time for fifteen takes."

The only tension was concern over Coral's health. Already suffering from the cancer that would claim her in 1991, the actress tired easily and needed frequent breaks to rest. John proved very solicitous: "She was a sick woman," he said, "and we had to look after her, so her state of mind and health were always of graver concern to us all than the actual problems of the film."

When the picture was screened for BBC officials and invited guests in the autumn of 1983, its witty dialogue prompted gales of laughter. "You couldn't hear half the jokes because you were still laughing at the previous ones," Bennett remembered. Great optimism prevailed, and when *An Englishman Abroad* was transmitted on 22 November, the reviewers were ecstatic. "Alan Bennett's recreation of Coral Browne's encounter with Guy Burgess has been turned by John Schlesinger into a beautifully controlled exploration of a secret life in a secret world," wrote Michael Church in *The Times*. "Alan Bates' portrayal of this moral outcast of the islands is as memorable a performance as one could wish."

American critics were equally as impressed. *Variety* called it "modestly conceived but richly textured," adding that "one is tempted to think that Schlesinger, who himself has been an Englishman abroad, warmed to the theme of cultural isolation and has consequently been inspired to make one of his best films."

At just 65 minutes it's hard to compare *Englishman* to the major features in Schlesinger's canon, yet there is no doubt it is a gem, at once haunting and droll, and sometimes – as that first BBC screening attested – laugh-out-loud funny. Just watch Browne as she realizes on stage that it was none other than the infamous Guy Burgess who'd burst into her dressing room looking for a place to be sick. Then there's the moment when Burgess' London tailor accepts a suit order with utter deadpan and typically English discretion: "Mum's always the word here," he tells Browne. "Moscow or Maidenhead, mum is always the word."

Browne proved Schlesinger and Bennett right: age has no bearing on the story, and being older and wiser may even have contributed to the actress' compelling portrayal of herself. Bates, after several bad films, found himself, like John, redeemed in public opinion. As he stands silently weeping to the music in a Russian orthodox church, all his brittle, ironic defenses disappear and we see the true face of loneliness and exile.

An Englishman Abroad was heralded as one of the best BBC films in recent memory, and John basked in the kind of critical acclaim he hadn't known since *Sunday, Bloody Sunday*. Free of a corresponding concern over box office, this was an unmitigated triumph. The film won a slew of BAFTA awards, including Best Single Drama, awarded to the director, while Bates and Browne took the top acting prizes. In addition, John shared the Broadcasting Press Guild Award with Alan Bennett and Innes Lloyd. "It restored a good deal of confidence," he said. "Certainly in my case, as I'd lost it."

Schlesinger's own years as an Englishman abroad had prepared him for guiding, with such an unerring eye, Burgess' story of cultural disconnection and loneliness. Loyalty to one's country was a concept that that had intrigued him ever since he'd taken up residence in Los Angeles, when he had been forced to confront his own allegiances and values. *The Falcon and the Snowman*, the script of which he was studying while making *Englishman*, was another treatise on the subject of spying; in the early 1980s, the ideas of patriotism, citizenship and betrayal were in the forefront of his mind.

It was no coincidence that such thoughts should come at this particular stage in John's life. In a broader sense, the concept he was grappling with wasn't so much about disloyalty to one's country, although that was a superficial consideration; rather, it was the larger ideas of challenging assumptions and defying authority, basic tenets of John's existence since he was a child. This was the man, after all, who had made *Sunday, Bloody Sunday*, and other films that subverted the norm and over-turned old bromides, and who, in a more rebellious decade, had been lauded for doing so. But in the era of Margaret Thatcher and Ronald Reagan, such an anti-establishment worldview had gone decidely out of fashion. Is it any wonder that John's thoughts, consciously or not, now turned toward stories of those who sought to undercut, overthrow, devalue, debunk?

He was fascinated by the story of Christopher Boyce and Daulton Lee, two friends from Palos Verdes, California, former altar boys who, for different reasons, had betrayed their country. Boyce, a former CIA employee, had done so with a sense of purpose, with a desire to enforce some balance upon a system he saw as inherently flawed. Lee, on the other hand, had gone along almost as a joyride, intoxicated by the kind of money that could be made from the enterprise – a very capitalistic attitude, in fact. Like Burgess, neither Boyce nor Lee is essentially a villain; certainly, John didn't see them that way: "I know there are people who feel that selling government secrets is the worst type of crime imaginable, worse than cold-blooded murder or the rape of a child and therefore no time should be wasted – string them up or let them rot," John said. "Well, I don't know."

In *An Englishman Abroad*, Guy Burgess admits, "I can say I love London. I can say I love England. I can't say I love my country because I don't know what that means." Alan Bennett would claim those thoughts as his own, and indeed believed they were shared by many of his countrymen: "There is a sense that an ironic attitude towards one's country and a skepticism about one's heritage are a part of that heritage. And so, by extension, is the decision to betray it. It is irony activated."

In spite of the browbeating given to *Honky Tonk Freeway*, John was once again tweaking the values of middle America. "I always felt the Christopher Boyce character in *Falcon* was really the voice of John," said Wally Nicita, the film's casting director. "It was John questioning the black-and-white world that America loves to live in."

Screenwriter Steven Zaillian remembered John's enthusiasm for the subject. "We had a lot of meetings up at his house. We talked about the story over and over and over. He was looking to me for the truth in the culture of the story because I was more familiar with it than he was. I was the same age as the characters in the film. I was an American. One thing that he always used to say was that Americans have no sense of irony. Now, John's films have always had a kind of an irony that was very close to his sensibility and his personality, and it was very frustrating to him when that wasn't recognized."

With Zaillian, John found his last perfect writing

partnership. Young and eager, without as yet any real credits behind him, Zaillian was happy to collaborate, to listen and to learn, to participate in what was Schlesinger's favorite aspect of filmmaking: the "what if" stage, the time when the director cross-pollinated his ideas with those of his writer. "He spoiled me forever," Zaillian would say. He would go on to write, among others, *Schindler's List*, *Searching for Bobby Fischer*, and *Gangs of New York*, but never quite rediscovered the magic of his first film experience again. In a letter to John he later reflected on the creative process and what Schlesinger had taught him: "Anything we could imagine was possible. Creativity without the annoyances of reality. Just the story and the two of us. Dreaming."

The script was completed in late 1983; then came the truly difficult part. Acting as their own producers, John and Michael had to convince a studio to back the film. Fox had withdrawn its interest, so they struck a deal with Hemdale Film Corporation, then in the midst of a prosperous working relationship with Orion Pictures (*The Terminator*, *Platoon*). "I wanted to work with John Schlesinger," said Mike Medavoy, one of Orion's founders. "What I had always admired about John was his honesty. What you saw was what you got."

Timothy Hutton, then riding a crest of popularity with *Ordinary People* and *Taps*, was cast as Boyce and threw himself into researching the part. He got to know the real Christopher Boyce, visiting him in jail, sometimes speaking to him on the telephone from the set. John, concerned with "objectivity," kept his own contact with Boyce to a minimum. He also didn't want to be hemmed in by a strict adherence to facts: "There was no way we could keep slavishly to the truth," John explained, "because of the problems of condensing time, of amalgamating characters, and having to take liberties with what they actually said."

More difficult was the casting of Daulton Lee. "He represents an outrageous fantasy," John said. As described in the book, Lee was a loveable psychotic, a crazy man who inspired a mix of loyalty and loathing in those who knew him. In some ways, Lee reminded John of Paul Jabara, unpredictable, volatile, difficult – tons of fun but also hopelessly addicted to drugs. In fact, while Boyce was the "Falcon" because of his love of the ancient art of falconry, Lee was the "Snowman" because he trafficked in "snow," or cocaine.

John settled on Sean Penn for the role. He was taking a chance. Although Penn had a budding reputation as a brilliant, edgy young actor, his best known roles at that point had been the stoned-out Jeff Spicoli in *Fast Times at Ridgemont High* and the soldier-boy hero in the sentimental teen romance *Racing With the Moon*. It was, however, Penn's performance as the tough reform-school kid in *Bad Boys* that finally convinced John. "He saw something in Sean," said Medavoy. "I think he knew this guy was going to be one of our great actors."

Yet the experience of working with Penn would turn out to be the most testing of John's career, at least until Rupert Everett came along. "Sean and John were like oil and water," said Nicita. "Very combustible, because John had a very short trigger and Sean was playing a provocative character. He did everything he could to be a bad boy."

Much of the film was shot at Mexico City's Churubusco studios, chosen because it was cheap and the budget from Orion was stingy ($11.5 million). Almost from day one, Schlesinger and Penn clashed. John's diaries recount a steadily deteriorating relationship between director and star. "Sean tried heroin over the weekend and missed rehearsal because the effects were so bad," John recorded at the start of filming in December 1983. "Tuesday he was out of control. In over twenty years of directing I've never known a day quite like it. Yet I don't want a head-on collision with him because we've four months to shoot."

Penn was indulging in much the same kind of "method" acting that Dustin Hoffman had used on *Marathon Man*, inhabiting the character of Daulton Lee to search out experiences, sometimes mind-altering ones, that would give him insights into Lee's world. But perhaps he lacked the sense of humor about the process, John said, which had made Dustin's "methodology" bearable.

The problems only escalated from there. "Sean throws a childish fit when he's not allowed to do a stunt himself," John wrote in February. "His pique lasts all night. Immensely boring. I can now barely bring myself to talk to him."

He didn't need to: assistant director Patrick Crowley remembered Penn telling John at one point: "Just direct. You don't have to tell me how to act."

"John was crushed," Crowley said. "He had a whole bag of insights into that character that he was never able to get out. Here he was, known as an actor's director in both England and the States, with people going out of their way to work with him. If Sean had been just some pretty boy, somebody who was limited as an actor, it wouldn't have been so distressing to John. But here was this clay that John really wanted to work with but he just couldn't get through."

Penn, for his part, felt that he needed to protect the character from a script that seemed too focused on making commentary about America: "The American nuances got over the top and it became storytelling in quotes." He said with some amusement that after the first two weeks he and John no longer fought "because we never spoke again for the whole picture. I'd say to the guy standing next to John, 'Could you tell John . . . ?' and John would say, 'Could you tell Sean . . . ?' It was comic."

The most infamous tale from the set concerned Sean turning over a table in anger, or pushing John into it, or something like that. "Here's what happened," Penn told me. "One day I got upset and slapped a Scrabble game off the table. A couple of pieces hit John. I walked off the set and I heard John say, 'You are the most unprofessional actor I've ever worked with.' And I called Dustin who felt envious that I had stolen his throne."

To his diary John confided: "I have never disliked working with anyone more, including Atherton and Brian Cox."

In the beginning, it was quite the opposite with Hutton who, John observed, had "wonderful inner qualities as an actor." But soon a rivalry between the two actors had bubbled to the surface. Like Boyce and Lee, Hutton and Penn had been boyhood friends. But a couple of months into the shoot, Hutton could see he was being upstaged. John recorded in his diary how, after one scene, he had to walk Hutton around the set "to try and soothe him down and bolster his confidence and pay attention to him."

A few days later, John called Penn into his camper to "try to have a reasonable and private conversation with him . . . He seems obsessed with the idea that Tim is jealous of his showy part, which may in part be true."

Once, when Hutton got angry about what he saw as preferential treatment to Penn, he crumpled up his script and tossed it at the crew. "They're both neurotic children," John lamented. "I'm too bored with kindergarten to go on."

So unbearable did the tension on the set become that John began to feel physically sick. When Hutton came into the director's camper one day to complain about something, John found he had "to throw up — fortunately just out of sight."

"Look, it was miserably hot down there," Childers said. "People were acting up all over the place." Drug use was rampant, he said, and conditions at the studio and at their lodgings were primitive. Then an epidemic of bronchial infection laid everyone low for several weeks. "It was not a happy experience for anybody."

For the first time, John and Michael found themselves battling each other on the set. No longer were they just artists in pursuit of a creative vision; now they were producers as well, with all the financial and logistical headaches that came with producing a film. Working six days straight, sometimes seven, the crew finally approached John and asked for time off. John whipped out his wallet in anger and tossed it dramatically across the set. He was responsible for any overages, so days off would essentially be paid out of his own pocket. "But he understood the dynamic of the crew," said Pat Crowley. "He knew we needed time off. He realized people were starting to fall apart."

At the end of the shoot, however, Penn seemed conciliatory. He told Childers that he "really felt positively" about John. After hearing the comment, John wrote in his diary, "He must have been drunk." But later Sean would repeat the statement at the airport as he and Childers headed back to Los Angeles.

The reflective comments he made to me — saying he'd get down on his knees in gratitude if he had the chance to work with Schlesinger again — seem to suggest he was being genuine in his remark to Childers. "Looking back on it," Penn said, "John's singular vision was uncompromising. Whatever his mission was on that picture is the stuff that we as actors miss so much today with most directors. I was aware of that even then. He was, at his best, as good as a filmmaker gets. Let's face it. John had a set of balls on him."

W hat made the Mexican production even more difficult was the news that reached John on 25 January 1984, that his father had died in London at the age of 87. For the past few years Bernard Schlesinger had become increasingly frail. John confided to Gary Shaw that he feared the same fate: losing control of his body, being unable to walk, suffering incontinence. "Pray God that is not me," he said, which recalled the similar prayer he uttered after Jo Janni's stroke.

Trapped in Mexico, he was devastated not to be able to make it back to England in time for Bernard's funeral. The man whose pride and approval John had so long desired, so long wondered about, would go to his grave without his son in attendance.

Possibly even more difficult for John was being separated from his mother during this time. Winifred's own health had declined, and after her husband's death she seemed to lose all interest in life, according to John's diary. He would ring her at those odd moments of overlap between London time and Mexico City time, fretting about whether she could hear him, if she knew who was calling, if his words cheered her in any way. He agonized over her "terrible decline." Indeed, Winifred Schlesinger would not long outlive her beloved husband. She died in 1986 at age 89.

John was now the patriarch of the family, a role his nieces and nephews recalled with great affection. He doted on them, proving enormously generous with money and counsel. His brother, Roger, said he thought sometimes John mused about what it might have been like to have children of his own. Certainly his role of caretaker extended to his gay family as well: Michael, Noel, others. Sometimes it was a burden. In his diary John recounted with some annoyance having to bail Noel out of a possible bankruptcy, asking, "Why is he incapable of managing his affairs?"

But any burden in supporting family, gay or straight, was offset by the sense of community he fostered; it was far preferable to being alone, a recurring fear in his diaries. "There were always people about for whom John was a kind of godfather," said one friend. "He was the lord and master of the house, the provider. Sometimes he'd have to kick out a few 'hangers-on,' but mostly it was a family of friends who really cared about each other and, of course, about John. He felt good having people around."

With *Falcon* in post-production, John directed another opera at Covent Garden, Richard Strauss' *Der Rosenkavalier*, which opened in December 1984 starring Kiri Te Kanawa. Once again, John brought a filmic eye to the proceedings, a perspective not missed by his diva: "He certainly seemed to have a very cinematic view of the production," Dame Kim remembered. "He saw it all on a very grand scale. As a cast we found his sighting of the audience was not where we were used to it, and he wanted us often to be singing in the opposite direction to where the audience were, which took some getting used to."

As in *The Tales of Hoffmann*, John had plenty of instruction for his chorus; a videotape of the opera revealed that even behind a glass door, while Aage Haugland as Baron Ochs takes center stage, chorus members are engaged in bits of business. Few in the audience would have been able to see them, yet it added to the overall sense of activity and spectacle. And once again, John got high marks from the critics: Irving Wardle wrote "Mr. Schlesinger has wrought well with a production that will endure."

The notices for *Falcon*, however, which premiered in the U.S. in January 1985, were not so unanimous. Richard Corliss in *Time* said he missed the "wry, rueful way" John had handled the subject in *An Englishman Abroad*. Rex Reed, usually squarely in Schlesinger's corner (indeed, he was the only major critic to like *Honky Tonk Freeway*) summed up the core of much of the criticism: "If these guys disgraced their families, ruined their lives, and sullied their flag because one needed money for dope and the other had some naïve prejudice against the CIA, then I'm not sure they're worth making a movie about. I'm not talking banner-waving patriotism here. I'm talking about no trace of missing honor. They espouse no cause, they believe in nothing."

That's the fundamental flaw of the film. What really motivates these guys? We never really understand. We don't see the conflict. At least Guy Burgess, in Alan Bennett's script, ruminates on cause and effect. Chasing after a thriller – and box office success – John tried to shape *Falcon* more like *Marathon Man* than *An Englishman Abroad*. And on that level, he succeeded, at least partially. *The Falcon and the Snowman* is an exciting film, with excellent performances and some splendid plotting. The revelation, as John expected, was Sean Penn, a whirlwind of destructive energy on the screen. All that methodology and misbehavior in Mexico apparently worked to his advantage, because his presence commands our full attention. It's a bravura performance, haunting and disturbing, solidifying Penn's place in the ranks of the finest movie actors of the late twentieth century.

Certainly *Falcon* is the apex of Schlesinger's "second tier" films. Janet Maslin agreed, calling it John's "best work in a long while"; her colleague at the *New York Times*, Vincent Canby, reacted almost as positively, calling it "effective entertainment, a scathing social satire . . . [it] has the effect of being less about the vagaries of international espionage than about the all-pervasive second-rateness of United States Government functionaries and of the society that produced Boyce and Lee."

In the face of flag-waving Reaganism, John was once again thumbing his nose at the zeitgeist. Sean Penn was right: he *did* have a set of balls. And for a brief, heady couple of weeks, his defiance seemed to be paying off: *Falcon* opened very strong, debuting with $2.3 million at just 265 theaters, an auspicious per-screen average of nearly $9,000. For its first week of release, it was the second highest-grossing film in America, bested only by *Beverly Hills Cop*. Orion heralded its success in a full-page ad in *Variety*, proclaiming "The Falcon Soars!"

In its second week, however, a downward slide began: the picture dropped to fourth place, overtaken by *A Passage to India* and *The Killing Fields*. By the third week, with the opening of *Witness*, Schlesinger's film began to plummet steadily. It would end up making just $7.7 million in 1985; it would take a few years to make back its full cost, and John never really saw much profit.

"It was too ambitious," he said. "We didn't have time within the context of the movie to deal sufficiently with Hutton's youth, to set up the complexity of his motives." Artistically, that was indeed the film's chief flaw, yet its fatal mistake was to dare offer a challenge to the prevailing political winds. Where *Midnight Cowboy* had pegged the spirit of the times with uncanny precision, *The Falcon and the Snowman* was further proof that the old iconoclast was decidedly out of step with his audience. Part of him, of course, desperately wished to find the pace, to fall back into step, for that would have meant career security; but another part deplored the conventional wisdom of the 1980s with its emphasis on conformity and capitalism. "How can I make movies about *that*?" John lamented.

Yet for a moment he was back in favor in Hollywood; *Falcon* had performed respectably enough to erase memories of *Honky Tonk Freeway*, giving him the kind of comeback denied to Michael Cimino. In January 1985, coinciding with the release of the film, John was feted in a star-studded affair at the Museum of Modern Art in New York. Kathy Larkin of the *Daily News* gushed over "stretch limousines the length of city buses rimming the curbside" as celebrities arrived for the gala. Paparazzi snapped photographs of John flanked by his stars, past and present: Timothy Hutton and Lori Singer from *Falcon*, Dustin Hoffman, Richard Gere. Not to mention the gossip columnist's grab-bag of others – Diane Keaton, Bob Fosse, Sting, Jonathan Demme, Brian De Palma, Penny Marshall, Bianca Jagger, Nora Ephron – once again eager to be seen beside the director of *Midnight Cowboy*.

Around the same time, at an annual lunch for foreign directors given by the Directors Guild, John received a hearty round of applause from the many old-timers in attendance. In 1969, they had looked at him askance as a radical upstart, but he had won them over with his charm and with his movies. Sitting next to the veteran Rouben Mamoulian, John conversed warmly with Stanley Donen, Robert Wise, Fred Zinnemann.

He may not have been a fan of their pictures growing up, never citing American directors as influences, but he came to admire many of them as people, and some, like William Wyler, prompted him to reassess their work and influence. "I miss George Cukor," John wrote in his diary about his friend who had died in 1983. "It's the first time I've attended this lunch without him."

Old Hollywood was dying off, and New Hollywood was finding it difficult to hang on. John Schlesinger would make only two more pictures that he actually developed himself. The first was *The Believers*, which he plunged into immediately after *Falcon*. Again, it was Michael's influence; Childers would, in fact, step up from associate producer to producer on this one. Orion was once again backing the film, after Fox sent it into turnaround. Mike Medavoy remembered liking the initial idea very much, even if John admitted to a friend that the book on which it was based (*The Religion* by Nicholas Conde) "wasn't of the first class, which means that I can't be judged against a literary masterpiece." The script didn't turn out much better. John found himself constantly rewriting with screenwriter Mark Frost (from the television series *Hill Street Blues*). By the time they finished production, John said, "there wasn't a white page to be found in the script."

With its ritual sacrifice, voodoo curses, and insects crawling out of its leading lady's cheek, *The Believers* was, in truth, the flat-out horror picture John had been itching to do ever since he first rigged up that gibbet for *Black Legend* nearly forty years earlier. He was fascinated by the glimpse into Santeria, the Cuban-Puerto Rican religious mix of island voodoo and Catholicism, hiring a Santerian priestess, Carla Pinza, to play a small part in the film as well as serve as technical advisor.

Touring through East Harlem, he met with many of the sect's adherents, learning that Santeria was about more than just "trances and cutting up chickens." Some of the crew was spooked: a few walked off the set, while others, including John, wore beads given them by Carla Pinza to ward off evil spirits.

Principal roles were played by Martin Sheen and Helen Shaver; filming began in New York then shifted to Toronto. Sheen was aware of deficiencies in the script, as was John: "It was a constant concern," Sheen said. "He didn't have the confidence in the script that a director needs to have."

Still, all along, John believed that he was making a sure-fire commercial hit. For the first time in his interviews with the media, John didn't try to justify making a genre film. Like *Rosemary's Baby*, it was a horror film, he said, no more, no less, simply done with compelling style. Yet there was a sense that, as much fun as it might be, he didn't want to be accused, as he had been before, of "squandering" his talent. To Gene Phillips, he wrote in January 1987, "I am contemplating a couple of British projects, as I rather want to come back here and make a small film. As *The Believers* was one for 'them,' it is time I did one for 'me.'"

Such words, while not without truth, did position him rather high-mindedly with a writer who frequently reviewed his films and had written a book on his career. If *The Believers* was merely one for "them," as John seemed to want people to think, then he couldn't be held to as high a standard when it was judged.

But, as ever, there remained a part of him that might have preferred to continue making fun thrillers like this one, working with spider wranglers who blew the furry creatures out of a tube and into the faces of the actors. John loved antics like that. The truth is *The Believers* was as much for him as it was for "them." But where the macabre, suspenseful moments of *Marathon Man* had been written and executed with stunning precision, the whole hodgepodge of *The Believers* was doomed by a script that went nowhere, that seems merely an exercise in spectacle. It has great atmosphere, and the opening scene, in which a woman is electrocuted in her kitchen, is gripping, but most of the film is such a chaos of style and form that it's often embarrassing to watch.

"I hate it when John Schlesinger tries to get down and dirty," complained David Denby in *New York* magazine after *The Believers* was released in June. "The director of *Billy Liar*, *Midnight Cowboy* and *Sunday, Bloody Sunday* brings less skill to such genre assignments than a hack director who may really believe in what he's doing." Pondering the beetles that eat through Helen Shaver's cheek, Denby mused: "I wonder if these are the opportunities actors long for when they work with a man who is supposed to be a 'major director'?"

The film was universally panned. Opening in fifth place, John was again trounced by Eddie Murphy, with *Beverly Hills Cop II*; such other horror offerings as *The Witches of Eastwick* and *Predator* ranked higher than *The Believers*. Bad word of mouth spread fast; by its second week the film dropped to sixth, below *Benji the Hunted*. After that, it was in freefall, though in the end, it did only slightly worse business than *The Falcon and the Snowman*.

With the utter failure of *The Believers*, John lost any chance of redemption Hollywood may have been willing to grant him after *Falcon*. If there had been a moment when he might have reclaimed a position of influence in the American cinema, it was now gone. In an interview with *American Film* magazine at the time, he was asked what had made him switch from his earlier films, "which were more directly about human relationships" to his current "action pictures." John bristled. "Are they totally action-oriented?" he replied. "I don't think they are. In all my films, there is some kind of personal relationship going on."

To prove it, his next film was *Madame Sousatzka*, a much more satisfying coda to Schlesinger's days of developing his own projects. It was a project suggested by Robin Dalton, a former literary agent who had produced a small film in Australia, *Emma's War*, starring Lee Remick, and was now looking to move into larger features. Dalton was convinced of the cinematic possibilities of Bernice Rubens' novel. The story explored the triangular relationship between a gifted young piano student, his eccentric and possessive teacher, and his lonely, single mother who is afraid of losing him. John immediately recognized some shared sensibility with the project. "Music has always been very much a part of my life," he said. "Second, I've always liked extreme characters. I liked that it was about older people looking back and a younger person completely on the brink of both a career and awareness."

From the start, he was passionate about the project. So thoroughly did he enlarge upon the basic material that he was given a writing credit along with Ruth Prawer Jhabvala, the screenwriting partner of the Merchant-Ivory team, just off *A Room With a View*. It was John's idea to change the student in the film from a ten-year-old Jewish boy to a fifteen-year-old Indian immigrant. "Up-aging" the boy, John said, allowed an element of sexual tension to be added to the script, explaining the young man's occasional wandering interest and layering another dimension onto the character of Madame Sousatzka, whose involvement with her students was already extreme, bordering on obsession.

As the larger-than-life figure, John cast Shirley MacLaine, an inspirational choice. MacLaine was the key that allowed Dalton to secure financial backing from Cineplex-Odeon, the American company behind Martin Scorsese's *The Last Temptation of Christ* and Paul Newman's production of *The Glass Menagerie*. Once again, John was making a film in Britain with a largely British crew but without a penny of British money. The budget for *Madame Sousatzka* was set at £3.5 million – a shoestring when one remembers that *Yanks*, a full decade before, had been made for about the same cost. "We took what we could get," John said plainly.

He'd call *Madame Sousatzka* his "woman's picture," because producer, screenwriter and star were all women. His last go-round with a female screenwriter had been rife with conflict, but Jhabvala proved a happy and engaging collaborator. And while some of John's friends wondered about his famous aversion to women in authority, *Madame Sousatzka* turned out to be a thoroughly enjoyable collaboration for all concerned.

In addition to MacLaine, John cast Twiggy as a sexy upstairs neighbour and, in her third Schlesinger vehicle, Peggy Ashcroft as the aristocratic Lady Emily. "What a trio!" John crowed to another chum. "It's great fun and lovely to be working at home again." For the pivotal part of the young student John chose Navin Chowdhry, a young actor making his screen debut, and as his mother, Shabana Azmi, a top box-office draw of the Indian cinema.

Production began in September 1987. "Shirley MacLaine arrived last week and threw herself in body and soul trying to get it right," John wrote to a friend.

He wasn't kidding. "I am going to channel Sousatzka," MacLaine announced on the first day of shooting. "I am going to throw her up to the universe and let her play herself through me."

I could imagine John's wry, mocking grin, but MacLaine insisted that he was utterly fascinated by her process. "I told him I was using the body movement of Bella Abzug and the history of my relationship with my classical Russian ballet teacher. He was fine with all that. [Our collaboration] was more of a personal synergy over wine and cheese. I used to love watching him with his pigeon-chested kind of posture and he would just enjoy his wine and cheese over lunch and we'd talk about the world."

And when filming was complete, MacLaine said, he was just as fascinated with the process of how she let Sousatzka go. "I remember the last day, when we were doing my close-up watching the boy play – a five-minute close-up. John finally said, 'Wrap,' and Sousatzka just left me. Immediately, I got the flu, a 103-degree temperature, and John was very intrigued. He was very open-minded about the technique I had used of just channeling her basically and he wanted to know, 'So now she's left and you are sick. Why?' I didn't know why but we talked about it. It fascinated him."

"John was so determined to really make a good picture," said Twiggy. "He paid a lot of attention to the script and the performances. It was such an honor to work with him."

"It's gone pretty well," John acknowledged to a friend near the end of production. "But nowadays I hesitate to make any kind of prophecy as people told me *The Believers* was the best thing since sliced bread, and look what happened to that!" That beleaguered film had just opened in England after nearly a year's delay, and John felt the critics were "particularly vicious and personal." He was "battered and bloodied," he reported, "but unbowed."

The first major screening of *Madame Sousatzka* was held at the Venice Film Festival on 4 September 1988. It was clearly being touted as an "art film," with the next screening at the Toronto Film Festival a week later. It finally went on limited release in the United States during the second week of October. Not until the following March did it open in England, when it was chosen for a Royal gala performance with the Queen Mother and Princess Margaret in attendance. John reported to a friend that they "seemed to enjoy it a great deal."

But very few people ever saw *Madame Sousatzka*. Critics were largely unimpressed: Glenn Wein in the influential gay newspaper the *New York Native* called it "Madame Shnoozeatska." Janet Maslin reckoned the film was as much an antique as the title character herself. Stanley Kauffman took a broader look: "The once-interesting Schlesinger continues his descent with this crumbly-stale tearjerker. Earlier in his career he sometimes overreached and fumbled. No longer. *Madame Sousatzka* is so comfily trite that Schlesinger, once intelligently ambitious, seems only cynical."

As the final film of his "second tier" period, *Sousatzka* resembles his first, *Yanks*: lovely to look at it, with engaging performances, hard to dislike. But it attempts nothing new, offers no surprises, fails to challenge in any way. *Madame Sousatzka* opened in the United States on just twenty screens. It barely registered in the weekly box office receipts. Three weeks later, Universal, its American distributor, gave it a slightly wider release, with 74 screens. But without much of a buzz there was never any reason to expand it beyond that. The film ended up making just $1.4 million in the U.S. domestic market, John's worst showing since *Honky Tonk Freeway*.

Kauffman was wrong. John didn't make *Sousatzka* with any cynical motive, churning out a "feel-good" movie in a desperate gamble to recapture box-office success. The film was, plainly and simply, another piece of chamber music – quite literally this time. He made the picture because the subject interested him. He made it because he wanted to work in England. He made it for exactly the opposite reason Kauffman and others suggested. He made it because he was tired of chasing after the American dream of success, which had eluded him now for twelve years. He made it because he *could*.

"I must confess I haven't had such a good time making a film for many years," he wrote to a friend. "*Sousatzka* was very close to my heart and to my experience, so it was largely a labour of love."

It is at least a film about human relationships, about the ways in which people love and live with each other. Many directors have made far worse pictures as their last projects. And although John would direct another seven films, some of them excellent, *Madame Sousatzka* marked the end of an era. From now on, John Schlesinger would be a director for hire.

Seventeen

"Well, of course, he's a queen"

The last time I saw John Schlesinger was on 2 July 2003, a very hot day in Palm Springs. He was sitting inside, in the air-conditioning, but still had a view of the mountains. Although I knew he had reverted to silence, I'd made the drive out from Los Angeles to see him anyway. I was getting ready to start writing this book.

"John," I said, sitting beside him, "I'd like to share with you some of the points I'll be making in the book. Is that okay?"

He looked at me with that halfway glance of his, his head slumped down over his chest. No reply; not that I expected one. If he didn't want to be bothered, he'd start making that motion with his hand against the side of his head or he'd keep his eyes defiantly closed. Until I had such a sign, however, I figured I'd plow on with my notes.

"Well, in no particular order," I began, "I suppose I'll talk about your fascination with human relationships, how your films were about people on the outside, figures pushed to the edge in some way . . ." I studied him to see if he was listening. I thought he was. "I'll talk about survival, how that mattered to you, how it informed your choices, in life and in art. I'll talk about the idea of half a loaf, that you believed it was sometimes – maybe most of the time – the best that we could expect from life."

Michael had joined us, sitting behind John, his hand on his partner's shoulder.

"Then there's the idea that you never saw yourself as an artist out struggling at the end of your rope," I continued. "How you had little patience for pretentious people, how you loathed intellectuals, how you thought too much theory and too much arty-farty talk was a lot of stuff and nonsense – that you wanted, first and foremost, to tell a good story."

I checked to see if there was any flicker in his eyes. Maybe. Who could be sure?

"It was always the story that mattered to you," I went on. "Not just on film but in your life. You always had a brilliant sense of story. Yours is a good one, John. Your story. No great dramatics, just a life lived well."

The ending of that story, however, I still wasn't so sure about, how all the various pathways of his life had led here to this point. What these last two years meant still wasn't clear to me, but there was no question his life had been a good run.

"You're a man whose story tells us a great deal about the times you lived in," I said. "Not to mention how you moved with your times, John. How you and Michael lived as an openly gay couple, how you never tried to disguise who you were, even before there was an established precedent on how to be 'out.'"

"We're rather proud of that," Michael said softly, looking at John.

"I'm not going to sugarcoat anything," I added quickly. "To do that removes the life of a story, the very humanness you fought so hard for in your films. But no matter the highs and lows, your story, and yours and Michael's, will have resonance for many."

John was still silent. But he was alert and watching me. I had no idea whether my words were making sense to him, or if they were merely sounds to him now, like the static on a radio.

"I don't know if you'll still be here when the book comes out, John," I said, quieter now, "but I want you to know what a privilege it's been working with you, having the opportunity to tell your story. I'll be back in September sometime, and I should have a good chunk done by then. I'll read you some pages, see what you think."

There was nothing. Nothing except his eyes, fixed on me. I left that day to return to the East Coast to commence writing.

John Schlesinger died three weeks later.

"I owed it to him to give him the best life I could," Michael said to me about John's life, post-stroke. "He would have done it for me."

Indeed, for a time, it looked as if it might well have been the other way around, that it would have been John finding the nurses for Michael, John sitting beside Michael's bed. Because in 1986, Michael had tested positive for HIV.

AIDS ripped a hole through the fabric of John's life. Dozens of friends died. Famous, not famous: Paul Keenan, one of the Jeep boys from *Honky Tonk Freeway*, in 1986. John's old boyfriend Peter Buckley in 1991, Tony Richardson that same year. Peter Allen in 1992. Production designer Ferdinando Scarfiotti and Philip Corey, one of John's "mistresses," in 1994. And, of course, his beloved Paul Jabara, in 1992.

"They were very scary times," Michael said. "Everybody around us was dying. John and I, out of our phonebooks, counted 85 people we lost."

When Michael tested positive for the virus, there was little effective treatment for AIDS. The anti-viral medications AZT and ddI were too toxic, Michael felt, as did many; yet without them there was no alternative, no hope. And although his health was not yet terribly compromised, an AIDS diagnosis in 1986 meant certain death. "I didn't want to die," Michael said. "I was terrified. All I wanted at that point was to be with John."

Of course, John was tested as well; Michael said it was a miracle that his test came back negative. What it predicted, however, was that the nearly twenty-year-older John would outlive the young, spirited, golden boy he'd always assumed would survive him.

"John looked at me," Michael remembered, "and he said, 'I'll be there. I'll stand by you.'" He became emotional remembering John's words. "I knew he would take care of me, the way he'd always taken care of me."

He got up from his chair, a bundle of nervous energy. "And now I'm on the cocktail and it's been wildly successful. My [viral load] numbers the other day were the best I've ever had. Practically undetectable." He looked off toward John's room. "John took care of me. He gave me a life. He was not only a lover but really the father I never had as well. And now it's my turn and I love him and it's been hard. It's been two years of ups and downs. I've seen him more and more destroyed and less and less of the John I knew. But still there's a little bit of him there and sometimes it connects and that's why I'm here. I want him to feel he's surrounded by love. He would've been there for me."

For John, Michael's HIV diagnosis came like a thunderbolt. In 1986, he was 60 years old. To imagine that he would have to watch his much younger partner die from a long, debilitating illness was an unbearable thought but, given his propensity for doom, somehow foretold. One could never really have it all in life. Something was better than nothing. After all, he'd had two decades with Michael – he should expect more?

Yet that was just it: he did expect more. For the first time in his life, John had gotten used to having it all: a partner, a career, a flourishing social life, all things that he'd once despaired of ever achieving. Now his old maxim had come back to haunt him. *The Believers* was a flop and Michael was going to die. Survival, as ever, was the best he could hope for.

"Survivor's guilt" was a phenomenon marked by many sociologists of the period, a collective sense felt by those who had somehow managed to skirt the plague while so many loved ones perished. John fell into a dark, deepening depression as friends continued to die all around him, and the carefree, cavalier life he had so loved crumbled into bittersweet memory. To survive: what did that mean in the age of AIDS? Was the idea worth so much now, if all his friends would go before him? Hardy's vision of man being struck down only to get back up, the old chestnut of half a loaf being better than no bread at all – they had been such guiding principles of his life, but now, as he was forced to confront them directly, they seemed empty of meaning. John was bitter and angry: after 40 years of fruitless search, he had finally found love, but now he would grow old, denied the comfort his parents had known from each other. He'd grow old and die alone, just as he'd always imagined and feared.

Many couples in times of crisis have found that what might have pulled them together – the loss of a child, the decline of a career, a diagnosis of terminal illness – instead pushes them apart. In John and Michael's case, the separation they experienced in the late 1980s and early 1990s was neither official nor permanent, but it exposed their relationship to its most grueling test. In the immediate aftermath of Michael's diagnosis, John was in London more than he was in Los Angeles. Michael, meanwhile, depressed over his health and the failure of *The Believers*, lost himself for a time in a world of parties and nightclubbing. "We were better together," Michael said. "We were never as good when we were apart."

The "mistresses" began taking up more of their time; friends remembered John being particularly smitten with one young man who was very unsuitable for him, a drug-user and a golddigger, they said. Some of his friends faulted him for being too distant during some of Michael's more difficult times in the early 1990s; John himself, in his diaries, would admit to "not being very good at letting it all hang out" – in other words, talking intimately about the challenges they were facing.

Yet something kept them together, something kept them from breaking that bond; many other couples, gay and straight, facing far less severe crises, have called it a day. John's perseverance in the relationship was pinned by some friends on "Jewish guilt," but his letters reveal it was far more than that. Michael's health and wellbeing were never far from his thoughts. He was constantly expressing worries about his partner's frame of mind, asking friends to visit him and cheer him up. He felt guilty there had been no work for Michael on *Madame Sousatzka,* and he wished very much that Childers was with him in London. "He doesn't really want to stay here," John wrote, "where work for Americans is difficult."

During the winter of 1987-88 they did enjoy a holiday together in the Caribbean to mark their anniversary. John commented to a friend, "Michael and I have just celebrated twenty years of being together (kind of), although we spend many months apart since he prefers living in Los Angeles and New York while I'm very committed to home in England." Still, he told another friend, "I try to talk to Michael every week. He seems up and down in spirits, and I miss him." To his diary he added: "I think about MC all the time. So many years together, so many ups and downs but we have always pulled through."

Their relationship had changed fundamentally over the years, as most relationships do; but what remained was a deep and abiding commitment. "People always ask what keeps a couple together, when the answer is so obvious," said one friend. "John and Michael loved each other. Just because their relationship didn't look like somebody else's, that didn't mean they didn't love each other. It was John who kept Michael going, and in the end, it was Michael who kept John alive, who was there right until the end."

Few Hollywood directors of John's stature had been affected so intimately by AIDS. The crisis reshaped his priorities, both personally and professionally. In late 1989 he took no fee for making an AIDS prevention television spot for Project Angel Food featuring Bette Midler. "This is a very tragic time," he wrote to a friend, "and one I feel compelled to do something about on film. Not a very commercial proposition, but one that I very much want to tackle in time."

In John's cabinets, I discovered several files tabbed, "AIDS Project." Included within were descriptions of books he was considering for adaptation: *The Beautiful Room is Empty* by Edmund White, *Second Son* by Robert Ferro, *The Mysteries of Pittsburgh* by Michael Chabon, among others. When word got out that John Schlesinger was considering an AIDS film, Paul Monette sent him an advance copy of *Borrowed Time*, with a note saying John was "the single director who has dealt with a homosexual relation on film in a literate and truthful way." The idea of John working with any of these writers, particularly with Monette on *Borrowed Time*, leaves an ache for what might have been. To have once again worked with a writer of such exquisite grace on a project so close to his heart would have made all the difference in Schlesinger's later life and career.

The route John eventually chose to pursue might also have produced a classy result, a latter-day *Sunday, Bloody Sunday*, if only the fates had so ordained. In June 1988, Schlesinger met with the young American writer David Leavitt, then just 26 years old and a literary wunderkind, his acclaimed collection of stories, *Family Dancing*, having been published soon after he'd graduated from Yale. John was charmed by Leavitt's youthful passion and frankness. David had no qualms talking quite openly to the press about being gay, and indeed he saw gay visibility as a vital tool in the fight against AIDS. Leavitt, so in touch with the contemporary world, would be John's choice for screenwriter for his film about AIDS.

In September of that year, John drafted a treatment for the proposed picture. Reading it some fifteen years later, it seems simple, almost patronizing: the brilliant, sensitive young man cut down in his prime, with his straight female best friend taking care of him. Like so many early AIDS dramas, the man's lover leaves him; activists would cry foul at such portrayals, saying they hardly reflected reality. Indeed, although John would imbue his character with many of Michael's traits – attending Louise Hay seminars, finding optimism through spiritual exploration – he had removed *himself* entirely from the story, leaving it less a narrative about a man with AIDS than a story of how his straight friends dealt with it. With some logic, John argued it was the only way that the property might appear at least *somewhat* commercial to prospective backers.

Leavitt's eventual treatment, called "Someone's Son," took a much less obvious commercial route, focusing more on the actual AIDS patient. In January 1989, Orion contracted with Schlesinger and Leavitt to develop the project, but events were moving swiftly; a few months later, Leavitt was writing to John to say that they would have to rewrite a scene set at a research hospital, as such places were increasingly being phased out in favor of more humane drug trials conducted in the home. Another plot point, in which a man loses his apartment after his lover dies, also seemed outdated since American courts were increasingly recognizing a surviving partner's rights.

The film with Leavitt was, sadly, never made; Orion went bankrupt, and by then the script seemed out of touch. It became one more empty "might-have-been" in the last decade of Schlesinger's career. What did come of the connection, however, was the opportunity, taken as a lark, for John to return to acting after 34 years. He played a small supporting part, with typical Schlesinger geniality, in the BBC adaptation of Leavitt's *Lost Language of Cranes* in 1991. John found it amusing, an enjoyable holiday from directing.

The AIDS crisis pushed John toward a greater willingness to publicly confess to being gay. His character in *Cranes* was, in fact, a gay man in a longtime relationship. But where once Schlesinger had been in the vanguard in the public expression of his homosexuality – refusing to be photographed with starlets, living openly with Childers, unambiguously dealing with gay themes in his work – he was now increasingly seen as "old guard," part of that generation for whom talking about personal sexuality in the press was never done. "Why did I have to announce it?" John would recall of his feelings from an earlier time. "Wasn't it obvious?"

Perhaps. But by the 1990s the gay movement was demanding a specificity from celebrities that would have been unimaginable in previous decades. In 1975, a time when the construct of being an "out" celebrity was just beginning to be imagined, John was interviewed by Cliff Jahr, a writer from the *Village Voice*. It's a prickly interview, with John clearly uncomfortable with what he saw as Jahr's attempt to push his words into a "thesis." When asked if he was aware that Malcolm in *Darling* was a "landmark for gays," John replied with an exasperated, "Oh, really!" When Jahr confronted him with a critical assessment that Joe Buck was a "sex fantasy lifted from classic gay lore," John responded testily, "That's wishful thinking" – though it would, in fact, be something he'd acknowledge years later. When asked point-blank if audiences, given his films, could think of him as a "gay director," John replied, "I don't think that's necessarily true." Pushed, he added, "Some of my audience may think anything. I really can't tell what my audience may think."

His answers offer a clue to his 1970s-era mindset. Was he denying his gayness? Not really. His response to Jahr was a bit of semantic play, saying it wasn't "necessarily true" that audiences would think him gay, but that "some" might think so. Either way, he wasn't saying if they were wrong or right, although that was obviously what Jahr was hoping for. (Earlier, Guy Flatley in the *New York Times* had let John off the hook easier, observing that like Daniel Hirsh in *Sunday, Bloody Sunday* John was Jewish and unmarried, "but he does not wish to pursue any further parallels.") That Jahr had a political axe to grind became obvious (though he denied it) when he issued a call for famous gay men and women to come out of their closets, suggesting America's "collective psyche would be better for knowing."

Until that point, John had not viewed himself as "in the closet" – certainly he hadn't lived his life in a state of denial or pretense in the way so many others had. But suddenly a closet had been built around him, constructed by activists who expected him to break out of what they had made. The rules were different; John was faced with a choice of either acquiescing or being branded a "closet case."

Of course, his career, his films, had created this dilemma for him. As Jahr pointed out, if Schlesinger was going to continue to imbue nearly every one of his films with some kind of gay element, he had to expect questions about it, and those questions were inevitably going to turn personal. Vincent Canby seemed, in somewhat coded parlance, to "out" the director as far back as 1971, when he observed that *Sunday, Bloody Sunday* brought "the homosexual phantoms that have existed in earlier Schlesinger films out of the closet into the fresh air." As his awkwardness in the Jahr interview demonstrated, however, John was not always comfortable in his role as pioneer, as one of the few undisguised gay directors making movies in the 1970s. But then how would he have known the best way to answer questions that had never been asked, really, of anyone else, ever before?

The onslaught of AIDS in many ways radicalized John's way of thinking. By 1988 the national gay American magazine *The Advocate* could run an interview with Schlesinger subtitled "An Oscar-Winning Director Looks at the Gay Elements in his Films." This time he didn't object to any "thesis" about his work. Though he didn't come out in the piece (the question wasn't asked), he spoke about reading names at the AIDS Memorial Quilt and about his desire to make a "gay-themed" film about AIDS.

It wasn't just the health crisis that shaped his perspective in these years. The notorious Clause 28, which became law in Britain in 1988, stated that no local authority could "intentionally promote homosexuality or publish material with the intention of promoting homosexuality." Stunned when a provincial film festival told him they had reconsidered showing *Sunday, Bloody Sunday* because of fear of the law's reach, John wrote in his diary: "It's abominable, playing into the hands of bigots. What have we come to, after so many years of progress?"

Although he'd curse Margaret Thatcher in private for not opposing the law, he wasn't sure how to respond publicly. Taking a stand on a compassionate, health-care issue like AIDS was one thing; gay rights was another step. Ian McKellen remembered sitting next to John at an awards ceremony and imploring him to come out and join the campaign against Clause 28. "Clearly I had stepped across some boundary," McKellen said, "because he turned on me and said, 'My dear, anyone who wants to know if I'm gay need only look at my work.' Which is a fair point, but *not* a fair point at the same time. Not then, not given what we were facing."

The real test came in 1991, when a knighthood for McKellen was announced in the Queen's New Year's Honours List. Derek Jarman, who John considered a self-righteous boor, publicly criticized McKellen in the *Guardian* for accepting a knighthood from the same Conservative government that had passed Clause 28. "Honors support a dishonorable social structure," Jarman proclaimed.

Immediately, a group of gay artists mobilized in support of McKellen. Antony Sher and Martin Sherman, the author of *Bent*, drafted a letter and began phoning various potential signatories. "I agreed to ring John," Sher said, "but I fully expected him to say no." Instead, to Sher's great surprise, Schlesinger agreed, saying he wanted "to stand up and be counted."

On 9 January the following letter ran in the *Guardian*: "As Gay and Lesbian artists, we would like to respectfully distance ourselves from Derek Jarman's article. We regard [McKellen's] knighthood as a significant landmark in the history of the British Gay Movement. Never again will public figures be able to claim that they have to keep secret their homosexuality in fear of it damaging their careers. Ian McKellen provides an inspiration to us all, not only as an artist of extraordinary gifts, but as a public figure of remarkable honesty and dignity."

It was signed, Simon Callow, Michael Cashman, Nancy Duguid, Simon Fanshawe, Stephen Fry, Philip Hedley, Bryony Lavery, Michael Leonard, David Lan, Tim Luscombe, Alec McCowen, Cameron Mackintosh, Pam St Clement, John Schlesinger, Antony Sher, Martin Sherman, Ned Sherrin, and Nick Wright.

"I was more surprised than anyone when that letter was signed by John," said McKellen. "He then took that as his coming out, and on other occasions made it perfectly clear that he was gay. He gave interviews about it, perhaps for the first time."

"I am an openly gay director," John remarked in an interview a few years later, "which I can say much more easily now."

Applauded as he was in January, John stunned many of those same gay and lesbian signatories later that year by filming a short campaign film for Prime Minister John Major. Hired by the firm of Saatchi & Saatchi, John took his cue from the Madison Avenue-style American political campaigns and crafted a film not so much about Major as about Britain itself. We see the sun rising and setting over pastoral green hills, cows grazing, a friendly game of cricket being played, all to the strains of Mozart's piano concerto No. 21. "That looks like a nice country," one viewer was quoted as saying in the *Daily Telegraph*. "May one go and live in it?"

Indeed, the economy of Britain, after rebounding in the 1980s, was in decline once more; Schlesinger's portrait of the nation seemed staggeringly out of touch. "I could only assume John had been out of the country for some time," Ian McKellen said after seeing it. But John knew what he was doing. The film was meant to counter the Labour message of anger and gloom. The Prime Minister himself makes only a brief appearance, talking about a "nation at ease with itself." More footage was given to a woman in childbirth, symbolizing, *The Times* said, "that something new and beautiful can only come after struggle."

John liked the fact that Major was distancing himself from the legacy of Mrs Thatcher and implying that the Conservatives were moving in a new direction. Still, the film infuriated many of his friends. "I don't want to talk about that," Julie Christie said when I raised the subject with her. But others confirmed that John's embrace of the Conservative cause in 1991 did cause a rift, however temporary, with his darling Julie.

"Everyone thinks I volunteered to make it," John would complain. "But they asked me, and I thought it would be interesting to do." He was approached by Saatchi & Saatchi to meet with the Prime Minister at Downing Street. "I found I liked him very much," John said, "so I went ahead and did it." It was a one-shot assignment – John was essentially brought in by the advertising agency as "a last-minute rejigger" to their campaign – whereas Hugh Hudson, the director of *Chariots of Fire*, directed a concurrent campaign film for Labour candidate Neil Kinnock as part of an ongoing involvement in the Labour cause.

Some of John's friends suggested, almost as a sort of apologia for the whole episode, that Schlesinger took the job simply because it was "an interesting idea." They offered as evidence the fact that in the early 1990s he returned to making commercials and didn't necessarily always believe in the product he was promoting: he made commercials for cigarettes, after all, though he didn't smoke. Presented this very scenario by BBC interviewer Jeremy Isaacs, however, John refuted the idea: "I believed in [Major] as a product, yes," he insisted. "I think he's a very good, honest, honorable man. I don't really trust politicians on the whole, but he was someone I did, and indeed, voted for."

It may have caused his leftist friends to shrink in horror, but to John it was not such a contradiction: Labour, after all, hadn't opposed Clause 28 either. Besides, John had always reveled in his contradictions. "For years I've been kind of a woolly-minded liberal, always finding that something one believed in has already been proven wrong," he once said. "If one said, 'I won't go to Greece because of the colonels,' well, then, one ended up in Spain." But when Julie Christie would bring her "strange liberal appendages" to his house, he'd rail in his diary about their superior airs and lack of humor. One such woman, he wrote, reminded him "quite horrendously of Penelope Gilliatt. Her way of talking and her attitudes caused me to move further to the right than ever over dinner."

Some friends would suggest John took on the Major campaign film simply "to piss off" his leftist friends, especially after the fuss over the McKellen letter earlier that year. There was another consideration, too; unlike Hugh Hudson, a committed socialist who gave his efforts to the Labour party free of charge, John was paid quite well for his services. Money was an issue; his last two films had been bombs, and he had two households (three, if one counted Strawberry Hole) of considerable size to maintain. That's not to mention the staggering healthcare costs Michael was accumulating in the United States, where problems with his health insurance meant much had to be paid directly out of their own pockets. Noel Davis, too, was once again in dire straits, living with John in London and dependent on his old friend's largesse.

In the spring of 1989, he was approached by the American producer Scott Rudin (*Flatliners*) to direct a thriller called *Pacific Heights*, about a young San Francisco couple terrorized by a tenant from hell. With its little twist of making the wife the stronger character, needing to rescue her husband, the script by

Daniel Pyne appealed to John. He and Rudin agreed on the star casting of Melanie Griffith, still riding a crest of fame from *Working Girl*, but casting the husband was less certain. They were considering Michael Keaton when they realized that the actor, then just off *Batman*, would be more interesting if he played against type as the psychopathic tenant. Accordingly, Keaton displaced Christopher Reeve, who'd wanted that part badly and had sent John a handwritten letter. Briefly, John considered using Reeve for the husband, but he needed an actor who seemed physically weaker than Melanie. That was the reason he eventually gave the part to Matthew Modine.

While casting was being finalized, John headed to Austria in the summer of 1989 for the annual Salzburg Festival to direct Verdi's opera *Un Ballo In Maschera*, again starring Placido Domingo. It had been an offer John couldn't refuse, made by the great conductor Herbert von Karajan himself. "What does that old Nazi want with this English faggot?" John asked incredulously when he learned of the invitation. It was with great apprehension that he went to meet the maestro, revered throughout Europe, but to John's great relief, they got along famously: "That severe demeanour," John wrote to a friend, "hides quite a nasty sense of humor, which makes him human."

Eleanor Fazan, once again choreographing movement for the opera, remembered, "Von Karajan would arrive and approach the stage with this great medieval king walk. He really was an absolute king but he was rather camp, too, and John and he used to make camp jokes together. Still, he was very frightening. He'd sit in the back row with a microphone. And if John were to ask one of us our opinion on something, Von Karajan would say, 'I don't understand this English parliament you have. When I want something I make up my own mind.'

And John would laugh and say, 'Well, maestro, maybe I'm not as clever as you are.'"

Ten days before the opening night, Von Karajan died unexpectedly, but the show went on, with Georg Solti stepping in as conductor. The reviews were good – John Higgins in *The Times* praised its "visual magnificence and dramatic sensibility," adding that "John Schlesinger certainly knows how to put on a party." So successful was *Un Ballo In Maschera* that John would return the following summer to remount the production with the same cast.

In January he flew to San Francisco to start shooting *Pacific Heights*. Perhaps because he hadn't developed the project, John felt uncomfortable with the material. Melanie Griffith, he wrote in his diary, "seems a little uncertain – as I am." He worried that her "little girl voice may be a bore," but he liked her personally very much.

He was also impressed with Michael Keaton, enjoying the sexual undercurrent that the actor was able to give the character. "He loved that kind of titillation and sexual danger," Keaton said. "He wasn't just shooting the script, he was going for the full colors."

As John's "third tier" films go, *Pacific Heights* isn't terrible, thanks mainly to Keaton's creepy performance. There are some moments of suspense and a few good scares, but the story is hard to sustain, especially with Griffith and Modine as the leads: they never really become people we care about. The early scenes intended to establish domestic bliss between the two of them fall flat; Schlesinger's skill was never in showing happy, contented relationships. However, the problem is chiefly with the script, which lacks any real characterization or interpersonal dynamics, despite some clumsy, obvious, last-minute attempts by both screenwriter and director to layer some on.

Critics weren't impressed when the movie was released in September. Like a voice from the past, Pauline Kael weighed in, accusing Schlesinger of "foisting his boredom on us." But the picture proved popular enough, opening at number one. Though it disappeared fairly quickly after that, *Pacific Heights* ended up making a respectable $29.3 million.

John's next venture brought a reunion with Alan Bennett and Innes Lloyd at the BBC. Bennett had written a companion piece to *An Englishman Abroad*, mounting the two as a double-bill at the National Theatre under the banner "Single Spies." Now the BBC was interested in pairing them as films. The new piece was *A Question of Attribution* and its spy Sir Anthony Blunt, the keeper of the Queen's pictures who, in 1979, had been exposed as the fourth man in the Burgess-Maclean-Philby spy ring. Stripped of his knighthood, Blunt aroused a certain amount of compassion from many Britons, who were left wondering why his misdeeds mattered so much so many years after the fact. Bennett incorporated this sentiment into his entertaining, literate script. When Blunt discovers the ghostly presence of additional sitters in a misidentified Titian, it is the playwright making a compelling analogy: identifying long-ago sitters, like long-ago Communists, is ultimately an exercise in pointlessness.

Bennett's intelligent script was a refreshing change from the pedestrian writing of *Pacific Heights*. The playwright himself had played Blunt on the stage; for the film, however, they brought in James Fox. If Fox comes across a bit reserved, that's the intent; as Lynne Truss in *The Times* would observe, the film was a play of ideas, not psychology, dealing far less with "Why did he do it?" than with "Why do you want to know?" In this it differs from the character study of *An Englishman Abroad*, and so is less immediately visceral. Still, it is impossible not to be moved by the sight of the serious, dignified man humbled at the end, thrown to a pack of snapping, shouting reporters waiting for him outside his door.

But the most talked-about aspect of the film was Prunella Scales' portrayal of the Queen – "HMQ" in the script – the first time any reigning monarch had been so depicted. It is Scales who has the best lines in the film, bantering with Blunt over forgeries and "fakes"; whether she's talking about art or his spying career, we're never quite sure. Scales perfected all of Her Majesty's little mannerisms, from the tilt of her head and the slight raising of her eyebrows to the determined clutch of her ever-present handbag. "It was even more believable in the theater with no close-ups," said Scales. "I actually had a letter from somebody who had worked at the Palace saying that he got to his feet when I came onto the stage. Very dramatic!"

One of John's signature moments that differed from the stage production was the use of corgis, which the director saw as essential in capturing the royal verisimilitude. The dogs are right on cue, too: when we see a corgi come scampering into the hall, we know who must be behind it.

Once again, John had a triumph on the small screen, although the acclaim for *A Question of Attribution* was sadly offset by the death of Innes Lloyd shortly before the film's transmission on 20 October 1991. With Lloyd and Bennett, John would share, for the second time, the BAFTA Award for Best Single Drama. The film also received praise when it was broadcast in the United States on *Masterpiece Theater* the following year, with John O'Connor in the *New York Times* calling it "exquisitely constructed."

In the summer of 1992, John went to Germany to begin an adaptation of Ian McEwan's novel *The Innocent*. Producer Norma Heyman (*Dangerous Liaisons*) brought him in to save the project after Paramount had put it in turnaround. The new backers were a German company, Studio für Spielfilme, which planned to shoot the film at Berlin's Deutsche Film Ateliers (DEFA), the historic site of Lang's *Metropolis* and von Sternberg's *The Blue Angel*. It would be the first time the studio was used for a big-budget international film since the fall of the Berlin Wall.

John accepted the assignment on the priviso that he could entirely recast. Out went Kyle MacLachlan, Willem Dafoe and Lena Olin; in came Campbell Scott, Anthony Hopkins and Isabella Rossellini. Schlesinger also insisted on script revisions, to which McEwan, who was adapting his own novel, acquiesced, shifting the focus of the story from its more "techno-thriller" elements onto the love affair between Scott and Rossellini. McEwan told the *Sunday Times* that he would have preferred to keep the emphasis on the secret spy tunnel under the Soviet sector of Berlin: "I would probably also have made the film darker and gone for a less happy ending," he said, "but I am prepared to trust people who have a more positive belief in human nature."

"Positive belief in human nature" certainly never described John Schlesinger. Rather, it was the producers who insisted on "less dark" elements. John quickly became embittered, struggling for control over the picture, lamenting in his diary about endless "back and forths" over the script. Was it a thriller? A black comedy? A love story? A tale of espionage? It didn't help that the actors were unhappy, performing completely out of sync with each other. Anthony Hopkins, playing an American, affects a very strange accent, while Scott, playing English, doesn't do much better. Hopkins was reclusive and withdrawn during the shoot; John would recall dining at a restaurant with others from the cast and crew and seeing Tony off by himself in a corner, declining their offer to join them.

John hated Germany. It might have been the home of his ancestors, but as a Jew he couldn't escape feeling bitter and resentful. Visiting a former concentration camp at Sachsenhausen, Schlesinger stood there "in the presence of what had been the past," realizing "what people witnessed and went through." He couldn't shake the feeling. "I had an enormous sense of how lucky I was, as a Jew, that I wasn't part of that, wasn't caught by that," he recorded for his diary. "I don't know how they endured it. It was very difficult for me to work in Germany with that thought."

Isabella Rossellini recalled John's biting black humor as they traveled one day in a car together: "He could see smokestacks on factories and said to me, 'I wonder who they're burning in there this time.'" Once, when his German crew had trouble filling some balloons with helium, John gruffly asked what the problem was. Told that they couldn't get the gas to work, John bellowed, "You people had no trouble with that fifty years ago!"

"*The Innocent* was a ghastly experience," John said. Fighting with the crew, with the producers, with an increasingly incoherent script, he knew even before the film was completed it would be a disaster. Later, he'd say it was "certainly not my best film but not my worst either." But if not *The Innocent*, what?

John couldn't leave the country fast enough. It would be a year before the film was released, and then just in German cinemas; British and American distributors showed a distinct lack of interest. John returned to London without a project, the first time in years he was completely at liberty. Banging around his big house on Victoria Road, he felt lonely and irrelevant, not to mention financially squeezed. He'd sell the house the next year, choosing a smaller place at Cranley Mansions in Gloucester Road, a wonderful two-storey flat with gorgeous views of the city.

Yet there was good news during that period as well: to John's great delight, Michael's life and health seemed back on track. In a new career as an events planner, Childers organized a spectacular AIDS fundraiser for Project Angel Food, "Divine Design," in September 1991, which raised more than a million dollars. "MC has outdone himself," John wrote in his diary. "He rightly glows. I haven't seen him so pleased and gratified for years."

There would still be difficult moments, but the trend was on an upswing by the mid-1990s, with John frequently noting in his diary how good Michael was looking, "newly muscled and suntanned." If there had been a moment when the relationship might have ended, it was past; their commitment to each other had prevailed.

"I remember John and Michael coming for dinner with Antonio [Banderas] and me," Melanie Griffith said. "And they were such a different couple. I didn't get it at first. I couldn't see how they'd stayed together all these years. John was so quiet and ironic, a little pessimistic. Michael was loud and outgoing and always laughing. But then I realized opposites attract. Someone picks up where the other leaves off. And you could see it with the two of them, how they just fit together, how it worked."

B ut John was an ageing man by now, tired, and somewhat discouraged. AIDS had taken many of his friends but age and infirmity were also taking an inevitable toll: Huw Wheldon died in 1986, Coral Browne in 1991, Richard MacDonald in 1993, Alan Cooke in 1994 – the same year Jo Janni finally passed away, ending an important chapter in John's life.

Himself now diagnosed as a diabetic, John had to take injections and a daily dose of prescription drugs. Isabella Rossellini remembered seeing him on the set of *The Innocent* one day, when he thought he was alone. "He was sitting in a prop wheelchair, trying it out," she said. "I had the impression he was imagining himself in it, wondering about his future."

When he became aware that Rossellini was watching, John laughed and said, "Tell me the truth, Isabella. Am I an old fart?"

He was 68 when he began filming yet another small television film, an adaptation of one of his cherished childhood books, *Cold Comfort Farm*, as a co-production for the BBC and Thames Television. It had now been twenty years since he'd had an unqualified big-screen success. Practicality had mitigated his previous intransigence against working in television: "Television is at least a way of getting something on a screen," he admitted, "albeit a small one, though it is never very satisfactory because it has such little shelf life."

He went through the early stages of production assuming that this project, too, like *An Englishman Abroad* and *A Question of Attribution*, might get good marks at transmission but then it would be over, the end, back to the BBC vault. VCRs were becoming more and more common, of course, and there might be a small afterlife for the film in home rentals, but what John longed for was the kind of big-screen release he had known during his heyday.

Certainly he recognized the quality of the material. The script by Malcolm Bradbury was bitingly funny, and a brilliant ensemble cast had been rounded up: Eileen Atkins, Ian McKellen, Stephen Fry, Joanna Lumley, Sheila Burrell. But for the lead of Flora Poste, the intrepid young city girl who transforms the household of her morose, eccentric relatives on Cold Comfort Farm, John wanted to discover a new star, the way he had in the old days. In came Kate Beckinsale, whose most notable role to date had been in Kenneth Branagh's *Much Ado About Nothing*. John liked her test but concluded she seemed a bit too young – an observation which prompted an extraordinary four-page handwritten letter from Beckinsale begging him to reconsider and pointing out that in Stella Gibbons' novel Flora is twenty. At 21 years of age, Beckinsale insisted, she might be too mature for the role, but certainly not too *young!*

The letter was exactly the sort of thing Flora would have done. John was charmed by Beckinsale's pluck and gave her the part. The actress lived up to her promises, too, delivering a spritely, quirky performance that is the perfect match to the oversized grotesqueries around her. A less capable performer might have been upstaged by such scene-chewers as Burrell, her old Ada Doom murmuring about "something nasty in the woodshed," or McKellen's Amos Starkadder bellowing "There'll be no butter in hell!" But Beckinsale holds her own – and the picture – together playing the role straight enough to set her apart but with enough wry, offbeat humor that Flora becomes one of the most memorable cinematic characters of the 1990s: "Nature's all very well in her place," she says, "but there's no reason to be untidy."

Cold Comfort Farm was filmed in Sussex, not far from Strawberry Hole, which meant John could live at the oast house for three straight weeks – a glorious experience, the longest he'd ever been there for one period. It was a happy shoot: "Twelve-hour days, six days a week," John wrote to a friend, "so by the end we were on our knees, but it was fun."

Eileen Atkins recalled taking John to a transsexual boutique to buy "huge wobbly tits" for Judith Starkadder. "You never really see them, just my face," Atkins said, laughing, "so all I'd done was land myself with these absolutely heavy breasts for the whole shoot."

They sparred over how best to interpret the character; Atkins saw Judith as an "earth mother" but John was insistent she be more powerful, more consuming. "It sounds as if you want Medea," Atkins said, to which John's face lit up and he said, "Yes! Exactly! I want Medea!" Atkins laughed. "I did about five takes and each time John was saying, 'More, more!' I thought he was nuts, but when I saw it [onscreen], he was right."

Whatever magic John exerted during the six weeks it took to shoot the film worked splendidly. *Cold Comfort Farm* is a joy from start to finish, from the sly opening banter between Beckinsale and the delicious Joanna Lumley to the exuberant ending – for once, an unqualified happy resolution to a Schlesinger film. John showed a cool authority with the material, proving to all the world he could direct comedy, providing he had a solid script. And Bradbury's script for *Cold*

Comfort Farm is perfectly timed, expertly balanced. It is also, significantly, warm-hearted where *Honky Tonk Freeway* had been mean-spirited, and driven less by the needs of the plot than by the peculiarities of the characters.

And what characters they are! All of them over-the-top, but that's the point. John believed that Ian McKellen's turn as a fire-breathing preacher in the Church of the Quivering Brethren would have netted him a Best Supporting Actor nomination had the film been made as a feature – which was exactly what the director had in mind as production wrapped in the autumn of 1994; *Cold Comfort Farm*, he was convinced, could be blown up to 35mm and distributed as a feature film in the United States.

"Something told me that this was the kind of comedy American audiences might like," John said. He wasn't too surprised when British critics proved somewhat tepid in their response to the film, which was first transmitted on New Year's Day, 1995. His eye was already on an American distribution, something he was pressuring Thames Television to support. He was met with skepticism. "They had no guarantee it would be picked up," John said, "and you have to take risks in this business." It wasn't a huge sum of money he was asking for – £8,000 – but only when Schlesinger agreed to pay half did Thames come up with the rest.

In the meantime, to keep working, John accepted another assignment, with some belief that this one might actually become the commercial smash he still hankered after. The property was *An Eye for an Eye*, being produced for Paramount by Michael Levy (*Prelude to a Kiss*), the harrowing story of a mother who seeks revenge for her daughter's murder after the criminal justice system fails. Based on Erika Holzer's novel, the script was being written by the team of Amanda Silver and Rick

Jaffa, just off their huge success with *The Hand That Rocks the Cradle*. The film would have a sizeable budget, about $20 million, and would star two-time Oscar winner Sally Field.

Production began in the spring of 1995, but "John really struggled with the script," said Field. "He kept trying to bring more to it, more psychological depth." Indeed, as with most of his later pictures, it is a substandard script that is the chief flaw. Not trusting the material, John seemed unwilling to let any shot last longer than a few moments. It was a stylistic break with his past that increasingly came to define his later work. "I remember seeing *The Believers, The Innocent, Pacific Heights*, and [feeling] there was something frantic about them," said Gavin Lambert. "But when he did trust his material, as in *Falcon, Yanks, An Englishman Abroad*, he allowed the shots and the scenes more time."

Eye for an Eye (the original article was eventually dropped) opens magnificently: Field, stuck in a traffic jam, hears on her mobile phone her daughter being murdered. It's an amazing performance, the frantic mother running through traffic, banging on car windows. Field is, in fact, remarkable throughout, delivering the right mixture of rage, grief, frustration, and despair. But for the picture, it's downhill after the powerhouse opening.

In John's files I found numerous script revisions, his notes scrawled all over them: "Something too long here," "This doesn't feel right," "Needs to be more compelling." The first rewrites had been done in November 1994, and pages were still being added and subtracted long after production began. Ed Harris rightly complained that his part as Sally Field's husband made no sense: "Why am I here? What purpose am I serving?" John brought in an outside writer, Patty Sullivan, to help reshape Harris' part, and encouraged the actor to layer as much nuance as he could onto the bare bones he was given.

It was John who came up with the opening they finally used, a reverie of his own childhood: Field comes into her daughter's room to catch a moth that is frightening her, letting the creature go into the night air. Meanwhile, in the darkness below, looms the killer, played with seething malice by Kiefer Sutherland, whose father Donald had, of course, played in *The Day of the Locust*.

Some of the criticism of the film would center around Sutherland's stark portrayal: he is pure evil with no trace of humanity. This wasn't a deficiency in the script; it was a deliberate choice by the director. "John and I agreed that it had to be done that way," said Sutherland. "Not a thread of a redeemable quality. It was a very black and white film, about the paranoia people had about the judicial system, especially after the O.J. Simpson trial."

Eye for an Eye is Schlesinger's most violent film. The scene in which Sutherland rapes and kills the girl is almost unbearable to watch. Olivia Burnette, who played Field's daughter, was just eighteen and looked far younger; Sutherland remembered rehearsing with her, trying to prepare her for the brutality of the scene. "Right before we filmed it, John pulled me aside and said, 'Really go for it,'" Sutherland said. "I had to carry this poor girl off the set when we were done, she was crying so hard."

The onscreen violence mirrored the tumult going on behind the scenes. John battled with the writers and with the producers; he could see, as he had with *The Innocent*, the film heading inexorably toward disaster. "John was being drained," said Sally Field. "I could see him taking it in, the problems, the fights. I felt very protective of him. I found myself always wanting to defend him."

Released in January 1996, the film was immediately attacked for its violence and simplistic narrative. "John Schlesinger, many hours past *Midnight Cowboy*, takes on a barn-door-size target – the much-maligned L.A. police department – and still misses," quipped *USA Today*. "Never has John Schlesinger made a film as mean-spirited and empty as this," commented Janet Maslin in the *New York Times*.

If the producers hoped at least the thriller aspects might pull in moviegoers, as had happened with *Pacific Heights*, they were disappointed: *Eye for an Eye* did decent business in its first couple of weeks, but faced with the more compelling Brad Pitt-Bruce Willis shocker, *Twelve Monkeys*, it quickly fell off the charts. The picture would eventually make back its cost, but barely.

The negative press for *Eye for an Eye* was compounded by the fact that it followed reviews nearly as bad for *The Innocent*, which had finally been released, first in Britain in June 1994 and then in the United States in September 1995. But there was a silver lining to all that, too: *Cold Comfort Farm* had been playing to rave reviews and rapturous audiences at film festivals all across the United States and Canada, and was finally given a theatrical release by Gramercy Pictures in May 1996. The chorus of praise that greeted the picture was the best music to John's ears since Von Karajan, with headlines proclaiming "Schlesinger Soars Back into Favor," "Not the End After All for Schlesinger," "Schlesinger Comeback," "Director Regains Focus." Roger Ebert said, "I thought we'd never see another good film from John Schlesinger."

John relished the renewed attention, especially after being

so recently battered over *Eye for an Eye*. He embarked on a massive North American promotional tour in the spring and summer of 1996. To one interviewer he described the film as having "a glow about it, a glow of pleasure," but that glow could have equally described him that glorious summer, delighting in having brought the English catchphrase, "There's something nasty in the woodshed," to American shores. "I think people in the industry are quite surprised that I've made this film," John said. "It's jolly nice to have made something which is 'feel-good.'"

Reversing the trend exhibited by his films for more than a decade, *Cold Comfort Farm* actually *climbed* rather than dropped on the box-office chart. Excellent word of mouth allowed it to break the top twenty by the first week of June, despite the fact that it had opened in only a limited number of theaters. By the early summer, the film was showing a staggering 339 percent increase in box-office; it ended up as Gramercy's second-highest grosser for 1996–1997, behind only *Fargo*. The final revenues ($5.5 million) weren't enough for the studio to fully recoup its various distribution costs, but the fact that *Cold Comfort Farm* had been a "sleeper hit," a favorite of both audiences and critics, gave John the kind of satisfaction he hadn't known in a very long time. The film was included on more than 50 American "Ten Best" lists at the end of the year, with the *Chicago Tribune* proclaiming it the "Number 1" film of 1996. John was exultant; after more than a decade of flops, he finally felt "rehabilitated" by Hollywood.

"If only I had stopped there," he would say to friends.

The failure of the majority of his later pictures had left John deeply disappointed; he believed firmly that had he been able to get the ones he'd been developing on his own off the ground, his later career would have been much less bleak. Certainly the "might-have-beens," as always, are an interesting lot: Eileen Atkins told me he had wanted to adapt her script about the love affair between Vita Sackville-West and Virginia Woolf. "My feeling was at that point [the mid-1990s] he was only really interested in choosing things that had something to do with being gay," Atkins said. "I think that was his *raison d'etre* in his last years."

A consideration of the projects he explored does reveal several that are gay-themed: an adaptation of the book *Say Uncle*, about a gay man who adopts a child; a proposal from Clive Barker to assemble fifteen short films by gay filmmakers set to the music of gay composers; and, of course, his continuing determination to make a film about AIDS. But John turned down the opportunity to direct the American television production of Armistead Maupin's gay classic *Tales of the City*, and among the projects that advanced the farthest was an adaptation of Edith Wharton's *The House of Mirth* which, although it may have had some gay sensibility, was definitely a mainstream affair. The project got as far as a preliminary deal with Dustin Hoffman's Punch Productions and a script by Freddie Raphael in the autumn of 1998. Another project John spent time with was *Flush*, Virginia Woolf's ironic portrait of the Barrett-Brownings as seen through the eyes of their cocker spaniel. It would have been produced by Lily Tomlin and Jane Wagner.

But his most impassioned project in these last years was *The Normal Heart*. In May 1996, in the midst of his triumph with *Cold Comfort Farm*, John signed on to direct the film adaptation of the searing AIDS drama written by his old friend Larry Kramer. For years, the rights had been held by Barbra Streisand; when she finally allowed the option to lapse, Kramer immediately enlisted Schlesinger as director and David Picker as producer. It was a happy reunion of old friends which might have gone even further: Jon Voight and Dustin Hoffman were suggested for leading roles.

In the gay press there was much rejoicing that the film version of the play would finally be made; Streisand's stubborn roadblocking had drawn much criticism. John was also promising to smash some barriers: "I'm very glad *Philadelphia* was successful," he said, "but I found it very flat in the personal department." Some had felt the Tom Hanks film was made "too palatable" for the benefit of mainstream audiences, emphasizing Hanks' relationship with his lawyer and his family over that with his lover (Antonio Banderas). *The Normal Heart*, on the other hand, would be a gay story told by an outspoken gay author and a newly politicized gay director.

During this period, John gave several interviews to the gay press, an unthinkable proposition a decade before. "I think if something doesn't make money, they probably use [my sexuality] as a hook," he told one reporter. "'Well, of course, he's a queen, so he doesn't have balls.' That makes me angry, makes me *very* angry."

Being so open about himself was liberating. Around this time he took another acting assignment, in another gay-themed television drama, Jonathan Tolins' *The Twilight of the Golds*. In 1997, he received a Lifetime Achievement Award from Outfest, the Los Angeles Gay and Lesbian Film Festival. "Strange how relaxed I am about all this now," John wrote in his diary. In another interview with the gay press, he spoke openly about

Michael for the first time: "I'm happy to have a companion of 28 years who's here with me, and we enjoy each other's company, and that's quite wonderful to have."

With *The Normal Heart*, John, at the age of 70, was moving into his most political role yet. Kramer's health, compromised by more than ten years with AIDS, compelled them to act quickly. "We're all rushing headlong to set it up," John told the press. Larry was working with him on the screenplay, and they hoped to be in production by summer.

They weren't. After all the excitement, *The Normal Heart* was not meant to be. "We couldn't get the money," Kramer said. "We needed bankable stars. We thought we had Sharon Stone, then she backed out. It all fell apart."

By the end of the year, with the innovative drug cocktail treatments changing the face of the epidemic, producers began calling the script "dated." John argued that it wasn't "dated," it was "history." But no one was listening. AIDS was over, according to Hollywood.

Instead of *The Normal Heart*, John began work on *The Tale of Sweeney Todd* for Showtime. His heart wasn't in it, and it shows. Gone was much of the black humor that marked Stephen Sondheim's West End and Broadway musical; here, John told the gruesome story of the Demon Barber of Fleet Street straight, complete with throat-slashings and the torture of a mute boy. Yet even his usually delicious penchant for the macabre fails here; Ben Kingsley as Todd is distinctly lacking in any charisma, with only Joanna Lumley as Mrs. Lovett, who bakes the barber's victims into pies, showing any spark. Lots of good visual details, but the production has no center, probably because John simply couldn't get very enthused about the material.

That's when he accepted Rupert Everett's offer to make *The Next Best Thing*.

"The last few years have been somewhat depressing," John wrote, in one of his last letters to Gene Phillips, "because projects close to me were canceled or didn't get off the ground, so in my anxiety to keep working, which provides me with my chief pleasure in life, I have perhaps accepted films which were wanting in some way just in order to keep going."

The call I'd been expecting came on 21 July 2003. "We've had to take John to the hospital," Michael said. "His breathing was becoming labored, and even with his oxygen his lips and fingernails were turning blue. He's on life support now, but we're not going to leave him on it. He wouldn't want to live that way."

No, he wouldn't. That night, I decided to watch *Cold Comfort Farm*. No matter what came afterward, this was John Schlesinger's true swan song.

"I must warn you," Stephen Fry as Mybug tells Flora Poste. "I'm a queer, moody brute, but there's some rich dirt in here if you're willing to dig."

Yes, a queer moody brute. And very rich dirt indeed.

Epilogue

2000–2003

"The one very strongly held belief that I have"

The power was out on 19 October 2003, the morning of John Schlesinger's memorial service at the Directors Guild in Los Angeles. If it didn't come back on, there'd be no lights, no sound. The opera singers wouldn't have any microphones. The film clips of John's career wouldn't be shown. Worst of all: there'd be no air conditioning. Some people were cursing, others were laughing.

Comedy or tragedy?

"We'll make do," said Michael York as emcee, his voice booming from the stage. "We're actors. We know how to project."

So the event went on as scheduled. Jerry Hellman sat quietly with his wife. Sally Field sat by herself. Lily Tomlin walked up to the podium and told the crowd how John and Michael had been role models for her and her partner, Jane Wagner. Peter

Bart pronounced from the stage that John had been the greatest English director of his generation, bar none. Kaye Ballard recounted a story of John joking that Madonna had given him a heart attack. "I wonder who will give me *mine*," Ballard said, her eyes scanning the audience comically. "Probably one of these new young Hollywood producers who ask, 'But what have you *done?*'"

New Hollywood, Old Hollywood – the terms had long since lost their meaning. Outside the auditorium a visitor was asking a Directors Guild employee who the service was for. "John Schlesinger," she was told. "An oldtime director."

Oldtime. A few of John's contemporaries had managed to hang on – Scorsese, Altman, Polanski – but most of them had faded away long before he did. And John, like Isherwood, had never quite surrendered his sense of still being a part of the here and now. Before his stroke, he was still out there trying, pitching *House of Mirth* to Julia Roberts, *Flush* to Cate Blanchett, a script called *Midday Moon* to Brad Pitt. And he almost, at long last, got *Hadrian VII* off the ground, with Jerry Hellman producing and Daniel Day-Lewis starring. It would have been a reunion all around: John had given Day-Lewis one of his first jobs, as a youthful extra in *Sunday, Bloody Sunday*. If not Day-Lewis, then Jerry was also negotiating with Geoffrey Rush . . .

But none of those projects happened. Not after the devastating reviews for *The Next Best Thing*. That John had, for once in his career, brought a film in on time and under budget mattered little: the film made just $15 million domestically, Paramount's third worst for 2000. (It would eventually make back its cost with European revenues, but only by a sliver.) At the premiere party at Saci, a Times Square nightclub, everyone had been smiling, but already the reviews were predicting oblivion. John arrived with Isabella Rossellini on one arm and Anjelica Huston on the other, almost as bodyguards. He was still weak from his heart surgery, but managed to share some banter with Gwyneth Paltrow and Salman Rushdie – though observers noted he kept to the opposite end of the room from Madonna and Rupert Everett.

Had John read the reviews, which he was insistent he did not, he might have found interesting what the *New York Daily News* concluded: that the film proved "half a loaf is *not* better than none at all." Was that his point? Had he truly reversed his old axiom?

At his memorial service, there were some who thought so. "John got what he wanted eventually," said Gary Shaw. "Look at how much these people loved him. John never settled for second best. He wanted it all."

Michael Childers was shaking hands and embracing those who were filing out of the sweltering hot auditorium. The power hadn't been restored in time to show any clips.

"It's John telling us, *enough already*," joked Shaw. "It's all been said. Now move on."

His last work wasn't a film, it was an opera: Benjamin Britten's *Peter Grimes*, staged first in June 2000 in Milan at the Teatro alla Scala, and scheduled for a second production in Los Angeles that autumn.

"John was far, far, far from his peak," said Eleanor Fazan. "He was so tired all the time. He would turn up late, which was so unlike him. He would sit there almost like a little boy, really regressed into himself. He'd be more interested in the ice creams and puddings. He wasn't at all well and he must have known it. I remember during rehearsals looking out into the theater and John had fallen asleep."

"He had no energy in Italy," agreed his assistant, Julien Lemaitre. "But I have to say he worked very hard, as best as he could. He remained very passionate about the music."

The Italian critics weren't kind when the opera opened on 15 June. Some in the audience actually booed. "Italians are snobs about their opera," said Lemaitre. "First of all, *Peter Grimes* was not their classic Italian opera, and secondly, John was English, and a filmmaker, too."

"He shouldn't have done it," said Childers. "But he wanted to prove that he could still put on a show."

The fiasco in Milan seemed to offer evidence to the contrary. Yet by the time the Los Angeles production was mounted in October, John had rediscovered some of his old reserves of strength. Maybe the fear of being seen to fail one more time in Hollywood was enough to galvanize him. "He was still quite weak," said Eleanor Fazan. "He could hardly walk, but he was right there. He was intent and focused. He was at every lighting rehearsal. He didn't let anyone get away with anything. No one was directing this opera but John."

On 18 October 2000, at the Dorothy Chandler Pavilion, John Schlesinger's final production was presented. It was the same place where, 30 years previous, he had won his Oscar for *Midnight Cowboy*. That night, he hadn't been present to collect his award, but now he was very much in attendance. He was there to receive finally the accolades and applause for an extraordinary career. And applaud they did – several ovations, with calls for the maestro no louder than the calls for Schlesinger. It was the first time that many of John's friends ever remembered seeing him moved to tears.

Interestingly, much of the praise for *Peter Grimes* was reserved not so much for the music, though the Los Angeles Opera was superb, but for the *story*: the edgy, subversive tale of Peter Grimes, the fisherman on trial for murdering a boy. Is he hero, villain, both? How are we supposed to respond to him? What does he tell us about human nature, about ourselves? Questions John might have asked, three decades earlier on film, but which now he could express only through opera. "*Peter Grimes*," observed critic Fred Goss, "is an opera obviously created to provoke thought, and Los Angeles Opera's production achieves that goal — and *more*, admirably. You probably won't leave the Dorothy Chandler Pavilion humming the music, but the story just may haunt you forever."

Story. It had always been Schlesinger's holy grail: to tell stories that explored the complexities of the human spirit, stories that provoked but also, just as importantly, entertained. The vulgarian in him could appreciate the "wonderful gross" humor of *There's Something About Mary* and he was intrigued by the "excellent commentary" of *The Opposite of Sex*, but it was Bill Condon's *Gods and Monsters* that he liked best of all the recent movies he had seen, because it told "such a compelling story."

About his own films, he remained defiant: *Eye for an Eye*, he insisted, wasn't as bad as the critics made out. *The Day of the Locust*, he believed, was his finest achievement. And after seeing *Honky Tonk Freeway* on television, he said, "I stand by every frame."

He'd called his work his "chief pleasure in life," but that was true only so far as it went. The sheer, sensual joy of *living* was what mattered most to him. To a friend writing to compliment him on *An Englishman Abroad*, John wrote back saying, as wonderful as it all was, he was tired of talking about it: "I am dying instead to talk about food or sex!" Asked at the Venice Film Festival to identify the themes of *Madame Sousatzka*, his answers reflected his own life: "Music, food, and sex, three of the most important things in life, in that order."

After thinking about it for a moment, he added also: "Success and failure – and the need for any artist to surmount the problems that accompany both."

On the morning of New Year's Day 2001, John Schlesinger woke later than usual, walking very slowly to the table out on the terrace of his Palm Springs home. Michael went inside to fix him his usual grapefruit, tea and toast. When he returned to the terrace he found John slumped over in his chair. He couldn't move.

An ambulance was called, which took John, over Michael's objections, to Desert Hospital. It was closer than Eisenhower Medical Center in adjacent Rancho Mirage, where John was officially a patient. Doctors quickly determined that he hadn't been compliant with taking the anti-stroke medications prescribed for him following his heart surgery. "I think if he had been compliant with the medication," Dr. Kaminsky mused, "the stroke maybe could've been prevented."

Depression, exhaustion, the pressures of directing the opera all may have contributed to John's non-compliance. Kaminsky had John transferred to Eisenhower Medical, where a more experienced stroke team was in place, but precious time had been wasted with the detour to Desert Hospital. Six hours is usually all that's allowed for performing the procedure that can sometimes reverse the effects of a stroke. Still, Kaminsky was hopeful: "The first films of John's brain showed where the obstruction was. There was no blood flow to that side of the brain. But then when they did the injection, it opened up like a sunburst. It was amazing. I felt very positive that John would recover."

He didn't, of course. For two years, he would sit in his wheelchair, staring at the mountains, going from a few whispered sentences to a life of silence.

His nurse, Maureen Danson, became part of the family, tending to John above and beyond the call of duty. "Once I asked him, 'John, are you happy to be here?' and he said yes, he was," Maureen remembered. "I think that for most of [those last two years] John was still, in his own way, finding some enjoyment from life. He enjoyed the parties Michael would have. He was always very excited getting dressed, asking who would be there."

A year before his stroke, John had befriended a young filmmaker, Ilo Orleans. Going to the movies with Ilo, bantering around thoughts and opinions afterward, became one of the final great joys of his life. Orleans would be a frequent visitor in John's last two years. "You could always gauge how alert John was by telling him Ilo was coming by to visit," Maureen said, laughing. "He so loved spending time with Ilo."

There was a sense that he was reliving his life, considering it from new perspectives, maybe even rethinking some of the old maxims. Not many people came to see him except for the devoted regulars. Brenda Vaccaro was often at the house, and called nearly every day, with Maureen holding the phone to John's ear so he could hear Vaccaro's unmistakable voice. Julie Christie visited frequently. One day both Lynn and Vanessa Redgrave came by. Jerry Hellman would sometimes get emotional as he sat beside his old partner, but he'd stay with him for hours, talking about the past. John's brother Roger and sister Hilary often flew in from England, and they telephoned several times a week. Roly Curram and Geoffrey Sharp also made the trip a couple of times.

And in early 2002, when Alan Bates was honored at the Palm Springs Film Festival, John sat in his wheelchair in the front row, tears streaming down his face as Bates said he wouldn't have had a film career if not for John Schlesinger.

The knighthood never came, despite the best efforts of Bates and Glenda Jackson, but other awards piled up. On 19 May 2002, at a gala, star-studded celebration at the Egyptian Theatre in Hollywood, John received the Lifetime Achievement Award from the British Academy of Film and Television Arts. Dustin Hoffman, Jon Voight, Jerry Hellman, Sally Field, Brenda Vaccaro, Conrad Hall, Steven Zaillian, David Picker and others paid tribute. The only disappointment of the evening was John's absence, due to a seizure a few days before. In November he was once again present in spirit only when the Directors Guild of Great Britain honored him in London, with Roger accepting the award on his brother's behalf. The gathering included Antony Sher, James Fox, Billy Williams, Jim Clark, Robin Dalton, William Dudley, Eleanor Fazan and Luciana Arrighi.

For one last honor, John did manage to appear: on 10 January 2003, a star in his name was dedicated along the Walk of Fame on Palm Springs' main boulevard. William Devane, Kaye Ballard, Stefanie Powers, and Franco Zeffirelli, in town for the film festival, were on hand. John, with Michael protectively behind his wheelchair, lifted his eyes one last time to the snapping cameras and gave a little smile in gratitude. It was his last public appearance.

The days were getting more difficult. At a party, too proud to get sick at the table, John chose instead to swallow, causing him to aspirate. It meant another short hospital stay. He withdrew more and more, but even still he found ways to be present. "Especially with music," Maureen said. "He'd be sitting there for the longest time listening and then he'd say, 'They changed the words.' Sometimes you'd think he wasn't present, but he'd surprise you."

Occasionally there were still flashes of the old John. As his birthday neared, Michael asked him what he might like. "A good fuck," John answered. It gave Michael the best laugh he'd had in months.

"At one point," Michael recalled, "I did go in to John and tell him it would be okay to go." Shirley MacLaine had suggested to him that John might be reluctant, after 36 years, to leave his partner, for whom he had been caretaker for so long. Now the roles were reversed. Certainly even before his stroke John had witnessed the rejuvenation of Childers' career. In addition to his successful events organizing, Michael had jumpstarted his photography with a series of new works as well as several major retrospectives, including the publication of a book, *Hollywood Voyeur*, featuring some of his most iconic photos. Now he needed to let John know he would be okay without him. "I made sure he understood that I'd be all right," Michael said, "even when he was no longer here with me."

In November 2002 Michael had to break the news to him that Noel Davis had died in London. For several days, John was silent, eating very little. Maureen thought Noel's death might have depressed him enough that he was starting to let go, but he rallied, still not apparently finished with this last stage of his life.

"I think he felt how much he was loved," Michael said.

"That's what I wanted for him. And I always made sure there was music. I wanted him always to have his music."

When finally in the summer of 2003 John's breathing simply could not sustain itself any longer, he was taken one last time to hospital. On the morning of 24 July, the life support systems were discontinued. For the rest of the day, however, John's heart went on beating strongly. Michael was at his bedside. At one point John opened his eyes, ascertained Michael was still there, and squeezed his hand.

Finally, at 5:30 a.m. the next morning, he died. He was 77 years old.

He hadn't been forgotten, as he'd sometimes thought. All the major American television networks carried stories on his death, with the *New York Times* and *Los Angeles Times* giving his obituaries front-page coverage. In Britain, John's death created a media flurry, with tributes appearing for days in *The Times* and the *Guardian*. Several hundred people turned out for a memorial service at the synagogue in St. John's Wood, with Alan Bates, Alan Bennett, Jim Clark and others taking turns eulogizing their old friend. In the audience were Roly Curram, Lisa Eichhorn, Eileen Atkins, Ann Skinner, and dozens more who had walked part of John's life with him. His ashes were carried back to London by Michael: finally John had come home to England. His ashes were interred beside John's parents in a small private ceremony. Michael kept a small vial that will be buried with him.

The end of John's story is, like the rest of it, about survival. "I am essentially a rather pessimistic person, although I'm not without hope," he said once. "There is something in me which says that we have got to cope with whatever is our lot, otherwise why go on? And most people do, and that's one of the incredible miracles of mankind."

A few years before his stroke, interviewer Jeremy Isaacs had asked him about his greatest fear. "Physical pain, perhaps," John answered. During the last two years of his life, John never seemed to be in any physical pain; if he had been, his friends believed, he never would have lasted as long as he did. Rather, he seemed during that period quiet and contemplative, the first time anyone could remember John Schlesinger described in such terms. He'd been a man who'd never had time to slow down – a man who, like his father, had turned away from opportunities for self-contentment – a man who had never taken no for an answer, who had refused to ever simply rest upon his laurels. Now he had no choice but to do so. It was either that, or die.

He had been right all along: survival was, in itself, a reward. "I do believe in – not organized religion," he said, shortly before his stroke, "but in providence, whatever they mean by that, because I think it is unthinkable that people endure what they endure and then they go on. How? What is the miracle of that? It *is* a miraculous thing. And that – survival – is the one very strongly held belief that I have."

In *Sunday, Bloody Sunday* there's a scene in which Daniel Hirsh consoles a couple over the condition of their relative, who's been in an accident. "You're not thinking she'd be better gone, doctor, are you?" the woman asks.

"No, I'm not," Hirsh says. "I'm certainly not."

"If she couldn't move?" the woman persists.

There is a pause, but then Daniel tells her: "People can manage on very little."

John's greatest fear wasn't pain. It was loneliness. "I am terrified of loneliness," he admitted once. "I have never lived alone. I like being alone in my room, I like to shut the world out – but I like the knowledge that there is someone else in the house."

In those last two years of his life, there was always someone else in the house. He was never alone. "Surrounded by love," was Michael's mantra. The end of John Schlesinger's story came only when survival, on its own, became too much of a burden. At the same time, significantly, he also came to realize that life hadn't required him to settle for half a loaf after all. He'd gotten the whole bloody thing.

In that last scene between Joe Buck and Ratso Rizzo in *Midnight Cowboy*, when they've almost made it to Florida, after Joe has cleaned up his friend and dressed him in happy, hopeful, colorful clothes, Ratso turns to him and says, very quietly, "Thank you, Joe." Those are the last words he speaks before he dies: *Thank you*. Life had, to his great surprise, given him far more than he'd ever believed possible.

In his last hours of life, lying in his hospital bed, John Schlesinger, his lips dry and parched, felt Michael's hand gently swabbing the inside of his mouth, giving him relief. And the last words he, too, ever uttered were ones of gratitude. He said, quite simply, "Thank you."

FILM AND TELEVISION PRODUCTIONS

DIRECTED BY JOHN SCHLESINGER

Productions that were shown only on television are listed in italics. John Schlesinger is the sole director unless otherwise credited. I am grateful to the staff of the BBC Archives, especially Erin O'Neill, for helping me compile, for the first time, the complete list of Schlesinger's work for the *Tonight* and *Monitor* programmes with credits assembled as best as possible from existing records. I am also indebted to Nancy J. Brooker's *John Schlesinger: A Guide to References and Resources* (Boston: G.K. Hall, 1978) and Jonathan Hacker's *Take Ten: Contemporary British Film Directors* (Oxford: Clarendon Press, 1991). Thanks also to my assistant Aaron Leventman for additional research, and to Roger Schlesinger for information on the early films.

1945   HORROR (16 mm)

PRODUCERS/DIRECTORS/EDITORS/WRITERS: John Schlesinger, John Marples. PHOTOGRAPHY: John Schlesinger. CAST: John Schlesinger (*escaped convict*), Roger Schlesinger (*escaped convict*), Paul Vaughan (*murderer*), Laura Ford (*victim*). 10 mins.

1948 BLACK LEGEND (Mount Pleasant Productions, 16 mm)

PRODUCERS/DIRECTORS/WRITERS: John Schlesinger, Alan Cooke. PHOTOGRAPHY: John Schlesinger. EDITOR: John Schlesinger. LIGHTING AND TITLES: Humfrey Wakefield. COSTUMES: Evelyn Lamb. CONTINUITY: Roger Schlesinger. CAST:

Ena Morgan (*Martha Broomham*), John Marples (*George Broomham*), Dela Bradshaw (*Dorothy Newman*), Nigel Finzi (*Robert Broomham*), Robert Hardy (*Mad Thomas*), Kate Lovelock (*Sarah Pummis, the gossip*), Laura Ford (*neighbour*), Bill May (*neighbour's beau*), Lev Bevan (*William Kimber*), Charles Lepper (*Ezra Daniel, also bicyclist in prologue*), Hilary Schlesinger, Christopher Hall, Michael Morgan, Eve Lear (*bicyclists in prologue*), Roger Schlesinger (*Sheriff of Newbury*), Wendy Schlesinger, Charlotte Fraisse (*farm girls*), Susan Schlesinger (*Penelope*), Lillian Painting (*Madge Daniel*), David Raeburn (*vicar*), Percy Billington (*hangman*), John Schlesinger (*judge*), Alan Cooke (*prosecutor*), Jean Tubb, Ethel Druce, Hilda Moorby, Hilda Whalley, Alf Brown, C.S Drummond (*villagers and extras*). 60 mins.

1950 THE STARFISH: A FAIRY TALE (Mount Pleasant Productions, 16 mm)
PRODUCERS/DIRECTORS/WRITERS: John Schlesinger, Alan Cooke. PHOTOGRAPHY: John Schlesinger. EDITORS: Malcolm Cooke, Richard Marden. ASSEMBLY: Alfred Cox. MUSIC: Roy Jesson. SOUND RECORDIST: Charles T. Parkhouse. TECHNICAL ADVISOR: Frances Kirk. MAKE-UP: Margaret Hoggarth. CONTINUITY: Joyce Finzi. PRODUCTION ADMINISTRATION: John Marples, Geoffrey Sharp. MUSIC: Roy Jesson. MUSICAL ASSISTANT: Hilary Schlesinger. CAST: Kenneth Griffith (*Jack Trevenick*), Nigel Finzi (*Tim Wilson*), Susan Schlesinger (*Jill Wilson*), Christopher Finzi (*Michael Wilson*), Ursula Wood (*Mother*), Stanley Webber (*Father*), Margaret Webber (*Witch Meg*), Thomas Arthur (*an old salt*), Hartley Tripp (*Mr. Nick, the café owner*), Fred Stevens, Harry Stevens, Buller Arthur, Llewellyn Stevens, Ernest Stevens, Benny Stevens, Avis Austin, David Raffin (*fishermen and extras*). 75 mins.

1956 SUNDAY IN THE PARK (Face of London Productions)
PRODUCERS/DIRECTORS/WRITERS: John Schlesinger, Basil

Appleby. PHOTOGRAPHY: John Schlesinger. MUSIC: Serge Lancen. CAST: Robert Stinson (*business man in bowler hat*), Roger Schlesinger, Barbara Webber (*loving couple*), Ian Buruma (*boy*). 15 mins.

1957 *PETTICOAT LANE* (*Tonight*, BBC)

FIRST BROADCAST: 23 April. PRODUCER: Donald Baverstock. ASSISTANT PRODUCER: Alisdair Milne. PHOTOGRAPHY: A.A. "Tubby" Englander. EDITOR: Jack Gold. COMMENTARY: Derek Hart.

RUSH HOUR (*Tonight*, BBC)

FIRST BROADCAST: 19 June. PRODUCER: Donald Baverstock. ASSISTANT PRODUCER: Alisdair Milne. PHOTOGRAPHY: A.A. "Tubby" Englander. EDITOR: Jack Gold. COMMENTARY: Derek Hart.

UPPINGHAM SCHOOL AT THE HOLIDAYS (*Tonight*, BBC)

FIRST BROADCAST: 9 August. PRODUCER: Donald Baverstock. ASSISTANT PRODUCER: Alisdair Milne. EDITOR: Jack Gold.

WAKES WEEK (*Tonight*, BBC)

FIRST BROADCAST: 16 August. PRODUCER: Donald Baverstock. ASSISTANT PRODUCER: Alisdair Milne. EDITOR: Jack Gold.

FLOWER SHOW (*Tonight*, BBC)

FIRST BROADCAST: 30 August. PRODUCER: Donald Baverstock. ASSISTANT PRODUCER: Alisdair Milne. EDITOR: Jack Gold. COMMENTARY: John Schlesinger.

DAY TRIP TO BOULOGNE (*Tonight*, BBC)

FIRST BROADCAST: 25 September. PRODUCER: Donald Baverstock. ASSISTANT PRODUCER: Alisdair Milne. EDITOR: Jack Gold. COMMENTARY: John Schlesinger.

HOLIDAY RESORT IN BAD WEATHER (*Tonight*, BBC)

FIRST BROADCAST: 1 October. PRODUCER: Donald Baverstock. ASSISTANT PRODUCER: Alisdair Milne. EDITOR: Jack Gold. COMMENTARY: Frank Phillips, Noel Davis.

SONG OF THE VALLEY (*Tonight*, BBC)
FIRST BROADCAST: 1 November. PRODUCER: Donald Baverstock. ASSISTANT PRODUCER: Alisdair Milne. EDITOR: Jack Gold. MUSIC: based on a song recorded by Dorothy Squires. CAST: F. Turner, T. Brooke.

ARMISTICE DAY (*Tonight*, BBC)
FIRST BROADCAST: 11 November. PRODUCER: Donald Baverstock. ASSISTANT PRODUCER: Alisdair Milne. EDITOR: Jack Gold.

1958 **THE CIRCUS** (*Monitor*, BBC)
FIRST BROADCAST: 2 February. PRODUCER: Huw Wheldon. PHOTOGRAPHY: John S. Turner. SOUND: R. Crawley. EDITOR: Allan Tyrer.

PARIS LEFT BANK (*Monitor*, BBC)
FIRST BROADCAST: 2 March. PRODUCER: Huw Wheldon. WRITER: Robert Robinson.

THE ITALIAN OPERA (*Monitor*, BBC)
FIRST BROADCAST: 30 March. PRODUCER: Huw Wheldon. PHOTOGRAPHY: Charles de Jaeger. EDITOR: Allan Tyrer.

YEHUDI MENUHIN (*Monitor*, BBC)
FIRST BROADCAST: 13 April. PRODUCER: Huw Wheldon.

BRUSSELS EXHIBITION (*Monitor*, BBC)
FIRST BROADCAST: 27 April. PRODUCER: Huw Wheldon. WRITER: Robert Robinson. EDITOR: Allan Tyrer.

CANNES FILM FESTIVAL (*Monitor*, BBC)
FIRST BROADCAST: 25 May. PRODUCER: Huw Wheldon. WRITER: Robert Robinson. PHOTOGRAPHY: Ken Higgins. EDITOR: Allan Tyrer. SOUND: Bob Saunders. COMMENTARY: Robert Robinson.

BENJAMIN BRITTEN (*Monitor*, BBC)
FIRST BROADCAST: 22 June. PRODUCER: Huw Wheldon. PHOTOGRAPHY: Ken Higgins. EDITOR: Allan Tyrer.

STUDENTS ORCHESTRA OF GREAT BRITAIN (*Monitor*, BBC)

FIRST BROADCAST: 20 July. PRODUCER: Huw Wheldon.

ON THE PIER (*Monitor*, BBC)

FIRST BROADCAST: 20 July. PRODUCER: Huw Wheldon. WRITER: John Schlesinger. COMMENTARY: Robert Robinson.

THE INNOCENT EYE (*Monitor*, BBC)

FIRST BROADCAST: 9 November. PRODUCERS: Huw Wheldon, Peter Newington. WRITER: Michell Raper. PHOTOGRAPHY: John McGlashan. EDITOR: Allan Tyrer. SOUND: Peter Jarvis, Bob Saunders. COMMENTARY: Geoffrey Keen, David Peel.

1959   *GEORGE SIMENON* (*Monitor*, BBC)

FIRST BROADCAST: 18 January. PRODUCER: Huw Wheldon, Peter Newington. WRITER: John Schlesinger, Huw Wheldon. EDITOR: Allan Tyrer. COMMENTARY: Huw Wheldon.

HI-FI FO FUM (*Monitor*, BBC)

FIRST BROADCAST: 12 April. PRODUCER: Huw Wheldon, Peter Newington. WRITER: Robert Robinson. COMMENTARY: Robert Robinson.

1960   *PRIVATE VIEW* (*Monitor*, BBC)

FIRST BROADCAST: 8 May. PRODUCER: Huw Wheldon. WRITER: Michell Raper. PHOTOGRAPHY: John McGlashan. EDITOR: Allan Tyrer. MUSIC: Freddie Phillips, Ken Jones. COMMENTARY: Huw Wheldon. CAST: Anthony Whishaw, James Howie, Sonia Lawson, Allan Rawlinson (*themselves*).

1961   TERMINUS (British Transport Films)

RELEASE DATE (UK): 1 April. PRODUCER: Edgar Anstey. WRITER: John Schlesinger. PHOTOGRAPHY: Ken Higgins (billed as Ken Phipps). EDITOR: Hugh Raggett. ASSISTANT EDITORS: David Gladwell, Nicholas Hale. ADDITIONAL PHOTOGRAPHY: Robert Paynter. ASSISTANT PHOTOGRAPHER: Jim Godfrey. ASSISTANT DIRECTOR: Nicholas Hale. MUSIC: Ron Grainer, Julian Cooper,

Michell Raper. SOUND RECORDING: Ken Cameron. CAST: Matthew Perry (*little lost boy*), Margaret Ashcroft (*mother*), Gertrude Dickin (*woman asking about train*). 30 mins.

THE CLASS (*Monitor*, BBC)

FIRST BROADCAST: 9 April. PRODUCER: Huw Wheldon. WRITERS: Michell Raper, John Schlesinger, Harold Lang. PHOTOGRAPHY: Tony Leggo. EDITOR: Allan Tyrer. SOUND RECORDING: Derek Dean, Bob Saunders. CAST: Harold Lang (*himself*), Angela Down (*herself*).

THE GUNS OF NAVARONE PROMOTION (*Columbia*)

RELEASE DATE (US): various short films from June to October. PRODUCER: Carl Foreman. WRITER: John Schlesinger.

1962 A KIND OF LOVING (Vic Films/Anglo-Amalgamated)

RELEASE DATE (UK): 12 April. PRODUCER: Joseph Janni. SCREEN-PLAY: Willis Hall, Keith Waterhouse, based on a novel by Stan Barstow. PHOTOGRAPHY: Denys Coop. EDITOR: Roger Cherrill. ART DIRECTION: Ray Simm. SET DECORATION: Maurice Fowler. PRODUCTION MANAGER: Charles Hammond. ASSOCIATE PRODUCER: Jack Hanbury. ASSISTANT DIRECTOR: Frank Ernst. MUSIC: Ron Grainier. SOUND: Don Sharpe, George Stephenson, Red Law. WARDROBE: Laura Nightingale. MAKE-UP: Bob Lawrence. CAST: Alan Bates (*Vic Brown*), June Ritchie (*Ingrid Rothwell*), Thora Hird (*Mrs. Rothwell*), Bert Palmer (*Mr. Brown*), Gwen Nelson (*Mrs. Brown*), Malcolm Patton (*Jim Brown*), Pat Keen (*Christine*), David Mahlowe (*David*), Jack Smethurst (*Conroy*). 112 minutes.

1963 BILLY LIAR (*Vic Films/Waterhall Productions/Anglo-Amalgamated*)

RELEASE DATE (UK): 13 August. PRODUCER: Joseph Janni. SCREENPLAY: Willis Hall, Keith Waterhouse, based on a novel by Keith Waterhouse. PHOTOGRAPHY: Denys Coop. EDITOR: Roger

Cherrill. ART DIRECTION: Ray Simm. SET DRESSER: Ken Bridgeman. PRODUCTION MANAGER: Charles Blair. ASSOCIATE PRODUCER: Jack Rix. ASSISTANT DIRECTORS: Frank Ernst, Jim Brennan. MUSIC: Richard Rodney Bennett. CONDUCTOR: John Hollingsworth. SOUND: Peter Handford, Tom Buchanan, Doug Barnett. WARDROBE: Laura Nightingale. MAKE-UP: Bob Lawrence. CAST: Tom Courtenay (*Billy Fisher*), Julie Christie (*Liz*), Wilfred Pickles (*Geoffrey Fisher*), Mona Washbourne (*Alice Fisher*), Ethel Griffies (*Grandmother*), Finlay Currie (*Duxbury*), Rodney Bewes (*Arthur Crabtree*), Helen Fraser (*Barbara*), Gwendolyn Watts (*Rita*), Leonard Rossiter (*Shadrack*). 98 minutes (cut to 96).

1965   DARLING (Vic Films/Anglo-Amalgamated)
RELEASE DATE (UK): 4 August. PRODUCER: Joseph Janni. SCREENPLAY: Frederic Raphael. STORY: Frederic Raphael, John Schlesinger, Joseph Janni. PHOTOGRAPHY: Ken Higgins. EDITOR: James Clark. ART DIRECTION: Ray Simm. SET DECORATION: David Ffolkes. PRODUCTION MANAGER: Ed Harper. ASSOCIATE PRODUCER: Victor Lyndon. MUSIC: John Dankworth. SOUND: Malcolm Cooke. COSTUMES: Julie Harris. MAKE-UP: Bob Lawrence. CAST: Julie Christie (*Diana Scott*), Dirk Bogarde (*Robert Gold*), Laurence Harvey (*Miles Brand*), Roland Curram (*Malcolm*), Alex Scott (*Sean Martin*), Basil Henson (*Alec Prosser-Jones*), Helen Lindsay (*Felicity Prosser-Jones*), Tyler Butterworth (*William Prosser-Jones*), Jose-Luis de Vilallonga (*Prince Cesare Della Romita*), Pauline Yates (*Estelle Gold*), Peter Bayliss (*Lord Grant*). 127 minutes (cut to 122).

1967   FAR FROM THE MADDING CROWD (Vic Films/ EMI/MGM)
RELEASE DATE (UK): 16 October. PRODUCER: Joseph Janni. SCREENPLAY: Frederic Raphael, based on a novel by Thomas Hardy. PHOTOGRAPHY: Nicolas Roeg. CAMERA OPERATOR: John

Harris. EDITOR: Malcolm Cooke (uncredited), James Clark. PRODUCTION DESIGN: Richard MacDonald. ART DIRECTION: Roy Smith. SET DECORATION: Peter James. PRODUCTION MANAGER: Ed Harper. MUSIC COMPOSITION: Richard Rodney Bennett. MUSIC CONDUCTOR: Marcus Dodds. ASSOCIATE PRODUCER: Edward Joseph. ASSISTANT DIRECTORS: Kip Gowans, David Bracknell. SOUND: Robin Gregory, John Aldred. COSTUMES: Alan Barrett. MAKE-UP: Bob Lawrence, Philip Leakey. CONTINUITY: Ann Skinner. CAST: Julie Christie (*Bathsheba Everdene*), Terence Stamp (*Sergeant Troy*), Peter Finch (*William Boldwood*), Alan Bates (*Gabriel Oak*), Fiona Walker (*Liddy*), Prunella Ransome (*Fanny*), Alison Leggatt (*Mrs. Hurst*), Paul Dawkins (*Henry Fray*). 169 minutes (cut to 143).

1969 MIDNIGHT COWBOY (Hellman/Schlesinger Production/UA)

RELEASE DATE (US): 25 May. PRODUCER: Jerome Hellman. SCREENPLAY: Waldo Salt, based on a novel by James Leo Herlihy. PHOTOGRAPHY: Adam Holender. CAMERA OPERATOR: Dick Kratina. EDITOR: Hugh A. Robertson, Jr.; James Clark (uncredited). PRODUCTION DESIGN: John Robert Lloyd. SET DECORATION: Philip Smith. MASTER SCENIC ARTIST: Edward Garsero. GRAPHIC EFFECTS: Pablo Ferro. MUSIC SUPERVISOR: John Barry. MUSIC PRODUCER: Toxey French. ASSOCIATE PRODUCER: Kenneth Utt. SECOND UNIT DIRECTOR: Burt Harris. ASSISTANT TO THE DIRECTOR: Michael Childers. SOUND: Abe Seidman, John Fitzstephens. COSTUMES: Ann Roth. WARDROBE SUPERVISOR: Max Solomon. MAKE-UP: Irving Buchman. CONTINUITY: Nicholas Sgarro. PRODUCTION MANAGER: Hal Schaffel. CAST: Dustin Hoffman (*Ratso Rizzo*), Jon Voight (*Joe Buck*), Jon McGiver (*Mr. O'Daniel*), Brenda Vaccaro (*Shirley*), Barnard Hughes (*Towny*), Sylvia Miles (*Cass*), Ruth White (*Sally Buck*), Jennifer Salt (*Crazy Annie*), Bob Balaban (*student in movie theater*), Viva (*Gretel*

McAlbertson), Gastone Rossilli (*Hansel McAlbertson*), Ultra Violet, Paul Jabara, International Velvet, William Dorr, Cecilia Lipson, Taylor Mead, Paul Morrissey, Paul Jasmin, Michael Childers (*party guests*). 119 minutes (cut to 113).

1971 SUNDAY, BLOODY SUNDAY (A Vectia Film/UA)

RELEASE DATE (UK): 29 June. PRODUCER: Joseph Janni. SCREEN-PLAY: Penelope Gilliatt; John Schlesinger, David Sherwin (uncredited). PHOTOGRAPHY: Billy Williams. EDITOR: Richard Marden. PRODUCTION DESIGN: Luciana Arrighi. ART DIRECTOR: Norman Dorme. MUSIC: Ron Geesin. MUSIC CONDUCTOR: Douglas Gamley. ASSOCIATE PRODUCER: Teddy Joseph. ASSISTANT DIRECTOR: Simon Relph. SOUND: Simon Kaye. COSTUMES: Jocelyn Rickards. MAKE-UP: Freddy Williamson. PRODUCTION MANAGER: Hugh Harlow. CAST: Glenda Jackson (*Alex Greville*), Peter Finch (*Dr. Daniel Hirsh*), Murray Head (*Bob Elkin*), Peggy Ashcroft (*Mrs. Greville*), Vivian Pickles (*Alva Hodson*), Frank Windsor (*Bill Hodson*), Thomas Baptiste (*Professor Johns*), Tony Bitton (*George Harding*), Harold Goldblatt (*Daniel's father*), Hannah Norbert (*Daniel's mother*), Bessie Love (*answering service operator*), Emma Schlesinger (*Tess Hodson*). 110 mins.

1973 THE LONGEST (Segment of *Visions of Eight*) (Wolper Productions/MGM-EMI)

RELEASE DATE (US): August 2. EXECUTIVE PRODUCER: David L. Wolper. PRODUCER: Stan Margulies. SCREENPLAY: John Schlesinger. PHOTOGRAPHY: Arthur Wooster. EDITOR: Jim Clark. PRODUCTION ASSISTANTS: Drummond Challis, Richard Richtsfeld. PRODUCTION MANAGER: Udo Lambsdorff. MUSIC: Henry Mancini. SOUND: Rene Borisewitz, Gerry Humphries. ELECTRONIC SOUND: Brian Hodgson of Electrophon. SOUND EDITOR: Frank Schreiner. CAST: Ron Hill, Avery Brundage, Frank Shorter (*themselves*). *Film runs* 110 mins./"The Longest" 25 mins.

1975   THE DAY OF THE LOCUST (Paramount)

RELEASE DATE (US): 7 May. PRODUCER: Jerome Hellman. SCREENPLAY: Waldo Salt, based on a novel by Nathanael West. PHOTOGRAPHY: Conrad Hall. EDITOR: Jim Clark. PRODUCTION DESIGN: Richard MacDonald. ART DIRECTOR: John Lloyd. SET DECORATOR: George Hopkins. MUSIC: John Barry. ASSOCIATE PRODUCER: Sheldon Schrager. SPECIAL EFFECTS: Tim Smyth, Albert Whitlock. SOUND: Tommy Overton. COSTUMES: Ann Roth. MAKE-UP: Del Armstrong. PRODUCTION ASSOCIATE: Michael Childers. DANCE SUPERVISION: Marge Champion. CAST: Donald Sutherland (*Homer Simpson*), Karen Black (*Faye Greener*), Burgess Meredith (*Harry Greener*), William Atherton (*Tod Hackett*), Geraldine Page (*Big Sister*), Richard A. Dysart (*Claude Estee*), Bo Hopkins (*Earle Shoop*), Pepe Serna (*Miguel*), Lelia Goldoni (*Mary Dove*), Billy Barty (*Abe*), Jackie Haley (*Adore Loomis*), Gloria LeRoy (*Mrs. Loomis*), Natalie Schafer (*Audrey Jennings*), William Castle (*director*), Madge Kennedy (*Mrs. Johnson*). 144 mins.

1976   MARATHON MAN (Paramount)

RELEASE DATE (US): 6 October. PRODUCER: Robert Evans, Sidney Beckerman. SCREENPLAY: William Goldman, based on his novel. PHOTOGRAPHY: Conrad Hall. EDITOR: Jim Clark. PRODUCTION DESIGN: Richard MacDonald. ART DIRECTOR: Jack De Shields. SET DECORATOR: George Gaines. MUSIC: Michael Small. ASSOCIATE PRODUCER: George Justin. SPECIAL EFFECTS: Richard E. Johnson, Charles Spurgeon. SOUND MIXER: David Ronne. SOUND EDITORS: Edward L. Sandlin, Freddie Stafford. COSTUMES: Robert De Mora. MAKE-UP: Ben Nye. ASSISTANT DIRECTORS: Howard W. Koch, Jr., Burtt Harris. SCRIPT SUPERVISOR: Nick Sgarro. ASSISTANT TO THE PRODUCERS: Michael Childers. CAST: Dustin Hoffman (*Babe Levy*), Laurence Olivier (*Christian Szell*), Roy Scheider (*Doc Levy*), William Devane (*Janeway*), Marthe Keller (*Elsa*), Fritz Weaver (*Professor*

Biesenthal), Richard Bright (*Karl*), Marc Lawrence (*Erhard*), Ben Dova (*Szell's brother*). 126 mins.

1979   YANKS (UA)

RELEASE DATE (US): 19 September. PRODUCER: Joseph Janni, Lester Persky. SCREENPLAY: Colin Welland, Walter Bernstein. STORY: Colin Welland. PHOTOGRAPHY: Dick Bush. EDITOR: Jim Clark. PRODUCTION DESIGN: Brian Morris. ART DIRECTOR: Milly Burns. MUSIC: Richard Rodney Bennett. ASSOCIATE PRODUCER: Edward Joseph. CONTINUITY: Zelda Barron. SOUND MIXER: Simon Kaye. SOUND EDITOR: Ian Fuller. COSTUMES: Shirley Russell. MAKE-UP: Wally Schneiderman. ASSISTANT DIRECTOR: Simon Relph. CHOREOGRAPHER: Eleanor Fazan. CAST: Richard Gere (*Matt*), Lisa Eichhorn (*Jean*), Vanessa Redgrave (*Helen*), William Devane (*John*), Chick Vennera (*Danny*), Wendy Morgan (*Mollie*), Rachel Roberts (*Mrs. Moreton*), Tony Melody (*Mr. Moreton*), Derek Thompson (*Ken*), Martin Smith (*Geoff*), Simon Harrison (*Tim*), Sue Robinson (*girl at dance*). 139 mins.

1981   HONKY TONK FREEWAY (EMI / Universal)

RELEASE DATE (US): 21 August. PRODUCER: Don Boyd. Howard W. Koch, Jr. SCREENPLAY: Edward Clinton. PHOTOGRAPHY: John Bailey. EDITOR: Jim Clark. ART DIRECTOR: Edwin O'Donovan. SET DECORATOR: Bruce Weintraub. MUSIC: Elmer Bernstein, George Martin. SPECIAL EFFECTS: Joe Day. SOUND MIXER: Larry Jost. SOUND EDITOR: Peter Horrocks. COSTUMES: Ann Roth. MAKE-UP: Gerry O'Dell. SECOND UNIT DIRECTOR: Jim Clark. CAST: William Devane (*Mayor Kirby T. Calo*), Beau Bridges (*Duane Hansen*), Beverly D'Angelo (*Carmen Odessa Shelby*), Hume Cronyn (*Sherm*), Jessica Tandy (*Carol*), Geraldine Page (*Sister Maria Clarissa*), Teri Garr (*Ericka*), Peter Billingsley (*Billie*), Paul Jabara (*T.J. Tupus*), Howard Hesseman (*Snapper*), Jenn Thompson (*Delia*), Ron Frazier (*David Kirk*). 107 mins.

1983 *SEPARATE TABLES* (HBO/HTV/Primetime Television)

FIRST BROADCAST (US): 13 March. EXECUTIVE PRODUCER: Colin Callender. PRODUCERS: Edie Landau, Ely A. Landau. SCREENPLAY: Terence Rattigan (1958 screenplay). PHOTOGRAPHY: Gary Penny EDITOR: Peter Buchanan. PRODUCTION DESIGNER: Julia Trevelyan-Oman. SET DECORATOR: Chris Cook. MUSIC: Phillip Smith. COSTUMES: June Robinson. CAST: Julie Christie (*Mrs. Shankland/Miss Railton-Bell*), Alan Bates (*John Malcolm/Major Pollock*), Claire Bloom (*Miss Cooper*), Irene Worth (*Mrs. Railton-Bell*), Sylvia Barter (*Lady Matheson*), Bernard Archard (*Mr. Fowler*), Liz Smith (*Miss Meacham*), Kathy Staff (*Mabel*). 125 mins.

AN ENGLISHMAN ABROAD (BBC)

FIRST BROADCAST (UK): 22 November. PRODUCER: Innes Lloyd. SCREENPLAY: Alan Bennett. PHOTOGRAPHY: Nat Crosby. EDITOR: XXX. PRODUCTION DESIGNER: XXX. PRODUCTION MANAGER: Tom Kingdon. MUSIC: George Fenton. COSTUMES: Amy Roberts. CAST: Alan Bates (*Guy Burgess*), Coral Browne (*Herself*), Peter Chelsom (*Giles*), Vernon Dobtcheff (*Guildenstern*), Charles Gray (*Claudius*), Judy Gridley (*Tessa*), Czeslaw Grocholski (*General*), Denys Hawthorne (*Tailor*). 65 mins.

1985 **THE FALCON AND THE SNOWMAN** (Hemdale Film Productions/Orion)

RELEASE DATE (US): 25 January. EXECUTIVE PRODUCER: John Daly. PRODUCERS: Gabriel Katzka, John Schlesinger. SCREENPLAY: Steven Zaillian, based on the book by Robert Lindsey. PHOTOGRAPHY: Allen Daviau. EDITOR: Richard Marden. PRODUCTION DESIGN: James D. Bissell. ART DIRECTOR (MEXICO): Agustin Ituarte. SET DECORATOR: Lisa De Scenna. ASSOCIATE PRODUCER: Michael Childers. MUSIC: Lyle Mays, Pat Metheny, David Bowie. SOUND MIXER: Rene Borisewitz. SOUND EDITOR: Nicholas Stevenson. COSTUMES: Albert Wolsky. MAKE-UP: Ken

Chase, Ester Oropeza. FIRST ASSISTANT DIRECTOR: Patrick Crowley. SECOND UNIT DIRECTOR: Michael Childers. CAST: Timothy Hutton (*Christopher Boyce*), Sean Penn (*Daulton Lee*), Richard Dysart (*Dr. Lee*), David Suchet (*Alex*), Lori Singer (*Lana*), Pat Hingle (*Mr. Boyce*), Dorian Harewood (*Gene*), Mady Kaplan (*Laurie*), Jerry Hardin (*Tony Owens*), Chris Makepeace (*David Lee*). 131 mins.

1987   THE BELIEVERS (Orion)

RELEASE DATE (US): 10 June. EXECUTIVE PRODUCER: Edward Teets. PRODUCERS: Michael Childers, John Schlesinger, Beverly J. Camhe. SCREENPLAY: Mark Frost, based on the novel *The Religion* by Nicholas Conde. PHOTOGRAPHY: Robby Müller. EDITOR: Peter Honess. PRODUCTION DESIGN: Simon Holland. ART DIRECTORS: John Kasarda, Carol Spier. SET DECORATORS: Susan Bode, Elinor Rose Galbraith. MUSIC: J. Peter Robinson. SOUND MIXER: Tod A. Maitland. SOUND EDITOR: Nicholas Stevenson. COSTUMES: Shay Cunliffe. MAKE-UP: Mickey Scott, Shonagh Jabour. SPECIAL MAKE-UP EFFECTS: Kevin Haney. SPECIAL EFFECTS: Connie Brink, Ted Ross. FIRST ASSISTANT DIRECTOR: Patrick Crowley. SECOND UNIT DIRECTOR: Michael Childers. CAST: Martin Sheen (*Cal Jamison*), Helen Shaver (*Jessica Halliday*), Harley Cross (*Chris Jamison*), Robert Loggia (*Lt. Sean McTaggert*), Elizabeth Wilson (*Kate Maslow*), Harris Yulin (*Robert Calder*), Jimmy Smits (*Tom Lopez*), Lee Richardson (*Dennis Maslow*), Richard Masur (*Marty Wertheimer*), Carla Pinza (*Carmen Ruiz*), Janet Laine-Green (*Lisa Jamison*). 114 mins.

1988   MADAME SOUSATZKA (Cineplex-Odeon/Universal)

RELEASE DATE (US): 1 October. PRODUCER: Robin Dalton. SCREENPLAY: Ruth Prawer Jhabvala, John Schlesinger, based on the novel by Bernice Rubens. PHOTOGRAPHY: Nat Crosby. EDITOR: Peter Honess. PRODUCTION DESIGN: Luciana Arrighi. ART

DIRECTORS: Stephen Scott, Ian Whittaker. MUSIC: Gerald Gouriet. SOUND MIXER: Simon Kaye. SOUND EDITOR: Bob Risk. COSTUMES: Amy Roberts. MAKE-UP: Sallie Evans. ASSOCIATE PRODUCER: Simon Bosanquet. FIRST ASSISTANT DIRECTOR: Chris Rose. CAST: Shirley MacLaine (*Madame Sousatzka*), Peggy Ashcroft (*Lady Emily*), Twiggy (*Jenny*), Shabana Azmi (*Sushita*), Navin Chowdhry (*Manek Sen*), Leigh Lawson (*Ronnie Blum*), Geoffrey Bayldon (*Mr. Cordle*), Lee Montague (*Vincent Pick*), Robert Rietty (*Leo Milev*), Sam Howard (*Edward*), Roland Curram (*menswear salesman*), Katharine Schlesinger (*piano student*). 122 mins.

1990 PACIFIC HEIGHTS (Morgan Creek Productions/ Twentieth Century Fox)

RELEASE DATE (US): 28 September. EXECUTIVE PRODUCERS: Gary Barber, David Nicksay, James G. Robinson, Joe Roth. PRODUCERS: Scott Rudin, William Sackheim. SCREENPLAY: Daniel Pyne. PHOTOGRAPHY: Amir M. Mokri. EDITORS: Mark Warner, Steven Ramirez. PRODUCTION DESIGN: Neil Spisak. ART DIRECTORS: Gershon Ginsburg, Sharon Seymour. SET DECORATORS: Clay A. Griffith, Debra Schutt. MUSIC: Hans Zimmer. SOUND EDITOR: Robert Grieve. COSTUMES: Bridget Kelly, Ann Roth. MAKE-UP: Valli O'Reilly. CO-PRODUCER: Dennis E. Jones. FIRST ASSISTANT DIRECTOR: Herb Gains. CAST: Melanie Griffith (*Patty Palmer*), Matthew Modine (*Drake Goodman*), Michael Keaton (*Carter Hayes*), Laurie Metcalf (*Stephanie MacDonald*), Mako (*Toshio Watanabe*), Nobu McCarthy (*Mira Watanabe*), Dorian Harewood (*Dennis Reed*), Beverly D'Angelo (*Anne*), Carl Lumbly (*Lou Baker*), Luca Bercovici (*Greg*), Tippi Hedren (*Florence Peters*), Sheila McCarthy (*Liz Hamilton*). 102 mins.

1991 *A QUESTION OF ATTRIBUTION* (BBC)

FIRST BROADCAST (UK): 20 October. PRODUCER: Innes Lloyd. SCREENPLAY: Alan Bennett. PHOTOGRAPHY: John Hooper.

EDITOR: Mark Day. PRODUCTION DESIGN: Barbara Gosnold. ASSISTANT PRODUCER: Martin Pope. MUSIC: Gerald Gouriet. SOUND MIXER: Aad Wirtz. COSTUMES: Amy Roberts. MAKE-UP: Daphne Croker-Saunders. CO-PRODUCER: Dennis E. Jones. SECOND ASSISTANT DIRECTOR: Tim Stevenson. CAST: James Fox (*Sir Anthony Blunt*), David Calder (*Chubb*), Geoffrey Palmer (*Donleavy*), Prunella Scales (*H.M.Q.*), Ann Beach (*Mrs. Chubb*), Edward de Souza (*Collins*), Mark Payton (*Phillips*), Jason Flemyng (*Colin*). 71 mins.

1993 THE INNOCENT (DEFA-Studio für Spielfilme/ Miramax)

RELEASE DATE (Germany): 1 September; (UK): 18 June, 1994. EXECUTIVE PRODUCER: Ann Dubinet. PRODUCERS: Norma Heyman, Wieland Schulz-Keil, Chris Sievernich. SCREENPLAY: Ian McEwan, from his novel. PHOTOGRAPHY: Dietrich Lohmann. EDITOR: Richard Marden. PRODUCTION DESIGN: Luciana Arrighi. ART DIRECTORS: Dieter Dohl, Philipp Hübner. SET DECORATORS: Philipp Hübner, Olaf Schiefner. MUSIC: Gerald Gouriet. SOUND EDITOR: Nicholas Stevenson. SOUND MIXER: Axel Arft. COSTUMES: Ingrid Zoré. MAKE-UP: Joan Hills. FIRST ASSISTANT DIRECTOR: David Tringham. CAST: Anthony Hopkins (*Bob Glass*), Isabella Rossellini (*Maria*), Campbell Scott (*Leonard Markham*), Hart Bochner (*Russell*), Ronald Nitschke (*Otto*), James Grant (*MacNamee*), Jeremy Sinden (*Captain Lofting*), Richard Durden (*Black*). 107 mins.

1995 COLD COMFORT FARM (BBC/Gramercy Pictures)

FIRST BROADCAST (UK): 1 January; RELEASE DATE (US): 10 May, 1996. EXECUTIVE PRODUCERS: Richard Broke, Antony Root. PRODUCER: Alison Gilby. SCREENPLAY: Malcolm Bradbury, from the novel by Stella Gibbons. PHOTOGRAPHY: Chris Seager. EDITOR: Mark Day. PRODUCTION DESIGN: Malcolm Thornton.

ART DIRECTOR: Jim Holloway. MUSIC: Robert Lockhart. SOUND EDITORS: Allan Fowle, Debbie Pragnell. COSTUMES: Amy Roberts. MAKE-UP: Anita Burger, Carmel Jackson. FIRST ASSISTANT DIRECTOR: Paul Judges. CAST: Eileen Atkins (*Judith Starkadder*), Kate Beckinsale (*Flora Poste*), Sheila Burrell (*Ada Doom*), Ian McKellen (*Amos Starkadder*), Stephen Fry (*Mybug*), Joanna Lumley (*Mary Smiling*), Miriam Margoyles (*Mrs. Beetle*), Rufus Sewell (*Seth Starkadder*), Ivan Kaye (*Reuben Starkadder*), Jeremy Peters (*Urk*), Christopher Bowen (*Charles Fairford*), Harry Ditson (*Earl P. Neck*). 95 mins.

1996   EYE FOR AN EYE (Paramount)

RELEASE DATE (US): 12 January. PRODUCERS: Michael I. Levy, Michael Polaire. SCREENPLAY: Amanda Silver, Rick Jaffa, from the novel by Erika Holzer. PHOTOGRAPHY: Amir Mokri. EDITOR: Peter Honess. PRODUCTION DESIGN: Stephen Hendrickson. ART DIRECTOR: David J. Bomba. SET DECORATOR: Jan K. Bergstrom. MUSIC: James Newton Howard. SOUND EDITORS: Terry Rodman. COSTUMES: Bobbie Read. MAKE-UP: Leslie Lightfoot. FIRST ASSISTANT DIRECTOR: Gregory Jacobs. CAST: Sally Field (*Karen McCann*), Ed Harris (*Mack McCann*), Kiefer Sutherland (*Robert Doob*), Joe Mantegna (*Det. Sgt. Denillo*), Olivia Burnette (*Julie McCann*), Alexandra Kyle (*Megan McCann*), Beverly D'Angelo (*Dolly Green*), Darrell Larson (*Peter Green*), Charlayne Woodard (*Angel Kosinsky*), Philip Baker Hall (*Sidney Hughes*), Keith David (*Martin*), Wanda Acuna (*Hispanic housewife*). 101 mins.

1998   *THE TALE OF SWEENEY TODD* (Showtime)

FIRST BROADCAST (US): 19 April. EXECUTIVE PRODUCERS: Gary Dartnall, Robert Halmi, Jr., Peter Shaw. PRODUCER: Ted Swanson. SCREENPLAY: Peter Buckman, Peter Shaw. PHOTOGRAPHY: Martin Fuhrer. EDITOR: Mark Day. PRODUCTION DESIGN: Malcolm Thornton. ART DIRECTOR: Stephen Simmonds. MUSIC: Richard

Rodney Bennett. SOUND EDITOR: Danny Longhurst. COSTUMES: Joan Bergin. ASSISTANT DIRECTOR: Jim Gorman. CAST: Ben Kingsley (*Sweeney Todd*), Campbell Scott (*Ben Carlyle*), Joanna Lumley (*Mrs. Lovett*), Selina Boyack (*Alice*), David Wilmot (*Tom*), Sean O'Flanagain (*Charlie*), Katharine Schlesinger (*Lucy*), John Kavanagh (*Rutledge*), Joe Savino (*Chambers*). 92 mins.

2000 THE NEXT BEST THING (Paramount)

RELEASE DATE (US): 3 March. EXECUTIVE PRODUCERS: Gary Lucchesi, Lewis Manilow, Ted Tannebaum. PRODUCERS: Tom Rosenberg, Richard Wright, Linne Radman, Leslie Dixon, Marcus Viscidi, Meredith Zamsky. SCREENPLAY: Tom Ropelewski, Mel Bordeaux, Rupert Everett (last two uncredited). PHOTOGRAPHY: Elliott Davis. EDITOR: Peter Honess. PRODUCTION DESIGN: Howard Cummings. ART DIRECTOR: David S. Lazan. ART DIRECTOR: Jan K. Bergstrom. CONDUCTOR: Gabriel Yared. SOUND EDITOR: Terry Rodman. COSTUMES: Ruth Myers. ASSISTANT DIRECTOR: Peter Kohn. CAST: Madonna (*Abby Reynolds*), Rupert Everett (*Robert Whittaker*), Benjamin Bratt (*Ben Cooper*), Ileana Douglas (*Elizabeth Ryder*), Malcolm Stumpf (*Sammy*), Lynn Redgrave (*Helen Whittaker*), Josef Summer (*Richard Whittaker*), Neil Patrick Harris (*David*), Michael Vartan (*Kevin Lasater*). 107 mins.

THEATER AND OPERA PRODUCTIONS

DIRECTED BY JOHN SCHLESINGER

Operas are listed in italics. John Schlesinger is the sole director or (in the case of the operas) producer. The names listed here are original casts.

1964 NO WHY (Royal Shakespeare Company, Aldwych Theatre)
PREMIERE: 2 July. PLAYWRIGHT: John Whiting. DESIGNER: Barry Kay. CAST: Tony Church (*Henry*), June Jago (*Eleanor*), John Steiner (*Max*), Garry Van de Peer (*Jacob*), Ken Wynne (*Gregory*), Caroline Maud (*Amy*), Elizabeth Spriggs (*Sarah*), Mary Allen (*servant 1*), Wyn Jones (*servant 2*).

1965 TIMON OF ATHENS (Royal Shakespeare Theatre, Stratford-on-Avon)
PREMIERE: 1 July. PLAYWRIGHT: William Shakespeare. DESIGNER: Ralph Koltai. MUSIC: Richard Rodney Bennett. CHOREOGRAPHER: John Broome. LIGHTING: John Bradley. CAST: Paul Scofield (*Timon*), Tony Church (*Flavius*), David Waller (*Lord Lucullus*), Timothy West (*Lord Lucius*), Stanley Lebor (*Lord Ventidius*), Jeffrey Dench (*Head of Senate*), Brewster Mason (*Alcibiades*), Paul Rogers (*Apemantus*), Charles Kay (*a poet*).

1966 DAYS IN THE TREES (Royal Shakespeare Company, Aldwych Theatre)

PREMIERE: 9 June. PLAYWRIGHT: Marguerite Duras, translated by Sonia Orwell. DESIGNER: Timothy O'Brien. CAST: Peggy Ashcroft (*Mother*), George Baker (*Son*), Brian Badcoe (*Dede*), Frances Cuka (*Marcelle*).

1972 I AND ALBERT (Piccadilly Theatre)
PREMIERE: 6 November. PRODUCER: Richard Pilbrow. MUSIC: Charles Strause. LYRICS: Lee Adams. BOOK: Jay Allen. DESIGNER: Luciana Arrighi. MUSICAL DIRECTOR: Gareth Davies. COSTUMES: Alan Barrett. CHOREOGRAPHER: Brian MacDonald. LIGHTING: Robert Ornbo. CAST: Polly James (*Queen Victoria*), Sven-Bertil Taube (*Albert*), Lewis Fiander (*Disraeli*), Aubrey Wood (*Lord Palmerston*).

1975 HEARTBREAK HOUSE (National Theatre Company at the Old Vic)
PREMIERE: 25 February. PLAYWRIGHT: George Bernard Shaw. DESIGNER: Michael Annals. CAST: Eileen Atkins (*Hesione Hushabye*), Colin Blakely (*Captain Shotover*), Patience Collier (*Nurse Guinness*), Graham Crowden (*Hector Hushabye*), Edward de Souza (*Randall Utterword*), Harry Lomax (*Burglar*), Alan McNaughton (*Mazzini Dunn*), Anna Massey (*Ariadne Utterwords*), Kate Nelligan (*Ellie Dunn*), Paul Rogers (*Boss Mangan*).

1977 JULIUS CAESAR (National Theatre, Olivier Theatre)
PREMIERE: 22 March. PLAYWRIGHT: William Shakespeare. DESIGNER: John Bury. MUSIC: Harrison Birtwistle. LIGHTING: David Hersey. CAST: John Gielgud (*Caesar*), Ronald Pickup (*Cassius*), Brian Cox (*Brutus*), Mark McManus (*Antony*), Gawn Grainger (*Casca*), Oliver Cotton (*Decius*).

1980 THE TALES OF HOFFMANN (Royal Opera House, Covent Garden)

PREMIERE: 15 December. MUSIC: Jacques Offenbach. LIBRETTISTS: Jules Barbier, Michel Carré. CONDUCTOR: Georges Pretre. DESIGNER: William Dudley. COSTUMES: Maria Bjornson. MOVEMENT: Eleanor Fazan. LIGHTING: David Hersey. CAST: Placido Domingo (*Hoffmann*), Robert Lloyd (*Lindorf*), Claire Powell (*Nicklaus*), Robert Tear (*Spalanzani*), Luciana Serra (*Olympia*), Siegmund Nimsgern (*Dappertutto*), Ileana Cotrubus (*Antonia*), Nicola Ghiuselev (*Miracle*), Deanne Bergsma (*Stella*).

1981 TRUE WEST (National Theatre, Cottesloe Theatre)
PREMIERE: 10 December. PLAYWRIGHT: Sam Shepard. DESIGNER: Grant Hicks. LIGHTING: Rory Dempster. CAST: Bob Hoskins (*Lee*), Antony Sher (*Austin*), Shane Rimmer (*Saul Kimmer*), Patricia Hayes (*Mom*).

1982 *THE TALES OF HOFFMANN* (Royal Opera House, Covent Garden)
PREMIERE: 14 January. MUSIC: Jacques Offenbach. LIBRETTISTS: Jules Barbier, Michel Carré. CONDUCTOR: Jacques Delacote. DESIGNER: William Dudley. COSTUMES: Maria Bjornson. MOVEMENT: Eleanor Fazan. LIGHTING: David Hersey. CAST: Placido Domingo (*Hoffmann*), Stafford Dean (*Lindorf*), Diana Montague (*Nicklaus*), John Dobson (*Spalanzani*), Luciana Serra (*Olympia*), Thomas Allen (*Dappertutto*), Leona Mitchell (*Antonia*), Nicola Ghiuselev (*Miracle*), Deanne Bergsma (*Stella*).

1984 *DER ROSENKAVALIER* (Royal Opera House, Covent Garden)
PREMIERE: 4 December. MUSIC: Richard Strauss. LIBRETTIST: Hugo Von Hofmannsthal. CONDUCTOR: Georg Solti. SET DESIGNER: William Dudley. MOVEMENT: Eleanor Fazan. LIGHTING: Robert Bryan. CAST: Kiri Te Kanawa (*The Marschallin*), Anne Howells (*Octavian*), Aage Haugland (*Baron Ochs*), Barbara Bonney (*Sophie*),

1989 *UN BALLO IN MASCHERA* (Salzburg Festival)
PREMIERE: 27 July. MUSIC: Giuseppe Verdi. LIBRETTIST: Antonio Somma. CONDUCTOR: Georg Solti, Gustav Kuhn. DESIGNER: William Dudley. MOVEMENT: Eleanor Fazan. LIGHTING: Helmuth Reichman. CAST: Placido Domingo (*Gustavo*), Josephine Barstow (*Amelia*), Leo Nucci (*Renato*), Florence Quivar (*Ulrica*), Sumi Jo (*Oscar*).

1990 *UN BALLO IN MASCHERA* (Salzburg Festival)
PREMIERE: 28 July. MUSIC: Giuseppe Verdi. LIBRETTIST: Antonio Somma. CONDUCTOR: Georg Solti. DESIGNER: William Dudley. MOVEMENT: Eleanor Fazan. LIGHTING: Helmuth Reichman. CAST: Placido Domingo (*Gustavo*), Josephine Barstow (*Amelia*), Leo Nucci (*Renato*), Florence Quivar (*Ulrica*), Sumi Jo (*Oscar*).

2000 *PETER GRIMES* (Teatro alla Scala, Milan)
PREMIERE: 15 June. MUSIC: Benjamin Britten. LIBRETTIST: Montagu Slater. CONDUCTOR: Jeffrey Tate. DESIGNER: Luciana Arrighi. LIGHTING: Gianni Mantovanini. MOVEMENT: Eleanor Fazan. CHORUS MASTER: Roberto Gabbiani. CAST: Philip Langridge (*Peter Grimes*), Patricia Racette (*Ellen Orford*), Alan Held (*Captain Balstrode*), Sarah Walker (*Mrs. Sedley*), Anne Collins (*Auntie*), Brett Polegato (*Ned Keene*), Donald George (*Bob Boles*).

PETER GRIMES (Los Angeles Opera, Dorothy Chandler Pavilion)
PREMIERE: 18 October. MUSIC: Benjamin Britten. LIBRETTIST: Montagu Slater. CONDUCTOR: Richard Armstrong. DESIGNER: Luciana Arrighi. LIGHTING DESIGNER: Mark Jonathan. MOVEMENT: Eleanor Fazan. CHORUS MASTER: William Vendice. CAST: Philip Langridge (*Peter Grimes*), Nancy Gustafson (*Ellen Orford*), Gregory Yurisich (*Captain Balstrode*), Suzanna Guzman (*Mrs. Sedley*), Judith Christin (*Auntie*), John Atkins (*Ned Keene*), Greg Fedderly (*Bob Boles*).

NOTES AND SOURCES

Quotes from John Schlesinger are from conversations I had with him over the course of a year and a half (December 2001 to July 2003) or from Schlesinger's private journals and diaries, written or tape-recorded; or else they come from the various published and unpublished sources referenced in the notes for each chapter. Quotes from others, unless otherwise indicated, are from interviews conducted by me during the two-year span from December 2001 to December 2003.

In some instances, in order to make reading easier, I have eliminated brackets ([ ]) and ellipses (. . .) from quotations, retaining them when their removal might interfere with accuracy or alter the thrust or intent of the person being quoted.

PROLOGUE

Articles and reviews:
The New York Times, 28 May, 1972; *The New Yorker*, 2 October, 1971.
Books:
Biskind, Peter. *Easy Riders, Raging Bulls: How the Sex, Drugs and Rock 'n' Roll Generation Saved Hollywood*. New York: Simon and Schuster, 1998.
Buhle, Paul and Wagner, Dave. *Hide in Plain Sight: The Hollywood Blacklistees in Film and Television, 1950–2002*. New York: Palgrave Macmillan, 2003.

ONE

Articles and reviews:

The Advocate, 16 April, 1999; *The New York Times*, 5 March, 2000; *Village Voice*, 21 March, 2000; *Variety*, 17 May, 1994, 28 February, 1995, 6 May, 1998, 5 June, 1998; *The Hollywood Reporter*, 30 October, 1996, 12 May, 1997; *The Los Angeles Times*, 31 July, 1999; *Interview*, March 2000.

Books:

Hacker, Jonathan. *Take Ten: Contemporary British Film Directors*. Oxford: Clarendon Press, 1991.

Additional John Schlesinger quotes from other sources:

MovieMaker, September 1995; *Penthouse*, June 1975; *Literature Film Quarterly*, Spring 1978; *New York Sunday News*, 24 October, 1976.

TWO

Original and unpublished sources:

1881, 1891, 1901 Censuses of England.

Letters between John Schlesinger and Gene Phillips, various dates, 1967–1997, courtesy Gene Phillips.

Letters from John Schlesinger to Hilary Schlesinger, various dates, courtesy Hilary Schlesinger.

Letter from John Schlesinger to Mrs. M.E. Schwab, 26 November, 1980, John Schlesinger private collection, now at the British Film Institute (hereafter JS/BFI).

Notes by John Schlesinger for his acceptance speech of the Shakespeare Award, 1981 (hereafter Shakespeare Award speech) (JS/BFI).

Books:

Buruma, Ian. *Voltaire's Coconuts, or Anglomania in Europe*. London: Weidenfeld & Nicolson, 1998.

Davies, Russell (ed.). *The Kenneth Williams Diaries*. London: HarperCollins, 1993.

Nichols, Peter. *Diaries, 1969–1977*. London: Nick Hern Books, 2000.

Rubens, Robert, "John Schlesinger," in Joseph F. McCrindle, ed. *Behind the Scenes: Theater and Film Interviews from the Transatlantic Review*. New York: Henry Holt, 1971.

Walker, Alexander. *Hollywood UK: The British Film Industry in the Sixties*. New York: Stein and Day, 1974.

Williams, Kenneth. *Just Williams: An Autobiography*. London: J.M. Dent and Sons, 1985.

Additional John Schlesinger quotes from other sources:

Los Angeles Village View, 25 Feb-3 Mar, 1994; Interview with Jeremy Isaacs broadcast on the BBC on 3 February 1993 and reprinted online (hereafter Isaacs interview); *Screen*, Summer 1970; *American Film*, November, 1987; *American Cinematographer*, June 1975; *Newsday*, 19 October, 1995; *Venice*, March 2000.

THREE

Original and unpublished sources:

Letter from Howard Rose to Pascoe Thornton, 23 January, 1948; Letter from E.A. Harding to Neil Hutchinson, 13 February 1951; Letter from John Schlesinger to E.A. Harding, 29 October, 1951, BBC Written Archives (hereafter BBC WA).

Production records, radio and television programming, 1951–1955 (BBC WA).

Notes written by John Schlesinger for the MacTaggart Lecture, Edinburgh International Television Festival, 16 August, 1985 (hereafter MacTaggart Lecture) (JS/BFI).

Articles and reviews:

The Times, 29 June, 1949; 17 June, 1949; 21 February, 1950; 1 March, 1950; 8 June, 1950; 7 February, 1949.

Books:

Griffith, Kenneth. *The Fool's Pardon*. London: Little Brown and Company, 1994.

Hacker. *Take Ten*.

Lambert, Gavin. *Mainly About Lindsay Anderson*. New York: Knopf, 2000.

Thomson, David. *A Biographical Dictionary of Film* (2nd ed.) New York: William Morrow, 1981.

Additional John Schlesinger quotes from other sources:

Los Angeles Village View, 25 Feb–3 Mar, 1994; *Screen International*, 9 July, 1977; *New York Daily News*, 20 January 1985; *Films and Filming*, November 1969; Isaacs interview; *Cineaste*, Vol. 20, No. 4, 1995; *Screen International*, 12 September, 1997; *Making Films in New York*, December 1970.

FOUR

Original and unpublished sources:

Letter from John Schlesinger to Douglas Cleverdon, 3 January, 1952; Letter from Rosemary Hill to John Schlesinger, 28 March, 1956; Memo from Ian Atkins, 29 June, 1956; Memo from Royston Morley, 7 August, 1956; Letter from Michael Barry to John Schlesinger, 16 July, 1956; Letter from John Schlesinger to Michael Barry, 4 January, 1957; Letter from Michael Barry to John Schlesinger, 14 January, 1957; Letter from John Schlesinger to Rudolph Cartier, 6 February, 1957; Memo from Kenneth Adam, 19 March, 1957 (BBC WA).

MacTaggart Lecture.

Articles and reviews:

BBC Quarterly, Vol. 6, No. 3, Autumn 1951; *Daily Telegraph Magazine*, 26 July, 1991; *Hollywood Reporter*, 8 January, 1952; 2 January, 1953; *Variety*, 17 September, 1952; 17 July, 1957; *Look*, 25 August, 1953; *Los Angeles Times*, 19 November, 1957; *Screen*

International, 9 July, 1977; *The Times,* 20 September, 1956; 8 January, 1958; *Daily Telegraph,* 19 February, 1957; *Tribune,* 18 March, 1957.

Books:

Brand, Neil. *Dramatic Notes: Foregrounding Music in the Dramatic Experience.* Luton: University of Luton Press, 1998.

Briggs, Asa. *The History of Broadcasting in the United Kingdom.* Oxford University Press, 1979.

Doherty, David, et. al. *The Last Picture Show? Britain's Changing Film Audiences.* London: The British Film Institute, 1987.

Hacker. *Take Ten.*

Phillips, Gene. *John Schlesinger.* Boston: Twayne Publishers, 1981.

McFarlane, Brian. *An Autobiography of British Cinema.* London: Methuen, 1996.

Wildeblood, Peter. *Against the Law.* London: Weidenfeld & Nicolson, 1955.

Additional John Schlesinger quotes from other sources:

Transcript of the Louis B. Mayer Film Library Seminar, given by John Schlesinger, under the auspices of the American Film Institute, 27 October, 1998 (hereafter AFI transcript); *The Village Voice,* 30 June, 1975; *New York Daily News,* 20 January, 1985; *Screen,* Summer 1970; Transcript of National Film Theatre interview with John Schlesinger, 1977 (hereafter NFT transcript).

FIVE

Original and unpublished sources:

Memo from A.G. Finch, Special Contract for Services, 25 July, 1958; Letter from John Schlesinger to Huw Wheldon, 10 April, 1960; Letter from Huw Wheldon to John Schlesinger, 7 April, 1960; Letter from John Schlesinger to Huw Wheldon, 13 February, 1960; Letter from John Schlesinger to Huw Wheldon, 2 April,

1960; Letter from John Schlesinger to Huw Wheldon, 21 March, 1960 (BBC WA).

Production file, "Private View," 1960 (BBC WA).

Articles and reviews:

Omni Magazine, June 1987; *Hollywood Reporter*, 25 October, 1961.

Books:

Hacker. *Take Ten*.

Additional John Schlesinger quotes from other sources:

The New York Times, 28 June, 1995; NFT transcript; *Venice*, March 2000; AFI transcript; *Screen*, Summer 1970; *American Cinematographer*, June 1975; *Films and Filming*, November 1969.

SIX

Original and unpublished sources:

MacTaggart Lecture.

Motion Picture Association of America files, *A Kind of Loving*, November 1962, Academy of Motion Picture Arts and Sciences (hereafter AMPAS).

Notes written by John Schlesinger for an article of appreciation of Joseph Janni, by John Schlesinger, for *Guardian* (JS/BFI).

Shakespeare Award speech (JS/BFI).

Articles and reviews:

Box Office, 7 January, 1963; *Guardian*, 2 January, 1994; *London Evening Standard*, 21 November, 1997; *International Herald-Tribune*, 11 November, 1972.

Books:

Ashby, Justin and Higson, Andrew. *British Cinema Past and Present*. London: Routledge, 2000.

Curran, James and Porter, Vincent. *British Cinema History*. Totawa, NJ: Barnes & Noble Books, 1983.

Hill, John. *Sex, Class and Realism*. London: British Film Institute, 1986.

Lay, Samantha. *Short Cuts: British Social Realism*. London: Wall-flower, 2002.

McFarlane. *An Autobiography* . . .

Murphy, Robert. *Sixties British Cinema*. London, British Film Institute, 1992.

Murphy, Robert. *The British Cinema Book*. London: British Film Institute, 2001.

Sussex, Elizabeth. *The Rise and Fall of British Documentary*. Berkeley: University of California Press, 1975.

Tonetti, Claretta. *Luchino Visconti*. New York: G.K. Hall, 1983.

Trevelyan, John. *What the Censor Saw*. London: Joseph, 1973.

Walker. *Hollywood UK*.

Additional John Schlesinger quotes from other sources:

NFT transcript; Isaacs interview; *Films and Filming*, November, 1969; *Screen International*, 8 July, 1978.

SEVEN

Articles and reviews:

Observer, 16 July, 1995; *The Times*, 14 August, 1963; *Observer*, 18 August, 1963; *Sight and Sound*, Autumn 1963; *Films in Review*, November 1963; *Observer*, 18 August, 1963; *Village Voice*, 19 December, 1963; *New Statesman*, 16 August 1963; *Time*, 20 September, 1963; *The New York Times*, 24 December, 1972; *The Times*, 25 July, 1963, 17 June, 1963.

Books:

Hall, Peter. *Making An Exhibition of Myself*. London: Oberon Books, 2000.

Additional John Schlesinger quotes from other sources:

Films and Filming, May 1963, July 1963.

EIGHT

Original and unpublished sources:

Memo from John Schlesinger to Frederic Raphael, 18 July, 1964; Letter from Frederic Raphael to John Schlesinger, 22 May, 1964; Letters from John Schlesinger to Frederic Raphael, 20 August, 1964; 27 August, 1964; 5 June, 1964; Letter from John Schlesinger to Jerome Hellman, 25 February, 1966; Letter from Jerome Hellman to John Schlesinger, 12 March, 1966 (JS/BFI).

Frederic Raphael notes to the script for *Darling* (JS/BFI).

Articles and reviews:

Daily Telegraph, 3 March, 1989; *The New Yorker*, 21 December, 1963; *Observer*, 30 December, 1962; *Daily Mail*, 14 September, 1965; *Evening Standard*, 17 September, 1965; *The Film Daily*, 17 August, 1965; Christian Century, 5 January, 1966;

The Times, 2 July, 1965, 13 August, 1965; *The Hollywood Reporter*, 10 February, 1966.

Books:

Curran and Porter. *British Cinema History*.

Hayward, Anthony. *Julie Christie*. London: Robert Hale Ltd., 2001.

Levy, Shawn. *Ready, Steady, Go! The Smashing Rise and Giddy Fall of Swinging London*. New York: Doubleday, 2002.

Mann, William J. *Behind the Screen: How Gays and Lesbians Shaped Hollywood*. New York: Viking, 2001.

Morley, Sheridan. *Dirk Bogarde: Frank Outsider*. London: Bloomsbury Publishing, 1999.

Phillips. *John Schlesinger*.

Raphael, Frederic. *Two For the Road*, London: Jonathan Cape, 1967.

Walker. *Hollywood, UK*.

Additional John Schlesinger quotes from other sources:

Screen, Summer 1970; *Venice*, March 2000.

NINE

Original and unpublished sources:

Letter from John Schlesinger to Jerome Hellman, 22 October, 1966; Letters from Jerome Hellman to John Schlesinger, 17 February, 1966; 12 March, 1966; 30 March, 1966; Letter from John Schlesinger to Jerome Hellman, 22 October, 1966; Letter from John Schlesinger to John Philip Law, 3 June, 1966; Letters from John Schlesinger to Jerome Hellman, 8 June, 1966, 12 September, 1966, 18 February, 1967; Letter from Jerome Hellman to John Schlesinger, 19 January, 1967; Letter from John Schlesinger to Jerome Hellman, 12 June, 1967 (JS/BFI).

MacTaggart Lecture.

Articles and reviews:

New York World Telegram and Sun, 2 August, 1965; *The New York Times*, 19 October, 1967, 5 November, 1967; *Village Voice*, 2 November, 1967; *The Observer*, 22 October, 1967.

Books:

McFarlane. *An Autobiography* . . .

Walker. *Hollywood, UK*.

Additional John Schlesinger quotes from other sources:

Screen, Summer 1970; *Films and Filming*, November 1969; *Film Comment*, May–June 1975; *American Cinematographer*, June 1975.

TEN

Original and unpublished sources:

Letter from John Schlesinger to Theo Cowen, 22 September, 1969; Letter from Richard Gregson to John Schlesinger, 11 August, 1966; Letter from John Schlesinger to Jerome Hellman, 3 January, 1967; Letter from John Schlesinger to Jack Gelber, 12 April, 1967; Letter from John Schlesinger to Jerome Hellman, 11 August,

1967; Letter from Jerome Hellman to John Schlesinger, 21 February, 1967 (JS/BFI).

Articles and reviews:

The Hollywood Reporter, 6 June, 1969; *Films and Filming*, September 1979.

Books:

Buhle. *Hide in Plain Sight*.

Additional John Schlesinger quotes from other sources:

Films and Filming, November 1969; *Newsday*, 19 October, 1995; *Screen*, Summer 1970; *American Film*, November 1987; *Making Films in New York*, December 1970; *Cineaste*, Vol. 20, No. 4, 1995; *Venice*, March 2000.

ELEVEN

Original and unpublished sources:

Letter from John Schlesinger to Patrick Duran, 3 April, 1970; Letter from John Schlesinger to Charlotte Levy, 29 May, 1969; Letter from John Schlesinger to Dustin Hoffman, 14 April, 1970; Letter from John Schlesinger to Jerome Hellman, 27 June, 1969 (JS/BFI). MacTaggart Lecture.

Articles and reviews:

New Republic, 7 June, 1969; *Look*, 20 June, 1969; *Esquire*, October 1969; *The New Yorker*, 27 September, 1969; *The Times*, 25 September, 1969; *Observer*, 28 September, 1969; *Time*, 30 May, 1969; *Playgirl*, August 1979; *Variety*, 27 May, 1970.

Books:

Biskind. *Easy Riders, Raging Bulls*
Phillips. *John Schlesinger*.
Russo, Vito. *The Celluloid Closet*. New York: Harper and Row, 1981.

Additional John Schlesinger quotes from other sources:

MovieMaker, September 1995; *Films and Filming*, September 1979; *Screen*, Summer 1970.

TWELVE

Original and unpublished sources:

Letter from John Schlesinger to Joseph Janni, 31 October, 1968; Letter from John Schlesinger to Penelope Gilliatt, 1 March, 1968; Letters from Joseph Janni to Penelope Gilliatt, 24 June, 1969; 28 July, 1969; Letters from John Schlesinger to Penelope Gilliatt, 15 August, 1969; 15 May, 1970; Memo from John Schlesinger to Joseph Janni, 10 January, 1972; Letter from John Schlesinger to Jean Nachbaur, 11 August, 1971; Letters from Jean Nachbaur to John Schlesinger, 5 August, 1971; 18 August, 1971; Letter from Joseph Janni to Penelope Gilliatt, 26 August, 1971 (JS/BFI).

Letters from John Schlesinger to Gene Phillips, 7 July, 1971; 29 November, 1972 (courtesy Phillips).

Revisions to *Sunday, Bloody Sunday* script by Ken Levison, 15 May, 1970 (JS/BFI).

Articles and reviews:

New York Post, 14 October, 1972; *Observer*, 4 July, 1971; *Punch*, 7 July, 1971; *The New Yorker*, 2 October, 1971; *The New York Times*, 3 October, 1971; *Time*, 27 September, 1971; *Guardian*, 15 June, 1971; *New York Post*, 29 November, 1971; *Life*, 8 October, 1971; *International Herald Tribune*, 11 November, 1971; *Los Angeles Herald-Examiner*, 11 November, 1971.

Books:

Dundy, Elaine. *Finch, Bloody Finch: A Life of Peter Finch*. New York: Holt, Rinehart and Winston, 1980.

Nichols, Peter. *Diaries*.

Phillips, Gene. *John Schlesinger*.

Sherwin, David. *Going Mad in Hollywood*. London: André Deutsch, 1996.

Additional John Schlesinger quotes from other sources:

Films and Filming, September 1979; *American Film*, December 1979;

Screen, Summer 1970; AFI transcript; Isaacs interview; *Literature Film Quarterly*, Spring 1978;
Penthouse, June 1975.

THIRTEEN

Original and unpublished sources:
Letter from John Schlesinger to Joseph Janni, 9 December, 1971; Letter from John Schlesinger to Stephen Murphy, 1 May, 1975; Letter from John Schlesinger to Tim Zinnemann, 15 October, 1974; Letter from Sidney Lumet to John Schlesinger, 9 May, 1975; Letter from John Schlesinger to Sidney Lumet, 15 May, 1975 (JS/BFI).
Letter from John Schlesinger to Gene Phillips, 29 November, 1972; 6 February, 1974 (courtesy Phillips).
Waldo Salt notes to the script of *The Day of the Locust*, 11 October, 1971 (JS/BFI).

Articles and reviews:
Screen International, 9 July, 1977; *The Times*, 7 November, 1972; *Penthouse*, June 1975; *American Cinematographer*, November 1972; *Time*, 17 September, 1973; *Sunday News*, 7 July, 1974; *Los Angeles Times*, 19 September, 1973; *The New York Times*, 8 May, 1975; *Film Comment*, May-June 1975; *Time*, 12 May, 1975; *The New Yorker*, 12 May, 1975; *Village Voice*, 12 May, 1975; *New York*, 12 May, 1975; *The Nation*, 24 May, 1975; *The Times*, 24 May, 1975; *Screen International*, 12 September, 1997.

Books:
Hacker. *Take Ten*.
Phillips, Gene. *John Schlesinger*.
Walker. *Hollywood UK*.

Additional John Schlesinger quotes from other sources:
Isaacs interview; *American Film*, November 1987; *Literature Film Quarterly*, Spring 1978; *Films and Filming*, September 1979; *Filmmakers Newsletter*, July 1975; *American Cinematographer*, June 1975.

FOURTEEN

Original and unpublished sources:

Letter from John Schlesinger to Brenda Vaccaro, 3 December, 1976; Letters from John Schlesinger to Sir Laurence Olivier, 6 June, 1975; 18 September, 1975 (JS/BFI).

Articles and reviews:

The Times, 26 February, 1975; *Observer*, 19 December, 1976; *Time*, 18 October, 1976; *The New Republic*, 30 October, 1976; *The New York Times*, 7 October, 1976; *Newsweek*, 11 October, 1976.

Books:

Evans, Robert. *The Kid Stays in the Picture*. Beverly Hills: New Millennium Press, 1994.

Goldman, William. *Adventures in the Screen Trade*. London: MacDonald & Co. Ltd., 1984.

Olivier, Laurence. *On Acting*. New York: Touchstone/Simon & Schuster, 1986.

Phillips. *John Schlesinger*.

Reed, Rex. *Travolta to Keaton*. New York: William Morrow and Co., 1979.

Additional John Schlesinger quotes from other sources:

American Cinematographer, June 1975; *Films and Filming*, November 1969; *City Limits*, 12–18 April, 1985; *Broadcast*, 23 August, 1985; *Los Angeles Times*, 31 December, 1994; *The Times*, 25 February, 1975; AFI transcript; *Venice*, March 2000; *Screen International*, 9 July, 1977; *American Film*, December 1979.

FIFTEEN

Original and unpublished sources:

Letter from John Schlesinger to Brenda Vaccaro, 25 March, 1977; Letter from Joseph Janni to John Schlesinger, 5 August, 1976; Letter from John Schlesinger to Brenda Vaccaro, 20 January,

1978; Letter from John Schlesinger to Howard Rosenman, 4 July, 1978; Memo from Joseph Janni to John Schlesinger, 1 June, 1978, Letter for John Schlesinger to Ferdinando Scarfiotti, 6 October, 1981 (JS/BFI).

Letter from John Schlesinger to Gene Phillips, 16 February, 1977 (courtesy Phillips).

Shakespeare Award speech (JS/BFI).

Articles and reviews:

The New York Times, 24 September, 1976; *The Times*, 23 March, 1977; *Variety*, 19 September, 1979; *The New York Times*, 19 September, 1979; *Village Voice*, 20 September, 1979; *New York Post*, 20 September, 1979; *Sight and Sound*, Winter 1979–1980.

Books:

McFarlane. *An Autobiography* . . .

Parker, John. *Richard Gere: The Flesh and the Spirit*. London, Headline, 1995.

Additional John Schlesinger quotes from other sources:

Screen International, 8 July, 1978; *The Times*, 19 March, 1977; *The Times*, 18 December, 1980; *The Times*, 7 January, 1981; *Screen International*, 25 October, 1980; *The New York Times*, 4 September, 1981; *New York Daily News*, 27 July, 1980; *The New York Times*, 21 August, 1981; *New York Post*, 21 August, 1981; *Screen International*, 25 May, 1985.

SIXTEEN

Original and unpublished sources:

Art Murphy's *Box Office Register*, 1985–1989 (AMPAS).

Letter from John Schlesinger to Howard Rosenman, 30 June, 1981; Letter from John Schlesinger to Ferdinando Scarfiotti, 6 October, 1981; Letter from Steven Zaillian to John Schlesinger, 28 November, 1983; Letter from John Schlesinger to Jeremy Zimmerman, 8 October, 1986; Letter from John Schlesinger to

John Robert Lloyd, 11 February, 1988; Letter from John Schlesinger to Ana Maria Quintana, 10 September, 1987; Letter from John Schlesinger to Jeff Seyfried, 8 April, 1988 (JS/BFI).

Letters from John Schlesinger to Gene Phillips, 27 February, 1981; 21 December, 1982; 28 January, 1987 (courtesy Phillips.)

MacTaggart Lecture.

Shakespeare Award speech.

Articles and reviews:

Variety, 6 August, 1980; *The New York Times*, 4 April, 1983; *The Times*, 25 August, 1992; 1 December, 1983; *Variety*, 30 November, 1983; *New York Daily News*, 20 January, 1985; *The Times*, 2 February, 1985; *The New York Times*, 25 January, 1985; 22 March, 1985; *Los Angeles Times*, 30 January, 1985; *New York*, 22 June, 1987; *The New Republic*, 17 October, 1988.

Books:

Bennett, Alan. *Writing Home*. London: Faber and Faber, 1994

Biskind. *Easy Riders, Raging Bulls*.

Hacker. *Take Ten*.

McFarlane. *An Autobiography* . . .

Medavoy, Mike. *You're Only as Good as Your Next One*. New York: Atria Books, 2002.

Sher, Antony. *Beside Myself*. London: Hutchinson, 2001.

Additional John Schlesinger quotes from other sources:

New York Post, 12 May, 1976; *Screen International*, 25 May, 1985; *American Film*, November 1987; *Los Angeles Times*, 7 June, 1987; *The New York Times*, 21 October, 1988.

SEVENTEEN

Original and unpublished sources:

Letter from John Schlesinger to Jeff Seyfried, 8 April, 1988; Letter from John Schlesinger to Ana Maria Quintana, 10 September, 1987; Letter from John Schlesinger to Rick Sinderman, 16

February, 1988; Letter from John Schlesinger to John Lloyd, 11 February, 1988; Letter from Michael Oliver to John Schlesinger, 11 April, 1988; Letter from John Schlesinger to Stewart Grimshaw, 5 September, 1984; Letter from John Schlesinger to David Geffen, 19 March, 1990; Letter from John Schlesinger to Antony Sher, 1 August, 1988; Letter from John Schlesinger to Dan Samuel, 30 March, 1989; Letter from John Schlesinger to Jeff Seyfried, 22 September, 1994 (JS/BFI).

Letters from John Schlesinger to Gene Phillips, 19 July, 1988; 22 September, 1994; 2 September, 1997 (courtesy Phillips).

Variety collection of box office records (AMPAS).

Articles and reviews:

Village Voice, 30 June, 1975; *The New York Times*, 3 October, 1971; *The New Yorker*, 6 January, 1992; *The Times*, 9 August, 1989; *The New Yorker*, 22 October, 1990; *The Times*, 21 October, 1991; *The New York Times*, 2 October, 1992; *Los Angeles Times*, 19 July, 1992; *The Sunday Times*, 19 June, 1994; *The Times*, 2 January, 1995; *Variety*, 20 May, 1996; *USA Today*, 15 January, 1996; *The Baltimore Sun*, 17 June, 1996; *The Plain Dealer*, 16 June, 1996; *The Austin Chronicle*, 14 June, 1996.

Additional John Schlesinger quotes from other sources:

Isaacs interview; *Penthouse*, June 1975; *Variety*, 9 February, 1989; *Los Angeles View*, 10–16 May, 1996; *Entertainment Today*, 10–16 May, 1996; *Etcetera*, 7 June, 1996.

EPILOGUE

Articles and reviews:

Variety, 6 March, 2000; *New York Daily News*, 3 March, 2000; *The Advocate*, 7 November, 2000.

Books:

Hacker. *Take Ten.*

Additional John Schlesinger quotes from other sources:

AFI transcript; Isaacs interview; *Los Angeles Village View*, 25 February–3 March, 1994.

Index